Qualitative Psychology

Qualitative Psychology

A Practical Guide to Research Methods

Second Edition

Edited by Jonathan A. Smith

Los Angeles | London | New Delhi
Singapore | Washington DC

First published 2008
Reprinted 2009, 2011

SAGE Publications Ltd
1 Oliver's Yard
55 City Road
London EC1Y 1SP

SAGE Publications Inc.
2455 Teller Road
Thousand Oaks, California 91320

SAGE Publications India Pvt Ltd
B 1/I 1 Mohan Cooperative Industrial Area
Mathura Road, New Delhi 110 044
India

SAGE Publications Asia-Pacific Pte Ltd
33 Pekin Street #02-01
Far East Square
Singapore 048763

Library of Congress Control Number available

British Library Cataloguing in Publication data

A catalogue record for this book is available
from the British Library

ISBN 978-1-4129-3083-3
ISBN 978-1-4129-3084-0 (pbk)

Typeset by C&M Digitals (P) Ltd., Chennai, India
Printed in Great Britain by the MPG Books Group
Printed on paper from sustainable resources

Contents

Notes on Contributors

Peter Ashworth is Emeritus Professor of Educational Research at Sheffield Hallam University, UK. He has published widely on the phenomenological approach to psychology – most recently, *Phenomenology and Psychological Science* (Springer, 2006; edited with Man Cheung Chung). He has written on such issues as the phenomenology of social participation, the lifeworld of the Alzheimer sufferer, and aspects of the experience of higher education including the meanings of student plagiarism. Dr Ashworth is a Fellow of the British Psychological Society.

Kathy Charmaz is Professor of Sociology and Coordinator of the Faculty Writing Program at Sonoma State University, USA. She is a sociological social psychologist who has written or co-edited seven books including *Good Days, Bad Days: The Self in Chronic Illness and Time*, which won awards from the Pacific Sociological Association and the Society for the Study of Symbolic Interaction, and *Constructing Grounded Theory: A Practical Guide Through Qualitative Analysis* and *The Handbook of Grounded Theory* (co-edited with Antony Bryant). She has received the 2001 Feminist Mentors Award and the 2006 George Herbert Mead award for lifetime achievement from the Society for the Study of Symbolic Interaction.

Paul Drew is Professor of Sociology at the University of York, UK, where he has taught and researched in Conversation Analysis since 1973. He has published journal and other articles on the basic practices underlying talk-in-interaction, as well as a range of aspects of conversational interaction, including repair; the management of such actions as invitations, requests and complaining; topic transition; and teasing. He has also published widely on what have come to be termed 'institutional' interactions, notably criminal court and medical (doctor-patient) interactions. His recent projects include communication between patients and medical professionals in a variety of primary and secondary care clinical settings; affiliation and disaffiliation in conversation; and indirectness in talk.

Amedeo P. Giorgi is Professor of Psychology at Saybrook Graduate School in San Francisco, USA. He is the founder and first editor of the *Journal of Phenomenological Psychology* and the author of *Psychology as a Human Science* (Harper Row, 1970).

He has written many articles on the relationship between phenomenology and psychology and is the originator of the descriptive phenomenological psychological method. He earned his Ph.D. at Fordham University, USA.

Barbro Giorgi is an adjunct professor of psychology at Saybrook Graduate School where she teaches courses on qualitative research methods and gives workshops on the application of the phenomenological approach to psychotherapy. Her research orientation is primarily phenomenological and she serves on doctoral dissertation committees for students using phenomenological research methods across the USA and in Scandinavia. Her own research focuses on the therapeutic process. She has also written theoretical articles on the application of Husserlian phenomenology to psychotherapy. She often joins her husband, Amedeo, in giving workshops on the descriptive phenomenological research method.

Michael Murray is Professor of Social and Health Psychology at Keele University, UK where he teaches health psychology and qualitative research methods. Previously he was at Memorial University of Newfoundland, Canada. He has published extensively on a range of issues in social and health psychology including narrative and social representation theory and critical and community health psychology. He has also written theoretical and methodological chapters on narrative psychology. Much of his current research uses participatory approaches designed to encourage community transformative action to promote health and well-being.

Mike Osborn is a Consultant Macmillan Psychologist at the Royal United Hospital in Bath, UK, working in both chronic pain and palliative care. His main research interest is in the phenomenology of chronic pain and the relationship between chronic illness, the self and the social world. He has also taught and written about the practicalities of doing qualitative research in psychology.

Peter Reason is Director of the Centre for Action Research in Professional Practice at the University of Bath, UK. His major academic work has been to contribute to the development of a participatory worldview and associated approaches to inquiry; and in particular to the theory and practice of co-operative inquiry. He is leading a large scale action research project exploring the introduction of low carbon technology in industry. Peter's major concern is with the devastating and unsustainable impact of human activities on the biosphere which, he believes, is grounded in our failure to recognize the participatory nature of our relationship with the planet and the cosmos.

Sarah Riley is a Lecturer in Psychology at the University of Bath, where she teaches qualitative methods and social constructionist/critical approaches to social psychology topics. Her research is concerned with the areas of identities (in particular, gender and youth culture) and research methods (visual methods, reflexivity and co-operative inquiry). She is a co-editor for *Critical Bodies: Representations, Practices and Identities of Weight and Body Management* (Palgrave/MacMillan, forthcoming).

Jonathan A. Smith is Professor of Psychology at Birkbeck University of London, UK where he teaches social psychology and qualitative research methods. He has written many articles applying interpretative phenomenological analysis to a range of areas in social and health psychology – for example, life transitions and identity, personal dilemmas around genetic testing, professionals' views on their practice. He has also written a number of methodological chapters on qualitative psychology. Much of his current research is in family and health and in psycho-social aspects of the new genetics.

Sue Wilkinson is Professor of Feminist and Health Studies at Loughborough University, UK. Previously she was at Simon Fraser University, Vancouver, Canada. She is the founding editor of the international journal *Feminism and Psychology* and has published widely in the areas of gender, sexuality, health and qualitative methods. Her current research interests are in conversation analysis, particularly in relation to healthcare interactions, support groups and telephone help-lines; the expression of emotion; and the mundane reproduction on sexism and heterosexism in and through the practices of talk-in-interaction.

Carla Willig lectures at City University, London. A major theme in her work to date has been a concern with method(ology). She has published empirical as well as theoretical papers and book chapters concerned with epistemological and methodological questions in general and discourse analytic concerns in particular. Much of this work constitutes an attempt to marry a social constructionist perspective with a critical realist epistemology. She is the editor of 'Applied Discourse Analysis. Social and Psychological Interventions' (1999) and the author of 'Introducing Qualitative Research in Psychology. Adventures in Theory and Method'(2001), both published by Open University Press. More recently, she has developed an interest in phenomenological approaches to research and has completed training in existential counselling psychology. Her current research is concerned with the role and function of interpretation, both in research and in the psychotherapeutic process.

Lucy Yardley is Professor of Health Psychology at the University of Southampton, UK, where she teaches qualitative methods to postgraduate psychology students. She has published studies using a wide variety of kinds of qualitative analysis, including grounded theory, thematic analysis, framework analysis and discourse analysis. She also carries out quantitative research, ranging from neuroscience experiments to large surveys, and has expertise in programmes of research that combine qualitative and quantitative studies. Her current interests include developing and evaluating web-based health interventions, and understanding and supporting adherence to rehabilitation.

First Edition Endorsements

'This excellent book introduces students to a wide range of qualitative methods. Its clear and engaging style makes the material particularly accessible to students who are unfamiliar with these topics. I will certainly be recommending it to my undergraduates.'

Chris McVittie, Senior Lecturer in Social Psychology, Queen Margaret University.

'*Qualitative Psychology*, edited by Jonathan Smith, draws together some of the most influential and important approaches in qualitative research. The contributors are experts in their field, hence students can be directed to the book confident in the knowledge that they will be accurately guided and informed. The style of each chapter is clear and accessible, and as such, is useful not only as an introduction but as a text which can support students throughout their studies.'

Mandi Hodges, Lecturer in Psychology, De Montfort University.

'*Qualitative Psychology: A Practical Guide to Research Methods* is an excellent introductory book introducing the reader to a variety of qualitative approaches commonly used in psychological research. It is an essential research methods book that students will find useful at either undergraduate or postgraduate levels. The contributors are all well-known international qualitative researchers who convey their area of expertise in a clear and very accessible manner to all. I would highly recommend this book for anyone who wants to grapple with qualitative research in psychology.'

Erika Borkoles, Exercise Psychologist, Carnegie Research Institute, Leeds Metropolitan University.

'Smith's text is a comprehensive and thoroughly practical guide to using a range of qualitative research methods in psychology; providing critical reflection as well as attending to the 'step-by-step' approach so craved by students.'

Sally Wiggins, University of Strathclyde.

'Smith's *Qualitative Psychology* has been the essential introduction to qualitative methods since its publication, a really accessible, informative and broad-ranging book, there is still nothing to compete with it.'

Carl Williams, Senior Lecturer in Psychology, Liverpool Hope University.

'In what is becoming a crowded field, Jonathan Smith's book offers a practical and persuasive route through a full range of qualitative methods available to researchers in psychology. It is not only the clarity of the writing throughout that distinguishes the book from many others in the area. The focus on practical concerns and applications of different methods also keeps the reader mindful that qualitative methods are a set of tools among many that are available to the modern researcher. It remains *the* text for applying qualitative methods in psychology – accessible, thorough, and above all an invaluable tool for studying social and psychological phenomena.' Patrick J. Leman, Royal Holloway University of London.

'I highly recommend this book to anyone with an interest in qualitative psychology, either student or not. It is written in an accessible and easy-to-understand style. To my knowledge, it is one of the best books available of its kind in the English language.'

Tomas Lindgren, Associate Professor, Department of Religious Studies, Umeå University, Sweden.

Preface to Second Edition

The guiding principle in preparing this second edition of *Qualitative Psychology* has been evolution rather than revolution. We wanted to retain all that was good about the first edition but also make a small set of discrete improvements. So nothing has been dropped from the first edition, but a number of significant enhancements are present:

- Each chapter introducing a method now has a box at the end illustrating three good examples of published research using the approach described. This will enable readers to follow up their reading, by seeing what a completed study using the approach looks like in practice.
- All chapters have been updated. As a result, the book remains authoritative and fresh.
- Peter Ashworth's chapter on the conceptual foundations of qualitative psychology has been extended to offer even clearer connections between that intellectual history and the approaches outlined in the book. Thus the chapter now offers the background to, as well as a mapping of, qualitative psychology.
- Sarah Riley has joined the team as co-author of the chapter on co-operative inquiry. In addition, that chapter has been modified to show more clearly its connections with action research.
- Lucy Yardley has been commissioned to write a much more extensive chapter on validity in qualitative psychology. Conceptions of quality and validity in qualitative research are a crucial issue for the field and this chapter gives a useful guide to the issues and how they can be addressed.

ONE

Introduction

Jonathan A. Smith

We are witnessing an explosion of interest in qualitative psychology. This is a significant shift in a discipline which has hitherto emphasized the importance of quantitative methodology. This change is reflected in a range of ways – for example, the large number of Ph.D. students completing qualitative projects; diverse conference presentations, symposia and workshops; the increasing numbers of qualitative articles appearing in peer-reviewed journals; and the establishing of psychology courses teaching qualitative methodologies.

This book aims to facilitate the further development of this active interest by offering practical guidance to those conducting qualitative research in psychology. It is written in an accessible manner and is primarily intended as a textbook for undergraduates and postgraduates, though it will also be useful to more advanced researchers. *Qualitative Psychology* covers the main qualitative approaches now used in psychology, and each chapter offers the reader a step-by-step guide to carrying out research using that particular method.

What is qualitative psychology? A dictionary definition might suggest that qualitative analysis is concerned with describing the constituent properties of an entity, while quantitative analysis is involved in determining how much of the entity there is. Indeed, much psychological research reflects the essence of that distinction. A great deal of qualitative research aims to provide rich or 'thick' (Geertz, 1973) descriptive accounts of the phenomenon under investigation, while quantitative research is more generally concerned with counting occurrences, volumes, or the size of associations between entities.

Qualitative and quantitative approaches clearly differ in terms of how the data are analysed. Quantitative research requires the reduction of phenomena to numerical values in order to carry out statistical analyses. Thus, although much quantitative research begins with verbal data – for example, answers to questionnaire items – the nature of the response is prescribed by the need for quantitative analysis, and this verbal material must be transformed into numbers for that quantitative analysis to be carried out.

By contrast, qualitative research involves collecting data in the form of naturalistic verbal reports – for example, interview transcripts or written accounts – and the analysis conducted on these is textual. Thus, the concern is with interpreting what a piece of text means rather than finding the numerical properties of it. The interpretation is then conveyed through detailed narrative reports of participants' perceptions, understandings or accounts of a phenomenon. For most qualitative researchers, this approach is consonant with a theoretical commitment to the importance of language as a fundamental property of human communication, interpretation and understanding. Given that we tend to make sense of our social world and express that sense-making to ourselves and others linguistically, qualitative researchers emphasize the value of analytic strategies that remain as close as possible to the symbolic system in which that sense-making occurs.

Qualitative approaches in psychology are generally engaged with exploring, describing and interpreting the personal and social experiences of participants. An attempt is usually made to understand a relatively small number of participants' own frames of reference or view of the world rather than trying to test a preconceived hypothesis on a large sample. For some qualitative researchers, the primary emphasis lies in how meanings are constructed and shaped discursively. Of course, there is a major theoretical underpinning to qualitative research, and the historical context of, and main themes in, that theoretical nexus is covered by Peter Ashworth in Chapter 2 of this book.

While it is true that qualitative and quantitative research projects usually differ considerably in terms of research question, orientation and execution, it is actually difficult to make categorical distinctions between qualitative and quantitative methods. Thus, for example, some quantitative researchers produce descriptive statistical accounts, and some qualitative researchers seek causal relationships. Similarly, Hayes (1997) argues that the process of analysis in qualitative research often invokes quantitative properties, as researchers make judgements, implicitly or explicitly, of the strength or otherwise of a category or property being reported, and individuals are compared with each other on various dimensions. Moreover, one can argue that quantitative research always involves interpretation by the researcher and that this process is essentially a qualitative one. So, while this book is written with a recognition of and commitment to qualitative research as a distinctive approach to psychological inquiry, it recognizes that the difference is not as categorical as sometimes portrayed.

It is also the case that qualitative psychology is not a homogeneous entity. There are a number of different approaches, each with overlapping but different theoretical and/or methodological emphases. And the growth of qualitative psychology has meant that recognizing this is increasingly important. Students need to know which particular type of qualitative method they are reading or working with, what its theoretical commitments are, and how it differs from other qualitative approaches they might encounter. So, for example, phenomenology and interpretative phenomenological analysis are concerned with exploring the lived experience of the participant or with understanding how participants makes sense of their personal and social world. On the other hand, discourse analysis and conversation analysis are concerned with describing the linguistic resources participants draw on during conversations, the patterns those conversations take, and the social interactional work being performed during them.

This book aims to help the reader navigate through these different perspectives and procedures. The intention is for the reader new to, but curious about, qualitative psychology to learn about the different qualitative approaches in terms of both their underlying theoretical assumptions and their practical procedures. Each chapter offers a short theoretical introduction to the approach and then offers a step-by-step guide to conducting psychological research by that method. The contributors are all recognized international experts; indeed, many of them are key figures in either the inception or development of their approach, and each has extensive experience using, teaching and writing about it. At the same time, the aim has been for the chapters to be written in an accessible fashion so that newcomers to the field can understand the main features of the particular method and be encouraged to try it out for themselves. Helping to set the scene for those practical chapters, the book begins with a chapter by Peter Ashworth outlining the conceptual foundations of qualitative psychology and their connection with the contemporary field. While qualitative psychology as a vibrant empirical force is relatively new, it actually has a long and distinguished intellectual history, and Peter Ashworth provides an entry to, and overview of, that history as well as a link to the approaches offered in the rest of the book.

TWO

Conceptual Foundations of Qualitative Psychology

Peter Ashworth

In this chapter, I want to point to the gradual unfolding in the history of psychology of certain ways of thinking which have, relatively recently, led to the emergence of specifically qualitative approaches to psychological matters. For, behind the use of qualitative methods lies a set of distinct conceptions of the nature of human psychology, and I will outline here some of the sources of these conceptions.

There are several different approaches to qualitative psychology, as the chapters in this book testify, but it is probably true to say that behind each approach is a concern with people's grasp of their world.

I use that ungainly term 'grasp of their world' to avoid terminology which would be unacceptable to one or other of the traditions within qualitative psychology. There are important differences in opinion about how the subject matter of qualitative research should be conceptualized. First, the 'qualities' sought in elucidating a person's grasp of their world may be seen as a system of objective *variables*. For some, qualitative research seems to aim at discovering the variables entailed in some human situation and does not dissent from the orthodox view of the person as being part of a natural system of causes and effects (in the positivist manner). Such an approach is not the focus of this book. Second, the person's grasp of their world may be conceptualized as a set of quasi-linguistic *propositions* (which may or may not be seen as open to personal choice) by which the person construes or constructs their world. Such qualitative psychologists often turn their attention to the range of social interpretations of events available to a person, arguing that these interpretations are what gives form and content to the individual's grasp of their world (gender, for instance, being ready-packaged for us in particular ways). These authors are likely to shy away from the use of terms like 'experience', feeling that it points too much to the individual; what should be studied, instead, is the social nature of the constructions of the world that guide thought and action. Third, qualitative psychologists may envisage the person's grasp of their world in terms of 'perceptions' or *meanings* (whether socially shared or idiosyncratic). This is a major aspect of the phenomenological viewpoint, in which qualitative researchers often speak of the personal 'lifeworld', and try to describe an individual's *experience* within this particular meaningful realm.

The Birth of Psychology and the Question of 'Experience'

Within contemporary psychology those who wish to investigate the person's grasp of their world in detail will tend to turn to qualitative methods. A concentration on human *experience* as the central topic of psychology or a focus on *construction* or *interpretation* seems to lead, for us, almost inevitably to qualitative research. Yet the history of psychology does not show a necessary link between the study of experience and qualitative methodology. It is sometimes forgotten that, when experimental psychology was founded in the second half of the nineteenth century, it was *defined* as the science of experience, and – maybe surprisingly – the methodology replicated as far as was possible that of the physical sciences. The philosophers and physiologists who began to establish psychology as a discipline had seen the immensely impressive strides in understanding the nature of the external world made by the physical sciences. Psychology would complement this by developing a scientific understanding of the inner world of experience, and this inner realm would be approached experimentally and quantitatively. The major interest of those early experimentalists, in fact, was in discovering what precisely the relationship was between the outer world and the inner world.

Gustav Fechner (1801–1887), for example, aimed to discover the laws relating the physical nature of an external physical stimulus to the internal experience of the sensation it produced. Fechner's *Elemente der Psychophysik* (1860/1966) could indeed be said to be the founding publication of experimental psychology. In it, Fechner reported his findings regarding such matters as the relationship between stimulus and sensation. For instance, a measured change in the intensity of light would be compared with the extent to which the person's experience of brightness altered. So variations in objective physical energy could be graphed against variations in the subjective sensation of brightness. The brightness of light is, in a certain sense, an experience.

The limitations of Fechner's psychophysics, from the point of view of contemporary qualitative psychology, are rather obvious. What was the meaning of 'experience' in experimental work such as Fechner's? It was simply the individual report of some aspect of a sensation. But we might well object that the experience of variations in brightness was within a very specific, controlled context, with a particular social meaning (the research participants lived in a culture and historical epoch in which it made sense to play the role of 'research subject' and to turn attention exclusively to the specified aspect of the sensation). We might wonder about the vocabulary available to the participants for reporting visual sensation. We might inquire about the relations of power between experimenter and subject. We might speculate about the perceived passage of time during these possibly tedious sessions. But these wider aspects of the experience in the round were of no interest to Fechner.

Right at the start, there was scientific controversy surrounding Fechner's book. Some of it was aimed at the details of the methodology. But William James was one of the distinguished psychologists who regarded the whole enterprise of 'psychophysics' as completely without value.

The human capacity to report verbally on sensations of the elementary kind investigated by Fechner ('Which light is brighter?' 'The one on the left.') could, it seems, appear unproblematic given the restricted focus of interest of the experimental investigation. When later investigators developed psychological studies which had more complex aims, the difficulties of the approach adopted by Fechner became increasingly insistent. A more elaborate attempt at the analysis of experience is found in Wundt's *Physiologische Psychologie* (1874/1904), in which various novel methods were used, but notably Wundt focused on laboratory investigation using trained and systematic *self-observation*. While systematic in the extreme and subject to careful experimental control, the method nevertheless depended on the research participants' verbal report of their (a question-begging term) *introspections*. The accounts of the structure of experience varied between laboratories as Wundt's approach began to be adopted by other workers in the new science.

It was not only because of the unreliability of the experimental self-observation method when applied to the description of the make-up of consciousness that Wundt's work on the structure of immediate experience was challenged. In particular, Franz Brentano (1838–1917) developed a quite different approach to immediate experience. He viewed conscious experience as a process; experiencing was an act, so that different kinds of experience are to be distinguished by the particular way in which we gain consciousness of the object of experience. In particular, the 'kind' of conscious act involved in relating ourselves to something so as to form a judgement about it is different from the conscious act by which we achieve a perception of something. So judgement and perception and other modes of conscious experience involve different orientations to the object.

The key feature of conscious activity, for Brentano (and this was taken up by Husserl and the phenomenologists), was its *intentionality*, a technical term pointing to the intrinsic 'relatedness' of consciousness to the object of its attention. The fact that consciousness uniquely has this attribute of intentionality was definitive, i.e. *all consciousness is consciousness of something*. And psychology, for Brentano, had the task of delineating the various ways in which consciousness could relate to its objects.

Brentano's act psychology did not gain a significant hearing outside Germany, though it had an impact on Gestalt theory. The psychology of Wundt, with its technique of self-observation and focus on mental content, gave way to functionalism and especially its behaviourist form in the Anglo-American world. But in the meantime the impressive psychological descriptions by William James (1842–1910) deserve attention.

Early Critique: William James and the 'Stream of Consciousness'

In volume I of James's *Principles of Psychology* (1890), he outlines a basic psychology of experience, primarily focusing on the stream of thought but also elaborating on two meanings of 'self'. James does not give us new research evidence, but he does detail quite systematic views on psychological matters that have in some ways been more influential than the work of James's experimentalist contemporaries.

The thing which distinguished James's description of experience from that of Wundt was that James rejected atomism in favour of the attempt to describe key features of the whole field of awareness taken in its entirety. James described consciousness as an ongoing process, having its own themes within which the current foci of attention get their meaning. So the content of consciousness is, at a particular moment, a phase of a personal 'stream'. The significance of a particular object of consciousness is due not just to its reference to the external thing but also to its relationship to the ongoing themes of my awareness – its personal relevance to me, the experiencer.

James builds up a general case for the importance of what he calls the 'fringe' of the focal object of which we are conscious. An object of awareness gains its meaning in large measure from the 'halo of relations' with which it is connected – its 'psychic overtone'. Husserl later also pointed to a similar idea: the 'horizon' of a phenomenon. That is, an object of awareness is affected intrinsically by the whole web of its meaningful connections within the world of experience. Choice is also a feature of consciousness for James. Of the available objects of attention, one becomes focal at a particular time, and others are reduced to the periphery of attention. Here we have something akin to the Gestalt psychologists' distinction between the figure and ground of awareness.

James's approach to consciousness is continued in the following chapter of the *Principles*, which is devoted to the self. James regards this as a very difficult topic, but he discusses in detail the distinction between the self as an object of thought (the self-concept, let us say), and the self as that *who* is aware of that self-concept. So the self is a 'duplex' (as James puts it) – involving both (a) the self which we can conceptualize, the self as known, the me, and (b) the self as that which 'has' that knowledge, the I. The *me*, in particular, is shown to have a complex structure. So James begins to develop a phenomenology of the self, which was elaborated on by such later authors as G.H. Mead and Gordon Allport.

The basic description of awareness and self was a valuable advance. James, much later, continued the descriptive tendency of his work in a way which also employed a form of qualitative research. This was in the ground-breaking *The Varieties of Religious Experience* (1902). In this book James draws on a wide range of texts and personal accounts, which are interpreted as subjective perceptions. Thus he sets aside the question of whether a person's account of their experience of God relates to any external reality and describes it in the terms employed by the person themselves.

James made a considerable contribution to the kind of thinking that lies behind qualitative psychology by his descriptions of the field of thought and his analysis of the notion of the self.

The Rejection of Experience in Behaviourism and Cognitivism

In the next generation of American theorists, we find the criticisms which James made of the kind of experimental self-observation undertaken by Wundt and his school, ripening into an alternative school of psychology, *behaviourism*. J.B. Watson (1878–1958) published a statement of position in the paper 'Psychology as a behaviorist views it' (Watson, 1913), in which he demanded a replacement of the self-observation method by the study of behaviour. It was asserted that mental processes could not be the object of scientific study because they were not open to observation. Partly this was an impatient reaction to the irresolvably contradictory findings of earlier psychologists. 'Objectivity' was the catchword, and this meant focusing on events which both (a) could be reported reliably and were not susceptible to idiosyncrasy, and (b) were open to observation by someone other than the person undergoing the experience.

Watson recognized that this meant that psychology would no longer be the science of consciousness (which, as we have seen, had been its definitive area of investigation), but he seems merely to have regarded this as a consequence of the requirement that psychology adopt a 'scientific' methodology. The apparent problem was neither that consciousness had previously been ill-formulated, nor that consciousness could be dismissed as unreal. Consciousness was simply not amenable to objective analysis. In the United States, especially, behaviourism was the dominant form of academic psychology for 40 or 50 years.

This historical shift was unfortunate, for it took out of play several lines of investigation which, when elaborated, are conducive to the development of qualitative psychology. When the psychologist concentrates on objective stimuli and measurable responses, attention is directed away from the following:

- *The 'first-person' perspective.* Propositions about psychological events can be stated only in the third person – from the viewpoint of the observer rather than that of the actor themselves.
- *The perceptual approach.* Behaviourism could not consider the perceptions of the research participant. Likewise other modes of intentionality of consciousness – thinking,

judging, paying or switching attention, etc. – could not be properly differentiated and researched because behaviourism could not permit itself to consider the relationship between consciousness and its objects of awareness.

- *Idiography*. Behaviourist research, though allowing for 'individual differences' due to variations in individuals' histories of reinforcement, could not regard the study of people in their uniqueness as a justifiable scientific enterprise. Objectivity would be threatened.
- *Meaning*. Meaning was sacrificed by behaviourism. In the search for the objective and observable causes of behaviour, the meaning that a situation has for the person disappeared as a topic of research. Similarly, people's own accounts of their experience were regarded as *verbal behaviour* – that is, responses which needed to be explained in terms of their causes – rather than understandable and meaningful in their own terms.
- *Social relatedness*. Other people are an important source of stimuli, and my responses to them are likely to have significant repercussions, but people were not seen as different in kind from the physical objects which constitute a person's environment. Behaviourists were not able to recognize the *social nature* of the human being. In particular, they were not able to recognize fully the social *construction* of human reality.

In effect, the catalogue of things which behaviourism neglected provides a valuable list of items which are, in varying degree, central to the qualitative sensibility in psychology.

However, within behaviourism, developments in a cognitive direction were made from time to time, in an attempt to re-establish psychology as, in some sense, a science of mental life. Perhaps *Plans and the Structure of Behavior* by Miller, Gallanter and Pribram (1960) is the most obvious of these attempts, in that the authors termed themselves 'cognitive behaviourists'. In time, a self-confident and autonomous cognitive psychology developed, importantly in Neisser's ground-breaking *Cognitive Psychology* (1967), effectively replacing behaviourism as the dominant tendency in experimental psychology.

Cognitive psychology can be seen as a critique of the denial of inner processes, in that it allows studies of perception, memory, thinking and so on. The work of Miller et al. and Neisser challenged behaviourism in its American heartland. In Britain, never so much in thrall to this theory, respected cognitive work had been going on – witness Bartlett (1932), Broadbent (1958) and Welford (1968). But, as I have shown in detail (Ashworth, 2000), cognitive psychology in general retains a quasi-behaviourist, methodological commitment to external, measurable and observable variables. In essence, the novelty of cognitive psychology lay in developing models of inner processes on the basis of what was externally observable. Viewing 'mental activity' as a process of *information flow*, cognitive psychologists began to test models of the operation of the mental mechanism (attention, perception, thought, memory, etc.)

The methodological approach of cognitive psychology is worth pondering, because it is often thought that this approach made an advance on the sterile objectivism of the behaviourists and allowed research to turn again to the scientific study of the whole breadth of the person's grasp of their world. But, if we look again at the list of matters which behaviourism refused to give place to in its research, we can see that cognitive psychology tackles only some of these directly. Additionally, both behaviourism and cognitivism share an underlying positivism (see Box 2.1).

Behaviourism's place in history lies in its paradigm-shattering critique of self-observation in psychology. Other lines of critique failed to capture the field at that time; we now turn to one alternative approach which did not reject experience but instead sought a more subtle approach to it. This viewpoint was one which immediately called for a qualitative psychology.

Box 2.1   Positivism

The methodological viewpoint generally taken for granted within the natural sciences, and dominant also in the social sciences, is positivist. The central idea is that only events which can be observed, or that only propositions which are (at least in principle) testable, have a claim to truth (unless, like logic, they are true by definition).

Among its characteristics – as seen in psychology – are the following:

- There is a single, unitary *real* world, within which the events of interest to psychology take place. This is realism.
- The individual is part of this real world, and so such processes as memory, emotion and thought are events in the real world with *definite enduring characteristics*.
- The purpose of science is to set up experimental situations in which the characteristics of these psychological processes can reveal themselves, and this will allow the processes to be modelled.
- The world can be described in terms of measurable variables which can interact with each other in determinate ways.
- The models (mathematically formulated if possible) will show how variables interrelate, especially how they relate to each other in a cause-and-effect fashion.
- The purpose of research is to test hypotheses regarding relationships between variables, and to reach, by closer and closer approximation, theories which can begin to be regarded as having the status of scientific laws. (This sense of an ongoing development gives positivism its characteristic historical optimism, and specifically the sense that each study, based on what is *known* and available in the established literature, is potentially a contribution to the 'total knowledge' of the future.)

In rejecting positivism in this sense, qualitative psychologists put on one side concern with the idea of an unequivocal real world, in favour of attending to the accounts that people formulate of *their* reality.

Phenomenology and Existentialism

The founder of phenomenology as a philosophical movement, Edmund Husserl (1859–1938), had a fundamental aim which it is necessary to have clearly in mind in assessing his work and its relevance to psychology. Although he was critical of both the experimental psychology of Wundt, and the subsequent behaviourist alternative, his purpose was not primarily to reform psychology. Rather, he wanted to provide a firm foundation for *all* the disciplines – sciences, arts and humanities – by establishing the meaning of their most basic concepts. For he believed not only psychology but all the scholarly disciplines lacked a method which would establish the nature of their fundamental concepts. What typically happened, according to Husserl, was that common-sense terms were pressed into use as if they were technical terms, or other rough-and-ready ways of developing concepts were employed. So, if asked what *perception* is, psychologists would have no precise account of the notion, but would have to answer in a way which arbitrarily built on unanalysed common-sense.

Husserl, then, proposed the method of *phenomenology*, which would enable basic concepts to be framed in a rigorous way that would give a firm basis to each science.

To take psychology specifically, Husserl (1925/1977; 1931/1960) regarded the discipline as flawed in its conceptual schemes by the tendency of psychologists to turn away from concrete experience and to develop prematurely abstract and unexamined concepts. Because the concepts were not grounded in experience, they were seriously lacking in clarity and appropriateness to the subject matter they were intended to reflect. What was the solution, then? In the Husserlian slogan, it was a *return to the things themselves*, as experienced.

The core philosophical basis of Husserl's programme was a rejection of the presupposition that there is something *behind* or *underlying* or *more fundamental than* experience, which should be immediately sought. No, Husserl maintained, what appears is the starting point; we should begin our investigation with what is experienced. In fact, phenomenology starts with the methodological move of suspending, or 'bracketing', the question of a reality separate from experience. Possibly later it will become necessary for the sciences to develop hypotheses about the underlying factors that account for what is experienced (the physical sciences have had to do this). But phenomenology is to be concerned with the primary reality, the thing itself as it appears: that is, the 'phenomenon'.

Though this gives a flavour of the work of phenomenological clarification of psychological concepts, it will be clear that a very arduous process is involved. Something akin to James's account of the web of meanings surrounding an experience must be described. The technical description of this process of attending to experience (Ashworth, 1996) goes beyond the scope of this chapter. Giorgi and Giorgi provide a careful account in Chapter 3.

It is important to note that, though phenomenology was initially concerned with the clarification of the basic concepts of each discipline, it is not surprising – given the way in which Husserl insisted on the importance of experience for this purpose – that the enterprise soon discovered special implications for the practice of psychological research. Husserl established that human experience in general is *not* a matter of lawful response to the 'variables' that are assumed to be in operation. Rather, experience is of a system of interrelated meanings – a Gestalt – that is bound up in a totality termed the 'lifeworld' (Husserl, 1936/1970). In other words, the human realm essentially entails embodied, conscious relatedness to a personal world of experience. The natural scientific approach is inappropriate. Human meanings are the key to the study of lived experience, not causal variables. In a nutshell, phenomenology insists that the daffodils are indeed different for a wandering poet than they are for a hard-pressed horticulturalist.

For phenomenology, then, the individual is a conscious agent, whose experience must be studied from the 'first-person' perspective. Experience is of a meaningful lifeworld.

Subsequently, 'existential phenomenologists', such as the early Heidegger (1927/1962), Merleau-Ponty (1962), and Sartre (1958; see Ashworth, 2000), developed phenomenology in a way which emphasized the lifeworld. At the same time, they tended to set aside Husserl's concern to develop, for each of the scholarly disciplines, a set of phenomenologically based concepts.

Tensions and divergences can be seen in phenomenological psychology. The emphasis may be on exhaustive *description* or on the development of essential structures of experience (see Giorgi, 1970; van Manen, 1997), and the descriptive emphasis may be idiographic (Smith et al., 1995). And there is debate about whether the empathic understanding required for phenomenological work might move towards interpretation (more of this below).

Especially in the American context, phenomenology and existentialism have been linked with 'humanistic psychology' (Misiak and Sexton, 1973). The purpose of this loose group of psychologists was to develop a way of pursuing the discipline which avoided the determinism of behaviourism and (as they believed) of psychoanalysis. What 'determinism' means here is the view that human behaviour and experience are to be regarded as the inevitable outcome of the set of variables (some internal, some environmental) which are in action on the person at a given time. In determinism, strictly understood, there is no place for a contribution of the person in how they will act. A profound concern that psychology should not be determinist in this sense led a number of authors, notably Bühler (1971), Maslow (1968) and Rogers (1967) – many of whom were psychotherapists – to call for a 'third force' of psychological thinking (Bugental, 1964) to counter the antihumanistic tendencies of the psychological mainstream.

The approach which I have personally espoused over nearly 30 years is existential phenomenology, with its fundamental concept of the lifeworld. In detail, people's lived experience of their situation may be quite specific, but all lifeworlds do have universal features such as temporality, spatiality, subjective embodiment, intersubjectivity, selfhood, personal project, moodedness, and discursiveness (Ashworth, 2006; Ashworth and Chung, 2006).

For existential phenomenology, human beings are taken as free by virtue of being conscious (consciousness entailing the capacity to envisage alternatives to what currently *is*), and resources such as language are tools for thought rather than, primarily, constraints on it. This is not to say that people are fully able to exercise the liberty which consciousness provides. Several authors within the existential-phenomenological tradition, such as Hannah Arendt (1998), have stressed that social arrangements (both local intersubjective ones and large-scale political structures) are required for the practical exercise of freedom.

In its broadest meaning, then, the phenomenological approach has the task of elucidating the taken-for-granted assumptions by which people navigate their lifeworld. To describe what everyone knows may seem a pretty empty ambition! But this impression is wrong. It has been argued: (a) that people *don't* 'know' – we act according to taken-for-granted understandings about our world which are for the most part pre-reflective, so elucidating them can often be a revelation; and (b) 'everyone' may have taken-for-granted understandings which enable a roughly shared communal life to take place – but there is scope for a great deal of idiosyncrasy.

In fact, the unique in human experience has been the focus of a further source of qualitative psychology.

Idiographic Psychology – G.W. Allport

Of the earlier writers to whom the humanistic psychologists look with particular admiration, Gordon Willard Allport (1897–1967) is notable for his concern that psychology should not neglect the unique in individual experience and behaviour. Allport was a member of a generation for whom behaviourism was almost definitive of, at least American, academic psychology, yet he was remarkably independent and, in contrast to anything that could be regarded as mainstream at the time, developed a theory of personality that stressed the distinct configuration of traits and tendencies which constitutes the uniqueness of each individual:

> I object strongly ... to a point of view that is current in psychology. Eysenck states it as follows: *To the scientist, the unique individual is simply the point of intersection of a number of quantitative variables.*
>
> What does this statement mean? It means that the scientist is not interested in the mutual interdependence of part-systems within the whole system of personality ... [and] is not interested in the manner in which your introversion interacts with your other traits, with your values, and with your life plans. The scientist, according to this view, then, isn't interested in the personality system at all, but only in the common dimensions. The person is left as mere 'point of intersection' with no internal structure, coherence or animation. I cannot agree with this view. (Allport, 1961: 8; his italics)

In this statement, the holism of Allport's approach is plain, and his interest in the *idiographic* approach to psychological research logically follows. The individual may be studied as a unique case. The psychology of personality does not need to be exclusively *nomothetic* (that is, restricting its attention to general dimensions on which individuals vary). The nomothetic approach assumes that the behaviour of a particular person is the outcome of laws that apply to all, and the aim of science is to reveal these general laws. The idiographic approach would, in contrast, focus on the interplay of factors which may be quite specific to the individual. It may be that the factors take their specific form only in this person; certainly, they are uniquely patterned in a given person's life (Allport, 1962).

As tends to be the case with psychologists who take a humanistic line, Allport considered in some depth the meaning of the *self*. He tried to cover a very great deal of what is linked in ordinary language in some way or other to the notion of self, using the coinage 'proprium' – to include both (a) people's *conception* of the self and the aspects of their world which they may be said to identify with; and (b) the 'integrative' mental function that may be labelled 'selfhood'.

Despite his insistence on the importance of the idiographic approach, Allport did not adopt an exclusively qualitative approach to research. Rather, his recommendation would be to study an individual person by using as many and varied means as possible. But he did pioneer some interesting qualitative approaches, such as the analysis of 'personal documents' and the use of 'self-reports' as a means of understanding the individual (Allport, 1961: 401–14; 1965).

Where Gordon Allport used qualitative methods, this largely reflected his concern with the study of the individual as a totality. He himself recognized that his holistic and idiographic interest had affinities with Gestalt theory and with existentialism. But Allport does not seem to have been interested in a qualitative psychology set up from the viewpoint of persons themselves. In the end, his is a psychology which will describe the person in individual complexity, certainly, but it would be carried out from the external vantage point of a psychologist for whom personal documents and other 'subjective' material can be used as evidence.

The World as Construction

What image of psychological life is suggested as a basis for qualitative research? We have seen James's description of consciousness, the focus on experience in existential phenomenology, and Allport's idiography. All these implicitly invite us to think of the person as a *perceiver*:

All other forms of conscious experience are in one way or another *founded* on perceptual, sensory consciousness. In general terms, Husserl contrasts the *self-givenness* of perception ... with that of a very large class of forms of consciousness that are 'representational' ... or work through a modification of presencing, which Husserl terms ... 'presentification', 'presentation' or 'calling to mind' (not just in memory, but in fantasy, wishing, etc.). When we remember, imagine or fantasize about an object, we do not have precisely the same sense of immediate, actual, bodily and temporal presence of the object. (Moran, 2005: 166–7)

And perception is not a construction or representation but provides direct access to the experienced object.

Of course, individuals are very active in their perceiving – they search, they pay attention selectively, they make choices, and their perception always has a meaning which is related to their lifeworld. But the approaches to be discussed in the rest of the chapter do not see the person as a perceiver so much as a *conceiver* or a *constructor*. Research focuses not so much on individuals' perception of a lifeworld as on their construction of it. The person is a sense-maker.

Two authors are indicative of the move to the idea of construction as the way many qualitative researchers approach the investigation of the individual's grasp of their world. I will deal with them in reverse historical order because the earlier, George Herbert Mead (1863–1931), has arguably a more deep-rooted ongoing influence on current qualitative research through the 'symbolic interactionist' movement than the later, George Kelly (1905–1967). Mead provides an appropriate link with later sections of this chapter.

George Kelly (1905–1967)

Kelly's (1955) approach centres on conception rather than perception. For Kelly, people act in accordance not with the way the world actually is but with their 'construction' of it. However, Kelly did not give us a detailed theory of the development in childhood of the capacity to construe the world, nor did he apparently prioritize the social basis of thought and selfhood (though he gives a great deal of attention to relations with others, and to the various ways in which an individual's way of seeing the world coincides with that of other people). So, though Kelly was undoubtedly a constructionist, it would be controversial to label him a social constructionist, and whether constructs are to be seen as falling within discursive structures or not is moot.

The 'fundamental postulate' of Kelly's theory of personal constructs expresses the constructionist outlook strongly – 'a person's processes are psychologically channellised by the way in which he [sic] anticipates events'. Kelly wants us to regard the person as acting as an informal scientist who views the world ('events') by way of categories of interpretation ('constructs') which are open to modification in the light of experience. Since reappraisal is thought to be possible by conscious reflection on one's construction of the world, we have here what Kelly called 'constructive alternativism'.

Kelly takes the view that we all have our own construction of events. But there are rather powerful limitations on the extent to which my construct system and yours can differ. Though each construct system is individual, Kelly speaks of the need for the contributors to a joint activity to be able to 'construe the construction processes' of the other participants. In other words, though we might not share the others' outlooks, for joint action to occur we must know what the others' outlooks *are*. So Kelly notes that individuals may include within their own system of cognition knowledge of the perspectives of others. To interact with another person, of course, requires knowledge of this sort. Many constructs *are* shared by people in common – indeed, to the extent that constructs can be communicated, they can be shared.

Essentially, Kelly views people as relating to reality (a notion which he strongly asserts) through their own developing system of constructs, and this system is materially affected by the person's coexistence and interaction with others. It is important to mention that Kelly does not dissent from the view of the self which we have noted in other authors. The *me* is a construct like any other.

Kelly provided a valuable new research technique, a logical scheme by which the researcher might specify in an organized way individuals' construct system. It was intended to facilitate assessment without sacrificing either individuality or changeability. This was the *role construct repertory grid* ('Rep Grid') in which the associations and dissociations between certain objects of experience – usually people well known to the individual – are mapped in terms of particular constructs (maybe one such construct would be kindly/cold). This exceedingly flexible tool has been used in a wide range of investigations (Bannister and Fransella, 1971). It may be used idiographically, but there are ways in which nomothetic procedures can be based on it. For instance, mathematical characteristics of grids can be derived, and the variation in such things as the complexity with which people construe a certain realm of experience can be investigated.

It is to be emphasized that Kelly saw the Rep Grid merely as a tool; he and subsequent personal construct psychologists value personal accounts as ways of eliciting personal constructs. It must also be said – in view of the fact that claims are made that Kelly represents the phenomenological position (e.g. Mischel, 1993) – that Kelly dissociated personal construct theory from phenomenology (though there is evidence in his work that he did not know the phenomenological literature in any depth, see Ashworth, 1973), and phenomenologists (e.g. Bolton, 1977) similarly distance themselves from his work, arguing (among other things) that it is too cognitive and that the fundamental postulate and corollaries entail presuppositions for which the phenomenological justification is absent. We can see, in any case, in the light of the argument that is being developed in this chapter, that Kelly's emphasis is on *construing*, not *perceiving*.

George Herbert Mead (1863–1931)

G.H. Mead's work is an important source of the constructionist orientation in qualitative psychology (Mead, 1934; see Ashworth, 1979, 2000); it was absorbed during the 1950s and 1960s into the school of social research referred to as 'symbolic interactionism'.

Symbolic interactionism is radically social. Mead (1934: 186) tells us:

What I want particularly to emphasise is the temporal and logical pre-existence of the social process to the self-conscious individual that arises within it.

Mind and self are products of social interaction, then. It is almost built into the name of the discipline, 'psychology', that the focus is on the individual person. Mead, instead, argued for the priority of the *relationship of communication* between caregiver and infant as the source of the mentality of the infant. He argued (he did not base his thinking on systematic evidence) that communication of a rudimentary kind between infant and carer comes before the development of the infant's capacity for thought. Indeed, it comes before the capacity for self-reflection. So infants interact with caregivers before they 'know what they are doing' or 'who they are'. The *meaning* of the infant's action becomes 'known' by the gradual internalization of expectations about how the others in the situation will react. So thought arises in a social process, and the *individualizing* of thought is a later development, which is in any case largely dependent on the use of the social tool, language.

It is important to notice how central language and other systems of symbols are to Mead. (It should be clear now why the school of thought is named 'symbolic interactionism'.) And, very importantly, linguistic symbols are a system of socially shared, not idiosyncratic, meanings.

There are two fundamental consequences of the idea that social interaction comes before thinking and selfhood, and that the latter are built from social materials. First, inner thought and external communication are basically similar. They are made of the same stuff. Mead expects no problem of translation of thought into word. Note also that, in internalizing language, the child is not just internalizing a symbol system but the system of activity. The process of conversation is being internalized; symbols are part of interaction, or discourse. Second, the self is part of this. Having acquired the capacity to reflect on one's own actions, one can build up a self-concept or identity. And the capacity for self-reflection develops through the reactions of others to the child's behaviour.

The view of Mead and the other symbolic interactionists – the term is due to Herbert Blumer (1900–1987) – contributes to qualitative psychology a highly social outlook: the person is first of all a member of society and only later (in the context of other people) becomes an individual. Hence it is appropriate for qualitative psychology to look to the symbolic systems of society – both those which are linguistic in the simple sense and those which are embedded in the forms of activity, the practices, of the culture. Mead's outlook is one important source of the approach of *discourse analysis* and *discursive psychology*. Other foundational thinkers in this area include Goffman (1959) (for the relation between Goffman and the existentialists, see Ashworth, 1985) and Garfinkel (1967). Qualitative methodology (often ethnographic, i.e. 'participant observation') is normally seen as the appropriate approach for research arising from symbolic interactionist and related theories.

One way of reading Mead, then, is as an early social constructionist theory. Individual selves and mental processes arise in a social context, and the 'content' of thought and selfhood is to be understood in the light of the meanings which are available within the culture in which the person is immersed. However, there is another emphasis, equally present in Mead (Ashworth, 1979;

Natanson, 1973). For, if mind and self are products of social interaction, it is equally true to say that it is individual interaction that constitutes society. Mead does not envisage a social milieu made up of roleplaying automatons – far from it. Having developed the capacity for mind and self as a result of interaction, the individual is then able, relatively autonomously – albeit in a continuing social context – to develop selfhood and personal tendencies of thought. Mead provides a social psychological theory with implications which include an element of individual agency. People are constructed *and are also* constructors.

The distinction between a *perceptual* and a *constructionist* outlook is not absolute. Berger and Luckmann (1967) in their influential book *The Social Construction of Reality* took their theoretical direction especially from the phenomenologist Alfred Schutz (e.g., 1972). Nevertheless, it is as well to note the different tendencies. Qualitative psychology may be more concerned with attempting to reveal the lifeworld (the perceptual tendency) or with how one's sense of reality is constructed.

Interpretation Theory: Hermeneutics

We have noted the distinction – rough and ready though it may be – between the forms of qualitative psychology that tend to adopt a perceptual approach and those that are constructionist in orientation. If we were to turn constructionist thinking back onto the question of the nature of qualitative research itself, we could hardly fail to find ourselves confronting the question, 'What processes of construction have the researchers themselves employed in coming up with the findings they have presented?' For a constructionist, all is construction. Both Mead and Kelly explicitly asserted that all science, including all forms of psychology, is a matter of construction. Further than this, the conclusions of a research activity have to be regarded as *interpretations*. Psychology is going to be an interpretive activity.

In his unrivalled study, *Freud and Philosophy: An Essay on Interpretation* (1970), Paul Ricoeur distinguished between two kinds of interpretation (using the term 'hermeneutics' to refer to the use of a theory of interpretation):

- The *hermeneutics of meaning-recollection* aims at faithful disclosure. For instance, studies concerned with the lifeworld of people with a certain disability, intended to inform others of the nature of their experience, would be instances of interpretation aimed at 'meaning-recollection'.
- The *hermeneutics of suspicion* aims to discover, behind the thing being analysed, a further reality which allows a much deeper interpretation to be made, and which can challenge the surface account. Plainly, psychoanalysis is definitively an instance of 'suspicion'; arguably, feminism can be as well.

The hermeneutics of meaning-recollection applies to any account of psychological life, surely. It is hardly explicit interpretation at all. In fact, though qualitative research adopting the *perceptual* model of psychological life would usually reject the hermeneutic label altogether, it certainly would be included within Ricoeur's broad definition of the hermeneutics of meaning-recollection. Indeed, it could be argued that this definition is too broad. Note that it would be in accord with the hermeneutics of meaning recollection for a psychological research methodology to involve interviewing research participants on some aspect of their experience, analysing the interview transcripts in such a way as to elicit their experience exceedingly faithfully, and then checking with the participants themselves after the analysis is done to ensure that the research account is faithful to their meaning. Of course, this is a frequent step in qualitative research.

Whether interpretation is the strong form that we see fully developed in psychoanalytic practice – the hermeneutics of suspicion – or not, Palmer (1969) usefully characterizes hermeneutics, the general theory of interpretative activity, as the method by which

> something foreign, strange, separated in time, or experience, is made familiar, present, comprehensible; something requiring representation, explanation or translation is somehow 'brought to understanding' – is 'interpreted'. (Palmer, 1969: 14)

Such interpretation may be a matter of elucidation (in the mode of 'meaning recollection'), or radical (in the mode of suspicion).

Martin Heidegger (1889–1976) has been mentioned in earlier pages, but a recognized early discussion of hermeneutic method is found in his early work. In *Being and Time* (1927/1962), he attempted an analysis of the everyday manner in which human beings go about their interpretative sense-making. For him, as with the constructionists, we live in an *interpreted world* and are ourselves *hermeneutic*; we are interpreters, understanders. For qualitative research, the hermeneutic approach provides a new view of the meaning of data. Interview research, for example, is the record of a process by which the researcher interprets the research participants' constructions of their world. This is reflected in Jonathan Smith's way of doing phenomenological analysis (see Chapter 4).

It was partly the divergence between Husserl and Heidegger, on the question of whether phenomenology is truly a disciplined description of experience or whether interpretation is inevitable, which led to a rift in phenomenology (similar to, but not precisely the same as, the perception/construction divide) that still affects phenomenological psychology.

The Discursive Turn and a Tendency to Postmodernism

The first half of the twentieth century saw a striking move in several very different modes of Western philosophy which began to focus on *language use* as somehow ontologically primary. The new understanding is that language does not just reflect the world of experience, but rather the world for us is constituted by our shared language. Language is in a sense the prime reality.

We have already seen one line of thought which takes this position – G.H. Mead and the symbolic interactionist tradition. A separate ancestral line also implicated in the rise of a discursive psychology is found in the ordinary language philosophy deriving from Wittgenstein's (1889–1951) later work (*Philosophical Investigations*, 1953). Wittgenstein's rejection of the idea that there can be a 'private language' – by which he criticized the view that understanding is an inner process – and his early avowal that the boundaries of my world are coextensive with the reach of my language are plainly important to discursive psychology. The Wittgensteinian account of the social world in terms of discrete 'language games' constituting or correlated with 'forms of life' is also important. (Austin, 1962, should be mentioned in this context.)

So, for Wittgenstein:

- A way of life and the language employed match, or are the same thing.
- We need to think of discourse use as a delimited language game appropriate to certain circumstances.
- It is in the nature of a language to be collective – there is no 'private language'.
- The idea of raw sensations on which language 'acts' to produce meaningful perceptions should be abandoned.

In a very different realm of philosophy to that of the ordinary language philosophers, we find Heidegger, dissident protégé of Husserl, putting forward the view that experience does not 'presence' the world directly, but that presencing is an act of interpretation in which language use is fundamental.

Language was once called the 'house of Being.' It is the guardian of presencing, inasmuch as the latter's radiance remains entrusted to the propriative showing of the saying. Language is the house of Being because, as the saying, it is propriation's mode. (Heidegger, 1957/1993: 424)

This quote gives a flavour of the writing of the later Heidegger. I read him as meaning that anything that we can say 'is' has linguistic form. It is language that, in this sense, 'houses' it and 'brings' it to vivid presence. The importance for us of this is that it, too, shows the discursive turn – but now in phenomenological philosophy. Interpretivism is involved in Heidegger's stance, then, but the discursive turn, most strongly emphasized in the chapters of this book – perhaps, in Chapters 6 to 8 – can also be seen in his thinking. Other sources of discourse analysis are mentioned by Willig in Chapter 8.

We can also see a link here with the constructionist turn discussed earlier. Here, however, a particularly 'strong' form of constructionism is implicated. In particular, (1) language and other cultural sign systems gain especial importance as at least the *means* by which the individual constructs reality, and maybe as the heart or foundation of that construction such that the individual's grasp of their world is *made* of the possibilities of such cultural resources; (2) the person is understood less as a unique individual, and more as a member of society, with ways of conceiving of reality that are typical of a historical epoch of a certain culture; and (3) the psychologist is very much part of this web of cultural construction. The third of these new emphases means that research has to be seen as a joint product of researcher and researched (part of what is often termed 'reflexivity'). It also means that psychology itself needs to be seen as part of cultural activity – a science which emerged from a particular period in the history of a certain society, and which cannot be detached from the interests and concerns of that society.

Social constructionism and the idea that interpretation is universal take us within a hair's breadth of *postmodern* thinking. Kenneth Gergen has summarized the constructionist stance, extending it to the entire postmodern movement, in the following statement:

> If one were to select from the substantial corpus of post modern writings a sin-
> gle line of argument that (a) generates broad agreement within these ranks and
> (b) serves as a critical divide between what we roughly distinguish as the mod-
> ern versus the post modern, it would be the abandonment of the traditional com-
> mitment to representationalism. (Gergen, 1994: 412)

By representationalism, Gergen seems to be pointing to the assumption, which I have previously called the 'perceptual tendency' that we can directly describe experience. Gergen asserts that this is not possible. Siding with the constructionists, he argues that experiences cannot but be shaped by our constructions of events. Indeed, he is making an even stronger statement than this. For Gergen, qualitative psychology does not strictly reveal a lifeworld, and a person's system of personal constructs does not relate the individual to reality. Instead, all that can be discovered by qualitative psychology is a kind of network of elements (let's call them segments of discourse), each of which gains its meaning purely from its position within the total system.

Gergen points out that this radicalization of the social constructionist perspective, whereby our conceptions do not touch the world, but all is construction or *all is text* (Derrida, 1976), is a central notion of postmodernism. It has many important implications for qualitative psychology.

One inescapable epistemological consequence is that the discursive turn undermines entirely the *correspondence theory of truth* which is assumed as a fundamental by much of psychology. This is the view that the truth of a hypothesis or theory or idea is to be found in its correspondence with 'outer reality'. Experimental design, for example, hinges on this notion. But if reality is not accessible except through discursive practices, then the separateness of idea and the real is lost. (Interestingly, lack of a separateness of the idea and the real is also the case with phenomenology, despite the fact that much phenomenology does not make the discursive turn, because 'reality' is bracketed and put out of play in order to reveal the structures of consciousness and the lifeworld.)

Modernism takes it for granted that our perceptions and constructions do relate to the real world and it allows the further assumption that ongoing *progress* is possible in research. This is because modernity has the fundamental notion that there is a non-negotiable, solid truth or reality about which it is possible to attain ever more accurate knowledge. The researcher can elaborate the structure of scientific constructs in a direction which approximates more and more to the truth of actual reality.

Modernism characterizes both the world of natural science and technology and the social and political world. It assumes that there are recognized criteria of scientific research or scholarly activity by which knowledge advances. In marked contrast, postmodernity can be viewed as a cultural movement for which such strong criteria of validity no longer exist (since the connection between 'reality' and human constructions has been dismissed). The idea of progress has nothing to refer to, because there is no standard against which to judge an innovation of theory, practice, product or policy that would enable one to see that it is an improvement over what previously existed.

Plainly, most psychology is modernist in its assumptions. There is a true reality to be uncovered by the activities of its researchers, and findings at one moment in time are the stepping-stones to refined findings later on. Postmodern thinking questions this (Kvale, 1992), and an important implication is that psychology can no longer present itself as 'outside human society, looking in'. It is not detached, but one among the many discourses within the culture – a discourse-space, a particular realm of social cognition and practical activity with its own rationality. In this view, qualitative psychology should not pretend to reveal progressively true, universal human nature, but should make us aware of the implicit assumptions (about 'human nature' and kinds of human experience) that are available to the members of a social group for the time being.

A key figure in this mode of thinking was Michel Foucault (1926–1984). Like other postmodern thinkers, he asserted the primacy of social constructions, or discourse (e.g., 1971; 1973a; 1973b). Foucault's constructionism (like that of all postmodernists) is a fully social one. The power of discourse does not come from the individual speaker-actor, but from the culture. And discourse *constitutes* the individual.

Perhaps Foucault's major contribution to postmodern social science was to emphasize the relationship between knowledge and power, or discourse and control. Foucault's last, uncompleted, work, *The History of Sexuality* (vol. 1, 1981), stresses control-through-discourse, arguing that the discourse-space of sexuality is one in which the individual defines himself or herself. Foucault finds it no accident that morality is treated most centrally as sexual morality, for, in the self-examination that awareness of sexuality entails, a process of personal self-monitoring is established.

Whereas Foucault was, at least at one stage, interested in the relationship between discourse and other features of the social world, Derrida (1981) regards all as, in the end, discourse. Such discursive sovereignty also contrasts with the hermeneutics of Freud, for whom interpretation is grounded in the primary, biological processes of libido. For Derrida, there is no hermeneutically privileged realm – there is no area of knowledge in which the certainty of absolute truth can be found.

Conclusion and Links to the Chapters in This Book

This chapter has shown the slow and subterranean development of ways of thinking which, together, constitute the qualitative sensibility in psychology. I have not strayed far over the borders of the established discipline, yet our scholarly neighbours in the social sciences have in some cases been the source of ideas that have been sparingly incorporated in qualitative psychology. One tendency that is to be encouraged, then, is qualitative psychologists' growing commerce with neighbours, both methodologically and in terms of subject matter. Disciplinary divisions do not stand up to phenomenological or discursive scrutiny.

Some historical currents within the discipline have been neglected for lack of space. The impact of psychoanalysis deserves proper recognition, both because of its focus on accounts of experience, and because of the dangers of the hermeneutics of suspicion to which it can succumb, which may pose dangers to qualitative psychology more broadly. Similarly, the strong relationship between phenomenology and Gestalt theory (Gurwitsch, 1964) was historically extremely important. I have neglected the impact of existential psychiatry (Binswanger, 1963; Boss, 1979; Laing, 1965). Finally, I have not discussed one of the strongest movements pressing the claims of the qualitative sensibility over the last few decades: Feminism (Gergen and Davis, 1997; Tong, 1991; Ussher, 1997; Wilkinson and Kitzinger, 1995) in its seizure of the high epistemological ground, in its quest for *voice*, in its concern that psychological thought and the process of psychological research should acknowledge the centrality of *power*, and with the need for equalization of the researcher/researched relationship.

I have used the phrase 'the qualitative sensibility' in this chapter, yet there is sufficient evidence to doubt the unity of mind of qualitative psychologists. The *perceptual* and the *discursive* tendencies seem rather distinct in their understanding of the human condition and the purpose of qualitative research. In fact, there are overlaps. Nevertheless, it would be roughly true to say that social constructionism moves in the postmodern direction, and that this leads to one form of qualitative psychology. A different form seems to originate from the Husserlian understanding of phenomenological research, which seeks universals of human experience (an undertaking which has modernist features). However, existential phenomenology, for example, is not quite characterizable in either modernist or postmodernist terms. Thus we can see a diversity of approaches, a flourishing of difference, but we can also see a unity, a qualitative sensibility.

Let me finish with a rough-and-ready mapping of the following chapters of this book in relation to the conceptual field I have laid out. Of course, this is not a definitive model and it is possible some of the authors would see some of this differently:

- The phenomenological psychology of Amedeo and Barbro Giorgi (Chapter 3) is Husserlian and treats experience or awareness in the broad meaning of the term of that philosopher (in which bodily relatedness to the world has characteristics of intentionality as well as the attentive 'mental' consciousness as commonly understood).
- Interpretative phenomenological analysis (outlined by Jonathan Smith and Mike Osborn in Chapter 4) focuses on experience, while allowing that both the research participant and the researcher are entering into interpretation. They also note the importance of attending to the idiographic.
- With Kathy Charmaz's Chapter 5 we are introduced to grounded theory – a technique of analysis emerging from the symbolic interactionist tradition in which 'what the people themselves say' is of utmost importance in founding the analysis. However, as Charmaz points out, there are different versions of grounded theory which mean the researcher can have one of a number of theoretical approaches which guide their understanding of the structures that emerge – they may be constructionist or experiential or even more positivistic in their outlook
- Michael Murray's piece on narrative psychology (Chapter 6) emphasizes the idea that it is a prime human characteristic to make sense of our circumstances by constructing stories. Narrative psychology is clearly at the intersection of the world as construction and the discursive turn
- In his account of conversation analysis (Chapter 7), Paul Drew takes the observation that the outcome of qualitative psychological research is a co-constitution of the researcher and the researched as a *theme* of research, drawing on the work of the ethnomethodologists. Here, perhaps, the prime reality is the process of interaction and the process of discourse.
- Carla Willig (Chapter 8) draws attention to two particular modes of discourse analysis, the approach of discursive psychology (in which the individual is an *agent* who draws on socially available discourses), and that inspired by the work of Michel Foucault in which the individual is *constituted* by the available discourses of the person. In the second case we can see the influence of the later Heidegger and his notion of *enframing*, in which a culture may have a mode of life such that there is a enveloping understanding of *what reality is like*.
- Focus groups are considered by Sue Wilkinson (Chapter 9) as a qualitative technique and, like the technique of grounded theory discussed in Chapter 5, there is some flexibility in the theoretical approach which the researcher may use. Again, we have a key issue of qualitative research generally: where does ontological priority lie – with the individual, the group, the interaction among the members of the group, the wider society?

- In Chapter 10, Peter Reason and Sarah Riley take this question of ontology further, for cooperative inquiry goes as far as it can in eliminating the distinction of role between the researcher and researched. Cooperative inquiry is usually an intensively practical matter – where *we* experiment on our situation and consider the outcomes.
- Finally, Lucy Yardley attempts, in Chapter 11, to address the question of validity as it arises anew for researchers who adopt a qualitative position.

It is worth underscoring the value of the variety of approaches within qualitative psychology. They have a number of emphases, but it is arguable that the richness of the human condition is such that no one tendency would encompass the whole. Allport's idiographic psychology is needed in order to approach the person's grasp of their world no less than the sociocentrism of some kinds of constructionism. Pluralism in qualitative psychology is to be valued. Pluralism of qualitative outlook and also awareness of human diversity.

It is in this context that qualitative psychology of whatever tendency should be judged. For it is usually only qualitative research that has a proper awareness of the diverse ways in which individuals (perceptually or constructively) grasp their world – and will, in particular, provide a hearing for the voices of the excluded.

THREE

Phenomenology

Amedeo Giorgi and *Barbro Giorgi*

Phenomenology is a philosophy initiated by Edmund Husserl (1900/1970) at the beginning of the twentieth century. One key aim of phenomenology was to ground radically the foundations of knowledge so that sceptical attacks on rationality and its procedures could be overcome. To build a secure basis for knowledge, Husserl decided to start with the problem of how objects and events appeared to consciousness since nothing could be even spoken about or witnessed if it did not come through someone's consciousness. It is to be noted here, however, that consciousness is to be understood not as limited to awareness, but in a much broader sense which would also include preconscious and unconscious processes. Husserl (1913/1983) also detailed a method for carrying out this project. Since psychology was also being founded about the same time as phenomenology, and since it, too, began as the 'study of consciousness', it was only natural that interaction between the two disciplines should take place. Unfortunately, the history of these interactions is filled with misunderstandings, and the reader is referred to other sources for details about this history (e.g., Cloonan, 1995; Merleau-Ponty, 1964; Spiegelberg, 1972). In this chapter, we will limit ourselves to an exposition of how the phenomenological method, adapted for scientific purposes, can help psychology make discoveries about the experiential world in psychologically significant ways.

How to determine precise psychological knowledge has been an issue for psychology ever since its founding as a modern discipline. When modern psychology was founded in the late nineteenth century, it began to seek secure knowledge according to the most prestigious criterion of that era, which was the experimental laboratory. Mainstream psychology has worked within this set of criteria with minor variations ever since. To be sure, some legitimate knowledge has been gained, but only in limited regions of the whole field of psychology, since most early studies focused primarily on sensory-perceptual experience or experiences tied to physiology because phenomena of that sort were highly amenable to the acceptable procedures and strategies of those times. Even when the so-called 'higher processes' were investigated, the idea of the natural science laboratory was still dominant since Ebbinghaus (1885/1964) invented an instrument for presenting nonsense material, and measured the time for learning and counted errors.

The advent of behaviourism and Gestalt theory were still laboratory-centred, but at least a few differences, in concession to the unique nature of psychological reality, were introduced by those theoretical movements. Radical behaviourism, in addition to focusing on behaviour, developed in such a way that it preferred to work in depth with a few subjects, within a functionalistic perspective, and it was more descriptive than quantitative in orientation (Day, 1976). Gestalt research was also almost exclusively laboratory-based, but it introduced the idea of phenomenal presences and behavioural environments, in addition to physical reality, and it tried to tie experience of them to the conditions of experimentation. In addition, Gestalt experiments often relied more upon careful descriptions than precise measurements (Koffka, 1935).

On the clinical side of the ledger, psychoanalysis established itself by 1900, but the setting for psychological knowledge was the therapist's room rather than the laboratory. The shift in setting led to a different type of knowledge. Psychoanalytic theoretical constructions were all based upon clinical case studies and the meanings that could be deduced from the observations and interpretations made by the clinician. However, psychoanalysis always suffered from the fact that it was not laboratory-based and, hence, not a true science in the eyes of mainstream psychology. Psychology is extremely conservative in its interpretation of science, and one departs from conventional criteria at great risk.

This chapter assumes not only that qualitative research yields useful knowledge but also that it is as legitimate a form of science as any other set of procedures acceptable to science. This is not the place to argue such a position, but we will demonstrate it by accepting certain generic operational criteria of scientific research and showing how the specific approach to qualitative research that we endorse, the phenomenological approach and method, can satisfy those criteria. While the perspective of science applied to human beings and human relationships is not identical to science as applied to things and processes, the strategies used are not oppositional. It is simply that strategic modifications are introduced because of the qualitative difference in subject matter. Many of the scientific issues concerning qualitative research are taken up by Giorgi (1986; 1989a; 1989b; 1992; 1994; 1997; 2000).

In general, phenomenological psychological research aims to clarify situations lived through by persons in everyday life. Rather than attempting to reduce a phenomenon to a convenient number of identifiable variables and control the context in which the phenomenon will be studied, phenomenology aims to remain as faithful as possible to the phenomenon and to the context in which it appears in the world. This means that, to study a particular phenomenon, a situation is sought in which individuals have first-hand experiences that they can describe as they actually took place in their life. The aim is to capture as closely as possible the way in which the phenomenon is experienced within the context in which the experience takes place. From this rich contextual example of the phenomenon as lived by the participant, phenomenological analysis attempts to discern the psychological essence of the phenomenon. In other words, phenomenology seeks the psychological meanings that constitute the phenomenon through investigating and analysing lived examples of the phenomenon within the context of the participants' lives. While persons' awarenesses are concomitant with these lived experiences, they are hardly ever totally coincident to what is being experienced by them. Usually, the capacity to live through events or respond to different situations greatly exceeds the capacity to know exactly what we do or why we do what we do. Consequently, an analysis of the meanings being lived by persons from a psychological perspective can be highly revealing. However, because phenomenology deals with experiences and meanings, its scientific status is often suspect. We intend to show, however, that phenomenological research can follow the general dictates of science.

Toward a Manageable Project

Most psychologists have issues or problems they would like to have the opportunity to research, but these are usually unformulated, vague and too impractical to carry out. It takes a careful honing and a disciplined attitude to convert an interest into a feasible research project. It takes a great use of knowledge and imagination to eliminate certain variables, control others and realize how to concretize still others in acceptable ways. In general, the more limited and more precise the research question is, the better the research is.

Since the primary purpose of this chapter is to demonstrate a specific type of qualitative research, we shall not dwell long on this first point. In order to test the method as it was developing, we used the phenomenon of learning as the vehicle for research because participants usually found it easy to describe, and they had few inhibitions about picking situations they did not mind sharing with others. In addition, for at least a half-century, learning was a key phenomenon for psychological research because of behaviourism and the verbal learning tradition. Thus, if phenomenological research could throw new light on learning, its usefulness could be demonstrated because of the long history of psychological research on learning.

However, in order to get as many perspectives on learning as possible, we also began to gather descriptions of failures to learn. Consequently, this phenomenon will be used to demonstrate the scientific phenomenological method. While the question may seem to be too general for precise research, it is not so from the phenomenological perspective that seeks the meanings of experiences; moreover, it parallels rather precisely the original questions dealing with descriptions of learning.

The Lifeworld of Learning

If one wants to understand a phenomenon in a better way than one can do spontaneously in everyday life, one, of course, has to study it more thoroughly. However, the way that such a phenomenon appears in everyday life – which phenomenologists call the 'lifeworld' – should still serve as a model or guide, or else the research situation may transform the original situation beyond recognition. This is an especially important problem when phenomena are so diverse that they can occur practically in any setting whatever, as is true of learning or failing to learn. One way around this difficulty is to have individuals describe situations in which they have learned or failed to learn, instead of trying to set up a specific laboratory situation in expectation that subjects will encounter the hoped-for experience. Instead of the researchers trying to come up with one alleged constant situation (alleged because different individuals bring different meanings to the one situation anyway), we decided to go to the participants and have them describe how they experienced situations in which they learned. Even though it is assumed that every situation, as well as the experiences, will be different, the various experienced situations can become the basis for higher-level invariable relationships between the persons and the situations in order to account for the phenomenon of learning.

The request made of the participants, after a general introduction about the purposes of the research, was this: 'Please describe for me a situation in which you failed to learn.' As mentioned, this parallels the original request, 'Please describe for me a situation in which you learned', most directly. Consequently, the psychological interest has to do with a better understanding of learning, and the specific research project is to contrast the experiences of failures to learn with the experiences of successful learning previously acquired.

The descriptions of two participants will be used in this chapter, and both sets of data represent original descriptive data rather than transcribed interviews. The data being used in this chapter came from workshops conducted by the authors. We try to limit workshop data to a page or two, because the analysis is usually a lengthy procedure, and the method is holistic in orientation, so it is practically impossible to select only a portion of data collected in published articles or dissertations. Sometimes MA thesis data are amenable, but Ph.D. dissertation data are consistently far too long to be used in a chapter of this size. (For other examples, see Giorgi, 1985.) The verbatim descriptions received from two participants are given in Box 3.1.

Box 3.1   Descriptions by participants

Participant no. 1

I learned how to copy a key several days before I actually had to make one./ Now, a customer had requested several copies of a round key. He was waiting. The person that usually cut the keys was not available, so I had to do it./ Material prepared, I placed the master key and the blank in their proper positions on the key machine (a small unit). I made sure both the keys were lined up just as I had observed when I was being taught to use the machine. I turned the unit on and began the process of duplication./ As I was turning the master key to each groove, I realized that the drill, which etches an identical groove onto the blank, was taking more time than seemed necessary to cut each edge. I was accustomed to the noise of the machine. I had observed the key-making process several times, but had 'listened to' the process more often. It just did not sound right to me./ By the time I had finished the first duplicate, I realized that I was doing something wrong./ I removed the copied key from its slot and compared it to the master. The grooves were not identical. The copied key had much longer and wider grooves./ I started over. I tried several more blanks. Each time I tried, I adjusted the blank's position a bit differently. I tried to remember exactly what position the blank had to be in. (There is a small spring which keeps the blank at a proper distance from the drill.)/ I was sure that the spring was to be left in a loosely coiled position. But the keys I kept making were not the same as the master./ I kept trying, each time adjusting the key so that the spring was a bit more tightly coiled./ By the time I was on my third try and blank, I was getting nervous. Someone was waiting for the copies I was trying to make./ I finally produced a duplicate that seemed to be like the master key. I gave the key to the customer and explained that it should be tested as I was not sure it would work./ Back at my desk, I felt miserable./ I had watched the key-making process so carefully: it was explained to me. Still, I had not learned. I wondered what I had done wrong./ (I found out later that the spring did in fact have to be coiled very tightly.) Had I not gotten nervous I might have figured this out myself eventually./

Participant no. 2

I was about 10 years old when I first attempted to ride a bike. We had only one./ My older brothers had learned long before, so I thought I would. We had

---

(Continued)

a large backyard where I lived with small hills or grades in it, so you'd think it would be easy for me to learn but for me it was disaster./ I'd try and fall over. I'd try again and use the brake too soon. Always something,/ and between fear of getting hurt and not catching on at how to do it, it was very frustrating./A couple of times I thought I was learning or at least getting over the fear when the family would say, 'Boy you must really be stupid: anyone can ride a bike, it doesn't take brains to do that.'/ But I just couldn't and the more I tried the more I failed and the more ridicule I got, but I had no success./The bike got a flat tyre, we never did get it fixed and it was the only bike we had. I don't know if I was glad or sad. I was glad at times because I could use the flat tyre as an excuse, but I was sad also because then I was left feeling dumb and stupid./

Well, many years later, after being married and all, I tried again to ride a bike here where I live now. The kids thought everyone should know how to ride a bike, 'What's your problem, Mom?'/Well, I did try, still without success, still the fear of getting hurt and the frustration of not being able to learn something that everyone says is so simple. I know all my children ride a bike and I do feel dumb not knowing how / but this is just a small failure in my life. I have bigger ones./ But failure is very frustrating and when you try over and over and still fail, you wonder./ But I think, in the case of the bike, fear and lack of confidence play a big part in it. Because if you fear and don't have confidence you won't succeed, but this comes a lot from the way you're brought up./ And maybe someday I'll try again and just maybe I'll succeed./

Determination of Data and Method

While these two procedures could be separated artificially, they are so intimately connected that it is better to treat them together. The first point to observe is that they both imply a certain slippage or contingency. That is, there are more methods available than the one actually chosen and more happens within a research setting than is recorded by 'data'. For example, if one chooses the phenomenological method, one cannot use grounded theory, and vice versa. Nor can one simply combine them. One has to accept the limits of the chosen method, and often this choice cannot be fully justified. Similarly, collecting verbal data means that non-verbal interactions are not accounted for. Collecting only non-verbal data through videotape still implies that only one perspective was utilized. In a face-to-face interview, some non-verbal data can also be noted in addition to the verbal account, but one can never catch up with the totality of what was 'lived through', and this kind of limitation must be weighed in all analyses. Consequently, all research requires that the researcher be ever mindful of co-determining contextual factors even if they are not blatantly manifest.

The intimate reciprocity between method and data should be obvious. If one wants to record behaviour, one needs instruments that will do so; if one wants voice registration, one would need different appropriate instruments. If one wants behaviour observation to be the basis of data, one must situate oneself accordingly; and, if one wants to use statistical procedures, one must respect the assumptions of the procedure chosen and be sure that appropriate numbers are obtained. Since what is key for phenomenology is how persons actually lived through and interpreted situations, the database often becomes retrospective descriptions. Moreover, since what drives the analysis of the descriptive data more than anything else is the search for psychological meaning as lived by the participant, the description of what it was like for the participant is an excellent database. Thus, there is a harmony among the raw data that is obtained, the method of analysis and the outcomes that are sought.

Perhaps this is a good place to clear up a possible misunderstanding. While retrospective descriptions are often the source of phenomenological data because of their convenience, they are not the only source. It is possible to obtain ongoing descriptions from participants by using the 'talking aloud' method (Aanstoos, 1985), and it is even possible to obtain descriptions of behaviour from others, so long as they are good descriptions from the perspective of everyday life rather than technical descriptions. Indeed, it is even possible to videotape the behaviour of others and then replay it and establish behavioural meaning units rather than verbal ones. Commentary can also be recorded while watching the videotapes, by either the recorder of the video, another researcher, or the participants themselves. These options are mentioned so that the reader knows that phenomenological analyses of data are not limited to retrospective descriptions.

The data presentation in Box 3.1 actually includes the first two steps of the method. It can do this because the first two steps of the method are straightforward and basically noninterventional with respect to the raw data. Consequently, before speaking about the first two steps of the procedure, we will pause momentarily to articulate some necessary concepts belonging to the phenomenological perspective.

A key notion of phenomenology is the idea of intentionality, which is not to be confused with our everyday sense of being 'goal-oriented' or 'deliberate'. Intentionality is the essence of consciousness, rather than awareness, and it means that consciousness is always directed toward some world or other (the real world, an imaginary world, the dream world, etc.). Strictly, intentionality means that all acts of consciousness are directed to objects that transcend the acts themselves (a perceptual act perceives a perceptual object; loving is directed towards a loved object, etc.). Moreover, phenomenologists insist that it is the object itself that is grasped by consciousness, not some representation of it. Representations in the ordinary sense exist, of course, but they are derived acts. Husserl upholds a presentational theory of consciousness. Most generically, what every person is present to is the world or some aspect of it. Consequently, if acts of consciousness grasp objects in the world, how is one to communicate these objects of consciousness or experience? Husserl's basic answer is 'by careful description'. However, Husserl was aware that description is a tricky matter. Achieving careful descriptions is much harder to do than to say. Unexpected biases lurk everywhere, especially in everyday life or with the 'common-sense' attitude.

Thus, to obtain the most precise data from descriptive practices, Husserl introduced certain attitudinal modifications, but, of course, they are not guarantees. One attitudinal shift is called 'epoche', or 'bracketing', and the other is called the phenomenological reduction, although sometimes both attitudinal shifts are discussed under the heading of the 'reduction'. Husserl was aware that a common error in description is simply to subsume later experiences under the rubrics of earlier ones. If one has been to one party, one has been to all of them, or if one can drive one car, one can drive them all. There is a grain of truth in this, but it is also obviously too sweeping a generalization. In order to help researchers be fresh and maximally open to the concrete experiences being researched, he recommended that one bracket knowledge about the phenomenon being researched that comes from other instances or indirect sources. To bracket does not mean to be unconscious of these other sources but rather not to engage them so that there can be no influence from them on the instance being considered. In addition, bracketing other instances of the same phenomenon possibly helps the researcher to notice different nuances or new dimensions of the phenomenon.

The second methodological aid that Husserl suggested was the phenomenological reduction. Husserl posited several types and levels of reduction, but there is only space to consider the one most relevant to the method under discussion. The one we will employ is the one that Husserl called the phenomenological psychological reduction, but which we prefer to call the scientific phenomenological reduction. The reduction that Husserl wanted philosophers to use he called the 'transcendental phenomenological reduction', and this reduction requires an attitude whereby one considers everything that is given to consciousness from the perspective of consciousness as such – that is, any creature's consciousness, and not specifically a human mode of consciousness. What we call the 'scientific phenomenological reduction' also requires the consideration of the given from the viewpoint of consciousness, but this consciousness is considered to be a human consciousness that is engaged with the world. The only difference that the scientific reduction introduces is the fact that the objects or states of affairs being considered are taken to be presences, not realities. They are taken to be exactly as they present themselves to be, but no claim is made that they actually *are* the way they present themselves to be.

Psychologists should be familiar with such phenomena, since we constantly deal with them. For example, we encounter hallucinations, images, dreams, false memories and so on that we recognize as experiential givens, but not as phenomena of the external world. This step helps us to resist the common error whereby we state that reality is just the way it presented itself to us. In other words, the epistemological claim reaches only as far as presence, not to actual existence.

Data Analysis: Four Basic Steps

We are now ready to confront the raw data of our research. The procedure basically involves four steps, and, as noted above, the first two are relatively straightforward.

To begin, the researcher must assume a psychological perspective, get within the attitude of the scientific phenomenological reduction, and be mindful of the phenomenon being studied (in this case, the failure to learn). Then the first actual step is to read the entire description written by the participant. This is an obvious step, but it needs to be made explicit because certain other methods analysing verbal data do not impose this requirement. The phenomenological perspective is a holistic one, and so one does need to know the global sense of the description before proceeding farther. Nothing more needs to be done here because the subsequent steps continue the work of the clarification of sense.

The second step of the method is the constitution of the parts of the description. This step is a bit of a luxury with the brief, demonstrative examples chosen for this chapter, but it is absolutely necessary when the original raw data cover over 100 pages. But, even with small sets of data, the constitution of parts is helpful because one can clarify implicit matters to an extent far beyond what would have been possible from a holistic perspective. Since we are doing psychological analyses, we would want to use the criteria most relevant to a psychological perspective, and since it is ultimately meanings that the analysis aims to discover, we use the criteria of meaning transitions to constitute the parts. Operationally, the 'meaning units' (the name applied to the parts) are formed by a careful rereading of the description, and every time the researchers experience a transition in meaning based upon the attitude we initially described, they place a slash in the text. That is why the original descriptions in Box 3.1 contain slashes.

It is important to note that there are no 'objective' meaning units in the texts as such; rather, they are correlated with the attitude of the researcher. Nor is it important that different researchers may constitute different meaning units. The making of meaning units is a practical step that will help the achievement of the subsequent step. Ultimately, what matters is how the meaning units are transformed, not their size or their comparison with those of other researchers.

Perhaps the third step is the time to say a word about the transformations that follow. Colleagues are often surprised to see what they consider to be active transformations of sense by the researcher in the method we are advocating. However, science almost always demands transformations or modifications of original data. What makes this difficult to comprehend very often is the laboratory tradition. It seems as though one goes into the laboratory and gets data rather directly. However, what is often overlooked is the fact that the laboratory itself is not a natural setting. It is a highly artificial environment constructed precisely in order to improve upon naturalistic settings. There are darkrooms, soundproof rooms, instruments for controlling stimulus intensity and quality, and other instruments for controlling participant responses, whether human or animal. In other words, the transformations take place initially in the situation so the data can be collected straightforwardly. With our method, the data are collected from an everyday perspective, but in order to make the raw data most relevant to psychology (or any other discipline) the transformations have to take place after the raw data are collected.

Why this difference between the laboratory tradition and experiential research? Basically, the difference depends on whether variables or factors are independent of each other and externally related, or interdependent and intrinsically related. The laboratory tradition began with research on 'things' or other phenomena that were fundamentally independent, and so the manipulation of variables was relatively easy. However, in so far as experiences belong to a given individual, they tend to be interdependent and intrinsically related. One can abstractly isolate experiential variables or factors, but one cannot do that actually without simultaneously modifying the structure of the experience. Where human beings are concerned, relationships are so primary that a person cannot be defined without referring to relationships. Consequently, by beginning with a description from the perspective of the lifeworld, one is picking up contextual and referential issues as they appear important to the participant. Since meanings are also basically relational, one begins to see how different dimensions of the experience relate to each other actually rather than hypothetically. Finally, the special relevance of these connections to psychology have to be made explicit, since it is obvious that the same set of raw data can be the basis for several disciplinary analyses.

The type of transformations being sought can be specified a bit more. One goal is to transform what is implicit to the explicit, especially with respect to psychological meaning. This aspect of the transformation is what allows the analysis to reveal meanings that are lived but not necessarily clearly articulated

Box 3.2   Analysis of participant 1's (P1) data

Participant no. 1

1. I learned how to copy a key several days before I actually had to make one.

1. P1 states that he had apparently acquired a certain skill several days before he was actually had to produce a product that required the skill.

1 + 2. P1 found himself in a situation where he had to execute a recently acquired skill, on his own (that is, without instructor guidance), in a 'real' situation with the potential user waiting. It is clearly among his first attempts to execute the skill in such a situation and P1 feels the pressure.

2. Now, a customer had requested several copies of a round key. He was waiting. The person that usually cut the keys was not available, so I had to do it.

2. P1 states that he had to exercise the recently acquired skill on his own because a potential user had requested the product that involved the skill and the potential user was waiting for the product. Since the person who ordinarily operates the machine that produced that product was not around, P1 reluctantly recognized that he had to do it.

3. Material prepared, I placed the master key and the blank in their proper positions on the key machine (a small unit). I made sure both the keys were lined up just as I had observed when I was being taught to use the machine. I turned the unit on and began the process of duplication.

3. P1 states that he got the material prepared, and since making the product involved an original and a duplicate, and a precise relationship between them, P1 claims that he lined up the relationship between the original and the duplicate as he remembered seeing them when being instructed. P1 says that he turned on the machine and began the process of making the product.

3. P1 relates that there was no apparent difficulty in getting the materials assembled, but, although not yet clear to P1, the first trouble point for P1 was the precise relationship between the original and the duplicate, which in the absence of the teacher who could have told him the answer, for P1 relied on his memory of the relationship as he observed it when he was first acquiring the skill. It is very likely that the relationship as originally lived and perceived was not as focused as P1 needed it to be in his present circumstances. P1 nevertheless began the process by turning on the machine.

4. As I was turning the master key to each groove, I realized that the drill, which etches an identical groove onto the blank, was taking more time than seemed necessary to cut each edge. I was accustomed to the noise of the machine. I had observed the key making process several times, but had 'listened to' the process more often. It just did not sound right to me.

5. By the time I had finished the first duplicate, I realized that I was doing something wrong.

6. I removed the copied key from its slot and compared it to the master. The grooves were not identical. The copied key had much longer and wider grooves.

4. P1 states that, as the process started and continued, he observed that one part was taking longer than seemed necessary and that the noise that the machine made did not seem right to him. P1 noted that, while he had observed the process several times before, he had 'heard' it more frequently, and this attempt did not sound right to his ears.

5. P1 states that, by the time he finished his first attempt at making the product, he knew that he was doing something wrong.

6. P1 states that he removed the product from the machine and compared it to the original and saw that the two were not identical. The product he produced was 'off' in a way that corresponded to his visual and auditory perception.

4. P1 states that, during the time that the process ensued and that he was operating the machine, he observed what appeared to be visual and auditory discrepancies, but he could not pinpoint just what the trouble was. The present experience of the process was contrasted to several previous observations now given memorially, and even more auditory prior instances also memorially contrasted, and all that he knew at this time was that the production process neither looked nor sounded right to him. The process also seemed longer than necessary to P1.

5 + 6. When P1 finished the product, he felt it was wrong and this was precisely confirmed when P1 compared his product with the original. The construction of his product implied more time (grooves longer and wider) just as his perception of the process had indicated and had given P1 a feeling of not performing correctly. Now he could confirm that the duplicate was indeed not a perfect match.

(Continued)

7. I started over. I tried several more blanks. Each time I tried I adjusted the blank's position a bit differently. I tried to remember exactly what position the blank had to be in. (There is a small spring which keeps the blank at a proper distance from the drill.)	7. P1 states that he started the process again and tried several more duplicates. With each attempt, P1 states that he used a different initial position as he groped in memory for the exact position the duplicate was supposed to be in. P1 then explains that there is a part of the machine which keeps the duplicate at a proper distance.	7. P1 then states that he started the process over again with different duplicates and each time he used random trial and error as the principle guiding the initial position of the duplicate since his memory, which was the reference point in the absence of precise knowledge or of a knowledgeable other, was only vague. P1 then explained that the concern was how to set the machine so that the relationship between the original and duplicate was correct.
8. I was sure that the spring was to be left in a loosely coiled position. But the keys I kept making were not the same as the master.	8. P1 states that he was sure that one device was meant to be loose, but the products he made were not the same as the original.	8 + 9. P1 states that one point of certitude for him was that a certain piece of the machine was meant to be loose; nevertheless, in contradiction of this alleged certitude, P1 varied the 'looseness' of this part of the machine as part of his experimental trial and error process.
9. I kept trying, each time adjusting the key so that the spring was a bit more tightly coiled.	9. Nevertheless, P1 states that he kept trying and one difference that he introduced each time was to tighten the device that he had kept loose a little bit more.	
10. By the time I was on my third try and third blank, I was getting nervous. Someone was waiting for the copies I was trying to make.	10. P1 states that when he was on his third attempt, and third duplicate, he began to get nervous. P1 became more conscious of the person waiting for his products.	10. P1 states that by his third attempt at making what he felt that he should have been able to do in the eyes of the other, who was waiting, he began to get nervous and he kept the tension in his phenomenal field between the task and awareness of the expectant, waiting other.

11. I finally produced a duplicate that seemed to be like the master key. I gave the key to the customer and explained that it should be tested as I was not sure it would work.

12. Back at my desk, I felt miserable.

13. I had watched the key-making process so carefully. It had been explained to me. Still, I had not learned. I wondered what I had done wrong.

14. (I found out later that the spring did in fact have to be coiled very tightly.) Had I not gotten nervous I might have figured this out myself eventually.

---

11. P1 states that he finally produced a duplicate that seemed like the original, but he wasn't sure. He gave the duplicate to the potential user with a sense of insecurity and explained to him that it should be tested since he was not sure it would work.

12. P1 then states that he returned to his own place at work and felt miserable.

13. P1 reflects on the process he just lived through. He was aware that he had watched the process of making the product carefully; the process had been explained to him. But he concluded that he had not learned, despite the fact that he made a product and he wondered what was wrong with the process he had just lived through.

14. P1 later found out that what he thought he was 'sure' about was precisely opposite to what the case was meant to be. The device had to be tight. P1 states that had he not become nervous, there was a chance that he could have figured that fact out on his own eventually.

---

11. P1 states that he finally produced an apparently acceptable duplicate but gave it to the waiting other with a sense of insecurity and with warning that the product might not be functional.

12 + 13. P1 then went to his own place in the work environment feeling miserable about his attempts to make the duplicate. P1 was aware that he had observed the process apparently carefully and had had it explained to him, but apparently he had not truly appropriated the process in an embodied, self-directed way, and, even though he had produced a duplicate, P1 knew he was not master of the process and wondered what there was about this living through of the procedure that was not correct.

14. P1 states that he later found out where the error was. He became aware that it was precisely what he was 'sure' about, and therefore explicitly not questioned, that was the source of the trouble since his remembered 'certainty' was the opposite of what it should have been. P1 reflects that had he not become nervous, and thus entered into a tense phenomenal field, he might have figured out the correct procedure on his own. That is, he might have also, in a knowing way, submitted to trial and error testing even the aspect that he thought he was sure about, and might possibly have discovered the correct procedure on his own.

Box 3.3   Analysis of participant 2's (P2) data

Participant no. 2

1. I was about 10 years old when I first attempted to ride a bike. We had only one.

1. P2 was a child when she first attempted to acquire a skill that many children seem to acquire easily (ride a bike). P2 states that her family had only one such object.

2. My older brothers had learned long before so I thought I would. We had a large backyard where I lived with small hills or grades in it, so you'd think it would be easy for me to learn, but for me it was disaster.

2. P2 states that her older siblings had learned the skill long before she did and so she thought that she would try. P2 described the environment for acquiring the skill as an apparently suitable one and one favourable for her efforts, but she says that the actual attempts were disasters.

2. It was implicit from the siblings that the achievement should have been easy for P2. The environment suggested the same.

3. I'd try and fall over. I'd try again and use the brake too soon. Always something,

3. P2 states that she would try and fail. She would try again and make one type of error or other, always something that prevented her from succeeding.

4. and between fear of getting hurt and not catching on at how to do it was very frustrating.

4. P2 states that, between fear of getting hurt in trying to acquire the skill and not ever being able to do it successfully, she found the experience to be frustrating. (She apparently does not relate the fear to the failure.)

4. P2's attempt to acquire the skill with a fearful attitude is not conducive to learning. Never experiencing a moment of success also is counterproductive for acquiring the skill, as is the consequent frustration.

5. A couple of times I thought I was learning or at least getting over the fear when the family would say, 'Boy, you must really be stupid: anyone can ride a bike; it doesn't take brains to do that.'

6. But I just couldn't, and the more I tried the more I failed and the more ridicule I got, but without success.

7. The bike got a flat tyre, we never did get it fixed and it was the only bike we had. I don't know if I was glad or sad. I was glad at times because I could use the flat tyre as an excuse, but I was sad also because then I was left feeling dumb and stupid.

5. P2 states that there were a couple of times when she was on the threshold of overcoming her fear of being hurt or 'catching on' to the correct performance, when P2's significant others would make derisive remarks regarding her in relation to her attempts to acquire the skill.

6. P2 states that for some reason she just could not acquire the skill, and the more she tried (performed?) the more she failed, and, the more she failed, the more ridicule she got from significant others – but without success.

7. P2 states that the object became nonfunctional, and so she could no longer attempt to acquire the skill without repairing the object. The actual state of the object left her feeling ambivalent – alternately glad and sad. P2 was glad because the object as dysfunctional was an excuse for her not to make new attempts (before ridiculing significant others). But P2 was sad because she realized that the state of affairs at the time the object became dysfunctional was one in which she felt 'dumb' for never succeeding in acquiring an apparently easy skill.

5. The attitude of significant others has a constraining effect on P2, especially at key moments. When encouraging words might have helped P2, she got negative remarks instead and these inhibited her attempts.

7. P2 seemed not motivated to bring her relation to the task to closure, and avoided confrontation with closure with excuses. However, the lack of closure of the experience left P2 with unresolved ambivalent feelings (relief from further challenge, but dissatisfaction in not completing the task).

(Continued)

(Continued)

8. Well, many years later after being married and all I tried again to ride a bike here where I live now. The kids thought everyone should know how to ride a bike, 'What's your problem, Mom?'	8. P2 states that many years later, as an adult with children of her own, she attempted to acquire the skill again because of the attitude of her children that anyone should be able to acquire the skill because it was perceived to be easy.
9. Well, I did try still without success, still the fear of getting hurt and the frustration of not being able to learn something that everyone says is so simple. I know all my children ride a bike and I do feel dumb not knowing how.	9. P2 states that she attempted once again to acquire the skill, but didn't succeed, acknowledged that she still had the fear of getting hurt and still experienced a frustration in not being able to perform a skill that relatives and acquaintances perceived as simple.
10. But this is just a small failure in my life. I have bigger ones.	10. However, P2 acknowledges that the failure to acquire the skill is merely a single failure in her life. She admits to having bigger ones. 10. P2 accepts this failure because she can point to others that overshadow it, thus creating a situation where there is no motive to change.
11. But failure is very frustrating, and when you try over and over and still fail, you wonder.	11. Nevertheless, P2 acknowledges that failure is very frustrating for her, and that failure after repeated attempts makes her wonder (about herself).

12. But I think that in the case of the bike, fear and lack of confidence play a big part. Because if you fear and don't have confidence you won't succeed, but this comes a lot from the way you're brought up.	12. P2 offers an interpretation of her failure to acquire the skill by suggesting that her fear of being hurt and lack of confidence in herself played big parts in her experience of failure. P2 then theorizes (generalizes) that if one does not have confidence and if one is afraid of possibly being hurt when trying to perform adequately on a task, one does not succeed. However, P2 relates this generalization to the way in which one is brought up, implying that it applies to her.	12. The failure experience seems in line with familiar self-interpretations on the part of P2 that seem to make it acceptable. Maybe that's why greater motivation to succeed is lacking.
13. And maybe someday I'll try again and just maybe I'll succeed.	13. Finally, P2 suggests that sometime in the future she could possibly be motivated to try to acquire the skill again, and expresses the (wishful?) hope that she may succeed the next time.	

or in full awareness. A second aim is to generalize somewhat so that the analyses are not so situation-specific. Seeking the psychological meaning of a situation in part means to go from the concrete lived situation as an example of something and clarify what it is an example of. Third, where possible, one is to describe what took place in ways that are psychologically sensitive. This does not mean 'labelling' meanings in terms of psychological jargon so much as genuinely articulating and rendering visible the psychological meanings that play a role in the experience.

Let us now turn to the analyses. For both participants 1 and 2 in Boxes 3.2 and 3.3, the left-hand column presents in their own words their description of a situation in which they failed to learn. The middle and right-hand columns represent the transformations performed by the researcher. (There is no fixed number of transformations; one does whatever is necessary.) The difference between the middle and right-hand columns is simply synthesis and highlighting of the psychological dimension.

Normally, one would not try to write a structure for a single case, but, since the purpose here is demonstrative, we have done so anyway. Writing a structure based upon a single example is the most difficult condition since there is minimal variation to help the researcher intuit what is common. (For an example of where two descriptions fit under one structure, see Giorgi and Giorgi, in press.) We mentioned above some of the specific reasons for transformation of the raw data. One of the points we made was that a certain degree of generalization should take place. Thus, in meaning unit 1 of Box 3.2, we see that 'making a key' was replaced by 'acquiring a skill', and we spoke about making a product that required the skill instead of a key. In meaning unit 7, participant 1 talked about 'blank keys' and how he adjusted their position differently, and we spoke about the 'process' that participant 1 was trying to achieve. In Box 3.3, for participant 2, in meaning unit 1 again, 'learning to ride a bike' becomes 'an attempt to acquire a skill' and, in meaning unit 7, participant 2 states that 'the bike got a flat tyre', and we express that point by saying 'the object became non-functional'. By our calling 'learning to make a key' and 'learning to ride a bike' 'skill acquisitions', the reader can see the potential for synthesis if all other constituents would fall into place as well. Yet, the claim is made that the psychological significance does not suffer from this kind of generalization. Indeed, one could argue that it clarifies the psychological by lifting it out of potentially confusing empirical details.

Box 3.4   General structure for participants P1 and P2

For P1, failure to learn the implementation of a recently acquired skill occurred when he had to apply his knowledge unexpectedly and prematurely and without

---

the presence of a reliable expert other to guide him, but in the presence of a waiting user. During the process, P1 was aware of auditory and visual discrepancies between a correct performance of the task and his own performance and did not have a detailed and precise memory available to correct this discrepancy. P1 had to rely upon faulty memories and unguided trial and error, and he had to cope with a self-imposed anxiety precipitated by the waiting user. In such circumstances, he managed to make a product, but he was uncertain of its effectiveness and frustrated by his performance.

For P2, the experience of failing to learn a skill occurred twice when she attempted a task that others claimed to be easy, but which for her involved a fear structure and difficulties and lack of proper support, such that the attempt at the task was experienced as primarily frustrating and led her to feel ambivalent about continuing the task. P2 experienced the attitudes of significant others as constraining and the whole experience was situated within a context of acceptance of failure that indicates that P2 lacked confidence in herself.

Another purpose of the transformations was to render the implicit explicit. In meaning unit 2 of Box 3.2, participant 1 recognizes that since the person who ordinarily cut keys was not there, and a potential user was expecting the key, 'he had to do it', and in the transformations we added 'reluctantly', since it is clear from other parts of the description that participant 1 would have preferred handing the task over to the person who normally did it. In meaning unit 10, we made it explicit that participant 1 felt that he was doing a task that, from the perspective of the potential user, he was able to do. It seems that he did not clarify the situation to the potential user, and so he experienced the situation as one of failure to learn. In meaning unit 2 of Box 3.3, we made explicit the fact that participant 2 assumed, because of the attitude of others, that learning to ride a bike would be easy – as implied by her siblings – and even the environment suggested that to participant 2.

A third purpose of the transformations mentioned above was to make them more descriptively articulate and better able to be the bearers of psychological meanings. For example, in meaning unit 7 (third column) of Box 3.2, it is made explicit that participant 1 relied on his memory of the relationship between the original key and the duplicate in the absence of the expert other, and it is also noted that it is quite probable that the initial perception as lived by participant 1 was not as focused as it needed to be in order for his recall to be successful in his present circumstances. For meaning unit 13 (third column of Box 3.2), we stated that participant 1 'had not truly appropriated the process in an embodied, self-directed way'. This was not explicitly stated by participant 1, but we would argue that this is the implicit psychological meaning embedded in the situation as he describes it.

The psychological expressions articulated by the researchers help clarify the psychological meaning in a more direct and pertinent way.

In Box 3.3, meaning unit 5 (third column) makes explicit that the attitude of significant others has a constraining effect upon participant 2 and the last meaning unit (13) makes explicit the idea that participant 2 was not motivated to keep trying to learn to ride a bike. While the constraint imposed by others and the ensuing lack of motivation to continue further are both implied in the empirical data, specifically tying constraining influences to the attitude of significant others and tying the lack of motivation to keep trying to learn to her historical self-interpretations are psychologically revealing dimensions of the concrete experience being reported.

Therefore, method and data are highly correlated and both are related to the purpose of the research as well as to assumptions regarding psychology. Our assumption is that psychology has to dip into the subjective world of the participant as much as possible. Collecting only behavioural data limits such access, although it is not without merit (in so far as behaviours reveal meanings), and the use of quantification tends to inhibit access to the subjective world of the other even more. One must not here confuse two separate issues: the world of the participant is subjective, but the means of capturing that world on the part of the scientist is intersubjective or objective.

The discussion of the structure of the experience also belongs to the relationship between data and method, and this is the fourth and last step of the procedures we are outlining. The structure is gained by going over the last transformations of meaning units and attempts to determine what constituents are typically essential in order to account for the concrete experiences reported. By 'typically essential', we mean that the structures obtained are not universal, but only general because of the role of context. One always tries to obtain one structure for all of the data, but that is not always possible, and one should not try to force the data to fit one structure. The necessity of several structures to account for the data means a fairly high degree of variability. For our examples in this chapter, a single structure was not possible; consequently, a structure was written for each example (see Box 3.4). However, usually, as more cases are added, the types of structures solidify, become enriched and trail far behind the cases. For example, one might have four or five types for 20 or 25 cases.

It is important to realize that a structure refers not only to the key constituents but also to the relationships among them. It is also possible for structures to have common constituents but still not be identical. A holistic view has to be taken in order to appreciate the relationship among the constituents. For example, frustration is part of each of the structures we are considering, but, for participant 1, his frustration was over not getting right what he thought he knew. However, participant 2's frustration was related to the seeming impossibility of success, and it led her to have ambivalent feelings about continuing the task. In other words, the psychological meanings of the frustration were not identical. Moreover, participant 1 experienced pressure and anxiety, but participant 2 was fearful, and the significant others were actively detrimental for participant 2 whereas participant 1 was desiring an absent other, and, while he felt pressure from the potential user, the latter was not vocally and actively detrimental. These differences are too great to be considered merely intrastructural, and, as interstructural, they require different structures to do justice to them.

Communicating Our Findings

The true closure of a research process is when the published material is read by a competent colleague. Without the reading of a research report, the entire process becomes practically useless. Thus, how the data are interpreted and communicated is also critical, and undoubtedly many contingencies enter into this process, especially for those who have a minority perspective. However, many of the difficulties encountered in this phase of the research process are not unique to phenomenology but are generally true for any minority perspective. Consequently, we do not think that these difficulties need to be discussed in this chapter.

Issues to Think About

All experienced researchers know that there is no perfect method. Each method has strengths and limits, and the research process itself can be enhanced only when limitations of methods are made explicit so that proper limits on ensuing interpretations of findings can be established. Obviously, this truth also holds for the phenomenological method as inspired by Husserlian phenomenology.

The first thing to be noted when retrospective descriptions are obtained as the raw data is the possibility of error or deceit on the part of the participant. Honest errors can obviously occur, but they are not as crucial for the psychological analysis as might at first appear. After all, the psychological perspective implies that the descriptions obtained are subjectively dependent ones, not objective reports. The interest is in how the participant experienced situations even if they come through memorial modes, because the manner in which situations stand out in memory is also psychologically revealing. This double possibility of error (memory and perception of original situation) certainly should make the researcher wary, but it does not present an insurmountable obstacle in so far as no claims for the objective reality are made. Rather, epistemological claims are based solely on how situations were experienced or remembered by the participant. In phenomenological research, this step is heightened because of the use of the scientific phenomenological reduction. The reader should recall that, within the reduction, strong epistemological claims are made only for how things presented themselves to the experiencers, not for how they actually were. But this is precisely what a psychological perspective tries to do – to depict how situations are experienced. With this emphasis, the objective reporting of a situation can serve as an aid in detecting the psychological profile, but the objective account should not serve as a substitute for the latter.

The question of deceit is more problematic in the sense that a research interviewer can be deceived over a short period of time or with descriptions that are as brief as the demonstrations presented in this chapter. However, with longer interviews such as are used in doctoral dissertations or sustained research, the fact that something is awry is usually detectable. One may not know just why the narratives are stilted or 'off', but the fact that a participant is trying to control a description usually comes through. Again, the use of the phenomenological reduction is helpful here since the epistemological claim is only for the experiential structure, not for the objective reality. Still, one was seeking authentic experiential structures, not deceitfully contrived ones. The latter only offer how someone construed the phenomenon to be.

Another possible prohibitor of deceit is the fact that in phenomenological research one is merely trying to find out what happened. That is, no specific hypothesis or theory is being advanced, so it is difficult to know why deceit would motivate the participant, unless it was simply to cover up personal failures or embarrassments. The research within the phenomenological attitude is usually discovery oriented rather than hypothesis proving or theory testing (Giorgi, 1986).

It would be fair to point out that these vulnerabilities are not unique to phenomenological research. All qualitative research dependent upon participant accounts of situations is equally vulnerable. Indeed, more objective approaches that depend on instruments such as questionnaires or test items would be equally vulnerable even though the participant only makes check marks on sheets of paper. There are checks and balances, but no foolproof strategy for detecting deception. In addition, one should not forget that all 'talk therapy' is equally vulnerable, although the establishment of a relationship over a lengthier period of time can establish a type of trust that research situations rarely allow.

Another vulnerability that is rather transparent with this method is the fact that the whole process seems to be dependent upon the researcher's subjectivity. This is especially true with respect to the third step of the method, the one in which expressions take on psychological sensitivity. We have already explained why this transformation is necessary because all science transforms raw data in some fashion, either a priori through the research setting or instruments, or a posteriori. Since the phenomenologist's transformation is a posteriori, and since it is concerned with precise expressions of psychological meaning, it often appears to be arbitrary or heavy-handed. Nevertheless, there are rigorous guidelines for such transformations, but their processes cannot be intersubjectively checked: only the outcomes can. And, of course, through dialogue with other researchers, greater clarity can be achieved, but that usually requires a special effort beyond the primary purpose of the research.

The inevitable fact that all psychologists seeking a scientific pursuit of the subject matter must face is that 'neutral' total access to their subject matter is lacking. One may believe that one has full access to one's own experiential processes, but, even if true, this access is not fully shareable with the critical other, and this attitude does not account for unconscious dimensions. If one turns to the behaviour or experience of the other as subject matter, again total access of any type is lacking since experiences are not directly shareable. Traditional psychology has tried to overcome this gap by means of quantification – numbers are precise and exactly shareable – or objectification. However, the conversion of psychological meaning to numbers loses a lot, and, in any case, to be psychologically rich, the process has to be reversed. That is, one has to go from the numbers back to the subjective psychological reality, and this is usually accomplished entirely subjectively by each researcher. Objectification participates in the same process, but perhaps not so radically. The difficulty is that the objectification of the subjective is not the same as comprehending the subjective as subjective. Ironically, to do so is closer to an authentic objective understanding of the subjective than the two previous strategies offer.

The phenomenological approach recognizes this lack of totalness. Consequently, since the critical other cannot directly share the phenomenological researcher's intuitions, meaning discriminations and transformations, the researcher leaves as complete a track record of the process as is possible. The phenomenological researcher shows the critical other the meaning unit discriminations that are made; the researcher shows the transformations that are correlated with each of the meaning units, although it is understood that contextual factors also operate with every transformation. Also clearly visible are the final transformations for each meaning unit that are the basis for the articulation of the structure of the experience. It is true that some critical processes remain invisible even though outcomes do not, but, through dialogue with the critical other, even some of these processes can become accessible.

Finally, it should be pointed out that the analysis should be done from an intersubjective attitude. That is, the researcher does not remain in a purely biographical attitude. Rather, he or she assumes a psychological attitude, the researcher's role, and is constantly conscious of the fact that a critical other will be reviewing the intuitions being described. The intuitions are not so much *person* based as *role* based. Again, these are not guarantees, but they are checks and balances, and they offer principles for believing in the possibility of objective outcomes.

Basically, both traditional researchers and qualitative researchers recognize the same dilemma, but different strategies are employed to overcome the problem of lack of total access. The traditional laboratory or measurement psychologists following a pre-established tradition err on the side of getting intersubjective agreement among researchers (of course, even with this bias, problems persist), but often the price paid is the reduction of the psychological richness of a phenomenon. Qualitative researchers would rather err on the side of 'fidelity to the phenomenon' and struggle with intersubjective agreement. In any case, both biases have some legitimation and they ought to be able to coexist with each other. Arbitrary exclusion of one of these positions by the other is the great error that should be avoided. After all, psychology is still a developing discipline that is trying to find its essential definition.

Box 3.5 presents three examples of phenomenological psychology in action.

Box 3.5   Three good examples of phenomenological psychology

Living through some positive experiences of psychotherapy

In this article by Giorgi and Gallegos (2005) three clients were asked to describe some alleviation of symptoms that they may have experienced in psychotherapy. The descriptions were broad enough so that they were able to be characterized as positive experiences. Positive experiences were easy to come by but they took place within a context of ongoing therapy that also included negative experiences and lack of progress. Instrumental to the existence of the positive experiences was a high quality relationship with the therapist that was safe, trusting, caring and non-judgmental. Phenomenological reflections on the empirical findings: (1) indicated that focused symptom relief was not necessarily the best strategy for outcome evaluation of therapy; (2) threw doubt on the termination of therapy as a good criterion for the experience of therapy; and (3) concluded that the relationship between therapist and client is complex but unified in a way that needs further clarification.

The acquisition of bulimia: childhood experience

This article by Day (2004) is concerned with the childhood experience that seems to be preparatory for the onset of bulimia. Three women's serial experiences of bulimia (reported in four interviews describing specific binge–purge episodes) were investigated and one pattern of experiencing that leads to bulimia emerged. As the interview process deepened (interviews 1–4), the data moved from symptom-related to life-related. The general structure that captured

---

(Continued)

the essence of the lived experiences varied as these women live out their unique lives. In understanding the totality of the phenomenon of bulimia, it is important to remember that each of the six key constituents merges with the others as they interact with each other and with the whole of the experience. These bulimic women reported having family backgrounds in which they experienced a sense of diminished self and dissatisfaction in interactions with significant others and self. They found themselves pressured to maintain a less than integrated life, and in rapid transition from 'awareful' behaving to automatic and anonymous functioning. A psychological hunger seems to possess them and this is lived out during the anonymous phase of their existence. Their need for the mastery and control ordinarily lacking in their lives becomes a symptomatic expression that has relevance for them in respect to the deep psychological pain that is only partially expressed. The phenomenal body and self are given priority over objective reality, resulting in distorted perceptions of 'fatness' and feeling of terror of fat.

The lived experience of spontaneous altruism: a phenomenological study

A significant amount of research has been conducted examining the social, psychological and behavioural aspects of altruism as well as the characteristics and practices of eminent altruists but very little research has been done that seeks to understand the nature of the lived experience of spontaneous altruism. In Mastain's (2006) study, three participants wrote descriptions of situations in which they engaged in spontaneous acts of altruism. Altruism was defined as a motivational state with the ultimate goal of increasing another's welfare. These descriptions were then expanded and clarified through a follow-up interview. The results of the phenomenological analysis produced a structure of the lived experience of spontaneous altruism consisting of 15 constituent themes. These themes detail the complex emotional, psychological and mental processes that work together in the experience of spontaneous altruism. They also point to the possible roles of love, spirituality, ego-autonomy and creativity in the experience of altruism.

Further Reading

Cloonan, T.F. (1971) 'Experiential and behavioral aspects of decision-making', in A. Giorgi, W. Fisher and R. van Echartsberg (eds), *Duquesne Studies in Phenomenological Psychology*. Pittsburgh, PA: Duquesne University Press, pp. 112–31.
Another exemplification of the application of the descriptive phenomenological method on a different phenomenon.

(Continued)

(Continued)

Creswell, J.W. (1998) *Qualitative Inquiry and Research Design. Choosing among Five Traditions.* Thousand Oaks, CA: Sage.
A comparison of five different qualitative methods with some theoretical foundation for each, along with concrete examples from each tradition.

Giorgi, A. (ed.) (1985) *Phenomenological and Psychological Research.* Pittsburgh, PA: Duquesne University Press.
The book within which Giorgi first articulated the phenomenological method, including a sustained theoretical justification in the second chapter.

Giorgi, A. (1994) 'A phenomenological perspective on certain qualitative research methods', *Journal of Phenomenological Psychology*, 25: 190–220.
A comparison of the phenomenological method with several other qualitative methods being utilized.

Kohák, E. (1978) *Idea and Experience: Edmund Husserl's Project of Phenomenology in Ideas*, I. Chicago, IL: University of Chicago Press.
An excellent commentary on Husserl's *Ideas* (1913/1983), I expressed in terms that make the original work more graspable for non-philosophers.

FOUR

Interpretative Phenomenological Analysis

Jonathan A. Smith and Mike Osborn

The aim of interpretative phenomenological analysis (IPA) is to explore in detail how participants are making sense of their personal and social world, and the main currency for an IPA study is the meanings particular experiences, events, states hold for participants. The approach is phenomenological (see Chapter 3) in that it involves detailed examination of the participant's lived experience; it attempts to explore personal experience and is concerned with an individual's personal perception or account of an object or event, as opposed to an attempt to produce an objective statement of the object or event itself. At the same time, IPA also emphasizes that the research exercise is a dynamic process with an active role for the researcher in that process. One is trying to get close to the participant's personal world, to take, in Conrad's (1987) words, an 'insider's perspective', but one cannot do this directly or completely. Access depends on, and is complicated by, the researcher's own conceptions; indeed, these are required in order to make sense of that other personal world through a process of interpretative activity. Thus, a two-stage interpretation process, or a double hermeneutic, is involved. The participants are trying to make sense of their world; the researcher is trying to make sense of the participants trying to make sense of their world. IPA is therefore intellectually connected to hermeneutics and theories of interpretation (Packer and Addison, 1989; Palmer, 1969; Smith, 2007; see also Chapter 2 this volume). Different interpretative stances are possible, and IPA combines an empathic hermeneutics with a questioning hermeneutics. Thus, consistent with its phenomenological origins, IPA is concerned with trying to understand what it is like, from the point of view of the participants, to take their side. At the same time, a detailed IPA analysis can also involve asking critical questions of the texts from participants, such as the following: What is the person trying to achieve here? Is something leaking out here that wasn't intended? Do I have a sense of something going on here that maybe the participants themselves are less aware of? We would say that both styles of interpretation are part of sustained qualitative inquiry but that the degree of emphasis will depend on the particularities of the IPA study concerned. The ordinary word 'understanding' usefully captures these two aspects of interpretation–understanding in the sense of identifying or empathizing with and understanding as trying to make sense of. Allowing for both aspects in the inquiry is likely to lead to a richer analysis and to do greater justice to the totality of the person, 'warts and all'. IPA also acknowledges a debt to symbolic interactionism (Denzin, 1995) with its concern for how meanings are constructed by individuals within both a social and a personal world.

IPA has a theoretical commitment to the person as a cognitive, linguistic, affective and physical being and assumes a chain of connection between people's talk and their thinking and emotional state. At the same time, IPA researchers realize this chain of connection is complicated – people struggle to express what they are thinking and feeling, there may be reasons why they do not wish to self-disclose, and the researcher has to interpret people's mental and emotional state from what they say.

IPA's emphasis on sense-making by both participant and researcher means that it can be described as having cognition as a central analytic concern, and this suggests an interesting theoretical alliance with the cognitive paradigm that is dominant in contemporary psychology. IPA shares with the cognitive psychology and social cognition approaches in social and clinical psychology (Fiske and Taylor, 1991) a concern with mental processes. However, IPA strongly diverges from mainstream psychology when it comes to deciding the appropriate methodology for such questions. While mainstream psychology is still strongly committed to quantitative and experimental methodology, IPA employs in-depth qualitative analysis. Thus, IPA and mainstream psychology converge in being interested in examining how people think about what is happening to them but diverge in deciding how this thinking can best be studied.

Indeed, we would argue that IPA's commitment to the exploration of meaning and sense-making links it quite closely to the original concerns of cognitive psychology in its rejection of the behaviourist paradigm that had thus far dominated the discipline. It is interesting to see how Bruner (1990), one of the founders of the cognitive approach, regrets how it swiftly moved from a central concern with meaning and meaning making into the science of information processing. For more on the theoretical foundations of IPA, see Smith (1996a) and Eatough and Smith (in press).

The aim of this chapter is to provide for the reader new to this way of working a detailed presentation of the stages involved in doing interpretative phenomenological analysis. It gives details of each stage and illustrates them with material taken from a study conducted by the authors. At the same time, it should be recognized that, as is generally the case with qualitative research, there is no single, definitive way to do IPA. We are offering suggestions, ways we have found that have worked for us. We hope these will be useful in helping the newcomer to IPA to get under way, but remember that, as you proceed, you may find yourself adapting the method to your own particular way of working and the particular topic you are investigating. We would also point the reader to related writing on interpretive phenomenology (Benner, 1994; Van Manen, 1997).

Constructing a Research Question and Deciding a Sample

As will be apparent, IPA is a suitable approach when one is trying to find out how individuals are perceiving the particular situations they are facing, how they are making sense of their personal and social world. IPA is especially useful when one is concerned with complexity, process or novelty. Box 4.1 illustrates the type of research questions that have been addressed by IPA. Research questions in IPA projects are usually framed broadly and openly. There is no attempt to test a predetermined hypothesis of the researcher; rather, the aim is to explore, flexibly and in detail, an area of concern.

Box 4.1   Examples of psychological research questions addressed in IPA studies

- How do gay men think about sex and sexuality? (Flowers et al., 1997)
- How do people with genetic conditions view changing medical technologies? (Chapman, 2002)
- What is the relationship between delusions and personal goals? (Rhodes and Jakes, 2000)
- How do people come to terms with the death of a partner? (Golsworthy and Coyle, 1999)
- How does a woman's sense of identity change during the transition to motherhood? (Smith, 1999)
- What model of the person do priests have? (Vignoles et al., 2004)
- How do people in the early stage of Alzheimer's disease perceive and manage the impact on their sense of self? (Clare, 2003)
- What influences the decision to stop therapy? (Wilson and Sperlinger, 2004)
- What forms of social support are helpful to people in pain? (Warwick et al., 2004)
- How does being HIV impact on personal relationships? (Jarman et al., 2005)

IPA studies are conducted on small sample sizes. The detailed case-by-case analysis of individual transcripts takes a long time, and the aim of the study is to say something in detail about the perceptions and understandings of this particular group rather than prematurely make more general claims. This is not to say that IPA is opposed to more general claims for larger populations; it is just that it is committed to the painstaking analysis of cases rather than jumping to generalizations. This is described as an idiographic mode of inquiry as opposed to the nomothetic approach which predominates in psychology (Smith et al., 1995). In a nomothetic study, analysis is at the level of groups and populations, and one can make only probabilistic claims about individuals: for example, there is a 70 per cent chance that person x will respond in this way. In an idiographic study, because it has been derived from the examination of individual case studies, it is also possible to make specific statements about those individuals.

IPA researchers usually try to find a fairly homogeneous sample. The basic logic is that if one is interviewing, for example, six participants it is not very helpful to think in terms of random or representative sampling. IPA therefore goes in the opposite direction and, through purposive sampling, finds a more closely defined group for whom the research question will be significant. How the specificity of a sample is defined will depend on the study; in some cases, the topic under investigation may itself be rare and define the boundaries of the relevant sample. In other cases where a less specific issue is under investigation, the sample may be drawn from a population with similar demographic/socio-economic status profiles. The logic is similar to that employed by the social anthropologist conducting ethnographic research in one particular community. The anthropologist then reports in detail about that particular culture but does not claim to be able to say something about *all* cultures. In time, of course, it will be possible for subsequent studies to be conducted with other groups, and so, gradually, more general claims can be made, but each founded on the detailed examination of a set of case studies. It is also possible to think in terms of theoretical rather than empirical generalizability. In this case, the readers make links between the findings of an IPA study, their own personal and professional experience, and the claims in the extant literature. The power of the IPA study is judged by the light it sheds within this broader context. A final note on sampling: it should be remembered that one always has to be pragmatic when doing research; one's sample will in part be defined by who is prepared to be included in it!

There is no right answer to the question of the sample size. It partly depends on several factors: the degree of commitment to the case study level of analysis and reporting, the richness of the individual cases, and the constraints one is operating under. For example, IPA studies have been published with samples of one, four, nine, fifteen and more. Recently there has been a trend for some IPA studies to be conducted with a very small number of participants. A distinctive feature of IPA is its commitment to a detailed interpretative account of the cases included, and many researchers are recognizing that this can only realistically be done on a very small sample – thus in simple terms one is sacrificing breadth for depth. Recently the first author has been arguing the case for the single case study (Smith, 2004) and for recent examples of IPA case studies, see Eatough and Smith (2006a; 2006b). In the recent past, five or six has sometimes been recommended as a reasonable sample size for a student project using IPA. Our current thinking is that, for students doing IPA for the first time, three is an extremely useful number for the sample. This allows sufficient in-depth engagement with each individual case but also allows a detailed examination of similarity and difference, convergence and divergence. The danger for the newcomer is that if the sample size is too large they become overwhelmed by the vast amount of data generated by a qualitative study and are not able to produce a sufficiently penetrating analysis. We express an intellectual debt to George Kelly here (see Bannister and Fransella, 1971; Smith, 1990; and Chapter 2 in this volume). To facilitate accessing an individual's personal constructs, Kelly suggested considering three elements at a time, allowing the individual to focus closely on the relationship between the elements in considering a way in which two were similar to and different from the third. IPA doesn't prescribe a technique in the same way but our thinking is clearly related.

Collecting Data: Semi-structured Interviews as the Exemplary Method for IPA

IPA researchers wish to analyse in detail how participants perceive and make sense of things which are happening to them. It therefore requires a flexible data collection instrument. While it is possible to obtain data suitable for IPA analysis in a number of ways – such as personal accounts, and diaries – probably the best way to collect data for an IPA study and the way most IPA studies have been conducted is through the semi-structured interview. This form of interviewing allows the researcher and participant to engage in a dialogue whereby initial questions are modified in the light of the participants' responses and the investigator is able to probe interesting and important areas which arise. Therefore, we will discuss semi-structured interviewing in detail in this chapter. For discussion of other data collection methods either used in or consonant with IPA, see Smith (1990) and Plummer (2000). It is useful first to contrast the primary features of a semi-structured interview with those of a structured interview.

The Structured Interview

The structured interview shares much of the rationale of the psychological experiment. Generally, the investigator decides in advance exactly what constitutes the required data and constructs the questions in such a way as to elicit answers corresponding to, and easily contained within, predetermined categories, which can then be numerically analysed. In order to enhance reliability, the interviewer should stick very closely to the interview schedule and behave with as little variation as possible between interviews. The interviewer will aim to:

- use short specific questions
- read the question exactly as on the schedule

- ask the questions in the identical order specified by the schedule
- ideally have precoded response categories, enabling the questioner to match what the respondent says against one of those categories.

Sometimes the investigator will provide the respondent with a set of possible answers to choose from. Sometimes the respondent is allowed a free response, which can then be categorized.

Thus, in many ways, the structured interview is like the questionnaire; indeed, the two overlap to the extent that often the interview is simply the investigator going through a questionnaire in the presence of a respondent, with the interviewer filling in the answers on the questionnaire sheet based on what the respondent says.

The alleged advantages of the structured interview format are control, reliability and speed. That is, the investigator has maximum control over what takes place in the interview. It is also argued that the interview will be reliable in the sense that the same format is being used with each respondent, and that the identity of the interviewer should have minimal impact on the responses obtained.

The structured interview has disadvantages which arise from the constraints put on the respondent and the situation. The structured interview deliberately limits what the respondent can talk about – this having been decided in advance by the investigator. Thus, the interview may well miss out on a novel aspect of the subject, an area considered important by the respondent but not predicted by the investigator. And the topics which are included are approached in a way which makes it unlikely that it will allow the unravelling of complexity or ambiguity in the respondent's position. The structured interview can also become stilted because of the need to ask questions in exactly the same format and sequence to each participant.

This section has offered only a brief introduction to the structured interview, the aim being to provide a context in which to place a discussion of semi-structured interviewing. For more on the different types of interview used by researchers, see Brenner et al. (1985) and Breakwell (2006).

Semi-structured Interviews

With semi-structured interviews, the investigator will have a set of questions on an interview schedule, but the interview will be guided by the schedule rather than be dictated by it. Here then:

- There is an attempt to establish rapport with the respondent.
- The ordering of questions is less important.
- The interviewer is freer to probe interesting areas that arise.
- The interview can follow the respondent's interests or concerns.

These differences follow from the basic concerns of an approach such as IPA. The investigator has an idea of the area of interest and some questions to pursue. At the same time, there is a wish to try to enter, as far as possible, the psychological and social world of the respondent. Therefore, the respondent shares more closely in the direction the interview takes, and the respondent can introduce an issue the investigator had not thought of. In this relationship, the respondents can be perceived as the experiential expert on the subject and should therefore be allowed maximum opportunity to tell their own story.

Thus, we could summarize the advantages of the semi-structured interview. It facilitates rapport/empathy, allows a greater flexibility of coverage and allows the interview to go into novel areas, and it tends to produce richer data. On the debit side, this form of interviewing reduces the control the investigator has over the situation, takes longer to carry out, and is harder to analyse.

Constructing the Interview Schedule

Although an investigator conducting a semi-structured interview is likely to see it as a co-determined interaction in its own right, it is still important when working in this way to produce an interview schedule in advance. Why? Producing a schedule beforehand forces us to think explicitly about what we think/hope the interview might cover. More specifically, it enables us to think of difficulties that might be encountered, for example, in terms of question wording or sensitive areas, and to give some thought to how these difficulties might be handled. Having thought in advance about the different ways the interview may proceed allows us, when it comes to the interview itself, to concentrate more thoroughly and more confidently on what the respondent is actually saying. For example, Box 4.2 presents a schedule from a project one of us conducted on kidney disease patients' response to their illness. The participants are undergoing dialysis treatment for their kidney disease – an extremely demanding treatment regimen which involves going to hospital three or four times a week and being attached to a dialysis machine for about three hours.

Box 4.2   Interview schedule: patient's experience of renal dialysis

A. Dialysis

1) Could you give me a brief history of your kidney problem from when it started to your beginning dialysis?
2) Could you describe what happens in dialysis, in your own words?
3) What do you do when you are having dialysis?
4) How do you feel when you are dialysing?
   prompt: physically, emotionally, mentally.

(Continued)

(Continued)

5) What do you think about?
6) How do you feel about having dialysis?
   prompt: some people/relief from previous illness/a bind.
7) How does dialysis/kidney disease affect your everyday life?
   prompt: work, interests, relationships.
8) If you had to describe what the dialysis machine means to you, what would you say?
   prompt: What words come to mind, what images? Do you have a nick-name for it?

B. Identity

9) How would you describe yourself as a person?
   prompt: What sort of person are you? Most important characteristics: happy, moody, nervy.
10) Has having kidney disease and starting dialysis made a difference to how you see yourself?
   prompt: If so, how do you see yourself now as different from before you started dialysis? How would you say you have changed?
11) What about compared to before you had kidney disease?
12) What about the way other people see you?
   prompt: members of your family, friends? changed?

C. Coping

13) What does the term 'illness' mean to you? How do you define it?
14) How much do you think about your own physical health?
15) Do you see yourself as being ill?
   prompt: always, sometimes? Would you say you were an ill person?
16) On a day-to-day basis, how do you deal with having kidney disease (the illness)?
   prompt: do you have particular strategies for helping you? ways of coping, practical, mental.
17) Do you think about the future much?

The following list suggests a sequence for producing an interview schedule. This is intended to be only suggestive, not prescriptive. Note also that doing this sort of work is often iterative rather than linear, and you may find your ideas of what the interview should cover changing or developing as you work on the schedule.

1. Having determined the overall area to be tackled in the interview, think about the broad range of issues you want your interview to cover. The three issues in the kidney dialysis project are description of dialysis, effect on the self and coping strategies.
2. Put the topics in the most appropriate sequence. Two questions may help here. What is the most logical order in which to address these areas? Which is the most sensitive area? In general, it is a good idea to leave sensitive topics until later in the interview to allow the respondent to become relaxed and comfortable speaking to you. Thus, an interview on political affiliations might begin with questions on what the different political parties represent, and then move on to the question of societal attitudes to politics before, in the final section, asking about the person's own voting behaviour – thus leaving the most personal and potentially most sensitive area until last. In the dialysis project, one could say that all the material is sensitive – but then the respondents know the project is about their health condition and have agreed to talk about it. It was decided that talking about the illness itself was the best way into the interview, and to allow discussion of the effect on the respondent's sense of self to come later.
3. Think of appropriate questions related to each area in order to address the issue you are interested in.
4. Think about possible probes and prompts which could follow from answers that might be given to some of your questions.

Constructing Questions

A strategy often employed in this type of interviewing is to encourage the person to speak about the topic with as little prompting from the interviewer as possible. One might say that you are attempting to get as close as possible to what your respondent thinks about the topic, without them being led too much by your questions. Good interview technique therefore often involves a gentle nudge from the interviewer rather than being too explicit. This aspect of the methodology runs counter to most of the training received for more orthodox psychology methodologies. Thus, you may well find that, in the course of constructing your schedule, your first draft questions are too explicit. With redrafting, these become gentler and less loaded but sufficient to let the respondents know what the area of interest is and recognize that they have something to say about it. It may be useful to try out possible questions with a colleague and get some feedback on the level of difficulty and tone.

Sometimes this initial question will be insufficient to elicit a satisfactory response. This may be for various reasons – the issue is a complex one or the question is too general or vague for this particular participant. To prepare for this, you can construct *prompts* that are framed more explicitly. Indeed, some of your first draft questions may serve as these prompts. You do not have to prepare prompts for every question, only those where you think there may be some difficulty. So, for example, after question 4 in the dialysis schedule (Box 4.2), there is a prompt to remind the interviewer to ask about each of these domains. After question 8, a prompt is provided in case the respondent has difficulty with the main question itself.

Thus, the interviewer starts with the most general possible question and hopes that this will be sufficient to enable the respondent to talk about the subject. If respondents have difficulty, say they do not understand, or give a short or tangential reply, the interviewer can move to the prompt, which is more specific. Hopefully, this will be enough to get the participant talking. The more specific level questions are there to deal with more difficult cases where the respondent is more hesitant. It is likely that a successful interview will include questions and answers at both general and more specific levels and will move between the two fairly seamlessly. If an interview is taken up with material entirely derived from very specific follow-up questions, you may need to ask yourself how engaged the respondent is. Are you really entering the personal/social life world of the participants, or are you forcing them, perhaps reluctantly and unsuccessfully, to enter yours?

Funnelling is a related technique. For certain issues, it may well be that you are interested in eliciting both the respondents' general views and their response to more specific concerns. Constructing this part of the schedule as a funnel allows you to do this. Thus, in Box 4.3, the first question attempts to elicit the respondent's general view on government policy. Having established that, the interviewer probes for more specific issues. The general point is that by asking questions in this sequence, you have allowed the respondents to give their own views before funnelling them into more specific questions of particular concern to you. Conducted in the reverse sequence, the interview is more likely to produce data biased in the direction of the investigator's prior and specific concerns. Of course, it is possible that when answering the first question the respondent may also address the targeted issue and so make it redundant for you to ask the more specific questions.

Box 4.3   Funnelling

1) What do you think of current government policies?
2) What do you think of the current government policies towards health and welfare issues?
3) Do you think the government record in this area is okay, or should it be doing anything different?
4) If so, what?
5) It has been suggested that government policy is moving towards one of self-reliance, the welfare system being there only as a safety net for people unable to finance their own provision. What do you think of this as a policy?

Below we provide some more tips on good practice for constructing the interview schedule:

- *Questions should be neutral rather than value-laden or leading.*
    Bad: Do you think that the prime minister is doing a good job?
    Better: What do you think of the prime minister's record in office so far?
- *Avoid jargon or assumptions of technical proficiency.* Try to think of the perspective and language of the participants in your study and frame your questions in a way they will feel familiar and comfortable with.
    Bad: What do you think of the human genome project?
    Better: What do you know about recent developments in genetics?
    Obviously, the first question would be fine if one were talking to biologists!
- *Use open, not closed, questions.* Closed questions encourage Yes/No answers rather than getting the respondent to open up about their thoughts and feelings.
    Bad: Should the manager resign?
    Better: What do you think the manager should do now?
    It all depends on intent and context, however. It is possible to ask what seems like a closed question in such a way and at such a point in the interview that it is actually unlikely to close down the response.

Having constructed your schedule, you should try and learn it by heart before beginning to interview so that, when it comes to the interview, the schedule can act merely as a mental prompt, if you need it, rather than you having constantly to refer to it.

Interviewing

Semi-structured interviews generally last for a considerable amount of time (usually an hour or more) and can become intense and involved, depending on the particular topic. It is therefore sensible to try to make sure that the interview can proceed without interruption as far as possible, and usually it is better to conduct the interview with the respondent alone. At the same time, one can think of exceptions where this would be neither practical nor sensible. For example, it may not be advisable with young children. The location of the interview can also make a difference. People usually feel most comfortable in a setting they are familiar with, as in their own home, but there may be times when this is not practicable and a different venue will need to be chosen.

It is sensible to concentrate at the beginning of the interview on putting respondents at ease, to enable them to feel comfortable talking to you before any of the substantive areas of the schedule are introduced. Hopefully, then, this positive and responsive 'set' will continue through the interview.

The interviewer's role in a semi-structured interview is to facilitate and guide, rather than dictate exactly what will happen during the encounter. If the interviewer has learnt the schedule in advance, he or she can concentrate during the interview on what the respondent is saying, and occasionally monitor the coverage of the scheduled topics. Thus, the interviewer uses the schedule to indicate the general area of interest and to provide cues when the participant has difficulties, but the respondent should be allowed a strong role in determining how the interview proceeds.

The interview does not have to follow the sequence on the schedule, nor does every question have to be asked, or asked in exactly the same way, of each respondent. Thus, the interviewer may decide that it would be appropriate to ask a question earlier than it appears on the schedule because it follows from what the respondent has just said. Similarly, how a question is phrased, and how explicit it is, will now partly depend on how the interviewer feels the participant is responding.

The interview may well move away from the questions on the schedule, and the interviewer must decide how much movement is acceptable. It is quite possible that the interview may enter an area that had not been predicted by the investigator but which is extremely pertinent to, and enlightening of, the project's overall question. Indeed, these novel avenues are often the most valuable, precisely because they have come unprompted from respondents and, therefore, are likely to be of especial importance for them. Thus quite a lot of latitude should be allowed. On the other hand, of course, the interviewer needs to make sure that the conversation does not move too far away from the agreed domain.

Here are a few tips on interviewing techniques.

- *Try not to rush in too quickly*. Give the respondent time to finish a question before moving on. Often the most interesting questions need some time to respond to, and richer, fuller answers may be missed if the interviewer jumps in too quickly.
- *Use minimal probes*. If respondents are entering an interesting area, minimal probes are often all that is required to help them to continue, for example: 'Can you tell me more about that?' or 'How did you feel about that?'
- *Ask one question at a time*. Multiple questions can be difficult for the respondent to unpick and even more difficult for you subsequently, when you are trying to work out from a transcript which question the respondent is replying to.
- *Monitor the effect of the interview on the respondent*. It may be that respondents feel uncomfortable with a particular line of questioning, and this may be expressed in their non-verbal behaviour or in how they reply. You need to be ready to respond to this, by, for example, backing off and trying again more gently or deciding it would be inappropriate to pursue this area with this respondent. As an interviewer, you have ethical responsibilities toward the respondent. For more on interviewing, see Taylor and Bogdan (1998), Breakwell (2006) and Burgess (1984).

Tape Recording and Transcription

It is necessary to decide whether to tape record the interview or not. Our view is that it is not possible to do the form of interviewing required for IPA without tape recording. If one attempts to write down everything the participant is saying during the interview, one will only capture the gist, missing important nuances. It will also interfere with helping the interview to run smoothly and with establishing rapport.

Of course, the respondent may not like being taped and may even not agree to the interview if it is recorded. It is also important not to reify the tape recording. While the record it produces is fuller, it is not a complete 'objective' record. Non-verbal behaviour is excluded, and the recording still requires a process of interpretation by the transcriber or any other listener.

If you do decide to tape and transcribe the interview, the normal convention is to transcribe the whole interview, including the interviewer's questions (see Box 4.4 for a sample). Leave a margin wide enough on both sides to make your analytic comments. For IPA, the level of transcription is generally at the semantic level: one needs to see all the words spoken including false starts; significant pauses, laughs and other features are also worth recording. However, for IPA, one does not need the more detailed transcription of prosodic features of the talk which are required in conversation analysis (see Chapter 7). Transcription of tapes takes a long time, depending on the clarity of the recording and one's typing proficiency. As a rough guide, one needs to allow between five and eight hours of transcription time per hour of interview.

Box 4.4   Sample of transcription from dialysis project

Q Right, okay, em, so I would like to start with some questions about dialysis, okay? And a very basic one just to start with, can you tell me what you do, physically do, when you're dialysing?

R What I actually do with myself while I'm sat there?

Q Yeah.

R Well, what I tend to do is, I always have a paper, or I watch TV, you mean actually just sat there?

Q Yeah.

R I read the papers, I always take two papers from work or a magazine and read those.

Q Do you mean work papers or?

R No, just normal everyday papers cos the problem I've got is because I'm right-handed and the fistula (?) is on the right-hand side, which is the one annoyance but I can't write.

Q Because you can't write, yeah.

R Or else I would be able to, so I read the papers or take as many magazines as I can and I always keep myself busy or watch TV. If I'm getting a good enough sound from the television point I watch the news, I always do it the same way, get in, get on, read the news daily papers, any magazines I've got, then if I've got a good enough sound on the TV I watch the news from half 6 to half 7, that's during the week when I'm in there, on the Sunday now I do it on a morning, I just buy a Sunday paper and I always read the paper or read a magazine. Always the same, just so I can keep my mind occupied. I always need to do that.

(Continued)

(Continued)

Q   So you are able to concentrate enough to be able to do?

R   Yeah. And sometimes if I'm tired I can go to sleep for an hour.

Q   Right.

R   Or if I've run out of papers and sometimes I just shut me eyes for an hour, and I can fall asleep but normally if I can I always make sure I get a magazine or a paper and read that and do something.

Q   And that sounds as though you're, that's quite a determined routine.

R   Yeah.

Q   Do you, what's behind that, what what why do you feel the necessity to be so methodical?

R   I think what I try and do is, yeah, so that I treat it as part of normal routine, I think that's what I do it for, I'm sometimes, I always get a paper from work, the same papers, always try and borrow a magazine and read and keep myself, a way not thinking about it while I'm on, that is why I do it and watch TV, so I don't think about the machine or I get bored if I'm just sat there doing nothing, but mainly not so I don't think about it, so I can just think about reading the paper, and I read the paper from top to bottom even if I've, I just read everything, it's the same things in the same papers in the daily paper, but I always read the same things, even if it's just reading the same things again I read the papers from top to bottom all the way through, and any magazines I always read them and read it from the beginning to the end or watch the TV, always keep myself busy thinking about something rather than that, that's what I feel I do it for.

Analysis

The assumption in IPA is that the analyst is interested in learning something about the respondent's psychological world. This may be in the form of beliefs and constructs that are made manifest or suggested by the respondent's talk, or it may be that the analyst holds that the respondent's story can itself be said to represent a piece of the respondent's identity (Smith, 2003). Either way, meaning is central, and the aim is to try to understand the content and complexity of those meanings rather than measure their frequency. This involves the investigator engaging in an interpretative relationship with the transcript. While one is attempting to capture and do justice to the meanings of the respondents to learn about their mental and social world, those meanings are not transparently available – they must be obtained through a sustained engagement with the text and a process of interpretation.

The following section describes a step-by-step approach to the analysis in IPA, illustrated with a worked example from a study on the impact of chronic benign pain on the participant's self-concept. Chronic benign low back pain is a useful subject for IPA, as the context and personal meanings of the pain to the sufferers are critical to their experience. The example is taken from a project using IPA to try to understand the experience of chronic back spain by patients from one clinic in northern England. Participants were interviewed in the style outlined above and the transcripts subjected to IPA. For more on the study, see Osborn and Smith (1998) and Smith and Osborn (2007).

This is not a prescriptive methodology. It is a way of doing IPA that has worked for us and our students, but it is there to be adapted by researchers, who will have their own personal way of working. It is also important to remember that qualitative analysis is inevitably a personal process, and the analysis itself is the interpretative work which the investigator does at each of the stages. The approach is both similar to and different from phenomenology and grounded theory (Chapters 3 and 5) as, hopefully, will become apparent.

A project may take the form of a single case design or involve a number of participants. For the latter, it is advisable to begin by looking in detail at the transcript of one interview before moving on to examine the others, case by case. This follows the idiographic approach to analysis, beginning with particular examples and only slowly working up to more general categorization or claims (see Smith et al., 1995).

Looking for Themes in the First Case

The transcript is read a number of times, the left-hand margin being used to annotate what is interesting or significant about what the respondent said. It is important in the first stage of the analysis to read and reread the transcript closely in order to become as familiar as possible with the account. Each reading has the potential to throw up new insights. This is close to being a free textual analysis. There are no rules about what is commented upon, and there is no requirement, for example, to divide the text into meaning units and assign a comment for each unit. Some parts of the interview will be richer than others and so warrant more commentary. Some of the comments are attempts at summarizing or paraphrasing, some will be associations or connections that come to mind, and others may be preliminary interpretations. You may also find yourself commenting on the use of language by the participants and/or the sense of the persons themselves which is coming across. As you move through the transcript, you are likely to comment on similarities and differences, echoes, amplifications and contradictions in what a person is saying.

The extract which follows shows this first stage of analysis for a small section of the interview with Helen, who was the first participant in our study:

Int. How long has it been like that?

Aggression	*H.* Since it started getting bad, I was always
Not who I am – identity	snappy with it but not like this, it's not who I
	am it's just who I am if you know what I mean,
Being mean	it's not really me, I get like that and I know like,
Can't help it – no control	you're being mean now but I can't help it. It's
Me doing it but not me	the pain, it's me, but it is me, me doing it but
Conflict, tension	not me do you understand what I'm saying, if

	I was to describe myself like you said, I'm a nice person, but then I'm not am I, and there's other stuff, stuff I haven't told you, if you knew you'd be disgusted I just get so hateful.

Me vs nice
Shame, if you knew – disgust
Fear of being known

Int. When you talk about you and then sometimes not you, what do you mean?

Not always me, part of
himself that is rejected
– hateful, the 'not me'

H. I'm not me these days, I am sometimes, I am all right, but then I get this mean bit, the hateful bit, that's not me.

Int. What's that bit?

Not me = pain, defending
against implications that
it is 'me'
Helpless
Mean/sour – worse than the pain

H. I dunno, that's the pain bit, I know you're gonna say it's all me, but I can't help it even though I don't like it. It's the mean me, my mean head all sour and horrible, I can't cope with that bit, I cope with the pain better.

Int. How do you cope with it?

Tearful/distressed,
avoidant/resistant

Unbearable, shocked at self

H. Get out the way, [tearful] sit in my room, just get away, look do you mind if we stop now, I didn't think it would be like this, I don't want to talk any more.

This process is continued for the whole of the first transcript. Then one returns to the beginning of the transcript, and the other margin is used to document emerging theme titles. Here the initial notes are transformed into concise phrases which aim to capture the essential quality of what was found in the text. The themes move the response to a slightly higher level of abstraction and may invoke more psychological terminology. At the same time, the thread back to what the participant actually said and one's initial response should be apparent. So the skill at this stage is finding expressions which are high level enough to allow theoretical connections within and across cases but which are still grounded in the particularity of the specific thing said. From Helen's account, related above, the following themes emerged and were noted:

Int. How long has it been like that?

H. Since it started getting bad, I was always snappy with it but not like this, it's not who I am it's just who I am if you know what I mean, it's not really me, I get like that and I know like, you're being mean now but I can't help it. It's the pain, it's me, but it is me, me doing it but not me do you understand what I'm saying, if I was to describe myself like you said, I'm a nice

Anger and pain
Struggle to accept self and identity – unwanted self

Lack of control over self

Responsibility, self vs pain

person, but then I'm not am I, and there's other stuff, stuff I haven't told you, if you knew you'd be disgusted I just get so hateful.

Shameful self – struggle with unwanted self
Fear of judgement

Int. When you talk about you and then sometimes not you, what do you mean?

H. I'm not me these days, I am sometimes, I am all right, but then I get this mean bit, the hateful bit, that's not me.

Unwanted self rejected as true self

Int. What's that bit?

H. I dunno, that's the pain bit, I know you're gonna say it's all me, but I can't help it even though I don't like it. It's the mean me, my mean head all sour and horrible, I can't cope with that bit, I cope with the pain better.

Attribution of unwanted self to the pain

Defence of original self

Int. How do you cope with it?

Ranking duress, self vs pain

H. Get out the way, [tearful] sit in my room, just get away, look do you mind if we stop now, I didn't think it would be like this, I don't want to talk any more.

Shame of disclosure

This transformation of initial notes into themes is continued through the whole transcript. It may well be that similar themes emerge as you go through the transcript and where that happens the same theme title is therefore repeated.

We have presented the two stages for a small extract above to show the way in which the transformation into themes works. To illustrate this process further, here is another section of the transcript, showing first the initial notes and then the emergent themes:

Resistance to change

Avoidance

Struggle against being 'bad person', depression

H. No, not really, well, you don't want to think you've changed at all, and I don't think about it, you've asked me and I'm trying to think and yeah, I don't want to, but I think I'm not a bad person, perhaps, yeah, it brings you down, and then you end up spoiling things.

Int. How do you mean?

Fear of exposure/public knowledge

H. No one is going to hear this tape, right?

Int. Like we agreed, anonymous and confidential, you get the tape after I'm done.

Mean, unsociable, undesirable
Schadenfreude
Loss of care, bitter against will

H. Right, [pause] the pain makes me mean. I don't want to be, but I get like, mean, I don't care about other people, nothing's funny, and I get mad if they try to be nice, like pity. It's not

Rejected as true self
Confusion, lack of control

really me, but it is me if know what I mean, I don't like it but I do it, do you understand, and I end up saying sorry, if I've snapped like, it's the pain it's killing, it does that sometimes.

The emergent themes for this extract were noted in the right-hand margin:

H. No not really, well, you don't want to think you've changed at all, and I don't think about it, you've asked me and I'm trying to think and yeah, I don't want to, but I think. I'm not a bad person, perhaps, yeah, it brings you down, and then you end up spoiling things.

Rejection of change
Avoidance of implications
Struggle to accept new self

Undesirable, destructive self

Int. How do you mean?

H. No one is going to hear this tape, right?

Shame

Int. Like we agreed, anonymous and confidential, you get the tape after I'm done.

H. Right, [pause] the pain makes me mean. I don't want to be, but I get like, mean, I don't care about other people, nothing's funny, and I get mad if they try to be nice, like pity. It's not really me, but it is me if you know what I mean, I don't like it but I do it, do you understand, and I up saying sorry, if I've snapped like, it's the pain it's killing, it does that sometimes.

Undesirable behaviour ascribed
to pain

Lack of compassion

Conflict of selves, me vs not me
Living with a new 'me'

At this stage, the entire transcript is treated as data, and no attempt is made to omit or select particular passages for special attention. At the same time, there is no requirement for every turn to generate themes. The number of emerging themes reflects the richness of the particular passage.

Connecting the Themes

The emergent themes are listed on a sheet of paper, and one looks for connections between them. So, in the initial list, the order provided is chronological – it is based on the sequence with which they came up in the transcript. The next stage involves a more analytical or theoretical ordering, as the researcher tries to make sense of the connections between themes which are emerging. Some of the themes will cluster together, and some may emerge as superordinate concepts. Imagine a magnet with some of the themes pulling others in and helping to make sense of them.

The preliminary list of themes that emerged from Helen's transcript and were noted in the right-hand margin are shown in Box 4.5. These were clustered as shown in Box 4.6. In this particular case, it will be seen that all the themes listed were present in the two extracts selected. This is because, in this particular case, we have specifically chosen these two extracts for their richness. They encapsulate each of the important issues in our analysis.

Box 4.5   Initial list of themes

Anger and pain
Struggle to accept self and identity – unwanted self
Lack of control over self
Responsibility, self vs pain
Shameful self – struggle with unwanted self
Fear of judgement
Unwanted self rejected as true self
Attribution of unwanted self to the pain
Defence of original self
Ranking duress, self vs pain
Shame of disclosure
Rejection of change
Avoidance of implications
Struggle to accept new self
Undesirable, destructive self
Shame
Undesirable behaviour ascribed to pain
Lack of compassion
Conflict of selves, me vs not me
Living with a new 'me'

Box 4.6   Clustering of themes

Undesirable behaviour ascribed to pain
Struggle to accept self and identity – unwanted self
Shameful self – struggle with unwanted self, fear of judgement
Shame of disclosure
Struggle to accept new self
Undesirable, destructive self
Conflict of selves, me vs not me
Living with a new 'me'
Unwanted self rejected as true self
Attribution of unwanted self to the pain
Defence of original self
Lack of control over self
Rejection of change
Avoidance of implications
Responsibility, self vs pain
Shame
Lack of compassion
Anger and pain
Ranking duress, self vs pain
Shame of disclosure

As the clustering of themes emerges, it is checked in the transcript to make sure the connections work for the primary source material – the actual words of the participant. This form of analysis is iterative and involves a close interaction between reader and text. As a researcher one is drawing on one's interpretative resources to make sense of what the person is saying, but at the same time one is constantly checking one's own sense-making against what the person actually said. As an adjunct to the process of clustering, it may help to compile directories of the participant's phrases that support related themes. This can easily be done with the cut and paste functions on a standard word- processing package. The material can be printed to help with the clustering, and as the clustering develops so the extract material can be moved, condensed and edited.

The next stage is to produce a table of the themes, ordered coherently. Thus, the above process will have identified some clusters of themes which capture most strongly the respondent's concerns on this particular topic. The clusters are themselves given a name and represent the superordinate themes. The table lists the themes which go with each superordinate theme, and an identifier is added to each instance to aid the organization of the analysis and facilitate finding the original source subsequently. The identifier indicates where in the transcript instances of each theme can be found by giving key words from the particular extract plus the page number of the transcript. During this process, certain themes may be dropped: those which neither fit well in the emerging structure nor are very rich in evidence within the transcript. The final table of themes for Helen is presented in Box 4.7. Because most of the themes recur in this transcript, the identifier in this case points to a particularly good example of the relevant theme.

Box 4.7   Table of themes from first participant

1. *Living with an unwanted self*
- Undesirable behaviour ascribed to pain   1.16   'it's the pain'
- Struggle to accept self and identity –
     unwanted self   24.11 'who I am'
- Unwanted self rejected as true self   24.24 'hateful bit'
- Struggle to accept new self   1.8   'hard to believe'
- Undesirable, destructive self   5.14   'mean'
- Conflict of selves, me vs not me   7.11   'me not me'
- Living with a new self   9.6   'new me'

2. *A self that cannot be understood or controlled*
- Lack of control over self   24.13 'can't help'
- Rejection of change   1.7   'still same'
- Avoidance of implications   10.3   'no different'
- Responsibility, self vs pain   25.25 'understand'

(Continued)

3. *Undesirable feelings*		
– Shame	5.15	'disgusting'
– Anger and pain	24.09	'snappy'
– Lack of compassion	6.29	'don't care'
– Confusion, lack of control	2.17	'no idea'
– Ranking duress, self vs pain	25.01	'cope'
– Shame of disclosure	25.06	'talk'

(1.16 = page 1, line 16)

Continuing the Analysis with Other Cases

A single participant's transcript can be written up as a case study in its own right or, more often, the analysis can move on to incorporate interviews with a number of different individuals. One can either use the themes from the first case to help orient the subsequent analysis or put the table of themes for participant 1 aside and work on transcript 2 from scratch. Whichever approach is adopted, one needs to be disciplined to discern repeating patterns but also acknowledge new issues emerging as one works through the transcripts. Thus, one is aiming to respect convergences and divergences in the data – recognizing ways in which accounts from participants are similar but also different.

In the study illustrated here, the superordinate list from Helen's account was used to inform the analysis of the other transcripts. By remaining aware of what had come before, it was possible to identify what was new and different in the subsequent transcripts and at the same time find responses which further articulated the extant themes. Evidence of the superordinate themes 'living with an unwanted self' and 'undesirable feelings' emerged in other transcripts in ways which helped to illuminate them further. The first stage of the process with Tony's transcript follows:

T. Yeah, you know that *Desert Island Discs?*

Int. The radio show?

Withdrawal, relief

T. I'd love that, don't get me wrong I'd miss my kids and I don't mean it, but to be away from people and not have to be something else you're not, that would be bliss.

Change in role, putting on an act
No people = bliss

Int. You'd be happier that way?

T. Yeah, no, well, no I'd still be a miserable old git but it wouldn't matter, it's only when other people come around that it matters, if you can just be yourself it doesn't matter what you do, I'd probably shout and swear

Miserable but no cost
People = duress

People = cannot be yourself

Front, façade, demands *of social role and convention*	all day but it wouldn't matter I wouldn't have to put on that front so it'd be easier. *Int.* So a lot of how you feel depends on who's around? *T.* I suppose it does, but not the pain, that just happens. Dealing with the pain, I sup-
Pain and relationships, *kids affected experience*	pose, is different. You could say if I didn't have kids I wouldn't be like this.

These initial comments were transformed into the following themes.

T. Yeah, you know that *Desert Island Discs?*	
Int. The radio show?	
T. I'd love that, don't get me wrong I'd miss my kids and I don't mean it, but to be away from people and not have to be something else you're not, that would be bliss.	*Pain and social context* *Conflict in identity* *Conforming to role despite pain*
Int. You'd be happier that way?	
T. Yeah, no, well, no I'd still be a miserable old git but it wouldn't matter, it's only when other people come around that it matters, if you can just be yourself it doesn't what you do, I'd probably shout and swear all day but it wouldn't matter I wouldn't have to put on that front so it'd be easier.	*Self in public domain* *Managing the self in public* *Destructive social consequences of pain*
Int. So a lot of how you feel depends on who's around?	
T. I suppose it does, but not the pain, that just happens. Dealing with the pain, I suppose, is different. You could say if I didn't have kids I wouldn't be like this.	*Self independent of pain* *Self/identity and relationships* *define pain experience*

One can see here how the analysis of pain and identity is evolving and, as the analytic process in this example continued, the theme of 'living with an unwanted self' and 'undesirable feelings' transmuted to become 'living with an unwanted self in private' and 'living with an unwanted self in public'. As we said earlier, the researcher can choose to either use the table of themes from the first transcript to orient the analysis of the subsequent ones, or start the analysis of each case as though it was the first. If one is working with a very small number of cases (for example, a sample of three as we are now suggesting for students' first IPA projects) then we would recommend that the latter strategy is adopted. When the number of cases is very small, it is best to start analysis of each from scratch and then look for convergence and divergence once one has done each case separately.

Once each transcript has been analysed by the interpretative process, a final table of superordinate themes is constructed. Deciding which themes to focus upon requires the analyst to prioritize the data and begin to reduce them, which is challenging. The themes are not selected purely on the basis of their prevalence within the data. Other factors, including the richness of the particular passages that highlight the themes and how the theme helps illuminate other aspects of the account, are also taken into account. From the analysis of the cases in this study, four main superordinate themes were articulated. The fourth one, 'a body separate from the self', emerged late in the analysis. Consonant with the iterative process of IPA, as the analysis continued, earlier transcripts were reviewed in the light of this new superordinate theme, and instances from those earlier transcripts were included in the ongoing analysis. Box 4.8 shows the identifiers for the themes for the two participants looked at in the chapter. In practice, each of the seven participants in the study was represented for each superordinate theme. Sometimes students are worried because they cannot find convergences between their individual case tables of themes. In our experience, this can be seen as an intellectual opportunity rather than a difficulty. It is often possible to see higher level convergences across seemingly disparate cases, and so this process pushes the analysis to an even higher level. The resulting analysis respects both theoretical convergence and, within that, individual idiosyncrasy in how that that convergence is manifest.

Box 4.8   Master table of themes for the group

	Helen	Tony
1. Living with an unwanted self in private		
Undesirable behaviour ascribed to pain	1.16	3.27
Struggle to accept self and identity – unwanted self	24.11	2.13
Rejected as true self	6.3	7.15
Undesirable, destructive self	5.14	2.17
Conflict of selves	7.11	12.13
Living with a new self	9.6	2.14
2. Living with an unwanted self, in public		
Shame	5.15	10.3
Lack of compassion	6.29	3.7
Destructive social consequences of pain	8.16	10.9
3. A self that cannot be understood		
Lack of control over self	24.13	11.8
Rejection of change	1.7	4.16
Responsibility, self vs pain	25.15	13.22
4. A body separate from the self		
Taken for granted	21.15	15.14
Body excluded from the self	23.5	16.23
Body presence vs absence	18.12	19.1

Writing Up

The final section is concerned with moving from the final themes to a write-up and final statement outlining the meanings inherent in the participants' experience. The division between analysis and writing up is, to a certain extent, a false one, in that the analysis will be expanded during the writing phase.

This stage is concerned with translating the themes into a narrative account. Here the analysis becomes expansive again, as the themes are explained, illustrated and nuanced. The table of themes is the basis for the account of the participants' responses, which takes the form of the narrative argument interspersed with verbatim extracts from the transcripts to support the case. Care is taken to distinguish clearly between what the respondent said and the analyst's interpretation or account of it. And when one sees the extracts again within the unfolding narrative, often one is prompted to extend the analytic commentary on them. This is consonant with the processual, creative feature of qualitative psychology.

Two broad presentation strategies are possible. In the first, the 'results' section contains the emergent thematic analysis, and the separate 'discussion' links that analysis to the extant literature. An alternative strategy is to discuss the links to the literature as one presents each superordinate theme in a single 'results and discussion' section. In the back pain study, the themes are presented together in one analysis section while a separate section is devoted to exploring their implications in relation to the existing literature. A brief extract from the final version is shown in Box 4.9. This was subsequently revised and the final version can be found in Smith and Osborn (2007).

Box 4.9   Extract from final write-up of the back pain study

Participants were asked to talk as widely as possible about the different ways their pain had affected or influenced their feelings, attitudes or beliefs about themselves. The participants' accounts clustered around four superordinate themes: living with an unwanted self, in private; living with an unwanted self, in public; living with a self that cannot be understood; and living with a body separate from the self.

Living with an unwanted self, in private

All of the participants related how, as a consequence of living with their chronic pain, they had experienced a deterioration in their sense of self, and were engaged in a struggle to manage that process. The phrase 'self-concept' was not used by the interviewer; the participants were asked to describe in their own words how they felt living with their chronic pain had affected the way they saw

---

(Continued)

or felt about themselves, 'as a person'. None of the participants reported any problems understanding this concept, referring to it as 'me' and 'who I am'.

Helen's account captured much of the participants' despair in relation to the deterioration in their self-regard, and their struggle to assimilate that aspect of their experience of living with pain into their self-concept. The changes Helen reported were associated with significant distress that, at times, outweighed that caused by the pain sensation, and prompted her to withdraw from social contact for fear of harsh judgement:

Int.	How long has it been like that?
H:	Since it started getting bad, I was always snappy with it but not like this, it's not who I am, it's just who I am if you know what I mean, it's not really me, I get like that and I know like, you're being mean now but I can't help it. It's the pain, it's me, but it is me, me doing it but not me do you understand what I'm saying, if I was to describe myself like you said, I'm a nice person, but then I not am I, and there's other stuff, stuff I haven't told you, if you knew you'd be disgusted I just get so hateful.
Int.	When you talk about you and then sometimes not you, what do you mean?
H:	I'm not me these days, I am sometimes, I am all right, but then I get this mean bit, the hateful bit, that's not me.
Int.	What's that bit?
H:	I dunno, that's the pain bit, I know you're gonna say it's all me, but I can't help it even though I don't like it. It's the mean me, my mean head all sour and horrible, I can't cope with that bit, I cope with the pain better.
Int.	How do you cope with it?
H:	Get out the way, [tearful] sit in my room, just get away, look do you mind if we stop now, I didn't think it would be like this, I don't want to talk any more.

Helen's account emphasized the distress she felt as she struggled to manage or comprehend her situation. Helen referred to behaviours and feelings she had about herself since having pain, of being 'hateful', that she found disturbing and alarming. They gave her feelings of self-disgust, and a fear that if others were aware of them they, too, would share that disgust:

H:	There's other stuff, stuff I haven't told you, if you knew, you'd be disgusted I just get so hateful.

Helen was not explicit about what she does that is so 'hateful', but showed that it was sufficiently threatening to warrant its concealment. Her use of the term 'hateful' was not explicit, but implied that she felt that, in being 'mean', she was both full of feelings of hate toward others, and also worthy of hate by others.

She showed a need to see herself in a positive light, as a 'nice person', but struggled to do so. This was reflected in her confusion about her sense of self, and her attempts to separate the undesirable behaviour from her self-concept, and attribute it to the pain:

(Continued)

Interpretative Phenomenological Analysis | **77**

(Continued)

> H: It's not who I am it's just who I am if you know what I mean, it's not really me … It's the pain, it's me, but it is me, me doing it but not me.

Helen appeared to be engaged in an ongoing process of defending her self-concept to retain a sense of self-worth, but she could not reject completely the implication that her 'disgusting' behaviour was not just a function of her pain but also related to herself, 'I know you're gonna say it's all me'. The battle to retain a sense of self-worth in the face of her confusing experience of her deteriorating physical and emotional state, and disability, was more difficult to bear than the sensation of pain itself:

> H: It's the mean me, my mean head all sour and horrible, I can't cope with that bit, I cope with the pain better.

Conclusion

This chapter has aimed to present the reader with an accessible introduction to IPA. We have outlined a series of steps for conducting a research study using the approach. Doing qualitative research may seem daunting at first, but, ultimately, it is extremely rewarding. We hope you may be encouraged by what we have written to attempt a project using IPA yourself.

Box 4.10 presents three good examples of IPA in action.

Box 4.10   Three good examples of IPA

Migration and threat to identity

This paper by Timotijevic and Breakwell (2000) explores the impact of migration on identity. Immigrants to the UK from the Former Yugoslavia were interviewed about their perceptions of the countries they had left and the one they had joined and the decision to move. Their accounts point to a rich patterning of identifications. Different people used different category membership strategies in relation to their former home. Some stressed their own ethnic identity at the expense of the greater national Yugoslavian while others identified as Yugoslavian and emphasized their own ethnic group as being an important element in that Yugoslavian identity. Thus the category Yugoslavian was not fixed and could therefore be invoked in different ways as part of the process of asserting ones identity. Their relationship to the UK was similarly complex. The paper neatly captures this multifaceted and dynamic process of identification and relates it to various theories of identity, including identity process theory and social identity theory.

(Continued)

Hepatitis C infection and well-being

Dunne and Quayle (2001) conducted focus groups with patients who had iatrogenically acquired Hepatitis C infection – that is, they became infected from contaminated blood infusion. The authors make a persuasive case for the use of focus groups here in that they argue the style of group facilitation and the fact that members were connected as members of a patients advocate group meant that the data obtained were still able to tap into personal lived experiences. The paper illustrates how difficult patients find it to make sense of their symptoms before they are given a diagnosis. And, when diagnosis comes, their reactions are mixed, partly because with it comes awareness of the seriousness of their condition. The paper also explores the negative impact on their primary social relationships. The authors discuss their results in terms of identity and life career and make links to the extant work of Charmaz and Goffman.

Anger and aggression in women

Eatough and Smith (2006b) present a detailed case study of one woman's account of anger and aggression. It is therefore a useful illustration of IPA's commitment to the idiographic. The paper aims to show how the individual attempts to find meaning for events and experiences within the context of their life and how this meaning making can be hard and conflictual. The analysis begins by demonstrating how dominant cultural discourses are used to explain anger and aggression. These include hormones, alcohol, and the influence of past relationships on present action. It then goes on to examine how the participant's meaning making is often ambiguous and confused, and how she variously accepts and challenges meanings available to her. Finally, the analysis shows how meaning making can break down and the consequences of this for the individual's sense of self.

Further Reading

Smith, J.A. (1996) 'Beyond the divide between cognition and discourse: using interpretative phenomenological analysis in health psychology', *Psychology and Health*, 11: 261–71.
This paper provides a summary of the theoretical basis for IPA.

Smith, J.A., Flowers, P. and Osborn, M. (1997) 'Interpretative phenomenological analysis and health psychology', in L. Yardley (ed.), *Material Discourses and Health*. London: Routledge, pp. 68–91.
This chapter illustrates IPA applied to three different areas in the psychology of health.

Smith, J.A. and Eatough, V. (2006) 'Interpretative phenomenological analysis', in G. Breakwell, C. Fife-Schaw, S. Hammond and J.A. Smith (eds) *Research Methods in Psychology*, (3rd edn). London: Sage. pp. 322–41.
This chapter gives an alternative discussion of the IPA method illustrated with material from a project on anger and aggression.

Eatough, V. and Smith J.A. (in press) 'Interpretative phenomenological analysis', in C. Willig and W. Stainton Rogers (eds) *Handbook of Qualitative Psychology*. London: Sage.
This chapter discusses the theoretical foundations of IPA and considers a range of current issues.

FIVE

Grounded Theory

Kathy Charmaz

Consider the following statement from an interview of a 47-year-old woman, Susan Nelson, who has diabetes, depression, vision loss, and congenital myopathy (a disease affecting her muscles).[1] In response to the first question about her health, Susan explained what this kind of myopathy meant:

> Mine was adult onset, so it's milder – it's most common in children. But they don't live to adulthood because it eventually affects the muscles of the respiratory system and – and so then they die because they can't keep breathing. Mine just affects basically my extremities. Extreme muscle pain, extreme fatigue. Any repetitive use of any set of muscles just causes almost instant pain and fatiguing. Now I have managed to work around it – working and resting and working and resting and working and resting – um, but I couldn't get on an exercise bike and pedal it for 30 seconds. Just, it's – I never understood why when I would go on walks with my friends, you know, you're supposed to increase your endurance, you know, and I never got to feeling better. I always hurt so hard after I got home, I'd have to lie down and the next day I was, you know, just real, you know I wasn't able to do a whole lot of anything, and I thought this is really weird, you know. I don't understand this, and I complained about a lot of symptoms for a lot of years and it took me a long time for the doctors to take me seriously. Because I'm a Lab Tech, all my conditions, I've discovered on my own by running my own blood tests.

Susan's short statement contains detailed information, reveals feelings, implies a perspective on self and situation, and offers insights about her illness history. Note her clarity when she first explains her condition and her bewilderment as she later describes experiencing symptoms. Susan's words foretell an interview filled with detailed information and clear ideas.

What does gathering and analysing rich qualitative data entail? After collecting a stack of transcripts and field notes, what do you do with them? How can you make sense of them? How can you give all your data a fair reading, rather than selecting only what interests you? How can you recognize multiple frames of reference and avoid misinterpreting data which flow from a frame of reference different from your own? As a novice researcher, how can you make analytic sense of your participants' experiences without either trivializing them or producing superficial reports? What guidelines can you use to analyse your material?

This chapter answers these questions. Grounded theory methods offer you a flexible set of inductive strategies for collecting and analysing qualitative data. These methods emphasize building inductive theories through data analysis. Hence, you create theoretical categories that are directly 'grounded' in your data. Grounded theory is a comparative and interactive method. You begin to construct your analysis by comparing bits of data – ideas and incidents – with each other. Your comparisons involve you in the analysis. Grounded theory keeps you interacting with the data and your emerging ideas about it.

A grounded theorist starts with gathering focused data and stays close to the data, while developing concepts that synthesize and conceptualize the collected data – in short, make analytic sense of these data. You study research participants' meanings, intentions, actions, and situations – whether you observe your study participants directly, construct life histories with them, engage them in intensive interviewing, or use other materials such as clinical case histories or autobiographies. Thus, you build levels of abstraction directly from the data and, subsequently, check and refine them by gathering further data. You gain a dense conceptual analysis about the empirical problem that you study. Grounded theory methods demystify the conduct of qualitative inquiry – and expedite your research and enhance your excitement about it.

Throughout this introduction to grounded theory, I provide examples from my social psychological studies of the experience of chronic illness. I begin by outlining the basic premises of grounded theory, the strategies it includes, and its history within qualitative research. Next, I introduce data collection strategies for generating useful data. Then I describe coding qualitative data, a technique for pinpointing what you see in each bit of data, making comparisons with other data, and providing short-hand labels for segments of data. I explain how early data analysis shapes subsequent data collection. Afterwards, I describe memo-writing, the crucial intermediate step between data collection and writing drafts of papers. Last, I comment on how scholars have used grounded methods, and outline criteria for evaluating studies conducted with them.

What Is Grounded Theory?

These methods consist of systematic guidelines for gathering, synthesizing, analysing, and conceptualizing qualitative data to construct theory (Charmaz, 2001). You begin with a topic or general research questions to explore and build a theoretical analysis from what you discover through your research. In my study, I started with general questions about what life was like for people with serious chronic illness and how they experienced time. I moved on to develop more refined ideas about self, identity, time and suffering.

You start inductively with individual cases, incidents or experiences and progressively create more abstract categories that explain what these data indicate. Thus, your categories synthesize data and, moreover, interpret them and identify patterned relationships within them. After you have some tentative categories, you gather specific data to refine and develop their properties and to delineate relationships between categories. At this point, you entertain all possible theoretical explanations for your data and then pursue the most promising theoretical direction. The distinguishing characteristics of grounded theory methods (see Glaser, 1992; Glaser and Strauss, 1967) include:

- simultaneous involvement in data collection and analysis phases of research
- developing analytic codes and categories from the data, not from preconceived hypotheses
- constructing middle-range theories to understand and explain behaviour and processes
- memo-writing – that is, analytic notes to explicate and fill out categories
- making comparisons between data and data, data and concept, concept and concept
- theoretical sampling – that is, sampling for theory construction to check and refine conceptual categories, not for representativeness of a given population
- delaying the literature review until after forming the analysis.

What kinds of research questions can grounded theory methods address? Barney G. Glaser and Anselm L. Strauss, the creators of grounded theory (1967), might answer, 'every kind'. They contend that researchers can adopt grounded theory to study diverse processes. Psychologists can use grounded theory methods to study individual processes, interpersonal relations, and the reciprocal effects between individuals and larger social processes. For example, you can study typical psychological topics such as motivation, personal experience, emotions, identity, attraction, prejudice, and interpersonal cooperation and conflict.

A Brief History of Grounded Theory Methods

Grounded theory methods emerged from the sociologists Glaser and Strauss's (1965; 1967) collaboration during the 1960s. Sociology has had a long tradition of ethnographic fieldwork, interview, and case studies from its beginnings to the present (see, for example, Allahyari, 2000; Dunn, 2002; Fine, 1986; Glaser and Strauss, 1965; Goffman, 1959; Thomas and Znaniecki, 1918; Whyte, 1943/1955). However, that tradition had eroded by the 1960s, as sophisticated quantitative methods gained dominance. These methods were rooted in positivism, or the assumption of a unitary scientific method of observation, experimentation, logic and evidence. Positivistic beliefs in scientific logic, objectivity and truth supported and legitimized reducing qualities of human experience to quantifiable variables. Positivistic methods assumed an unbiased and passive observer, the separation of fact from value, the existence of an external world separate from scientific observers and their methods, and the accumulation of knowledge about this world. Hence, positivism led to a quest for valid instruments, replicable research designs, and reliable findings. Most quantitative methodologists of the 1960s in the US ignored human problems that did not fit positivistic research designs. If they acknowledged qualitative research at all, proponents of quantification considered it to be a preliminary exercise for refining quantitative instruments. Simultaneously, the division between theory and research grew. At that time, theory informed quantitative research through the logico-deductive model of inquiry, which relied on deducing testable hypotheses from an existing theory. Yet this research seldom led to new theory construction.

In their initial statement of grounded theory, Glaser and Strauss (1967) challenged:

- the arbitrary division of theory and research
- prevailing views of qualitative research as a precursor to more 'rigorous' quantitative methods
- beliefs that qualitative methods were impressionistic and unsystematic
- separation of data collection and analysis phases of research
- assumptions that qualitative research could not generate theory
- views that limited theorizing to an intellectual elite.

Glaser and Strauss built on their qualitative predecessors' implicit analytic procedures and research strategies and made them explicit. Earlier qualitative researchers had taught generations of students through mentoring and immersion in field experience (Rock, 1979). Glaser and Strauss's written guidelines for conducting qualitative research changed that oral tradition. The epistemological assumptions, logic and systematic approach of grounded theory methods reflects Glaser's rigorous quantitative training at Columbia University. Strong links to symbolic interaction, with its stress on human reflection, choice and action, stem from Strauss's training at the University of Chicago with Herbert Blumer and Robert Park. Through their influence, Strauss adopted both the pragmatist philosophical tradition with its emphasis on studying process, action and meaning (Blumer, 1969; Mead, 1934) and the Chicago legacy of ethnographic research (Park and Burgess, 1921).

Grounded theory contains both positivistic and interpretive elements. Its emphasis on using systematic techniques to study an external world remains consistent with positivism. Its stress on how people construct actions, meanings and intentions is in keeping with interpretive traditions. Some grounded theorists join me (see, for example, Bryant, 2003; Clarke, 1998, 2003, 2005) in assuming that a researcher's disciplinary and theoretical proclivities, relationships, and interactions with respondents all shape the collection, content, and analysis of data. Grounded theory can bridge traditional positivistic methods with interpretive methods in disciplines such as psychology that have embraced quantification. These methods allow psychologists to study aspects of human experience that remain inaccessible with traditional verification methods. The grounded theory emphasis on process enables psychologists to study how individual and interpersonal processes develop, are maintained, or change.

Generating Data

With grounded theory, you begin by exploring general questions about a research topic of interest. You collect data about what relevant people for this topic say and do about it. How might you devise your initial research questions? Grounded theorists' background assumptions and disciplinary interests alert them to certain issues and processes in their data from which they can develop research questions. Consistent with Blumer's (1969) depiction of 'sensitizing concepts', grounded theorists often begin their studies with certain research interests and a set of general concepts. These concepts give you open-ended ideas to pursue and questions to ask about your topic. For example, I began my studies of people with chronic illnesses with an interest in how they experienced time and how their experiences of illness affected them. My guiding interests brought concepts such as self-concept, identity, and duration into the study. But that was only the start. I used those concepts as *points of departure* to form interview questions, to look at data, to listen to interviewees, and to think analytically about the data. Guiding interests should provide you with such points of departure for developing, rather than limiting, your ideas. Then you develop specific concepts by examining your ideas through successive stages of analysis and studying your data.

Thus, sensitizing concepts provide a place to start, not to end. A thorough foundation in a discipline provides such concepts, but we must use them with a critical eye. Professional researchers already hold epistemological assumptions about the world, disciplinary perspectives, and often an intimate familiarity with the research topic and the pertinent literature. Yet every grounded theory researcher should remain as open as possible to new views during the research.

Hence, grounded theorists develop their sensitizing concepts in relation to the processes they define in their data. In contrast, the logico-deductive model of traditional model of research necessitates operationalizing the previously established concept as accurately as possible.

In grounded theory research, you begin analysing what you gather early in your data collection. Simultaneous involvement in data collection and analysis means that your emerging analysis shapes your data collection decisions. Early analytic work leads you to collect more data around emerging themes and questions. For example, we sense Susan Nelson's efforts to account for her pain and fatigue in the interview excerpt above. Her remarks alert the interviewer to ask how she discovered her other conditions and how other people responded to both her search and her conclusions. Following up on an interview participant's comments allows for building further questions into subsequent interviews with other participants.

Through simultaneous involvement in data collection and analysis, you avoid being overwhelmed by volumes of general, unfocused data that do not lead to anything new. If you already have collected a substantial amount of data, begin with it, but subsequently collect additional data about your emerging analytic interests and themes. That way, you can follow up topics that are explicit in one interview or observation but remain implicit or absent in others. For example, a woman with multiple sclerosis mentioned having 'bad days'. She said, 'I deal with time differently [during a bad day when she felt sick] and time has a different meaning to me' (Charmaz, 1991a: 52). When we discussed meanings of time, I saw how she connected experiencing time with images of self. On a bad day, her day shortened because all her daily routines – such as bathing, dressing, exercising and resting – lengthened substantially. As her daily routines stretched, her preferred self shrunk. After I saw how she defined herself in relation to mundane daily routines, I asked interview questions that directly addressed this relationship. Her comment provided a valuable source of comparison, along with ideas to corroborate in other interviews. This data allowed me to compare what other people called 'a bad day' with the properties of lengthened daily routines, shortened time for valued activities, and a shrunken self and to frame new questions about research participants' meanings and actions. To what extent do people view themselves as separated from or embedded in their daily routines? Which daily routines? How does sickness affect their views? When do they claim the self that they experience while ill? When do they reject it?

The core components of grounded theory studies are analytic categories developed while studying the data rather than preconceived concepts or hypotheses. These categories move your study toward abstract analyses yet simultaneously elucidate what happens in the empirical world.

From the beginning, researchers actively construct their data with study participants. The first question to ask is, 'What is happening here?' (Glaser, 1978, 1992; Glaser and Strauss, 1967). Then you have to think of ways to find out. Perhaps their enthusiasm for developing an inductive methodology that anchored emergent theory in data led Glaser and Strauss (1967; Glaser, 1978) to imply in their early works that categories inhere in the data and may even leap out. I disagree. Rather, categories reflect interactions between the observer and observed. Certainly, social researchers' world-views, disciplinary assumptions, theoretical proclivities, and research interests shape what they create (see also, Charmaz, 2006; Clarke, 2005; Dey, 1999) by influencing their observations and emerging categories. What happens if the data do not illuminate your initial interests? Grounded theorists evaluate the fit between their initial research interests and the emerging data. We do not force preconceived ideas and theories directly upon our data. However, what might stand as a viable means of gathering data to one grounded theorist might be defined as forcing the data into a preconceived framework to another. For example, Glaser (1998: 94) cautions against preconceiving 'interview guides, units for data collection, samples, received codes, following diagrams, rules for proper memoing and so forth'. In contrast, I find that we can use such methodological tools when they fit our research design and our emergent analytic needs. For example, I see constructing interview guides with open-ended questions as particularly helpful for novices. A well-constructed guide fosters asking open-ended questions, provides a logical pacing of topics and questions, avoids loaded and leading questions, and gives you direction as well as your interview participants.

Grounded theorists do agree on starting analysis with the data. We follow leads that we define in the data. Thus, I started with research interests in time and self-concept but also pursued other topics that my respondents defined as crucial. For example, I felt compelled to explore their concerns about disclosing illness, which I had not anticipated studying but which had emerged as a significant theme in the data. I studied how, when and why ill people talk about their conditions. However, my interest in time alerted me to see whether people's accounts of disclosing their conditions changed over time.

What kind of data should you gather for grounded theory studies? To the extent possible, I advocate going inside the studied phenomenon and gathering extensive, rich data about it, while simultaneously using grounded theory strategies to direct my data collection. Rich data reveal participants' thoughts, feelings, intentions and actions as well as context and structure. My call for rich, detailed data means seeking full or 'thick' description (Geertz, 1973) such as writing extensive field notes of observations, collecting respondents' written personal accounts, and compiling detailed narratives of experience (such as transcribed tapes of interviews). Seidman (2006) advocates sequential intensive interviewing to build trust and to elicit detailed data. Transcribed tape recordings of interviews provide details for nuanced views and reviews of data. I find that studying the transcriptions gives me new insights and more codes with which to work. In contrast, Glaser (1998) argues that transcribing wastes time and fosters becoming lost in data.

Grounded theorists take different, sometimes contradictory approaches to data collection, although all assume that the strength of grounded theory lies in its empirical foundation. Glaser (1992; 1998) consistently stresses discovering what is happening in the setting without forcing the data into preconceived categories through such errors as applying extant theories to it, assuming the significance of demographic variables (such as age, sex, race, marital status, and occupation; also called face-sheet variables) *before* beginning the study, imposing evidentiary rules (a priori prescriptions about what stands as sufficient evidence) on the data, or failing to make theoretical distinctions with empirical description. However, he also advocates short cuts such as moving quickly from one empirical world to another to develop a category, not transcribing interviews, and until recently urged accepting a group's overt statements about itself, a practice which may obfuscate members' fundamental concerns. Such short cuts can cause problems. Researchers may obtain only a surface view of a group when they move quickly from one research site to another. In addition, people may not offer much beyond a public relations viewpoint until they trust the researcher. Furthermore, members may reveal their most important values and priorities through actions and assumptions, not careful statements. In effect, short cuts may curtail discoveries, miss basic social processes, overlook subtle meanings, and force data into categories prematurely.

Situate your data within settings and scenes, collective meanings, and individual interpretations, actions, and processes. Then, your descriptions will have more substance and form than mere observed behaviour. Even if you have detailed raw data, such as the typed transcription of a patient conference, elaborate on it. Provide the context by describing the structure of the conference, the events preceding it, the players in it, and their unstated concerns (if known or implicit in their non-verbal behaviour). Similarly, place a personal interview into perspective by describing the situation, the interaction, the person's affect, and your perception of how the interview went. Thorough written texts give you data to study. In short, get as much material down on paper as possible.

Rich data afford views of human experience that etiquette, social conventions, and inaccessibility hide or minimize in ordinary discourse. To obtain rich data:

- describe participants' views and actions in detail
- record observations that reveal participants' unstated intentions
- construct interview questions that allow participants to reflect anew on the research topic
- look for and explore taken-for-granted meanings and actions.

'Tell me about', 'how', 'what' and 'when' questions yield rich data, particularly when you buttress them with queries to elaborate or to specify, such as 'Could you describe … further' (for a sample interview guide, see Charmaz, 2001). Look for the 'ums' and 'you know's; explore what they indicate. How might they reflect a struggle to find words? When might a 'you know' signal taken-for-granted meanings? What do long pauses indicate? When might 'you know' seek the interviewer's concurrence or suggest that the respondent is struggling to articulate an experience? In my research, however, respondents' stories about illness often spilled out non-stop. For example, Christine Danforth stated:

If you have lupus, I mean one day it's my liver; one day it's my joints; one day it's my head, and it's like people really think you're a hypochondriac if you keep complaining about different ailments. … It's like you don't want to say anything because people are going to start thinking, you know, 'God, don't go near her, all she is – is complaining about this.' And I think that's why I never say anything because I feel like everything I have is related one way or another to the lupus but most of the people don't know I have lupus, and even those that do are not going to believe that ten different ailments are the same thing. And I don't want anybody saying, you know, they don't want to come around me because I complain. (quoted in Charmaz, 1991a: 114–15)

Through obtaining rich data, researchers gain thorough knowledge of their studied empirical worlds or research problems. Glaser (1998) advocates moving across different empirical settings quickly to seek comparative data about an emerging category. Instead, I recommend that novices gain a thorough empirical grounding in one arena before exploring another. Then you may discern what participants mean and how they define their experiences, and subsequently interpret these data starting from your respondents' points of view. You may see other things in the data as well, because you bring different perspectives and concerns to it than do your participants. (Here I adopt the assumption that to the best of their ability researchers should find out what is 'happening' and that we can find out because we share language and meanings with those we study, or we can learn them. Ultimately, however, our interpretations shape whatever we find and record and we must be cognizant of our interpretive processes as well as those of the people we study.) Rich data allow you to trace events, delineate processes, and make comparisons.

Throughout a grounded theory research project, you increasingly focus your data collection because your analytic work guides you to gather more specific data. *The grounded theorist's simultaneous involvement in data gathering and analysis is explicitly aimed toward developing theory.* Grounded theory ethnographers, for example, move from attempting to capture the whole round of life to focused areas to explore, observe, and analyse. Grounded theory interviewers adapt their initial interview guides; they add areas to explore and delete extraneous questions.

Grounded theorists follow leads to develop their emerging theoretical categories (Glaser, 1978). Other qualitative researchers may produce thick description of concrete behaviour without filling out, extending, or refining theoretical concepts or making theoretical connections. In contrast, grounded theorists use thick description to ask theoretical questions. For example, young adults agonized over telling room-mates, acquaintances, and dates about their conditions. Their stories sparked my interest in dilemmas of disclosing illness. Rather than obtaining thick description only about their difficulties in disclosing, I began to ask analytic questions about disclosing as a process and then gathered data that illuminated that process. These questions included:

- What are the properties of disclosing?
- Which social psychological conditions foster disclosing? Which inhibit it?
- How does disclosing compare with other forms of telling?

- How, if at all, does disclosing change after the person becomes accustomed to his or her diagnosis?
- What strategies, if any, do people use to disclose? When do they use them?

Researchers may adopt several grounded theory strategies to gather descriptive accounts without following the analytic steps that make their work theoretical. Listen closely to your respondents; attempt to learn unstated and assumed meanings of their statements; and shape your emerging research questions to obtain data that illuminate your theoretical categories. Then you will be doing grounded theory.

Defining Meanings and Processes

The grounded theory emphasis on studying processes moves research away from static analyses. We emphasize what people are doing, an emphasis which also leads to understanding multiple layers of meanings of their actions. These layers could include a person's (1) stated explanation of his or her action, (2) unstated assumptions about it, (3) intentions for engaging in it, (4) effects on others, and (5) consequences for further individual action and interpersonal relations. Throughout the research process, look at action in relation to meaning to help you obtain thick description and develop your categories. How do you study meaning?

Some grounded theorists believe they can readily discover what is significant in the research setting simply by looking or asking. However, the most important issues to study may be hidden, tacit or elusive. We probably struggle to grasp them. The data we 'find' and the meanings we attribute to them reflect this struggle. Neither data nor meaningful interpretation of them simply await the researcher. I assume that we are part of the meanings that we observe and define. In short, our understanding of respondents' meanings emerges from a particular viewpoint and the vocabulary that we invoke to make sense of them.

A researcher has topics to pursue; research participants have goals, thoughts, feelings, and actions. Your research questions and mode of inquiry shape your subsequent data and analysis. Thus, you must become self-aware of why and how you gather data. You learn to sense when you are gathering rich, useful data that do not undermine or demean your respondent(s). Not surprisingly, then, I believe the grounded theory method works best when the grounded theorist engages in data collection as well as data analysis phases of research. This way, you can explore nuances of meaning and process that hired hands might easily miss.

Respondents' stories may tumble out or the major process in which people are engaged may jump out at you. Sometimes, however, respondents may not be so forthcoming nor may major processes be so obvious. Even if they are, it may take more work to discover the subtlety and complexity of respondents' intentions and actions. The researcher may have entered the implicit world of meaning, in which participants' spoken words can only allude to significance, but not articulate it.

For example, many of my participants spoke of incidents in which their sense of social and personal worth was undermined. They complained, told stories, and expressed incredulity. I began to see their accounts as stories of suffering (Charmaz, 1999). These stories reflected more than a stigmatized identity – but what? Gradually, I pieced their stories together in a hierarchy of moral status that catapults downward as health fails, resources wane, and difference increases. Sufferers talked about loss, not moral status. Yet everything they said relied on assumptions of moral status.

The further we go into implicit meanings, the more we may conceptualize them with abstract ideas that encapsulate the experiences that gave rise to these meanings. For example, when exploring implicit meanings of 'bad days', I defined them according to my participants' evaluations of intensified intrusiveness of illness; reduced control over mind, body and actions; and curtailed choices and actions. I synthesized, condensed, and conceptualized participants' statements to make their tacit understandings explicit. Thus, we speak in our categories at this point, rather than reproduce participants' words. Some meanings are so well understood that they remain unstated and assumed; others are felt, but participants have no words to voice them.

For certain topics, close study and direct questioning may suffice. For other topics, you may need to redirect inquiry. Because our language contains few words with which to talk about time, many of my research participants' attitudes toward and actions concerning time remained unspoken and taken for granted. Yet their stories about illness often depended on conceptions of time and referred to implicit qualities of experienced time. For example, Christine Danforth's statement above referred to the quality and unevenness of her days. If a researcher plans to explore such areas, then he or she often needs to devise ways to make relevant observations or to construct questions that will foster pertinent responses. To illustrate, I asked my respondents questions such as, 'As you look back on your illness, which events stand out in your mind?' and 'What is a typical weekday like for you?' Glaser (1992) might say I force the data here by asking preconceived questions of it. Instead, I *generate* data by investigating taken-for-granted aspects of life. At whatever level you attend to your participants' meanings, intentions, and actions, you can create a coherent analysis by using grounded theory methods. Hence, the method is useful for fact-finding descriptive studies as well as more conceptually developed theoretical statements.

Perhaps the most important basic rule for a grounded theorist is: *study your emerging data* (Glaser, 1978; 1992). Studying the data sparks your awareness of respondents' implicit meanings and taken-for-granted concerns. How do you study data? From the very start, transcribe your audiotapes yourself or write your own field notes rather than, say, dictating them to someone else. Studying your data prompts you to learn nuances of your research participants' language and meanings. Subsequently, you learn to define the directions where your data can take you. Through studying interview audiotapes, for example, you attend closely to your respondents' feelings and views. They will live in your mind as you listen carefully over and over to what they were saying. For example, one student in my class remarked:

What an impact the words had on me when I sat home alone transcribing the tapes. I was more able to hear and feel what these women were saying to me. I realized how, at times, I was preoccupied with thoughts of what my next question was, how my eye contact was, or hoping we were speaking loud enough for the tape-recorder. (Charmaz, 1991b: 393)

If you attend to respondents' language, you can adapt your questions to fit their experiences. Then you can learn about their meanings rather than make assumptions about what they mean. For example, when my respondents with chronic illnesses often talked about having 'good days' and 'bad days', I probed further and asked more questions around my respondents' taken-for-granted meanings of good and bad days. I asked questions such as: 'What does a good day mean to you?', 'Could you describe what a bad day is?', 'What kinds of things do you do on a good day?', and 'How do these activities compare with those on a bad day?' By comparing interview accounts, I discovered that good days meant that participants' temporal and spatial horizons expanded and that possibilities increased for realizing the selves they wished to be. But had I not followed up and asked respondents about the meanings of these terms, their specific properties would have remained implicit.

Certainly, starting the research with strong data-gathering skills helps. A skilled researcher knows when to ask more questions or to make more focused observations. Nevertheless, novices can make remarkable gains in skill during a brief time by attending closely to their methods and by studying their data. By gathering rich data and by making meanings explicit, you will have solid material with which to create your analysis.

Coding the Data

Coding is the process of defining what the data are about. Unlike quantitative data, in which *preconceived* categories or codes are applied to the data, grounded theorists *create* their codes by defining what they see in the data. Codes emerge as you scrutinize your data and define meanings within them. This active coding forces you to interact with your data again and ask questions of them. (Thus, the interactive nature of grounded theory research is not limited to data collection, but also proceeds throughout the analytic work.) As a result, coding may take you into unforeseen areas and new research questions.

Coding is the pivotal link between collecting data and developing an emergent theory to explain these data. It consists of at least two phases: an initial phase involving the naming of each line of data followed by a focused, selective phase that uses the most significant or frequent initial codes to sort, synthesize and organize large amounts of data.

While coding, you use 'constant comparative methods' (Glaser and Strauss, 1967) to establish analytic distinctions – and thus make comparisons at each level of analytic work. At first, you compare data with data to find similarities and differences. For example, compare interview statements within the same interview and compare statements in different interviews. When conducting observations of an activity, compare what happens on one day with the same activity on subsequent days. Next, you can ask Glaser's two important analytic questions that separate grounded theory coding from other types of qualitative coding:

- What category or property of a category does this incident indicate? (Glaser, 1992: 39).
- What is this data a study of? (Glaser, 1978: 57; Glaser and Strauss, 1967).

These questions prompt you to think analytically about the fragments of data or incidents that you are coding. You begin to link the concrete data to more abstract ideas and general processes from the beginning, rather than remaining at a topical or descriptive level. Even taking mundane statements apart and looking at their implicit meanings will deepen your understanding and raise the abstract level of your emerging analysis.

Initial coding entails examining each line of data and defining the actions or events that you see as occurring in it or as represented by it – line-by-line coding (see Box 5.1). Compare incident with incident; then, as your ideas take hold, compare incidents to your conceptualization of incidents coded earlier. The code gives you a tool with which to compare other pieces of data. That way you can identify properties of your emerging concept.

Box 5.1   Initial coding: line-by-line coding

Excerpt 1, *Christine Danforth, age 37, lupus erythematosus, Sjögren's syndrome, back injuries.* Lupus erythematosus is a systemic, inflammatory auto-immune disease of the connective tissue that affects vital organs as well as joints, muscles, and nerves. Sjögren's syndrome is a related auto-immune inflammatory disease characterized by dry mucous membranes of the eyes and mouth.

Shifting symptoms, having inconsistent days
Interpreting images of self given by others

Avoiding disclosure

Predicting rejection

If you have lupus, I mean one day it's my liver; one day it's my joints; one day it's my head, and it's like people really think you're a hypochondriac if you keep complaining about different ailments ... It's like you don't want to say anything because people are going to start thinking, you know, 'God, don't go near her, all she is – is complaining about this.'

(Continued)

Keeping others unaware	And I think that's why I never say anything because I feel like everything I have is related one way or another to the lupus but most of the people don't know I have lupus, and even those that do are not going to believe that ten different ailments are the same thing. And I don't want anybody saying, you know, [that] they don't want to come around me because I complain.
Seeing symptoms as connected	
Having others unaware	
Anticipating disbelief	
Controlling others' views	
Avoiding stigma	
Assessing potential losses and risks of disclosing	
	Excerpt 2, *Joyce Marshall, age 60, minor heart condition, recent small cerebral vascular accident (CVA) (stroke). In her case, the stroke left her with weakness, fatigue, and slowed responses when tired.*
Meaning of the CVA	I have to see it [her CVA] as a warning. I can't let myself get so anxious. I have to live one day at a time. I've been so worried about John [her husband who had had life-threatening heart attacks and lost his job three years before retirement] and preparing to get a job [her first in 38 years] … It's just so hard with all this stress … to concentrate on what I can do today. I always used to look to the future. I can't now; it upsets me too much. I have to live one day at a time now or else there may not be any me.
Feeling forced to live one day at a time	
Having a worried past	
Earlier losses	
Difficult living one day at time; concentrate on today	
Giving up future orientation	
Managing emotions through living one day at a time	
Reducing life-threatening risk	

Line-by-line coding means naming each line on each page of your written data (Glaser, 1978), although you may not always have complete sentences. Through line-by-line coding, you take an analytic stance toward your work and, simultaneously, keep close to your data. Coding leads directly to developing theoretical categories, some of which you may define in your initial codes. You build your analysis from the ground up without taking off on theoretical flights of fancy. Line-by-line coding also reduces the likelihood of imputing your motives, fears, or unresolved personal issues to your respondents and to your collected data. Some years ago, a young man in my undergraduate seminar conducted research on adaptation to disability. He had become paraplegic himself when he was hit by a car while bicycling. His ten in-depth interviews were filled with stories of courage, hope, and innovation. His analysis of them was a narrative of grief, anger, and loss. When I noted that his analysis did not reflect his collected material, he realized how his feelings coloured his perceptions of other people's disabilities. His was an important realization. However, had he assiduously done line-by-line coding, he might have arrived at it before he handed in his paper.

From the standpoint of grounded theory, each idea that you adopt from earlier theory or research should earn its way into your analysis (Glaser, 1978). If you apply theoretical concepts from your discipline, you must ensure that these concepts work. Do they help you understand what the data indicate? Can you explicate what is happening in this line of data? If they do not, use other terms that do.

Line-by-line coding forces you to think about the material in new ways that may differ from your research participants' interpretations. For Thomas (1993), a researcher must take the familiar, routine and mundane and make it unfamiliar and new. Line-by-line coding helps you to see the familiar anew. You also gain distance from both your own and your participants' taken-for-granted assumptions about the material, so that you can see it from new vantage points.

If your codes define another view of a process, action or belief than your respondents hold, note that. Your task is to make analytic sense of the material. How do you make analytic sense of the rich stories and descriptions you are compiling? First, look for and identify what you see happening in the data. Some basic questions may help:

- What is going on?
- What are people doing?
- What is the person saying?
- What do these actions and statements take for granted?
- How do structure and context serve to support, maintain, impede, or change these actions and statements?

Try to frame your codes in as specific terms as possible – and keep them short. Make them active. Short, specific, active codes help you define processes in the data that otherwise may remain implicit. What you see in these data derives from your prior perspectives and the new knowledge you gain during your research. Rather than seeing your perspectives as truth, try to see them as representing one view among many. That way, you may gain more awareness of the concepts that you employ. For example, try not to assume that respondents repress or deny significant 'facts' about their lives. Instead, look for how they understand their situations before you judge their attitudes and actions through your own assumptions. Seeing the world through their eyes and understanding the logic of their experience brings you fresh insights. Afterwards, if you still invoke previously held perspectives as codes, you will use them more consciously rather than automatically.

In the example in Box 5.1 of line-by-line coding, my interest in time and self-concept comes through in the first two codes. Note how I kept the codes active and close to the data.

Initial codes often range widely across a variety of topics. Because even a short statement or excerpt may address several points, it could illustrate several different categories. I could use the excerpt in Box 5.1 to show how avoiding disclosure serves to control identity. I could also use it to show either how a respondent learns that other people see his or her illness as inexplicable or how each day is unpredictable. Having multiple interviews allows me to see how social and emotional isolation begins and progresses.

Initial codes help you to separate data into categories and to see processes. Line-by-line coding frees you from becoming so immersed in your respondents' world-view that you accept it without question. Then you fail to look at your data critically and analytically. Being critical about your data does not necessarily mean being critical of your research participants. Instead, being critical forces asking *yourself* questions about your data. These questions help you to see actions and to identify the significant processes. Such questions include:

- What process is at issue here? How can I define it?
- Under which conditions does this process develop?
- How does the research participant(s) think, feel, and act while involved in this process?
- When, why, and how does the process change?
- What are the consequences of the process?

Through coding each line of data, you gain insights about what kinds of data to collect next. Thus, you distil data and direct further inquiry early in the data collection. Line-by-line coding gives you leads to pursue. If, for example, you identify an important process in your fifteenth interview, you can return to earlier respondents and see whether that process explains events and experiences in their lives. If not, you can seek new respondents who can illuminate this process. Hence, your data collection becomes more focused, as does your coding.

After you have established some strong analytic directions through your initial line-by-line coding, you can begin focused coding to synthesize and explain larger segments of data. Focused coding means using the most significant and/or frequent earlier codes to sift through large amounts of data. Thus, focused coding is more directed, selective and conceptual than line-by-line coding (Glaser, 1978). Focused coding requires decisions about which initial codes make the most analytic sense and categorize your data most accurately and completely. Yet, moving to focused coding is not entirely a linear process. Some respondents or events make explicit what was implicit in earlier respondents' statements or prior events. An 'Aha! Now I understand' experience prompts you to study your earlier data afresh. Then you may return to earlier respondents and explore topics that had been glossed over, or that may have been too implicit or unstated to discern.

The strength of grounded theory coding derives from this concentrated, active involvement in the process. You *act* upon the data rather than passively read your material. Through your actions, new threads for analysis become apparent. Events, interactions and perspectives that you had not thought of before come into analytic purview. Focused coding checks your preconceptions about the topic.

In the first excerpt in Box 5.2, I selected the codes 'avoiding disclosure' and 'assessing potential losses and risks of disclosing' to capture, synthesize and understand the main themes in the statement. In the second, the following codes were most useful: 'feeling forced to live one day at a time', 'concentrating on today', 'giving up future orientation', 'managing emotions', and 'reducing life-threatening risk'. Again, I tried to keep the codes active and close to the data. Through focused coding, you can move across interviews and observations and compare people's experiences, actions and interpretations. Note how the codes condense data and provide a handle to them.

Box 5.2   Focused coding

Excerpt 1, *Christine Danforth, age 37, lupus erythematosus, Sjögren's syndrome, back injuries*

If you have lupus, I mean one day it's my liver; one day it's my joints; one day it's my head, and it's like people really think you're a hypochondriac if you keep complaining about different ailments … It's like you don't want to say anything because people are going to start thinking, you know, 'God, don't go near her, all she is – is complaining about this.' And I think that's why I never say anything because I feel like everything I have is related one way or another to the lupus but most of the people don't know I have lupus, and even those that do are not going to believe that ten different ailments are the same thing. And I don't want anybody saying, you know, [that] they don't want to come around me because I complain.

Avoiding disclosure

Assessing potential losses and risks of disclosing

Excerpt 2, *Joyce Marshall, age 60, minor heart condition, recent small CVA (stroke)*

Feeling forced to live one day at a time

I have to see it [her CVA] as a warning. I can't let myself get so anxious. I have to live one day at a time. I've been so worried about John [her husband who had had life-threatening heart attacks and lost his job three years before retirement] and preparing to get a job [her first in 38 years] … It's just so hard with all this stress … to concentrate on what I can do today. I always used to look to the future. I can't now; it upsets me too much. I have to live one day at a time now or else there may not be any me.

Concentrating on today
Giving up future orientation
Managing emotions
Reducing life-threatening risk

Strauss and Corbin (1990) also introduce a third type of coding, axial coding, to specify the dimensions of a category. The purpose is to sort, synthesize and organize large amounts of data and reassemble them in new ways after open coding (Cresswell, 1998). When engaged in axial coding, the researcher also links categories with sub-categories, and asks how they are related. Whether axial coding helps or hinders remains a question. Whether it differs from careful comparisons also is questionable. At best, it helps to clarify; at worst, it casts a technological overlay on the data. Although intended to obtain a more complete grasp of the studied phenomena, axial coding may make grounded theory cumbersome (Robrecht, 1995).

Axial coding is an a priori procedure to apply to the data. In contrast, you may find that emergent methodological directions and decisions occur when you study your data. For example, when studying disclosure of illness, I re-examined the data I had coded during open coding. Then I coded for the range between spontaneous statements and staged pronouncements. I linked forms of telling explicitly to the relative absence or presence of strategizing. After discovering that people invoked different forms of telling, I looked more closely at the context of their telling and the conditions affecting how and whom they told, as well as their stated intentions for telling. I coded for how, when and why they changed their earlier forms of telling. These strategies may lead to charting causes and conditions of the observed phenomenon.

Raising Focused Codes to Conceptual Categories

Focused coding moves your analysis forward in two crucial steps: (1) it establishes the content and form of your nascent analysis; and (2) it prompts you to evaluate and clarify your categories and the relationships between them. First, assess which codes best capture what you see happening in your data. Raise them to conceptual categories for your developing analytic framework – give them conceptual definition and analytic treatment in narrative form. Thus, you go beyond using a code as a descriptive tool to view and synthesize data.

Categories explicate ideas, events or processes in your data – and do so in telling words. A category may subsume common themes and patterns in several codes. For example, my category of 'keeping illness contained' included 'packaging illness' – that is, treating it 'as if it were controlled, delimited and confined to specific realms, such as private life', and 'passing' – which means 'concealing illness, maintaining a conventional self-presentation, and performing like unimpaired peers' (Charmaz, 1991a: 66–8). Again, make your categories as conceptual as possible – with abstract power, general reach, analytic direction, and precise wording. Simultaneously, remain consistent with your data. By making focused codes active (to reflect what is happening or what people are doing) and brief, you can view them as potential categories. Processes gain visibility when you keep codes active. Succinct focused codes lead to sharp, clear categories. That way, you can establish criteria for your categories to make further comparisons.

Grounded theorists look for substantive processes that they develop from their codes. 'Keeping illness contained', 'packaging illness', and 'living one day at a time' above are three such processes. As grounded theorists create conceptual handles to explain what is happening in the setting, they may move toward defining generic processes (Prus, 1987). A generic process cuts across different empirical settings and problems; it can be applied to varied substantive areas. The two codes above, 'avoiding disclosure' and 'assessing potential losses and risks of disclosing', reflect fundamental, generic processes of personal information control. Although these processes describe choices people with illness make in disclosing information, people with other problems may treat information control similarly. For sociologists, generic processes are basic to social life; for psychologists, generic processes are fundamental for psychological existence. Thus, a grounded theorist can elaborate and refine the generic process by gathering more data from diverse arenas where this process is evident. For example, personal information control and choices in disclosing are often problematic for homosexuals, sexual abuse survivors, drug users, and ex-convicts, as well as for people with chronic conditions. Concentrate on analysing a generic process that you define in your codes; then you can raise codes relevant to theoretical categories that lead to explanations of the process and predictions concerning it. These categories reflect what you think about the data as well as what you find in them. As Dey (1999) observes, categorization in grounded theory is more complex and problematic than its originators suggest and involves making inferences as well as classifications.

As you raise a code to a category, you begin to write narrative statements in memos, as I outline below, that:

• explicate the properties of the category
• specify the conditions under which the category arises, is maintained, and changes
• describe its consequences
• show how this category relates to other categories.

Categories may consist of *in vivo* codes that you take directly from your respondents' discourse, or they may represent your theoretical or substantive definition of what is happening in the data. For example, my terms 'good days and bad days' and 'living one day at a time' came directly from my respondents' voices. In contrast, my categories 'recapturing the past' and 'time in immersion and immersion in time' reflect theoretical definitions of actions and events. Furthermore, categories such as 'pulling in', 'facing dependency', and 'making trade-offs' address my respondents' substantive realities of grappling with a serious illness. I created these codes and used them as categories, but they reflect my respondents' concerns and actions. Novice researchers may find that they rely most on *in vivo* and substantive codes. What results is often a grounded description more than a theory. Nonetheless, studying how these codes fit together in categories can help you treat them more theoretically.

Through focused coding, you build and clarify your category by examining all the data it covers and by identifying variations within it and between other categories. You also will become aware of gaps in your analysis. For example, I developed my category of 'existing from day to day' when I realized that 'living one day at a time' did not fully cover impoverished people's level of desperation. In short, I had data about a daily struggle to survive that were not subsumed by my first category of living one day at a time. The finished narrative can be seen in Box 5.3.

Box 5.3   The category of 'existing from day to day'

Existing from day to day occurs when a person plummets into continued crises that rip life apart. It reflects a loss of control of health and the wherewithal to keep life together.

Existing from day to day means a constant struggle for daily survival. Poverty and lack of support contribute to and complicate that struggle. Hence, poor and isolated people usually plummet further and faster than affluent individuals with concerned families. Loss of control extends to being unable to obtain necessities – food, shelter, heat, and medical care.

The struggle to exist keeps people in the present, especially if they have continued problems in getting the basic necessities that middle-class adults take for granted. Yet other problems can assume much greater significance for these people than their illness – a violent husband, a runaway child, an alcoholic spouse, or the overdue rent.

Living one day at a time differs from existing from day to day. Living one day at a time provides a strategy for controlling emotions, managing life, dimming the future, and getting through a troublesome period. It involves managing stress, illness, or regimen, and dealing with these things each day to control them as best one can. It means concentrating on the here and now and relinquishing other goals, pursuits, and obligations (Charmaz, 1991a: 185).

Note the comparisons between the two categories above. To generate categories through focused coding, you need to compare data, incidents, contexts and concepts. Making the following comparisons helps:

- comparing different people (in terms of their beliefs, situations, actions, accounts or experiences)
- comparing data from the same individuals at different points in time
- comparing specific data with the criteria for the category
- comparing categories in the analysis with other categories.

As I compared different people's experiences, I realized that some people's situations forced them into the present. I then looked at how my rendering of living one day at a time did not apply to them. I reviewed earlier interviews and began to seek published accounts that might clarify the comparison. As is evident in the distinctions between these two categories above, focused coding prompts you to begin to see the relationships and patterns between categories.

Memo-writing

You may have thought of memos as business communications to state policies, procedures and proposals. However, in grounded theory, memos serve analytic purposes. Memo-writing consists of taking your categories apart by breaking them into their components. It is the pivotal intermediate step between defining categories and the first draft of your completed analysis. This step spurs you to develop your ideas in narrative form and fullness early in the analytic process. Memo-writing is the logical next step after you define categories; however, it is also helpful for clarification and direction during coding. Writing memos prompts you to elaborate processes, assumptions and actions covered by your codes or categories. Memos also help you to identify which codes to treat as analytic categories, if you have not already defined them. (Then you further develop your category through more memo-writing.)

Think about including as many of the following points in your memos as is possible and useful:

- defining each code or category by its analytic properties
- spelling out and detailing processes subsumed by the codes or catgories
- making comparisons between data and between codes and categories
- bringing raw data into the memo
- providing sufficient empirical evidence to support your definitions of the category and analytic claims about it
- offering conjectures to check through further empirical research
- identifying gaps in the analysis.

Grounded theorists look for patterns, even when focusing on a single case (Strauss and Glaser, 1970). Because they stress identifying patterns, grounded theorists typically invoke respondents' stories to illustrate points – rather than provide complete portrayals of their lives. By bringing raw data right into your memo, you preserve telling evidence for your ideas from the start of your analytic narratives. Through providing ample verbatim material, you not only ground the abstract analysis, but also lay the foundation for making claims about it. Including verbatim material from different sources permits you to make precise comparisons. Thus, memo-writing moves your work beyond individual cases through defining patterns.

Begin your memo with careful definitions of each category. That means you identify its properties or characteristics, look for its underlying assumptions, and show how and when the category develops and changes. To illustrate, I found that people frequently referred to living one day at a time when they suffered a medical crisis or faced continued uncertainty. So I began to ask questions about what living one day at a time was like for them. From their responses as well as from published autobiographical accounts, I began to define the category and its characteristics. The term 'living one day at a time' condenses a whole series of implicit meanings and assumptions. It becomes a strategy for handling unruly feelings, for exerting some control over a now uncontrollable life, for facing uncertainty, and for handling a conceivably foreshortened future. Memo-writing spurs you to dig into implicit, unstated, and condensed meanings.

Start writing memos as soon as you have some interesting ideas and categories to pursue. If at a loss about what to write, elaborate on codes that you adopted repeatedly. Keep collecting data, keep coding, and keep refining your ideas through writing more and further developed memos. Some researchers who use grounded theory methods discover a few interesting findings early in their data collection and then truncate their research. Their work lacks the 'intimate familiarity' with the setting or experience that Lofland and Lofland (1995) avow meets the standards for good qualitative research. Cover your topic in depth by exploring sufficient cases and by elaborating your categories fully.

Memo-writing frees you to explore your ideas about your categories. Treat memos as partial, preliminary, and eminently correctable. Just note where you are on firm ground and where you are making conjectures. Then go back to the field to check your conjectures. Memo-writing is much like free-writing or prewriting (Elbow, 1981). Use memos to help you think about the data and to discover your ideas about them. You can write memos for your eyes only. Do not worry about verb tense, overuse of prepositional phrases, or lengthy sentences at this point. Just get your ideas down as quickly and clearly as you can. You are writing to render the data, not to communicate it to an audience. Later, after you turn your memo into a section of a paper, revise the material to make it accessible to a reader. Writing memos quickly without editing them fosters developing and preserving your natural voice. Then your memo reads as though written by a living, thinking, feeling human being rather than a pedantic social scientist. You can write memos at different levels of abstraction – from the concrete to the highly theoretical. Some of your memos will find their way directly into your first draft of your analysis. Set aside others with a different focus and develop them later.

Direct much of your memo-writing to making comparisons, what Glaser and Strauss (1967: 105) call 'constant comparative methods'. This approach emphasizes comparing incidents indicated by each category, integrating categories by delineating their relationships, delimiting the scope and range of the emerging theory, and writing the theory. Hence, you compare one respondent's beliefs, stance, actions or situations with another respondent's, or one experience with another. If you have longitudinal data, compare a participant's response, experience, or situation at one point in time with that at another time. Then, as you become more analytic, start to make detailed comparisons between categories and then frame them into a theoretical statement. Through memo-writing, you distinguish between major and minor categories. Thus, you direct the shape and form of your emergent analysis.

At each more analytic and abstract level of memo-writing, bring your data right into your analysis. Show how you build your analysis on your data in each memo. Bringing your data into successive levels of memo-writing ultimately saves time; you do not have to dig through stacks of material to illustrate your points. A section of a memo is provided in Box 5.4. Note that I first defined the category, 'living one day at a time', and pointed out its main properties. Then I developed aspects of living one day at a time such as its relationship to time perspective, which is mentioned here, and to managing emotions. The memo also covered how people lived one day at a time, the problems it posed as well as those it solved, and the consequences of doing so.

Box 5.4   Example of memo-writing

Living one day at a time

Living one day at a time means dealing with illness on a day-to-day basis, holding future plans and even ordinary activities in abeyance while the person and, often, others deal with illness. When living one day at a time, the person feels that his or her future remains unsettled, that he or she cannot foresee the future or whether there will be a future. Living one day at a time allows the person to focus on illness, treatment and regimen without becoming entirely immobilized by fear or future implications. By concentrating on the present, the person can avoid or minimize thinking about death and the possibility of dying.

Relation to time perspective

The felt need to live one day at a time often drastically alters a person's time perspective. Living one day at a time pulls the person into the present and pushes back past futures (the futures the person projected before illness or before this round of illness) so that they recede without mourning [their loss]. These past futures can slip away, perhaps almost unnoticed. [I then compare three respondents' situations, statements and time perspectives.]

Theoretical Sampling

Memo-making leads directly to *theoretical sampling* – that is, collecting more data to illuminate your theoretical categories. Here, you sample for the purpose of *developing* your emerging theory, not for representation of a population or increasing the generalizability of your results. Thus, you seek more cases or ask earlier participants about experiences that you may not have covered before. You need more data to be sure that your category accurately describes the underlying quality of your respondents' experiences. In contrast, quantitative researchers need to have random samples whose characteristics are representative of the population under study. Whereas survey researchers want to use sample data to make statistical inferences about the target population, grounded theorists are interested primarily in the fit between their data and the emerging theory.

When I was trying to figure out how people with chronic illnesses defined the passage of time, I went back to several participants whom I had interviewed before and asked them more focused questions about how they perceived times of earlier crisis and when time seemed to slow, quicken, drift, or drag. Because such topics resonated with their experiences, they even responded to esoteric questions. For example, when I studied their stories, I realized that chronically ill adults implicitly located their self-concepts in the past, present or future. These time-frames reflected the form and content of self and mirrored hopes and dreams for self as well as beliefs and understandings about self. Hence, I made 'the self in time' a major category. Thereafter, I explicitly asked more people whether they saw themselves in the past, present or future. An elderly working-class woman said without hesitation:

I see myself in the future now. If you'd asked where I saw myself eight months ago, I would have said, 'the past'. I was so angry then because I had been so active. And to go down-hill as fast as I did – I felt life had been awfully cruel to me. Now I see myself in the future because there's something the Lord wants me to do. Here I sit all crumpled in this chair not being able to do anything for myself and still there's a purpose for me to be here. [Laughs.] I wonder what it could be. (Charmaz, 1991a: 256)

Through theoretical sampling you can elaborate the meaning of your categories, discover variation within them, and define gaps between categories. Theoretical sampling relies on comparative methods for discovering these gaps and finding ways to fill them. By the time you conduct theoretical sampling, you already have a set of categories that you can treat as tentative concepts to be further delineated – and tested – through rigorous scrutiny of your new data. These concepts are useful to understanding many incidents or issues in your data (Strauss and Corbin, 1990). I recommend conducting theoretical sampling later in the research to ensure that you have already defined relevant issues and allowed significant data to emerge. Otherwise, early theoretical sampling may bring premature closure to your analysis.

Variation within the studied process will probably become apparent as you engage in theoretical sampling. It requires being selective about which data you seek and from whom you seek it. You may focus on certain experiences, events or issues, not on individuals per se to develop your theoretical categories and to define how and when they vary. However, you are likely to gain more knowledge about the experiences, events, or issues that you seek to treat theoretically through observing or talking with individuals. For example, one of my main categories was 'immersion in illness' (Charmaz, 1991a). Major properties of immersion include recasting life around illness, slipping into illness routines, pulling into one's inner circle, facing dependency, and experiencing an altered (slowed) time perspective. However, not everyone's time perspective changed. How could I account for that?

By going back through my data, I gained some leads. Then I talked with more people about specific experiences and events that influenced their time perspective. Theoretical sampling helped me to refine the analysis and make it more complex. I then added a category, 'variations in immersion', to highlight and account for different experiences of immersion in illness. I filled out this category through theoretical sampling because I sensed variation earlier when comparing the experiences of people with different illnesses, different life situations, and different ages but had not made clear how immersion in illness varied and affected how these people experienced time. Subsequently, for example, I sampled to learn how illness and time differed for people who spent months in darkened rooms and how both varied when people anticipated later improvement or faced continued uncertainty. Thus, initial demographic variations in immersion led to useful theoretical understandings of variations in immersion itself. Making comparisons explicit through successive memos enabled me to draw connections that I did not initially discern. The memo became a short section of a chapter that begins as in Box 5.5 and then goes on to detail each remaining point.

Box 5.5   Variations in immersion

A lengthy immersion in illness shapes daily life and affects how one experiences time. Conversely, ways of experiencing time dialectically affect the qualities of immersion in illness. The picture above of immersion and time has sharp outlines. What sources of variation soften or alter the picture of immersion and time? The picture may vary according to the person's (1) type of illness, (2) kind of medication, (3) earlier time perspective, (4) life situation, and (5) goals.

The type of illness shapes the experience and way of relating to time. Clearly, trying to manage diabetes necessitates gaining a heightened awareness of timing the daily routines. But the effects of the illness may remain much more subtle. People with Sjögren's syndrome, for example, may have periods of confusion when they feel wholly out of synchrony with the world around them. For them, things happen too quickly, precisely when their bodies and minds function too slowly. Subsequently, they may retreat into routines to protect themselves. Lupus patients usually must retreat because they cannot tolerate the sun. Sara Shaw covered her windows with black blankets when she was extremely ill. Thus, her sense of chronological time became further distorted as day and night merged together into an endless flow of illness (Charmaz, 1991a: 93).

Theoretical sampling focuses further data collection to refine key categories in your research. You can then define them explicitly and identify their properties and parameters. Your subsequent memo-writing becomes more precise, analytic, and incisive. Theoretical sampling keeps you moving between targeted data collection and analytic memo-writing. You follow leads, check out hunches, and refine your ideas. Because theoretical sampling forces you to check ideas against direct empirical realities, you have solid materials and sound ideas with which to work. You gain confidence in your perceptions of your data and in your developing ideas about them.

When do you stop gathering data? The standard answer is that you stop when your categories are 'saturated'. And categories are 'saturated' when new data no longer spark new insights. But researchers disagree about the meaning of saturation. As Janice Morse (1995) suggests, researchers proclaim saturation rather than prove that they have achieved it. Thus, like other qualitative approaches, the grounded theory approach shares the hazard of assuming that categories are saturated when they may not be. The kinds of research questions and the analytic level of the subsequent categories matter. Mundane questions may rapidly produce saturated but common categories, whereas novel questions may demand more complex categories and more sustained inquiry.

Writing the First Draft

After defining your theoretical categories fully, supporting them with evidence, and ordering them by sorting the memos you have written about them, you start writing the first draft of *your* paper. Writing is more than mere reporting. Instead, the analytic process proceeds through the writing of your report. Use your now developed categories to form sections of the paper. Show the relationships between these categories. When you have studied a process, your categories will reflect its phases. Yet you still need to make an argument for your reader as to why this process is significant. That means making *your* logic and purpose explicit. That may take a draft or two. Then outline your draft to identify your main points and to refine how you organize them. (But do not start your draft from an outline – use your memos.) As your argument becomes clearer, keep tightening it by reorganizing the sections of your paper around it. What place do raw data such as interview excerpts or field notes have in the body of your paper? Grounded theorists generally provide enough verbatim material to demonstrate the connection between the data and the analysis, but give more weight to the concepts derived from the data. To date, qualitative researchers do not agree on how much verbatim material is necessary. Compared to those qualitative studies that primarily synthesize description, grounded theory studies are substantially more analytic and conceptual.

Our analytic focus encourages making theoretical relationships explicit and subordinating verbatim material to it (Glaser, 1978). Unlike some grounded theorists, I prefer to present many detailed interview quotations and examples in the body of my work. I do so to keep the human story in the forefront of the reader's mind and to make the conceptual analysis more accessible to a wider audience.

After you have developed your conceptual analysis of the data, go to the literature in your field and compare how and where your work fits in with it – be specific. At this point, you must cover the literature thoroughly and weave it into your work explicitly. Then revise and rework your draft to make it a solid finished paper. Use the writing process to sharpen, clarify, and integrate your developing analysis. Through writing and rewriting, you can simultaneously make your analysis more abstract and your rendering and grounding of it more concrete. In short, you hone your abstract analysis to define essential properties, assumptions, relationships, and processes while providing sufficient actual data to demonstrate how your analysis is grounded in people's experience.

Conclusion

The inductive nature of grounded theory methods assumes an open, flexible approach that moves you back and forth from data collection to analysis. Hence, you shape your methodological strategies while engaged in your research rather than having them planned before beginning the data collection. Similarly, you shape and alter the data collection to pursue the most interesting and relevant material.

The purpose of grounded theory is to develop a theoretical analysis of the data that fits the data and has relevance to the area of study. The systematic procedures of grounded theory enable qualitative researchers to generate ideas. In turn, these ideas may later be verified through traditional quantitative methods.

Nonetheless, as Glaser and Strauss originally claimed, grounded theory qualitative works stand on their own because: (1) they explicate basic (generic) processes in the data; (2) they analyse a substantive field or problem; (3) they make sense of human behaviour; (4) they provide flexible, yet durable, analyses that other researchers can refine or update; and (5) they have potential for greater generalizability (for example, when conducted at multiple sites) than other qualitative works. But do most researchers who claim to do grounded theory research actually construct theory? No, not at this time. At present, most construct conceptual analyses of a particular experience instead of creating substantive or formal theory. These researchers pursue basic questions within the empirical world and try to understand the puzzles it presents. They emphasize analytic categories that synthesize and explicate processes in the worlds they study rather than tightly framed theories that generate hypotheses and make explicit predictions. Many researchers engage in grounded theory coding and memo-making but do not conduct theoretical sampling or pursue extensive analysis of their categories. However, grounded theory methods provide powerful tools for taking conceptual analyses into theory development. For this reason, grounded theory methods offer psychologists exciting possibilities for revisioning psychological theory as well as useful strategies for rethinking psychological research methods.

Box 5.6 presents three examples of grounded theory studies in action.

Box 5.6   Three examples of grounded theory studies

Regions of the mind: brain research and the quest for scientific certainty

Susan Leigh Star (1989) analyses how localization theory gained acceptance as the dominant explanation of how the brain functions. By studying the routine work of early brain researchers, Star questions the foundational assumptions of science. Localizationists faced opposition but Star shows that their theoretical take-over did not rest on unassailable scientific proof. Gaps in their research and reasoning can be discerned. The localizationist take-over occurred because of their claims and sustained strategic actions during a particular historical context in which scientists faced and tried to resolve several types of uncertainties, such as the pressure to standardize criteria for disease categories and diagnoses. Star explains how localizationists' routine actions and strategies created definitions of certainty. They controlled the terms of the debate, shifted uncertainties from one realm to another, combined dissimilar data, generalized case results, focused on select problems, and ignored ambiguous findings. Through their routine efforts, localizationists established boundaries that prevented other theories of brain function from gaining credibility. By explicating the interactive and developmental processes that advanced localizational theory, Star constructs a new theoretical explanation for change and stability in scientific theorizing. Her study concludes that scientific theorizing does not result from unassailable evidence but instead arises from scientists' ideological proclivities and the exigencies of their routine work.

The body, identity, and self: adapting to impairment

Kathy Charmaz (1991a) outlines the process of altering life and self to accommodate to physical losses and to reunify body and self. This process begins with how chronically ill people experience noticeable physical changes and diminished bodily functions, define them as real, and cope with changes in bodily appearance. Bodily changes and their meanings affect the identity goals of people with chronic illnesses and foster making identity trade-offs. The views and

---

actions of other people figure prominently here. When chronically ill people feel devalued, they weigh interactional costs and balance necessary activities against possible identity trade-offs. During illness crises, however, the struggle to realize identity goals may cease and people may surrender to their sick bodies. At this point, the quest for control over illness ceases and the ill person flows with his or her body. Perhaps paradoxically, people who described this kind of surrender felt at one with themselves and able to face uncertainty and the possibility of death. This study shows how relationships between embodiment and identity goals shift as illness progresses and questions common beliefs in struggling against illness during crises.

The other side of help: negative effects in the help seeking processes of abused women

Lora Bex Lempert (1997) studies women who have suffered domestic violence. Lempert shows how telling helper providers about their abuse initiated a chain of unintended negative consequences, despite these providers' good intentions. Telling meant that the women's former fictions of relationship intimacy disintegrated and thereby affected their definitions of their relationships, as well as changing other people's views of the couple. Help providers reduced complex domestic relationships to incidents of violence and viewed leaving the abusive partner as the solution while the abused women held complex interpretations of their relationships. Subsequently they sought help to cope with or change these relationships, not only to leave them. To understand the conditions accounting for when, how and why abused women seek help, Lempert argues that the simultaneity of affection and abuse has to be analysed. If the women accepted providers' prescriptions to leave, they also had to accept images of themselves as passive, masochistic, and complicit in the violence. Paradoxically, providers' definitions and prescriptions relegated the women to a powerless position analogous to that which they had experienced with their abusive partners. Lempert's study demonstrates a larger problem in the helping professions: when service providers hold narrow definitions of the client's self and situation, they can negate potential benefits of receiving their services.

Note

1 The interview was conducted by a trained student assistant for a mini-grant entitled, 'Identity Hierarchies and Identity Goals: Adaptation to Loss Among the Chronically Ill', awarded by Sonoma State University. All names of interview participants have been changed.

Acknowledgement

This chapter has undergone several iterations. I am indebted to Judith Abbott, Tina Balderrama Emiliano Ayala, Lynn Cominsky, Jennifer Dunn, Carole

Heathe, Jane Hood, Sachiko Kuwaura, Erich Lehmann, Catherine Nelson, Jonathan Smith, and anonymous reviewers for comments on earlier versions.

Further Reading

Charmaz, K. (2001) 'Grounded theory: methodology and theory construction', in N.J. Smelser and P.B. Baltes (eds), *International Encyclopedia of the Social and Behavioral Sciences*. Amsterdam: Pergamon. pp. 6396–9.
This article provides a succinct statement of the logic of theory construction in grounded theory.

Charmaz, K. (2006) *Constructing Grounded Theory: A Practical Guide through Qualitative Analysis*. London: Sage.
This book provides a detailed introduction of the grounded theory method and offers clear guidelines and examples throughout.

Clarke, Adele E. (2005) *Situational Analysis: Grounded Theory after the Postmodern Turn*. Thousand Oaks, CA: Sage.
This book takes the implications of postmodernism and presents a revised version of grounded theory that builds on the pragmatist legacy of Anselm Strauss.

Glaser, B.G. (1978) *Theoretical Sensitivity*. Mill Valley, CA: Sociology Press.
This book contains the most definitive statement of the original grounded theory method.

Glaser, B.G. and Strauss, A.L. (1967) *The Discovery of Grounded Theory*. Chicago: Aldine.
This book provides the first statement of the grounded theory method and presents the rationale for it and for qualitative research, more generally.

Strauss, A.L. (1987) *Qualitative Analysis for Social Scientists*. New York: Cambridge University Press.
This book provides a 'hands-on' description of how Anselm Strauss taught grounded theory to graduate students through group participation.

SIX

Narrative Psychology

Michael Murray

Recently, the British writer A.S. Byatt published a collection of essays about narrative in which she argued that narrative lies at the heart of being human. Narration, she claimed, 'is as much part of human nature as breath and the circulation of the blood' (Byatt, 2000: 21). Narrative pervades our everyday life. We are born into a narrative world, live our lives through narrative and afterwards are described in terms of narrative. Until recently, the study of narrative was considered as being of interest only to literary or folklore critics (e.g., Brooks, 1985; Propp, 1968), but it increasingly has assumed greater importance in the social sciences. Narrative is concerned with the human means of making sense of an ever-changing world. It is through narrative that we can bring a sense of order to the seeming disorder in our world, and it is though narrative that we can begin to define ourselves as having some sense of temporal continuity and as being distinct from others. The aim of this chapter is to consider some of the theoretical issues around narrative psychology and some methodological issues around forms of narrative research.

Narrative Psychology

History of Narrative Psychology

Recent interest in the study of narrative arose as part of the general turn to language that occurred in the social sciences in the 1980s. Within psychology, three classic texts marked the specific narrative turn. The first was *Narrative Psychology: The Storied Nature of Human Conduct*, edited by Theodore Sarbin (1986). This collection amounted to a manifesto for the transformation of psychology. Sarbin contrasted the machine metaphor that, he argued, underlay much of mainstream psychology with that of the narrative metaphor. He summarized the implications of this alternative model:

In giving accounts of ourselves or of others, we are guided by narrative plots. Whether for formal biographies or autobiographies, for psychotherapy, for self-disclosure, or for entertainment, we do much more than catalog a series of events. Rather, we render the events into a story. (ibid.: 23)

In a later interview with Heaven (1999), Sarbin described how this idea arose in his discussion with theorists in the humanities. At first, he recalled, he did not distinguish between narrative as a mode of representation and narrative as an ontological form. However, over time, he became convinced that the latter stronger form of narrative was more appropriate. As he emphasized in his interview with Heaven (1999), 'stories have ontological status. We are always enveloped in stories. The narrative for human beings is analogous to the ocean for fishes' (ibid.: 301). According to this argument, narratives are not just ways of seeing the world; we actively construct the world through narratives and we also live through the stories told by others and by ourselves – they have ontological status.

The book edited by Sarbin (1986) also contains a chapter by Ken and Mary Gergen (1986) on the structure of narratives in which they argued that narratives are social constructions that are developed in everyday social interaction. They are a shared means of making sense of the world. They also have a certain structure. Gergen and Gergen identified three primary structures: the progressive, in which there is movement towards a goal; the regressive, in which the reverse occurs; and the stable, in which there is little change. This analysis is similar to the classic division of narrative into comedy, romance, tragedy and satire (Frye, 1957). Comedy is a story of progress towards a happy ending, romance is also a progressive tale in which the protagonist overcomes adversity and regains what has been lost, tragedy is more a regressive tale in which the protagonist suffers adversity despite the best of intentions while satire adopts a more stable stance and considers the absurdity of life. The second important book was *Acts of Meaning* by Jerome Bruner (1990), which followed his earlier *Actual Minds, Possible Worlds* (Bruner, 1986). In these books, Bruner argued that there are two forms of thinking: the paradigmatic and the narrative. The former is the method of science and is based upon classification and categorization. The alternative narrative approach organizes everyday interpretations of the world in storied form. The challenge of contemporary psychology is to understand this everyday form of thinking. Bruner identified a number of defining properties of narrative, including the following:

1. It is composed of a unique sequence of events, mental states and happenings involving human beings as characters or actors.
2. It can be 'real' or 'imaginary'.
3. It specializes in the forging of links between the exceptional and the ordinary.

These properties help us understand narrative as ways of constructing reality, of bringing sense to something that is obscure or unusual.

The third influential book was *Narrative Knowing and the Human Sciences* by Donald Polkinghorne (1988). While this book is wide-ranging in its scope, perhaps one of its most important features was the opening up of hermeneutic philosophy, in particular the work of Paul Ricoeur, to more widespread discussion within psychology. Ricoeur has developed an immense body of work on the centrality of narrative for meaning making. In his classic work *Time and Narrative*, Ricoeur (1984) has argued that, since we live in a temporal world, we need to create narratives to bring order and meaning to the constantly changing flux. Further, not only do we create narratives about the world but also narrative is central to how we conceive of ourselves, to our identity. It is through narrative that we not only construct a particular connectedness in our actions but also distinguish ourselves from others.

During the 1980s and 1990s, the study of narrative became much more extensive within various fields of psychology. Within personality and human development studies, Dan McAdams (1985) argued that narrative is central to our self-definition: 'We are all tellers of tales. We each seek to provide our scattered and often confusing experiences with a sense of coherence by arranging the episodes of our lives into stories' (ibid.: 11).

He also developed an approach to the study of narrative based upon a developmental model. The earliest form is the *narrative tone* which can be either optimistic or pessimistic. The former is characteristic of comic and romantic narratives whereas the latter is characteristic of tragedy and satire. This is followed by *imagery* which he described as a 'treasure trove of personalized symbols and fantasized objects' (ibid.: 55) that develops as we mature. At a more advanced level is the story *theme*, which is the 'recurrent pattern of human intention' (ibid.,: 67), and the *ideology*, which is revealed in the values and beliefs underlying the story. Each of these characteristics needs to be considered in investigating narrative.

Within clinical psychology, there was a movement towards the development of a form of narrative therapy (e.g., Mair, 1989; Neimeyer, 1995) that is based upon exploring alternative stories. Within health psychology, several researchers (e.g., Crossley, 1999; Murray, 1997a) argued that narrative is an everyday means of making sense of the disruption of illness. Of particular note, the study of narrative within psychology encouraged the growth of greater contact with the humanities (e.g., Fulford, 1999; Joy, 1997) and with the other social sciences (e.g., Maines, 1993).

Definition of Narrative

According to narrative theory (e.g., Murray, 1999; Sarbin, 1986), we are born into a storied world, and we live our lives through the creation and exchange of narratives. A narrative can be defined as an organized interpretation of a sequence of events. This involves attributing agency to the characters in the narrative and inferring causal links between the events. In the classic formulation, a narrative is an account with three components: a beginning, a middle and an end. Indeed, Bettina Becker (1999) has argued that in our world the number *three* has a special quality. For example, unlike the open-ended nature of a straight line, a triangle is enclosed, finished. In the same way, a narrative offers an integrated account of an event. Unlike an open-ended piece of discourse, a narrative has a finished structure. The full dimensions of this structure may not be detailed in everyday conversation. Rather, depending upon the context, certain endings may be left unfinished, and it is the job of the audience/reader to complete the narrative. Since we live in a storied world, we can draw upon more established social narratives to explain an event or to complete a particular story. This is not a process of which we are always conscious.

Function of Narrative

The primary function of narrative is that it brings order to disorder. In telling a story, the narrator is trying to organize the disorganized and to give it meaning. This is not a straightforward task. As Ricoeur (1987) says:

> The narrative ... is a synthesis of the heterogeneous. But concord cannot be without discord. Tragedy is paradigmatic for this: no tragedy is without complications, without fickle fate, without terrible and sad events, without irreparable error committed in ignorance or by mistake rather than through evil-mindedness. If then concord wins out over discord, surely it is the battle between them that makes the story. (ibid.: 436)

The ongoing tension continues as we try to give meaning to the various challenges to the order of our everyday life. Indeed, the tension intrinsic to narrative continues into the analysis of narrative accounts. This is often tentative and open to further challenge.

The use of narrative is particularly pronounced in everyday understandings of disruption (e.g., Becker, 1997). We all encounter disruptions to our everyday routines. Such disruptions include personal problems, family problems, financial problems and health problems. These challenges to our daily routines encourage attempts by us to restore some sense of order. Narrative is a primary means of restoring this sense of order.

The classic experiment by Heider and Simmel (1944) is an illustration of what can be described as this human urge to narrative. In that experiment, participants were shown a sequence of pictograms of abstract shapes in different positions. When asked to describe the pictograms, the participants replied with short stories. Since Heider and Simmel were interested in how the participants attributed causal connections; they did not consider the structure of the stories they developed. Fortunately, some of these stories were included in their report of the experiment, and it is apparent that, although they were brief, the stories contained the basic elements of the classic narrative with a beginning, a middle and an end.

Although we can use narratives to describe the movements of inanimate objects, such as in Heider and Simmel's experiment, it requires that we give those objects agency. Humans are action centres that strive within bounds to create their own worlds. They provide narrative accounts of their experiences that imply their role or lack of role in shaping these events. The converse of agency is suffering (Ricoeur, 1984). When we are denied the opportunity to express our agency, we experience suffering. Accounts of suffering reveal this restraint on our free agency. Suffering can be due to some personal misfortune, but it can also be due to social oppression that denies the opportunity for true agency.

The need to restore a sense of order following disruption is especially pronounced in Western society, which is bounded by order and rationality. Gaylene Becker (1997) has argued that Western ideas about the life course emphasize linearity. Living in such a world, we try to make sense of inconsistencies. Further, when we try to explain our disruptions to another, we are particularly keen to emphasize our reasonableness.

The central process of bringing order has been termed 'emplotment' by Ricoeur (1984), to denote the organizing of a sequence of events into a plot. This sequence of events can be brief or limitless. We can tell the story of going shopping or the story of the creation of the universe (cf. Polkinghorne, 1996). The common theme is the attempt to give these events a narrative shape. Events do not just happen. In the narrative, there is an interconnected sequence that leads from start to finish. However, the event has ended before the narrator has started to construct a narrative. Freeman (1993) has alerted us to this process: 'Consider again the word 'recollection' itself: while the 're' makes reference to the past, 'collection' makes reference to a present act, an act ... of gathering together what might have been dispersed or lost' (ibid.: 40). In telling the story, the narrator is aware of the ending and constructs the account from there. In life, all narratives are provisional; they are subject to change as new information becomes available. It is not that the narrator is trying to mislead the listener but rather, from a more extended perspective, different pieces of information become available for the story.

Narrative Identity

Narrative not only brings order and meaning to our everyday life but also, reflexively, provides structure to our very sense of selfhood. We tell stories about our lives to ourselves and to others. As such, we create a narrative identity. 'Subjects recognize themselves in the stories they tell about themselves' (Ricoeur, 1988: 247). We can hold a variety of narrative identities, each of which is connected to different social relationships. Each narrative identity not only connects us to a set of social relationships but also provides us with a sense of localized coherence and stability. At times of instability, we can make connections to other aspects of our narrative identities.

It is through narrative that we begin to define ourselves, to clarify the continuity in our lives and to convey this to others. We are active agents who recall the actions we have achieved and also those that have been suppressed by others. Narrative enables us to describe these experiences and to define ourselves. In constructing a personal narrative, we are selecting certain aspects of our lives and connecting them with others. This process enables us to assert that our lives are not a disconnected sequence of events but have a certain order.

This process of narrative identity formation is dynamic and occurs in a changing social and personal context. The values attached to different experiences in that context influence the character of events recalled and thus the shape of the story told. As Ricoeur (1987: 437) emphasized, this indicates 'we learn to become the *narrator of our own story* without completely becoming the author of our life'. While we can tell our life story, the actual pattern our life takes and indeed the very structure of the story we tell are shaped by a multiplicity of social and psychological forces both conscious and unconscious (Hollway and Jefferson, 2000).

Social Dimensions of Narratives

Narrative accounts are not emitted in a vacuum; rather, they are encouraged and shaped by a certain social context. Although the narrator tells the story, the character of the story told will depend upon to whom the story is being told, the relationship between the narrator and the audience, and the broader social and cultural context (Murray, 1997a). Thus, the study of narrative breaks down the traditional psychological/social distinction and develops a more complex psycho-social subject. The narrator is an active agent who is part of a social world. Through narrative, the agent engages with that world. Through narrative analysis, we can begin to understand both the narrators and their worlds.

Although narrative is often considered in individual or personal terms, we can also consider group, community or societal narratives. These are the narratives that particular collectives tell about themselves, their histories and their aspirations. In the same way as personal narratives are involved in the creation and re-creation of personal identities, these social narratives define the history of a collective and distinguish it from other collectives. Further, these collective narratives overlap with personal narratives such that individuals can define themselves as part of the group. In discussing narrative analysis, we should think about the level of analysis we are considering (Murray, 2000). Moreover, in analysing the personal narrative, we should attempt to consider the character of the broader social narrative within which it is being created.

In sum, we are enmeshed in a world of narrative; we understand our world and ourselves through narrative. As such, the study of narrative provides the researcher with a means to understand how we make sense of the world and of ourselves. The meaning of different narratives is not always apparent and can be approached in different ways by different researchers.

Narrative Research

Collecting Narratives

The primary source of material for the narrative researcher is the interview. Unlike the traditional structured interview that has a detailed series of questions to be answered, the narrative interview is designed to provide an opportunity for the participant to give a detailed narrative account of a particular experience. The life-story interview is the most extended version of the personal narrative interview. Gerontologists have particularly favoured this life-story approach as a means of exploring the experience of ageing (e.g., Birren et al., 1996).

As its name implies, the aim of the life-story interview is to encourage the participants to provide an extended account of their lives. The researcher will explain at the outset of the interview that the aim of the study is to learn about the person's life. While this may seem a simple invitation, the participant may, in practice, often be wary and uncommunicative at the outset. It is for this reason that the interviewer may need to meet with some participants on a number of occasions to win their confidence and to encourage them to reflect on their life experiences.

However, narratives are not just life stories in the most general sense but also stories about everyday experiences, especially disruptions of daily life. We can in the interview setting encourage participants to tell stories about particular experiences of change or disruptive episodes in their lives. Flick (2002) has termed this approach the *episodic* interview. Given the time and the opportunity, participants are often very willing to provide extended narrative accounts of different experiences. See Box 6.1 for examples of interview guides. It is obvious from these that the researcher has a particular focus for the interview but provides lots of latitude for the participant to develop the narrative account.

Box 6.1   Sample interview guides

1. I would like you to tell me about yourself – where you were born, where you grew up, that sort of thing. You should not be in any way inhibited about what to say, but just tell me as much as possible about yourself.
2. I am interested in finding out what happened during the selection interview. You can begin at the time you left home for the meeting and just tell me as much as you can remember.

A challenge for researchers is to convince the participants that they are interested in their narrative accounts but at the same time present a neutral stance so as not to encourage a particular narrative. Thus, the researcher should give encouraging nods and remarks but refrain from overt commentary since this may disturb the narrative. At the close of the interview the researcher may review the participant's narrative and introduce supplementary questions designed to obtain clarification, such as 'Why do you think that is the case?' or 'Could you give an example of that?' It is preferable to keep comment to the end of the interview when the participant's narrative account is reviewed (see Jovchelovitch and Bauer, 2000).

Sometimes it may be useful to invite participants to a group meeting where they can share in the telling of stories about an event. This focus group approach provides some participants with a greater sense of control and confidence (see Chapter 9 of this volume; also Wilkinson, 1998a; 1998b). These group interviews can be followed or supplemented with individual interviews. Another approach is for the researcher to provide the participant with details of the issue to be discussed. This helps to alleviate any suspicions the participant might have that there are some trick questions to come.

The interviewer can also use other methods such as encouraging the participants to keep a personal journal or to collect photographs or even to make a video. The aim is always to find a technique with which the participants are comfortable and which will allow them to develop their narrative account. Further, the researcher can analyse narrative material that is already available. For example, you can analyse published memoirs or films.

Since stories develop out of a particular social context and are told to a certain audience, it is important that such details are recorded when collecting narrative accounts. Mishler (1986) noted with reference to the importance of considering the interview setting:

The interviewer's presence and form of involvement – how she or he listens, attends, encourages, interrupts, digresses, initiates topics, and terminates responses – is integral to a respondent's account. It is in this specific sense that a 'story' is a joint production. (ibid.: 82)

The researcher should collect background material about the central participants as well as details about the interviewee. Such information is important when we begin to analyse the narrative accounts.

A useful strategy is for the researcher to keep a detailed log of each interview. This could include some basic demographic details of the participant and when and where the interview occurred. Sometimes after the interview has ended and the tape recorder has been switched off, the participant will make some additional comments that can substantially influence the interpretation of the whole narrative. It is important that the researcher pay careful attention. After the interview has ended, the researchers should record in their logs as much detail and commentary as they can recall about the interview. Even at this early stage the researcher should be considering what the key issues arising are and how the narrative is structured.

Some Logistical Issues

It is important that care be taken in setting up the interview. The researcher should make some initial contact with the participants, explain the purpose of the study and obtain their consent. At this stage, they can discuss when it would be most convenient to return for a more extended interview and clarify where would be the most comfortable setting. Sometimes the participants are happy to be interviewed at home; other times they prefer to attend the researcher's office or another setting. It is important to remember that it is the participants' choice and to accommodate their preferences as much as possible.

The researcher should practise using a tape recorder and test the quality of the recording. Sometimes the quality can be poor because of noise outside the interview room or the participants' speaking quietly. For these reasons, it is advisable to use an external microphone. If possible, the researcher should also attempt to ensure that the power is not interrupted during the interview by connecting the tape recorder to the electricity supply or by ensuring that extra batteries are available. It is a sign of respect to the participant for the researcher to ensure that the narrative is carefully recorded. Make sure to use the best available recording equipment and check that it works. Finding that the batteries fail halfway through the interview or discovering afterwards that the microphone did not pick up the participant's voice can be very frustrating.

Often the novice interviewer will be apprehensive about using a tape recorder and think that this will inhibit the participant. Fortunately, the reverse is often the case. After the researcher has carefully explained the study and assured the participant of confidentiality, the participant is often very enthusiastic. Sometimes after an initial hesitation, the participants will proceed to talk at length about their various experiences. The very fact that they have an audience for the story can act as a spur to more sustained reflection. It is surprising that even when the interview is being videotaped and requires additional technical personnel, many people, once they have agreed to participate, will be only too generous with their time and will be surprisingly frank and revealing. It is for this reason that the researcher should treat the participant with the utmost respect and courtesy. In addition, if the participant becomes distressed, the researcher should be prepared to stop the interview and, if necessary, ensure the participant is aware of appropriate support services.

Afterwards, it is important that the interview be transcribed carefully. It is a great advantage to have a professional transcriber, but this does not mean that the researcher does not have a role to play in the transcription process. Rather, the researcher should carefully review the transcript with the tape recording, correcting any errors in the transcription. This should be done as soon as possible after the interview, since it is easy to forget what the person had to say, especially when interviewing a number of people.

There are different ways of preparing interview transcripts for analysis. This depends upon the analytic frame preferred by the researcher (cf. Chapter 7). In narrative analysis, the focus is on getting the main narrative account. The narrative transcription should include, where possible, exclamations, pauses and emphases. You can underline certain parts of the text that the participants have stressed in their speech or add notes to mark such paralinguistics as sighs. The aim is to convey the detail and tenor of the story or stories. The transcription should also include the words of the researcher such that the character of the conversational exchange is apparent. We will see this more clearly in the example given below.

Analysing Narratives

The analysis of narrative accounts can be divided into two broad phases – the first descriptive and the second interpretive. A thorough reading of the transcribed narrative precedes both phases. In reading the narrative accounts, the aim is to familiarize oneself with both their structure and their content. A useful strategy is to prepare a short summary of the narratives that will identify the key features, such as the beginning, the middle and the end. The analysts can highlight key issues in the text and identify narrative linkages that connect different parts. They can also discern sub-plots within the broader narrative and consider connections between these. The summary will highlight the particular features in which the researcher is interested. In reading across the summaries, it is then possible to begin to get an idea of what the main issues being raised are (Mishler, 1986). It is through this process of close reading that a coding frame can be developed that can be applied to the various narratives. This coding frame is designed to capture the overall meaning of the narratives and the various particular issues raised within each.

The second step is to connect the narrative with the broader theoretical literature that is being used to interpret the story. Thus, the researcher goes beyond the descriptive phase to develop the interpretation. This requires a simultaneous familiarity with the narrative accounts and with the relevant literature such that the one can begin to connect with the other. This phase of the analysis can lead to labelling certain accounts as being of a certain type that illustrates their theoretical content. For example, we might be interested in how certain people handle particular crises in their lives. In the reading of the narratives, the central concern is how the narrators describe the various crises in their lives, how they draw on particular sources of support, and how they orient the story to the listener. Each story is examined for particular narrative elements – how the elements in the narrative are linked together (the structure and tone), what issues are the main themes, what images and metaphors are used, and what are the underlying beliefs and values.

Role of the Reader

The process of narrative analysis is not a passive process. Rather, the researchers bring to the text certain assumptions and beliefs that they use to analyse the narrative. In discussing the process of reading a text, Ricoeur (1987) makes the same point: 'The meaning or the significance of a story wells up from the intersection of the world of the text and the world of the reader' (ibid.: 430). Ricoeur (1972) used the term 'appropriation' to describe the process of narrative interpretation. He defined this process as making one's own what has been alien. This is not a one-way process. Not only does the researcher bring to the narrative certain ideas but also, simultaneously, the narrator is trying to convince the audience of the character of his or her story. As Ricoeur stresses:

> We play with a project, with an idea, we can equally be played. What is essential is the 'to and fro' (*Hin und Her*) of play. Play is thereby close to dance, which is a movement that carries away the dancer. (1972: 90)

Thus, rather than imposing a framework and rather than simply describing the narrative account, narrative analysis requires that the analyst play with the account. In conducting the narrative analysis, it is important to be aware of what theoretical assumptions are guiding the analysis while at the same time being open to new ideas and challenges.

Narrative Structure and Content

A particular concern in narrative analysis is how the narrative is structured or organized. Various schemes have been developed to convey the temporal quality of narratives. The threefold classification scheme developed by Gergen and Gergen (1984) is a useful analytic tool, but it is important to apply it not in a schematic way but rather in a flexible manner so as to encapsulate the various shifts in any narrative account. For example, the tragic narrative begins with a progressive structure, but then, despite struggle, the central character is overcome and the narrative becomes regressive. This regression can be overcome by changing the broad interpretive dimensions that are being used to frame the event. For example, people who are upwardly mobile in their career will probably present a progressive career narrative. However, if they are dismissed from their jobs they may develop a more regressive narrative unless they can redefine their goals and so continue to present a progressive narrative. This redefinition of goals, this turning point in a narrative, is similar to an epiphany. This is the moment in the account when the narrator sees the world in a different way. Conversely, a comedy is when a regressive narrative is transformed into a progressive narrative, as narrators redefine their values and realize the positive features of the changed life.

In his analysis of the personal narratives of people with multiple sclerosis (MS), Robinson (1990) used this temporal scheme. He found that the MS narratives could be organized into three broad categories. There were those who thought that their lives were ended due to the onset of MS (regressive narrative), those who thought that life had changed but was ongoing (stable narrative) and those who thought that the disease provided new opportunities (progressive narrative).

As mentioned earlier, this concern with narrative structure is similar to the concept of narrative tone that McAdams (1993) and Crossley (2000) place at the centre of narrative analysis. Whereas the structure is concerned with the major components of the narrative and how they are connected, the tone is concerned with the overall emotional flavour of the narrative. Thus a regressive narrative would have an overall pessimistic tone whereas a progressive narrative would have an optimistic tone, while a stable narrative would have a more objective tone and would be more like a chronicle or a listing of events.

Gee (1991) described the value of exploring the poetic structure of popular narrative accounts. He argued that verses are an intrinsic part of everyday narrative accounting and that poetry is merely a more developed form of that accounting. In particular, he was concerned about the use of rhythm and metaphor in popular narratives. The study by Becker (1999) is an example of the successful use of this strategy to explore personal narratives. In reading through the pain narrative of an elderly person, she noted that it had a certain poetic quality. She was then able to recast the narrative account as a series of poetic stanzas that each had a similar structure. In recasting the narrative, the interviewer's questions are omitted and the text is organized into verses by the researcher. This form of analysis requires attention to the overall rhythm that underlies the narrative and the metaphors used to describe particular experiences. For example, the narrator may repeat certain phrases within her account (such as 'and then I') which provide a certain rhythm.

Besides the structure of the narrative there is also the imagery used, the major themes and the values underlying the account. McAdams (1993) argues that the two central themes in life histories centre around power and love, which emphasize the importance of agency and having relationships. The importance of these themes varies across individuals and situations. These themes also underlie the major beliefs and values in a person's narrative account. Thus a focus on agency and power places an emphasis on individual rights and autonomy while a focus on relationships values the group and interpersonal relationships.

The researcher can also consider the personal, interpersonal, group and societal contexts (Murray, 2000). The personal context is concerned with how narrative draws on the experience of the individual. According to McAdams, the early experiences of attachment and loss colour how we react to situations in our later life. The interpersonal and group context takes into consideration the audience and the co-construction of narrative; and the societal context considers the broader social narratives which structure our everyday accounts. While it is difficult to integrate all these contextual levels into a single analysis, attention to one or the other may be particularly important in understanding the structure of certain narrative accounts.

In this chapter, we will consider the structure of a personal narrative account and the value of different analytic strategies. We will begin by summarizing the case, proceed to how the narrative is structured, and then consider how the narrative is located within a particular social context. Although we will consider in detail only one case, it is useful in developing an argument to explore contrary cases. We will consider briefly a contrary case. This process enables the researcher to clarify particular strategies used by the participants in constructing their narratives.

An Example: A Breast Cancer Story

The example is taken from a study of how women handle the disruption of their lives as a consequence of having had breast cancer (Murray, 2002). We were interested in how the women integrated the disease into their everyday lives – how they gave it meaning. We were also interested in how these stories were constructed in a particular social and interpersonal context. In this sense, we were interested in how the broader social context intersects with the personal narratives.

All the women interviewed had had surgery for breast cancer. At their last check-up, there was no sign of recurrence and they had agreed to be interviewed about the experience. The interviews took place in the women's homes or in the researcher's office. A young female research assistant who had no personal experience of breast cancer conducted them. For many of the women, the interview was an emotional experience. Several of them mentioned that they had had limited opportunity to discuss the operation with others. They felt that they had to present a strong face to their husbands and family members. The opportunity to talk freely about the event was largely welcomed. It is important that inexperienced researchers are briefed on the emotional intensity of some narrative interviews and that they have the opportunity to discuss the experience afterwards with their supervisor.

We can begin by preparing a summary of each of the narrative accounts. There were certain commonalties in all of the stories that gave them the standard narrative structure:

1. *Beginning*: this was life before cancer. Different women emphasized particular aspects of their lives – family life, marriage, work, children, etc. The main thing was that cancer did not play a part in their lives. Some of the women tried to identify early experiences that might have contributed to the later development of the disease.
2. *Middle*: the major part of the story centred around the diagnosis of cancer, the surgery (radical or otherwise) and the reaction of the patient and that of their family, friends or colleagues.
3. *End*: this involved looking back on the disruption in their lives; how they began to redefine themselves as a survivor of the disease, how their life expectations and experiences changed.

For some researchers, summarizing all the interviews can be a tedious task. However, it is an important task, as it makes the researcher familiar with the different narratives. It is also important in developing an analytic frame that can encapsulate all the narrative accounts. Thus, we develop an initial analytic frame and then engage with the other narrative accounts, all the time considering its adequacy and how it can be modified.

Having developed the analysis of the narratives, we can then proceed to writing a report or paper that is grounded in the interviews. It is important to have in mind what is the key argument or message that you want to convey from your reading of the narratives. It is then possible to select paradigmatic cases that best illustrate the central argument being developed by the researcher (Becker, 1997; Gray et al., 2002). In this chapter, I have chosen two cases that illustrate how people make sense of illness though connecting their current experiences with earlier life experiences. The selection of the narratives was guided by our understanding of Gergen and Gergen's (1984) temporal model and by McAdam's approach to the study of narrative which has been further developed by Crossley (1999). An initial reading of the narratives suggested that these models were a useful means of organizing much of the material.

The stable/regressive narratives were those with a pessimistic tone which portrayed life as being a litany of woes. In these narratives, childhood was described as being difficult with few improvements since becoming an adult. Despite many attempts to overcome various challenges, they seemed to be endless. Not only did these challenges recur but they also seemed to have little redeeming value. Cancer was another of these bleak challenges. The case of Mrs Brown, which is described in Box 6.2, illustrates this stable/regressive and pessimistic narrative. The dominant theme was that of attachment and loss. In her earlier life Mrs Brown had experienced separation and was now very anxious about the consequences of the cancer on the relationships enjoyed by her children. As a single parent she had a very close relationship with her children. The thought of them having similar childhood experiences as she had filled her with dread. She emphasized the lack of support she had received from others. A recurrent image was that of being alone: she had been alone as a child; she had not been able to establish a stable relationship with the father of her children or another partner; and she felt very alone when she was initially diagnosed with cancer.

Box 6.2 Stable/regressive/pessimistic narrative

Summary: Mrs Brown was a 50-year-old single mother. She described her upbringing as difficult. Her mother died when she was two, and she and her siblings were sent to different orphanages. There they were very badly treated by the guardians. On leaving the orphanage, she trained to be a nurse. She found it difficult to establish a secure relationship but wanted to have children. She had

---

(Continued)

three children by different partners but never married. Two of the children had grown up and left home. The third was aged 12 years. She had not held a full-time job for about ten years. About ten years ago, she had been diagnosed with breast cancer and had undergone a lumpectomy. Mrs Brown's life was difficult and the diagnosis of cancer was devastating. This summary can be extended into a three-part narrative to help clarify particular features.

Beginning: Throughout her account Mrs Brown emphasized her problems. She described her childhood in the orphanage as a very painful experience. Not only was she separated from her siblings but she also felt that the teachers were very harsh towards her. After she left the orphanage, she found it difficult to establish relationships. In general, her life was difficult.

Middle: The diagnosis of cancer was yet another ordeal. At the time, she was not working, she had three children and she was finding it difficult to make ends meet. When the surgeon told her she had cancer she was very upset:

Mrs B:	It really flipped me right out.
Int.:	Yeah.
Mrs B:	It really flipped me out, but it was so quick.
Int.:	Hmm, hmm.
Mrs B:	Like, I never had time to stop and think.
Int.:	Right.
Mrs B:	Like, they told me, and then I cried for three weeks, and then next week I was in hospital and had it all done.

She had a lumpectomy, and on discharge from hospital she found it very difficult to cope:

Int.:	Was it a mastectomy or a lumpectomy?
Mrs B:	No, it was just a lumpectomy.
Int.:	OK.
Mrs B:	Right, and so I went through all that, and then I went through a year of chemo and radiation and went through hell, but like by myself.
Int.:	Hmm, hmm.
Mrs B:	You know, no husband and three little kids. They were young then, right.
Int.:	Oh, it must have been hard.
Mrs B:	And it was terrible, it was absolutely terrible. I had no moral support. I had no one here to help.

Mrs Brown emphasized that, without any social support from family or friends and the fact that she had lost any religious belief because of her difficult child-hood experiences, the experience of cancer was frightening.

End:	Looking back, although she had survived, the whole experience was difficult. Sometimes she would blame God for her misfortune:

(Continued)

> *Int.:*   Did you ever think 'why me?'
>
> *Mrs B:* Oh many times.
>
> *Int.:*   Yeah?
>
> *Mrs B:* Many times, like holy, never stops, never stops. I be scrubbing the floor, I be scrubbing out a tub, I be bathing one of the kids, I be like 'why, why?' you know. There's no one here to take these kids.
>
> *Int.:*   Hmm, hmm.
>
> *Mrs B:* Why are You taking me? I thought I was going to die.
>
> *Int.:*   Yeah.
>
> *Mrs B:* Naturally.
>
> *Int.:*   Hmm, hmm.
>
> *Mrs B:* You know, somebody tells you 'you got cancer'. First thing, I'm dead.

The ongoing fear of death pervaded her everyday life: 'You have it, it never leaves you. I don't care what I'm doing. I could be baking bread and I'm always thinking. It was always there with me, maybe it's because I'm alone.' She was very anxious about the implications for her children if there was a recurrence of cancer:

> *Mrs B:* If it happens tomorrow, and he's only 12, I will flip. I will go really, really crazy.
>
> *Int.:*   Hmm, hmm.
>
> *Mrs B:* Yeah, because what's going to happen to him?
>
> *Int.:*   Yeah.
>
> *Mrs B:* Welfare would come and take him. [I] always worry about that kind of stuff. I worry about all that kind of stuff.

She felt despondent about her future life:

> *Mrs B:* Just give me more life and just keep it going and don't take it on me – that's the main thing.
>
> *Int.:*   Yeah.
>
> *Mrs B:* You know and like I don't aspire to any greatness or anything.
>
> *Int.:*   Hmm, hmm.
>
> *Mrs B:* I really don't. I don't aspire to going back to work and to make another life and to go travelling again. I never think of it. It seems like a dream.

A contrary narrative is one in which life is portrayed as a series of challenges that provide an opportunity for advancement. Even life-threatening events such as the diagnosis of cancer could be characterized as such an opportunity. The case of Mrs Jones, which is summarized in Box 6.3, illustrates this more progressive and optimistic narrative. She had given her 'heart to the Lord' at an early stage, and ever since she had felt her life to be a series of life-enhancing opportunities. Cancer was one of these opportunities. In Mrs Jones' case, attachment was secure, in particular through her attachment to religion. In view of the intensity of this attachment, the threat of cancer was minimized. She adopted a rather fatalistic stance and in some ways her story had tragic features. However, the crises she encountered were perceived as God's will and He would take care of things. Her recovery from cancer was evidence of His power. A recurrent image was that of security and comfort. The crises she experienced seem to strengthen rather than weaken her attachment to religion.

Box 6.3   Progressive/optimistic narrative

Summary: Mrs Jones was a 45-year-old married woman. She had six children. Although she had previously worked as a teacher, since the surgery for breast cancer she had devoted herself full-time to religious work. When she was young, she had not been particularly religious, although she had attended a Catholic church and school. When she was 16 years old, she met her future husband, who was a very devout evangelical Christian. Mrs Jones converted to his religion, and since then her devout religious belief has pervaded her whole life, including her experience of cancer. For her, having breast cancer was an opportunity to strengthen her faith and as such could be welcomed.

Beginning: Early in the interview, Mrs Jones provided a detailed account of her religious conversion: 'I started going to the Salvation Army church first and then started going to the Pentecostal church. So after we got married I kept going to the Pentecostal church and I gave my heart to the Lord and I have been going there since.'

Middle: She was diagnosed with breast cancer and underwent lumpectomy. Initially, the signs were good, but at follow-up there were signs of recurrence. Mrs Jones described the importance of her faith. The surgery was successful and at the time of the interview there were no signs of recurrence. Mrs Jones felt very optimistic: 'I feel that I'm healed. I feel that the Lord healed me.'

End: Looking back, Mrs Jones emphasized the positive experience of having cancer: 'I think that everything in life has been an experience to make me grow and I think it has brought me closer to the Lord.'

This narrative account was progressive. Although cancer was a major challenge, Mrs Jones had transformed this into an opportunity for heightened religious experience. Her narrative account became almost a testimony in itself. Throughout she gave praise to the Lord and all his glory. Her narrative was one of liberation. The disease strengthened her faith. Her recovery was confirmation of the power of religion.

In terms of narrative structure, Mrs Brown's story is both stable and regressive. Her whole life had been difficult and the diagnosis of cancer only served to highlight these problems. The lack of social support and the lack of religious faith left her feeling isolated. She felt she had substantial family responsibilities and cancer threatened her ability to live up to these responsibilities. Although she had managed so far, the potential recurrence of cancer remained a threat.

Connecting the Stories with the Context

This example of narrative accounts of the experience of cancer illustrates the way people can use narratives to forge 'links between the exceptional and the ordinary' (Bruner, 1990: 47). When given the opportunity in the interview, the women were eager to provide detailed narrative accounts. Indeed, once she had introduced the topic, the interviewer's role was minimal. Often the women were enthused at the opportunity of providing a detailed narrative account of their experience. Sometimes they mentioned that they felt that the giving of the account was therapeutic.

This eagerness to talk after surviving a personal threat is an established phenomenon. In religious terms, the phenomenon is known as 'giving witness', a term that in Greek is cognate with such terms as 'martyr' and 'testimony' (Scott, 1997). The public display of giving witness has spread from its original religious form to a more secular form in the modern world through the phenomenon of 'coming out', which has extensive currency not only in terms of sexual identity but also in terms of survivors of abuse and torture. This form of public narration is a means of developing a community of support and also of challenging certain repressive societal narratives.

In terms of structure, the women's stories had the classic beginning, middle and end. The beginning set the scene, the middle detailed the experience of breast cancer, and the end concerned the impact of the disease on their lives. In the example, the stable/regressive and pessimistic narrative connected the woman's account of cancer with her previous experiences, the interpersonal context and her broader social beliefs in creating a particular narrative identity. For Mrs Brown, life had been difficult. At a time when she felt she had little support, she was diagnosed as having cancer. This was just not fair. She felt that she did not ask for much out of life. Her narrative ended with almost an appeal to let her be healthy at least until her youngest child had grown.

At the personal level of analysis, the narrative reflects the different experiences of the women. Mrs Brown came from a broken family and felt very insecure in her relationships. The main concern for Mrs Brown was her responsibilities to her children. The onset of cancer was a major threat to this and thus was a threat to her life chances. In developing her narrative account, Mrs Brown works backwards from the present, describing earlier experiences of difficulties and lack of support. There is a coherence in the narrative identity that she presents.

At the interpersonal level, the narrative analyst is interested in how the participant conveys her story to the interviewer. In her story, what issues does she emphasize? Her whole life has been one of trials and she does not expect much in the future. 'I don't aspire to greatness', she says. In comparison to her, the young interviewer was fortunate. She seemed to be healthy and in good employment. The diagnosis of breast cancer was yet another tribulation for

Mrs Brown. During the interview, she spent considerable time detailing her childhood experiences of abuse and connecting this to her current circumstances. Her narrative account was developed in opposition to what was perceived as a less painful life history.

At the societal level, these narrative accounts reveal the underlying values of the women (McAdams, 1993). The dominant theme in the lives of the women described earlier was that of relationships emphasizing the importance of communal values. This finding accords with Gilligan's (1993) idea that women centre their discussions of moral issues around communal care and responsibilities. Thus, in the case of Mrs Brown, it was not right that her children's relationships could be jeopardized as hers had been. In the case of Mrs Jones, her relationship with God was secure and thus she was able to transform her illness into an opportunity for growth. Underlying this transformation was a belief in the agency provided by religious faith.

Further Analyses

This example provides an illustration of the process of narrative analysis. It is not the only way of conducting such an analysis. Unlike other forms of qualitative analysis that break the interviews down into themes, the aim of the narrative analysis is to take the full narrative account, to examine how it is structured and to connect it to the broader context. The important challenge is that the researcher is explicit in the initial theoretical formulation and then engages with the narrative account.

The narrative researcher can bring different theoretical frameworks to help make sense of the story told. Hollway and Jefferson (2000) compare the process of theoretical engagement with tossing a stone into a pond. An appropriate theory will spread its ripples out through the narrative account, revealing particular features that had been neglected by another theory. They used a psychodynamic framework that considers hidden anxieties as providing an underlying structure in narratives. Applying this framework to the breast cancer narrative previously discussed, we can begin to connect the woman's anxiety about her early experience of abandonment to her fear about the impact of the cancer on her children.

In narrative accounts developed in focus groups, it is important to note how collective stories are developed. The identification of collective terms such as 'we' and 'us' can assist in identifying these more social narratives. They can also be seen in the way some narratives are developed in contrast to the stories of the collective 'other' that are described using terms such as 'they' and 'them'. These terms are also apparent in individual narratives and illustrate to what extent the individual identifies with certain social stories or attempts to develop more oppositional narratives.

The researcher can also involve the participants in the process of narrative analysis. For example, one could ask them to review the narrative transcripts or their personal journals and to highlight certain features of interest, in a way for them to begin to develop a coding scheme. From this review, they, either as individuals or as part of a group, can begin the process of analysis. The researcher could also use the study of the narrative accounts as the beginning of a process of reflection for the participants. An extension to the cancer study described would be to invite the women to participate in a group setting to reflect upon their common experiences. Such a process could be emotionally charged for both the researcher and participants, but it also holds the possibility of converting the narrative research into a form of action research (see Chapter 10 of this volume; Lykes, 1997). In this form of research, the participants can begin to reflect upon the power of dominant societal narratives in shaping their experiences and, as a group, to consider alternative, more enhancing narratives.

In conclusion, the opportunities provided by narrative research are extensive and still being developed. In conducting a study, researchers should ask what are they trying to understand, what are the participants trying to say and why are they trying to say that? The aim is to reveal the underlying structure of narrative accounts that shape not only the way we account for our actions and those of others but also our very identity.

Box 6.4 presents three examples of narrative analysis in action.

Box 6.4   Three good examples of narrative analysis

Two Black men with prostate cancer: a narrative approach

Gray, Fergus and Fitch (2005) report details of a study which explored in detail the experiences of two Black men with prostate cancer. The two men participated in extensive interviews at four periods of time. The men were asked to provide details of their changing experience of cancer. The authors of the paper read and discussed the interview transcripts and agreed on the narrative structure and the core aspects of the narrative accounts of the two men. They were concerned to connect the men's accounts with their social experiences. They also considered the linear character of the narrative accounts, in particular, how time is framing the narratives. The authors also consider the issues of race and gender in interpreting the men's narratives. This paper is recommended because it illustrates in detail the process of conducting narrative analysis, the connection with theory, and the challenge of trying to consider the relevance of just two detailed case studies.

Cancer narratives and the cancer support group

This study by Yaskowich and Stam (2003) develops the idea of illness as biographical disruption. Interviews were conducted with 23 cancer patients who

---

(Continued)

participated in peer support groups. A biographical approach to the interview was adopted in which the participants were encouraged to provide details of their experience of being diagnosed and living with cancer. It also considered the unique role of the peer support group. The analysis followed the guidelines of grounded theory, an approach to qualitative analysis that is considered in a separate chapter. This analysis produced five preliminary categories and two transformed categories: 'biographical work' and 'a unique and separate culture'. The support group was considered a safe situation within which the participants could do the necessary biographical work which enabled them to integrate the diagnosis of cancer into their identities. This article is selected because it gives detailed information on all stages of the project from participant recruitment, conduct of interviews and analysis of interview transcripts. It is also important because it explicitly links grounded theory and narrative theory and clearly considers the use of grounded theory to explore narrative accounts.

Empowering social action through narratives of identity and culture

Williams, Labonte and O'Brien (2003) consider the use of narrative as a strategy for promoting social action in a community setting. Rather than accepting that narratives are a reflection of reality the researchers begin to explore their transformative potential. A sample of Pacific Islander women resident in a disadvantaged community in New Zealand agreed to participate in the project. This involved them sharing their stories of exclusion and oppression. Through dialogue and debate the members of the group began to see the commonalities in their stories. They identified a series of benefits of shared story-telling. These included confidence building, reconnection and pride in Tongan and Samoan identities and group building. They also identified two common narratives: struggles of immigrant women and shared experiences as women. From this process of shared narrative analysis the women began to explore strategies of resistance that brought some of them into conflict with family members. Discussion then moved to how to collectively resist such conflict. The reason why this paper was selected is because it shows the connection between narrative and participatory action research.

Further Reading

Bruner, J. (1990) *Acts of Meaning.* Cambridge, MA: Harvard University Press.
A short monograph that distinguishes paradigmatic and narrative modes of thinking.

Crossley, M. (1999) *Introducing Narrative Psychology: Self, Trauma and the Construction of Meaning.* Buckingham: Open University Press.
A succinct introduction to narrative theory and analysis.

(Continued)

Freeman, M. (1993) *Rewriting the Self: History, Memory, Narrative.* London and New York: Routledge.
A fascinating analysis of a range of classic autobiographies that illustrates the narrative construction of identity.

Mishler, E.G. (1986) *Research Interviewing: Context and Narrative.* Cambridge, MA: Harvard University Press.
A detailed introduction to narrative interviewing and analysis.

Sarbin, T. (ed.) (1986) *Narrative Psychology: The Storied Nature of Human Conduct.* New York: Praeger.
A collection of innovative articles on narrative psychology.

Valdes, M.J. (ed.) (1991) *A Ricoeur Reader: Reflection and Imagination.* Toronto: University of Toronto Press.
A selection of important articles on hermeneutic philosophy and narrative theory.

SEVEN

Conversation Analysis

Paul Drew

Researchers across a range of cognate disciplines – anthropology, sociology, communication, linguistics, sociolinguistics and pragmatics, as well as psychology – have in recent years increasingly turned to the perspective and methods of conversation analysis (CA). They have done so in order to investigate a wide variety of topics, some of which intersect with, or lie within, various fields of psychology. The sheer breadth and richness of these topics begin to give some idea of the adaptability of CA to a great variety of research sites. These topics include medical interaction, especially interactions between patients and doctors and other health-care professionals (Drew et al., 2001; Heath, 1986; Heritage and Maynard, 2006 ; Heritage and Sefi, 1992); child–adult interaction, and the development of mind (Wootton, 1997); news media, such as news interviews, political speaking and debate (Atkinson, 1984; Clayman, 1995; Clayman and Heritage, 2002); delusions and hallucinations (Palmer, 2000); speech disorders relating to aphasia, autism and cerebral palsy (Goodwin, 1995); sexual identity (Kitzinger, 2005a, 2005b); calls to the emergency services (Zimmerman, 1992); counselling of various kinds, including family systems therapy applied to HIV/AIDS counselling (Peräkylä, 1995; Silverman, 1997); and divorce mediation (Greatbatch and Dingwall, 1997). Underpinning the diversity of research in such 'applied' areas as these, however, is the programme of CA research into the basic processes of ordinary social interaction, with which this chapter will be concerned.

The origins of CA intersect more closely with psychology – at least with topics which have seemed intrinsically psychological in character – than is perhaps generally appreciated. Having first trained in the law, and then undertaken graduate study at the University of Berkeley, Harvey Sacks (1935–1975) began to develop CA in the course of his investigations at the Center for the Scientific Study of Suicide, in Los Angeles, 1963/64. Here he was interested initially in psychiatric and psychodynamic theorizing. But staff at the centre were recording suicide counselling telephone calls handled by a suicide prevention centre, in an attempt to understand more fully the problems which callers were facing and thereby to devise means of counselling callers effectively. It was these recordings which provided the stimulus for what was to become CA. Drawn by his interests both in the ethnomethodological concern with members' methods of practical reasoning (arising from his association with Harold Garfinkel), and in the study of interaction (he was taught at Berkeley by Erving Goffman), Sacks began to investigate how callers' accounts of their troubles were produced in the course of their conversations with Suicide Prevention Centre (SPC) counsellors. This led him, without any diminished sensitivity to the plight of persons calling the SPC, to explore the more generic 'machineries' of conversational turn-taking, and of the sequential patterns or structures associated with the management of activities in conversation. (For a definitive account of the origins of Sacks's work in CA, its subsequent development and the range of issues it spawned, see Schegloff, 1992a; Edwards, 1995, provides a clear and important review not only of Sacks's work, but also of the differences between his interactional approach and psychological perspectives, especially in cognitive psychology.) Through the collection of a broader corpus of interactions, including group therapy sessions and mundane telephone conversations, and in collaboration with Gail Jefferson (1938–) and Emanuel Schegloff (1937–), Sacks began to show that:

talk can be examined as an object in its own right, and not merely as a screen on which are projected other processes, whether Balesian system problems or Schutzian interpretative strategies, or Garfinkelian commonsense methods. The talk itself was the action, and previously unsuspected details were critical resources in what was getting done in and by the talk; and all this in naturally occurring events, in no way manipulated to allow the study of them. (Schegloff, 1992a: xviii)

At the heart of this is the recognition that 'talk is *action, not communication*' (Edwards, 1995: 579). Talk is not merely a medium, for instance, to communicate thoughts, information or knowledge: in conversation as in all forms of interaction, people are doing things in talk (Austin, 1962). They are engaged in social activities with one another – and what is beginning to emerge is a quite comprehensive picture of *how* people engage in social actions in talk-in-interaction. Sacks focused on such matters as the organization of turn-taking; overlapping talk; repair; topic initiation and closing; greetings, questions, invitations, requests, etc. and their associated sequences (adjacency pairs); agreement and disagreement; storytelling; and the integration of speech with non-vocal activities. Subsequent research in CA over the past 40 years has shown how these and other technical aspects of talk-in-interaction are the structured, socially organized resources – or methods – whereby participants perform and coordinate activities through talking together. Thus, they are the technical bedrock on which people build their social lives, or in other words construct their sense of sociality with one another.

Essentially, CA is a naturalistic, observation-based science of actual (verbal and non-verbal) behaviour, which uses audio and video recordings of naturally occurring interactions as the basic form of data (Heritage, 1984). CA is distinctive in its approach in the following kinds of ways.

First, in its focus on how participants understand and respond to one another in their turns at talk, CA explores the social and interactional underpinnings of intersubjectivity – the maintenance of common, shared and even 'collective' understandings between social actors.

Second, CA develops empirically Goffman's insight that social interaction embodies a distinct moral and institutional order that can be treated like other social institutions, such as the family, economy, religion, etc. By the *interaction order*, Goffman (1983) meant the institutional order of interaction; and CA explores the practices that make up this institution, as a topic in its own right.

Third, conversational organizations underlie social action (Atkinson and Heritage, 1984); CA offers a methodology, based on analysing sequences in which actions are produced and embedded, for investigating how we accomplish social actions.

Fourth, it is evident that the performance by one participant of certain kinds of actions – for instance, a greeting, question, invitation, etc. – sets up certain expectations concerning what the other, the recipient, should do in response. That is, recipients may be expected to return a greeting, answer the question, accept or decline the invitation, and so on. Thus, such pairs of actions, called in CA *adjacency pairs*, are normative frameworks within which certain actions should properly or accountably be done: the normative character of action, and the associated accountability of acting in accordance with normative expectations, are vitally germane to the moral order of social life, including ascriptions of deviance.

Fifth and last, CA relates talk to social context. CA's approach to context is distinctive, partly because the most proximate context for any turn at talk is regarded as being the (action) sequence of which it is a part – in particular, the immediately prior turn. CA also takes the position that the 'context' of an interaction cannot be exhaustively defined by the analyst a priori; rather, participants display in the 'design' of their turns at talk (this will be explained later) their sense of relevant context – including mutual knowledge, what each knows about the other, the setting, relevant biographical information, their relevant identities or relationships, and so on.

Underlying the methodology of CA is the attempt to capture and document the back-and-forth, or *processual*, character of interaction. The analytic aim is to show how conversational and other interactions are managed and constructed in real time, through the processes of production and comprehension employed by participants in coordinating their activities when talking with one another.

This involves focusing on the turn-by-turn evolution of conversations from one speaker's turn, to the next speaker's, and so on. Each participant in a dyadic (two-person) conversation (to take the simplest model) constructs or designs a turn to be understood by the other in a particular way – for instance, as performing some particular action. The other constructs an appropriate response, the other's understanding of the prior turn being manifest in that response. Hence, the first speaker may review the recipient's response to check whether the other has 'correctly' understood his or her first turn; and if the first speaker finds from that response that the other appears not to have understood his or her utterance/action correctly, that speaker may initiate repair to remedy the other's understanding (Schegloff, 1992b). The first speaker then produces a response, or a relevant next action, to the other's prior turn – and so the conversation proceeds, each turn being sequentially connected to its prior turn, but simultaneously moving the conversation forward by forming the immediate context for the other speaker's next action in the sequence (this is the 'context-shaped and context-renewing' character of conversational turns/actions described by Heritage, 1984: 242).

In broad terms, the objective of CA's methodological approach is to attempt to document and explicate how participants arrived at understandings of one another's actions during the back-and-forth interaction between them, and how they construct their turns so as to be suitably responsive to prior turns. In this way, conversation can be regarded as a co-construction between participants. CA's methodology is naturalistic and largely qualitative, and is characterized by four key features.

First, research is based on the study of naturally occurring data (audio or video recordings). These recordings are usually transcribed in considerable detail, though the precise level and type of detail (such as whether certain phonetic and prosodic features of production are included) will depend on the researcher's particular focus.

Second, phenomena in the data are generally not coded. The reason for this is that tokens which have the appearance of being 'the same' or equivalent phenomena may turn out, on closer inspection, to have a different interactional salience, and hence not to be equivalent. For example, repetitions might be coded in the same category, and hence regarded as undifferentiated phenomena. But different prosodic realizations of repeats (Couper-Kuhlen, 1996) or the sequential circumstances in which something is being repeated, and specifically what object is being repeated (Schegloff, 1996), can all crucially influence the activity being conducted through a repeat. Coding tokens on the basis of certain manifest similarities runs the risk of collecting, in the same category, objects which in reality have a quite different interactional significance.

Third, CA's methodology is generally not quantitative. This is not a rigid precept, but rather a corollary of the risks attendant on coding – following from which, it is clear that quantifying the occurrence of a certain object is likely to result in the truly interactional properties of that object being overlooked. Those interactional properties can be uncovered only by thorough qualitative analysis, particularly of the sequential properties of that object, and how variations in speech production are related to their different sequential implicature (on reasons for being cautious about, or avoiding, quantification, see Schegloff, 1993).

Fourth, CA's methods attempt to document and explicate how participants arrived at understandings of one another's actions during the back-and-forth interaction between them, and how in turn they constructed their turns so as to be suitably responsive to prior turns. Therefore, CA focuses especially on those features of talk that are salient to participants' analyses of one another's turns at talk, in the progressive unfolding of interactions.

But all this is pretty abstract. It is time to give a more concrete, practical picture of CA's methodology.

The Data Used in CA

I mentioned that the data which researchers in CA use are always recordings of naturally occurring interactions: data are not gathered though simulations, through experimental or quasi-experimental tasks, and are not fabricated. Nor, generally, are interviews treated as data, although, for certain analytic purposes or enterprises, some interviews may be considered as naturally occurring interactions. There is no easy guide to making recordings in the field, the difficulties of which include access (and the ethical standards of obtaining consent), technical aspects and attendant frustrations. (I once videotaped an open-plan architects' office in the north of England over one week: some of the best action was lost as data, as it turned out that for two days the sound had not been recorded; loose connections can drive you crazy! But see Goodwin, 1993, on technical aspects of recording.) And one can learn only from experience how to handle the personal relationships and expectations that can develop from extended involvement with those whom one is recording.

Once recordings have been obtained, the next step is to transcribe (all or some portions of) the data collected. Later, in the next section, I will begin to introduce CA's approach to analysing data by focusing on a brief extract from a telephone call between Emma (all names are pseudonyms) and a friend, Nancy, whom she has called. This extract begins about eleven minutes into the call when, after they have talked for some time about a class which Nancy is taking (as a mature student, in middle age) at a local university, Emma abruptly changes the topic. To give you some idea of what we try to put into and convey through our transcripts, Box 7.1, by contrast, shows a simple transcription of what the participants say to one another.

Box 7.1   Simple transcription

(1)   [NB:II:2:9]
Emma: … some of that stuff hits you pretty hard
Nancy: Yes
Emma: And then you think well do you want to be part of it What are you
        doing?
Nancy: What am I doing?
Emma: Cleaning?
Nancy: I'm ironing would you believe that
Emma: Oh bless its heart.
Nancy: In fact I I started ironing and I I somehow or another ironing just kind of
        leaves me cold
Emma: Yes
Nancy: You know
Emma: Want to come down have a bite of lunch with me?
Nancy: It's just
Emma: I've got some beer and stuff
Nancy: Well you're real sweet hon
Emma: Or do you have something else
Nancy: Let I No I have to call Roul's mother … .

This is the kind of transcript that might be produced by Hansard, as a record of Parliamentary debate, or by court stenographers as they write down what's said during a trial. It records, in standard orthography, the words that were spoken – or, rather, as they should have been spoken. But it does not record what was actually said. It does not, for instance, record the difference between words which were fully articulated, and those which were 'shortened' or run together (for instance, Emma does not say *bite of* in the thirteenth line: she runs them together, as *bahta*). Nor does it record the way in which things were said, the pacing, intonation and emphasis in their talk. Finally, it does not capture anything about the relationship between one person's turn at talk, and the next. In order to represent these and other aspects of talk, CA has developed a transcription system which aims to capture faithfully features of speech which are salient to the interaction between participants, including – as well as characteristics of speech delivery (such as emphasis, loudness/softness, pitch changes, sound stretching and curtailment, etc.) – aspects of the relationship between turns at talk. This relationship includes whether, and when, one speaker talks in overlap with another, and whether there is a pause between one speaker's turn and the next (see Atkinson and Heritage, 1984: ix–xvi; Jefferson, 1985; ten Have, 1999: ch. 5). To capture these features, we use the symbols shown in Box 7.2.

Box 7.2 Transcription symbols

The relative timing of utterances

Intervals either within or between turns are shown thus (0.7).

A discernible pause which is too short to be timed mechanically is shown as a micro-pause (.).

Overlaps between utterances are indicated by square brackets, the point of overlap onset being marked with a single left-hand bracket.

Contiguous utterances, where there is no discernible interval between turns, are linked by an equals sign. This is also used to indicate a very rapid move from one unit in a turn to the next.

Characteristics of speech delivery

Various aspects of speech delivery are captured in these transcripts by punctuation symbols (which, therefore, are not used to mark conventional grammatical units) and other forms of notation, as follows:

A period (full stop) indicates a falling intonation.

A comma indicates a continuing intonation.

A question mark indicates a rising inflection (not necessarily a question).

The stretching of a sound is indicated by colons, the number of which correspond to the length of the stretching.

.h indicates inhalation, the length of which is indicated by the number of h's.
h. indicates out breath, the length of which is indicated by the number of h's.

(hh) Audible aspirations are indicated in the speech in which they occur (including in laughter).

°° Degree signs indicate word(s) spoken very softly or quietly.

Sound stress is shown by underlining, those words or parts of a word which are emphasized being underlined.

Particularly emphatic speech, usually with raised pitch, is shown by capital letters.

Marked changes in pitch are shown by ↑ for changes to a higher pitch, and ↓ for a fall in pitch.

If what is said is unclear or uncertain, that is placed in parentheses.

Using these symbols to transcribe the same extract results in something that, although formidably difficult to comprehend at first sight, captures a considerable amount of detail that may be relevant to our analysis of the interaction between them. It is important to note in this respect that our transcriptions are 'preanalytic', in the sense that they are made before the researcher has any particular idea about what phenomena, patterns or features in the data that might be investigated. Indeed, the purpose of the transcript, used in conjunction with the recording, is that it should be a resource in developing observations and hypotheses about phenomena. The following is what the extract from the conversation between Emma and Nancy looks like transcribed in these symbols (this has been extended to include a little more of their conversation than was shown in Box 7.1). Try not to be put off by the detail, which, to begin with, will look like a mess: if you read it through a couple of times, you'll quickly begin to follow it.

```
(2)   [NB:II:2:9]
 1    Emm: ....... so[me a'° s]ome a'that stuff hits yuh pretty ha:rd=
 2    Nan:        [°Ye:ah° ]
 3    Emm: ='n then: °yuh thin:k we:ll d'you wanna be°
 4         (0.7)
 5    Nan: hhhhhh[hh
 6    Emm:       [↑PA:R:T of ut.w;Wuddiyuh ↑DOin.
 7         (0.9)
 8    Nan: What'm I do[in?
 9    Emm:           [Cleani:ng?=
10    Nan: =hh.hh I'm ironing wouldju belie:ve ↑tha:t.
11    Emm: Oh: bless it[s ↓hea:rt.]
12    Nan:            [In f a :c]t I: ire I start'd ironing en I: d-
13         I: (.) Somehow er another ahrning js kind of lea:ve me:
14         co:[ld]
15    Emm:     [Ye]ah,
16         (.)
17    Nan: [Yihknow,   ]
18    Emm: [Wanna c'm] do:wn 'av [a bah:ta] lu:nch w]ith me?=
19    Nan:                       [°It's js ] (    )°]
20    Emm: =Ah gut s'm beer'n stu:ff,
21         (0.3)
22    Nan: ↑ Wul yer ril sweet hon: uh:m
23         (.)
24    Emm: [Or d'y] ou'av sup'n [else °(    )°
25    Nan: [L  e  t] I  :  ] hu.   [n:No: i haf to: uh callo Roul's mother,h
26         I told'er I:'d call'er this morning I [ gotta letter ] from'er en
27    Emm:                                       [°(Uh huh.) ° ]
28    Nan: .hhhhhh A:nd uhm
29         (1.0)
30    Nan: .tch u.-So: she in the letter she said if you ca:n why (.)
31         yihknow call me Saturday morning en I jst haven't. h
32         [ .hhhh ]
33    Emm: [°Mm h]m:°=
34    Nan: ='T's like takin a beating.
35         (0.2)
36    Nan: kh[hh ↑hnhh hnh]-hnh- [hnh
37    Emm:   [°M m : : :, °]      [No one heard a wo:rd hah,
```

```
38   Nan:   >Not a word,<
39          (0.2)
40          Nan: Hah ah,
41          (0.2)
42   Nan:   n:Not (.) not a word,h
43          (.)
44   Nan:   Not et all, except Roul's mother gotta call .hhhhhh (0.3) °I
45          think it wuss:: (0.3) th'Mondee er the Tue:sday after
46          Mother's Da:y,
```

This telephone conversation is, of course, like any other, quite unique – in terms of time and place, and its having been held by these two participants, with whatever relationship and history they have with each other, and in whatever circumstances the call happened to be made. Notice that we can begin to see something of their relationship in Nancy's referring to 'Roul's mother', thereby assuming that Emma will recognize whom she is referring to when she names her ex-husband. Furthermore, it is evident that Emma already knows something about the circumstances associated with the difficulties Nancy is having with her ex-husband, when in response to Nancy's reference in line 34 to 'takin a beating', she (Emma) asks in line 37, 'No one heard a wo:rd hah,'. And finally, in lines 18–20, Emma invites Nancy over for lunch ('Wanna c'm do:wn 'av a bah:ta lu:nch with me?=Ah gut s'm beer'n stu:ff,'); presumably, there are not many people Emma could or would call mid-morning to invite over for an informal lunch that same day (that Roul is Nancy's ex-husband and that it is 11.15 am emerge later in the call). Thus, details in their conversation reveal something of their relationship and the uniqueness of what they know about each other.

Some First Steps in Analysing the Data

But against this (ethnographic) uniqueness, we can make out some familiar things in the data, things that we recognize to be happening in other conversations. Foremost among these is perhaps what seems central to this extract: Emma's invitation. There are various ways to begin to approach data for the first time (see Pomerantz and Fehr, 1996, for a useful and more extended outline than can be provided here). But an initial – and quite essential – starting point is to consider the ways in which participants are not 'just talking', but engaged in social activities. Whenever we are examining talk in conversation, we look to see what activity or activities the participants are engaged in – what are they doing? Here the activity being managed or conducted in this sequence is Emma's invitation. The *social character* of such an action or activity cannot be too strongly emphasized. People's engagement in the social world consists, in large part, of performing and responding to such activities. So again, when we study conversation, we are studying not language idling, but language employed in the service of doing things in the social world. And we are focusing on the social organization of these activities being conducted in conversation.

In referring to the *management* of Emma's invitation, I mean to suggest that we can see that Emma manages the interaction in such a way as to give herself the opportunity to make the invitation. Looking at what occurs immediately before, it is clear that Emma's invitation in lines 18–20 follows her having inquired about what Nancy was doing (line 6). It appears that Nancy's response – indicating that she *started* doing something (line 12) but might rather not continue it (*ironing just kind of leaves me cold*, lines 13–14) – encourages Emma to make her invitation. Now, we cannot be sure whether Emma asked what Nancy was doing with the intention of finding out whether she was free, and, if so, to invite her, or whether, having asked an innocent question, perhaps about their daily chores, and finding that Nancy was at a loose end, Emma decided at that point (that is, after Nancy's response) to invite her. This illustrates the difficulty in trying to interpret participants' cognitive or other psychological states, on the basis of verbal conduct. In short, we cannot know whether her inquiry in line 6 was 'innocent', and therefore that the invitation was interactionally generated by Nancy's response, or whether she made the inquiry specifically in order to set up the invitation she had already planned (and that, indeed, she might have made the call with the purpose of inviting Nancy over for lunch). All that we can say at this stage is that invitations, and similar actions such as requests, are regularly preceded by just such inquiries. Here are two quite clear cases, in which an initial inquiry receives an 'encouraging' response, after which the first speaker makes the invitation which the recipient might well have been able to anticipate.

(3) [:CN:1]
1   A: Watha doin'
2   B: Nothin'
3   A: Wanna drink?

(4) [JGII(b):8:14]
1   John: So who'r the boyfriends for the week.
2   (0.2)
3   Mary: .k.hhhhh- Oh: go::d e-yih this one'n that one yihknow, I jist,
4   yihknow keep busy en go out when I wanna go out John it's
5   nothing .hhh I don' have anybody serious on the string,
6   John: So in other words you'd go out if I:: askedche out one a' these
7   times.
8   Mary: Yeah! Why not.

Such inquiries as are made in the opening lines in extracts (3) and (4) are termed *pre-invitations*: they are designed to set up, as it were, the invitation which they presage – by finding out whether, if the invitation were made, it is likely to be accepted.

Whether or not Emma had in mind, when making her inquiry, to invite Nancy (and hence whether her inquiry in line 6 was designed as a pre-invitation), we can see that the invitation did not come out of the blue. It was preceded by, and arose out of, an interactional sequence (lines 6–17) from which Emma could discern that Nancy might be free to come for lunch. Another aspect of the management of her invitation is the way in which it is constructed or designed as a casual, spontaneous idea. This is conveyed, not only in the timing of the invitation (only an hour or so beforehand), but also in using phrases like 'come down' and 'bite of lunch'. The sociability being proposed is not portrayed as a luncheon party, an occasion to which others have been invited, or for which one should dress up, or an RSVP do: rather, it is an impromptu affair, on finding that Nancy might welcome some diversion from her chores. So the kind of invitation it is, and the concomitant expectations and obligations which might attach to the recipient of such an invitation, are manifest in the specific design of the turn in which the invitation is made.

Therefore, having outlined a first step in analysing data:

1. Look to see what activity or activities the participants are engaged in.
   We can add the second and third steps.
2. Consider the sequence leading up to the initiation of an action, to see how the activity in question may have arisen out of that sequence (and even whether a speaker appears to have laid the ground for the upcoming action).
3. Examine in detail the design (the specific words and phrases used, including prosodic and intonational features) of the turn in which the action is initiated.
   That latter point concerning turn design can be developed in the context of a fourth step:
4. Consider how the recipient responds to the 'first' speaker's turn/action.

In this respect, we can notice a number of features of Nancy's response. First, she does not answer immediately: there is a 0.3-second delay (line 21) before she begins to speak.

```
(5)   [From (2)]
18    Emm:    [Wanna c'm] do:wn 'av [a bah:ta] lu:nch w]ith me?=
19    Nan:                          [ °It's  is] (      )°]
20    Emm:    =Ah gut s'm beer'n stu:ff,
21            (0.3)
22    Nan:    ↑Wulyer ril sweet hon: uh:m
23            (.)
24    Emm:    [Or d'y] ou'av] sup'n else °(    )°
25    Nan:    [L e t-] l  :  ] hu.
```

Bearing in mind the first analytic step, to consider what action a speaker is doing in a turn (or sequence), we can notice here that, when she does respond, Nancy does an *appreciation* of the invitation (line 22, 'Wul yer ril sweet hon: uh:m'). She could, of course, simply have accepted Emma's invitation, with something like 'Oh, that'd be lovely', which would have simultaneously both *appreciated* and *accepted* the invitation. Here, though, Nancy appreciates the invitation without (at least yet) accepting. Two further observations about Nancy's turn/appreciation in line 22: it is prefaced with 'Wul' (that is, *Well*); and then she hesitates before continuing, as indicated by 'uh:m' and the slight (micro) pause (line 23) before she begins with 'Let-' (line 25).

Of course, having invited Nancy over for lunch, Emma is listening for whether Nancy will accept. It is quite plain from her turn in line 24, 'Or d'y ou'av sup'n else', that already Emma anticipates that Nancy might have some difficulty in accepting: having *something else to do* is a standard reason to decline an invitation.

A way to think about Emma's anticipating Nancy's difficulty/possible declining is that Emma *analyses* what Nancy has said. This again is fundamental to our investigations of conversation: we are focusing on *the analyses which participants make of each other's talk and conduct* – on how they understand what the other means or is doing. Looking at what it is that has led Emma to anticipate that Nancy might be going to decline, we can see that the only basis Emma has so far for making this analysis is the delay before Nancy speaks (in line 21), her appreciating the invitation without yet accepting it, and Nancy beginning her turn with 'Well'. Taken together, these three features indicate to Emma that Nancy might, after all, not be free to come over for lunch.

I mentioned before that, although this is a unique conversation, many features of their talk are quite familiar. Nancy's *appreciation* is one of the familiar features, and appreciations are familiar, particularly when one speaker is declining another's invitation (or offer).

Here is another example.

(6) [SBL:1:1:10:14]
```
1    Ros:   And uh the: if you'd care tuh come ovuh, en visit u
2           little while this morning I'll give you[cup a'coffee.
3    Bea:                                          [ khhh
4    Bea:   Uhhh-huh hh W'l that's awf'lly sweet of yuh I don't
5           think I c'n make it this morning, hheeuhh uh:m (0.3)
6           'tch I'm running en a:d in the paper 'nd an:d uh hh I
7           haftih stay near the pho::ne,
```

Bea's declination of Rose's invitation to come over for coffee that morning consists of three components:

[appreciation] + [declines] + [account]

Her [appreciation] is 'W'l that's awf'lly *sweet* of yuh' (line 4): she explicitly [declines] the invitation when she says 'I don't think I c'n *make* it this morning' (lines 4–5). (Note that Bea's declination is softened, or mitigated, by her saying 'I don't think', rather than just I can't make it'), after which she offers an [account] for being unable to make it, which is that 'I'm *running* en a:d in the paper 'nd an:d uh hh I haftih stay near the pho::ne' (lines 6–7). This illustrates the way in which an [appreciation] can be done to preface or lead into declining an invitation. One thing which the [appreciation] does is to delay the declination; and this is consistent with the 0.3-second pause (line 21) before Nancy's responds to Emma's invitation. So this is another feature of Nancy's response which may give Emma the clue that Nancy is about to decline: her 'decision' is delayed, both by the pause and by the prefatory [appreciation]. But it is important that the [appreciation] is itself prefaced by *Well*: it is possible to use an [appreciation] as a way to accept an invitation (as in *That's very good of you*), but in such cases the [appreciation] is not prefaced by the disjunctive *Well*.

Just parenthetically, before taking stock of where we are, it is worth noticing something about Emma's turn in line 24. Up to now, we have been considering what basis she had for anticipating that Nancy might be going to decline her invitation – focusing on details of what Nancy said in line 22, and the delays in her responding which are evident in lines 21 and 23. But when she anticipates Nancy's possible declination, Emma achieves something else: she also *pre-empts* that declination. If we compare the sequence in lines 24–37 of extract (2) with Bea's declination in lines 4–7 of (6), it is apparent that there is *no explicit declination of Emma's invitation*.

```
(7)     [from (2)]
22   Nan:    ↑Wul yer ril sweet hon: uh:m
23           (.)
24   Emm:    [Or d'y] ou'av] sup'n [else °(   )°
25   Nan:    [L e t-] I:] hu.         [n:No: i haf to: uh callo Roul's mother,h
26           I told'er I:'d call'er this morning I [ gotta letter ] from'er en
27   Emm:                                         [°(Uh huh.)° ]
28   Nan:    .hhhhhh A:nd uhm
29           (1.0)
30   Nan:    .tch u.-So: she in the letter she said if you ca:n why (.)
31           yihknow call me Saturday morning en I jst haven't. h
32           [.hhhh]
33   Emm:    [°Mm h]m:°=
34   Nan:    ='T's like takin a beating.
35           (0.2)
36   Nan:    kh[hh ↑hnhh hnh]-hnh- [hnh
37   Emm:      [°M m  : :  :, °]    [No one heard a wo:rd hah,
```

The square brackets at the beginning of lines 24 and 25 indicate that Emma and Nancy start to speak simultaneously. It appears that Nancy was going to continue with her response to Emma's invitation; but Emma manages to come in with her inquiry anticipating that she might have *something else* to do before Nancy does any more explicit rejection, of the kind which Bea does when she says 'I don't think I c'n *make* it this morning'. And the way in which the sequence develops finds them having moved on to the topic of Nancy's difficulties with her ex-husband (line 37), without having resolved the matter of whether Nancy is coming over for lunch. The point to notice here is not only that Emma's turn in line 24 displays her analysis or understanding of Nancy's response thus far, but also that she manages to forestall the declination that she anticipates. And if a declination has not been explicitly or officially made, then perhaps a decision about the invitation is still open (and, indeed, later in the call they do return to the possibility of Nancy's coming over for lunch).

A Reprise: the Analytic Steps so Far

In beginning to analyse this brief extract from a telephone call, I have suggested four initial steps. Focusing initially on a turn at talk, here on Emma's turn in lines 18–20 of extract (2), a way to begin to see *what* is going on in the talk, and *how* that is being done, is to:

1. Identify what activity or actions the participants are engaged in.

Here Emma has invited Nancy for lunch, so that we have an invitation sequence, in which Nancy's response should be to accept or decline the invitation.

2. Consider the sequence leading up to the initiation of an action, to see how the activity in question may have arisen out of that sequence (and even whether a speaker appears to have laid the ground for the upcoming action).

We saw that Emma's inquiry *may* have been a pre-invitation inquiry, designed to determine whether Nancy might be free to come for lunch. But we cannot be sure: her inquiry may have been 'innocent'. Nevertheless, she does make the invitation in an environment – after Nancy's less than enthusiastic report about a chore she would rather not be doing – which encourages her to believe that Nancy might be free/willing to take a break and come for lunch.

3. Examine in detail the design (the specific words and phrases used) of each of the participants' turns.

For instance, Emma designs her invitation so as to indicate that it is an impromptu, casual affair – which is a way of formulating the kind of occasion being proposed (which may have further implications as regards the recipient's 'commitment' or obligations).

4. Consider how the recipient responds to the 'first' speaker's turn/action.

This involves a combination of the first and third steps, applied to the next turn. Emma's invitation has set up an expectation concerning what Nancy will do next (that is, what action her next turn will constitute): she can be expected either to accept the invitation (preferably), or to decline it. Instead, what she does is to *appreciate* the invitation. That, coupled with two other aspects of the design of Nancy's turn – her delay before starting to speak, and prefacing her appreciation with the disjunctive *Well* – are all indications of her trouble in accepting, and are the basis on which Emma anticipates that Nancy might be going to decline.

In summary, we are looking at the data for the ways in which, through their turns at talk, participants manage activities. Our focus is on social conduct, and how conduct is constructed through precisely what participants say – through the *design* of their turns. Turn design involves speakers selecting from alternative possible ways of saying something. For instance, selecting the prefatory *Well* in line 22 gives Nancy's appreciation its declination-implicative character: without *Well*, and without the delay which precedes her response, the 'same' appreciation would presage acceptance. Finally, it is fundamental to CA's approach that we are investigating the ways in which speakers themselves, during the conversation, understand and analyse what the other is doing/meaning: so we focus on participants' analyses of one another's conduct.

In addition to these four analytic steps, another has been taken in what until now has been rather an implicit manner. The observations about the construction of turns at talk, and understandings of/responses to them, have supposed that what we are observing in this conversation are not features which are idiosyncratic to these speakers. I suggested that while this conversation was unique, in terms of its occurrence (time, place, participants and circumstances), nevertheless, what goes on in the talk, the activities the speakers are engaged in, and how they manage those activities are familiar – by which I was implying that these features of the data are *common* to a speech community, and are *systematic* properties of talk-in-interaction. The intelligibility of social action in conversation arises from participants employing intersubjective, common or shared forms and patterns of language. Recall that, at two points during these preliminary observations, I have introduced extracts from other conversations in which the same feature or pattern is evident. Extracts (3) and (4) are examples of inquiries which were plainly *pre-invitations*. Though the specific words and content of each are different, and the nature of the invitation is different in each case, the inquiries themselves serve the same function in terms of the sequence: the questions are asked in the service of an upcoming invitation, to see whether, if the invitation were made, it is likely to be accepted. And subsequently another extract (6) was shown to illustrate that a *Well*-prefaced [appreciation] was used in cases where the speaker is declining an invitation. It is evident that these observations draw on our knowledge about what occurs in other similar sequences of actions (here, invitation sequences) in other conversations between other participants. Hence, we are beginning to build a case for there being *patterns* in talk, and that these patterns are systematic, in so far as they arise from certain general contingencies which people face when interacting with one another. But, in order to explore and demonstrate this, we need to build *collections* of instances. This is the final and quite essential stage in the development of an analysis of a conversational phenomenon – so let us see what a collection can look like.

Systematic Patterns in Conversation (I): Collections

The aim of CA research is to investigate and uncover the *socially organized practices* through which people make themselves understood, and through which they manage social activities in talk. We can begin to see in the preliminary account of extract (2) that participants design their talk in ways which are organized (for instance, the combination of a delay in answering, together with prefacing an appreciation with *Well*) and shared (Emma anticipates from this that Nancy may be going to decline her invitation). These are not idiosyncrasies belonging to individuals, nor are these practices associated with the particular personalities of speakers. CA research aims to identify the shared organizations which are manifest in *patterns* of talk. Patterns only become apparent when one collects instances – as many instances as can be found – of a phenomenon, and examine these for the properties that cases have in common. Therefore, CA's methodology connects together (1) identifying a possible phenomenon; (2) making a collection; and (3) discerning the sequential pattern associated with the phenomenon. In order to illustrate how these are interconnected, and what a central role *collections* play in CA's methodology, I will take up something which happens to occur in the extract we have been considering in which Emma invites Nancy over for lunch. This is not directly related to the invitation itself, but arises from Nancy's account of having to call her mother-in-law. That is, the phenomenon I will examine is quite incidental to the invitation response which we have been looking at so far: it is something which initially caught my eye as curious, as in some respect puzzling.

Recall that Emma takes up the topic of the difficulties Nancy has been having with her ex-husband (parenthetically, managing thereby to consolidate the move away from an explicit or formal rejection of her offer).

```
(8)    [from (2)]
25    Nan:    n:No: I haf to: uh callo Roul's mother,h I told'er I:'d call'er
26             this morning I [ gotta letter ] from'er en
27    Emm:                    [°(Uh huh.)°]
28    Nan:    .hhhhhh A:nd uhm
29             (1.0)
30    Nan:    .tch u.-So: she in the letter she said if you ca:n why (.)
31             yihknow call me Saturday morning en I jst haven't. h
32             [.hhhh]
33    Emm:    [°Mm h]m:°=
```

```
34   Nan:   ='T's like takin a beating.
35          (0.2)
36   Nan:   kh[hh ↑ hnhh hnh]-hnh- [hnh
37   Emm:      [°M m : : :, °]      [No one heard a wo:rd hah,
38   Nan:   >Not a word,<
39          (0.2)
40   Nan:   Hah ah,
41          (0.2)
42   Nan:   n:Not (.) not a word,h
43              (.)
44   Nan:   Not et all, except Roul's mother gotta call .hhhhhh (0.3) °I
45          think it wuss:: (0.3) th'Mondee er the Tue:sday after
46          Mother's Da:y,
```

It is evident that Emma knows something of the situation involving Nancy's
ex-husband, when she asks 'No one heard a wo:rd hah,' (line 37). Nancy confirms this, in a fairly strong fashion. Nancy adds three further confirmations
(lines 40, 42 and at the start of 44). Notice that what Nancy repeats and confirms is a quite categorical version, 'no one' and 'not a word', both indicating
the completeness of her ex-husband's lack of communication. However, in line
44, she proceeds to qualify that, when she says '*except* Roul's mother gotta call'
(she then proceeds to tell what happened during this telephone call). Having
initially claimed that no one had heard from him, Nancy changes her story!
This, then, is what I found puzzling – how is it that Nancy comes up with what
are apparently inconsistent or contradictory versions?

   Now, one might attribute the change in her account, and the inconsistency
which results, to some kind of personal or psychological factor, such as a dis-
position to hyperbole, or that she forgot for the moment, or that her initial
version sprang from her being bitter about her ex-husband. Such attributions
would treat her 'inconsistency' as generated by factors associated with the
individual and her psychology, in the circumstances she finds herself in. But
once I had noticed Nancy's shift *from not a word* to *except Roul's mother got a
call* in this extract, I began to find many similar instances, in which a speaker
initially claims a strong, categorical or dramatic version, but then qualifies that
in some way which backs down from the strength or literalness of the initial
version. And, of course, once one begins to find a number of cases, the
phenomenon – the production of 'inconsistency' – begins to look less like a
psychological attribute, and more like something which, for some reason (or,
to deal with some contingency), is being systematically generated in interaction. Here are some of the other instances that I collected.

```
(9)    [Holt 289:1–2]
1      Sar:   1->   O:h yes (.) well we've done all the peaks.
2                   (0.4)
3      Les:         Oh ye:s
```

```
4                   (0.5)
5       Sar:        A::h
6                   (0.5)
7       Sar:    2-> We couldn't do two because you need ropes and that
```

```
(10)    [Holt:2:15:4–5]
1       Les:            Only: one is outst↓andingly clever wuh- an:' the other- .hh
2               1->     an:'°Rebecca didn't get t'college,°
3                       (0.4)
4       Joy:            Didn't ↓she:,
5       Les:    2->     Well she got in the end she scraped into a buh- business
6                       manogement,
```

```
(11)    [Drew:St:98:1] (Sandra's friends are going out that evening to a disco/night club; she has
        said she isn't going)
1       San:            I don't know hhh hu hu .hhh I dunno it's not really me
2       Bec:            Mw:rh
3       San:    1->     (     ) like it .hh I've never been to one yet,
4       Bec:            You ↑HAven't.
5       San:            No
6       Bec:            Not even t'Ziggy:s
7       San:    2->     Nope (.) I've bin twi- no ( ) a bin twi:ce at home to:: a place
8                       called Tu:bes which is really rubbi:sh and then I've been
9                       once to a place in ( ) Stamford called erm: (.) Crystals (.)
10                      which i:s o::kay: <b- n- Olivers> sorry Olivers (.) which is
11                      okay: ( ) but nothi:ng special,
```

```
(12)    [NB:IV:13:18]
1       Emm:    1->     I haven't had a piece a'mea:t.
2                       (1.0)
3       Emm:    2->     Over et Bill's I had ta:cos Mondee ni::ght little bitta
                        mea:t the*:re. B't not much.
```

In example (9), Sarah initially claims to have 'done' *all the peaks*, and then reveals that they did not do them all. In (10), Lesley first says that one of their friend's daughters did not get into college, but subsequently concedes that she did. Sandra first claims in (11) that she has *never been to one* (a disco/night-club), but then mentions some to which she has been. And, in (12), Emma first reports that she has not had a piece of meat recently, but then 'admits' to having eaten tacos a few nights before.

So, in each instance, there appears to be a discrepancy or inconsistency between the speaker's initial and subsequent versions – just as there was between Nancy's initially claiming that no one had heard from Roul, and her later statement that his mother heard from him a day or two after Mother's Day. In their subsequent versions, speakers seem to back down from their initial claims, revealing those to have been in some fashion incorrect, overstated, too strong and the like.

Here then is a phenomenon – a sequential pattern in which a speaker first claims something, and then retracts or qualifies that claim. We can collect cases of this phenomenon in whatever data we happen to be working with: you can listen for this, and find instances in data that you may collect – the phenomenon is not restricted to telephone calls, or conversations between friends, or even to 'ordinary conversation'. When we put together a collection of cases, we can begin to look for features they may have in common. This is the next analytic step.

Systematic Patterns in Conversation (II): Identifying Common Features in a Collection

We have now a corpus of five instances in which a speaker claims something and subsequently retracts that claim – our original case in (2)/(8), together with extracts (9)–(12) (though these are just a few of the many cases I have collected of this phenomenon). The next step is to examine the corpus, in order to determine whether instances have any features in common. In effect, this involves two of the analytic steps outlined earlier – namely, looking closely at how turns are designed, and considering how each participant responds to the other. Pulling these together, we can discern a number of features which these fragments have in common.

First, the initial versions are very strongly stated, categorical or dramatic – generally through descriptors which are extreme versions (Edwards, 2000; Pomerantz, 1986). Thus, in (9), Sarah claims to have done *all the peaks*; in (11), Sandra claims that she's *never been to one yet*; and, in (12), Emma claims that she *hasn't had a piece of meat* – each of which is an extreme version (and, in [10], Lesley claims categorically that Rebecca *didn't get to college*).

Second, the recipients avoid endorsing these initial versions. Indeed, in various ways, they display some (incipient) scepticism – either through initially not responding (silence), as in examples (9), (10) and (12); through only minimal acknowledgements (example (9)); or through interrogative elliptical repeats, such as Joyce's *Didn't she*, in (10) or Becky's *You haven't* in (11).

Third, the subsequent versions, in which the speakers appear to back down from the original claims, are characterized by explicitly contrasting elements when compared with the original versions. The sense of retraction is manifest, in part, through a direct contrast between the two versions – a contrast which is achieved through some lexical repetition. So *we've done all* in (9) becomes *we couldn't do two*: note the repetition of both the pronoun and the verb; in (10), *(Rebecca) didn't get* becomes *she got*; having claimed that *I've never been*, Sandra concedes *I've been*, in (11); and, in (12), *I haven't had* is changed to *I had*. The contrast exhibited through such repetition, and in extracts 9–12 through the simple switch between positive and negative forms (for example, *I've never been* becomes *I've been*), highlights the speakers' *retraction* of their initial claims. They begin by claiming something to be the case, and then retract their original claim.

(13)   (expanded form of (9) [Holt 289:1–2])
```
1    Les:         .hhh but there's some beautiful walks aren't the::[re
2    Sar:                                                           [O:h yes (.)
3                 well we've done all the peaks.
4                      (0.4)
5    Les:        Oh ye:s
6                      (0.5)
7    Sar:        A::h
8                      (0.5)
9    Sar: —>     We couldn't do two because you need ropes and that
10   Les:        Ye[:s.
11   Sar: —>       [It's a climbers spot
```

Nevertheless, fourth, the retractions are constructed so as to preserve some consistency with the initial versions, and hence the essential correctness of those first versions. They seem to back down from its strength, though not from the core truth of what is claimed or reported. I will outline this in just two cases.

Sarah and her family are just back from a holiday on a Scottish island, which Lesley has said is her daughter's favourite stamping ground. They are talking about walking (see line 1), in the context of which Sarah claims to have *done* all the peaks. In her subsequent version (lines 9 and 11), Sarah retracts that: they did not do two. However, she constructs this as their being *unable* to do two, explaining that they could not do two peaks because climbing gear is needed to get up them; they are not for walkers. She thereby constructs as *exceptions* the two peaks (note the specific enumeration of how many peaks, that being a small number – rather than that there were *some* they could not do) which they *could* not (rather than did not) do, thereby retaining her original claim as essentially true – they did all the peaks *which could have been walked.*

In example (10), there are more elaborate components through which the subsequent version is constructed so as to be consistent with the claim Lesley originally makes that *Rebecca didn't get to college.*

(13a)   From (10)
```
1    Les:        NO::↑: no they're not. Only: one is outst↓andingly clever
2                wuh- an:' the other- .hh an: '°Rebecca didn't get t'college,°
3                      (0.4)
4    Joy:        Didn't ↓ she:,
5    Les: -->    Well she got in the end she scraped into a buh- business
6         -->    management,
```

There are three components especially which 'reduce the distance' between this and her original claim. First, *she got in the end* portrays her as having had to search for a college to take her, and/or as having been accepted only at the last minute. This is consistent with, indeed merges into, the second component – *she scraped into* – depicting her as only just being sufficiently qualified to gain entry, and therefore as being in that sense among the last to be accepted. These components together portray her as having considerable difficulty in getting a place in college. The final component, *into business management*, depicts her, moreover, as only having been able to get a place to study that discipline: only having scraped into *business management* portrays that discipline as being in the academic bargain basement. The ways in which subsequent versions are designed to be exceptions to, and thereby essentially consistent with, the initial versions are, of course, quite explicit in the case with which we began, Nancy's claim 'Not et all, *except* Roul's mother gotta call'.

Systematic Patterns in Conversation (III): an Analytic Account of the Phenomenon

So far, we have identified a pattern in which speakers make a strong claim about something, but subsequently – in the face of the other's implicit scepticism (even if that is expressed only through failure to respond) – back down from that claim: however, their retractions are designed so as to preserve the essential correctness of their original versions (through constructing the subsequent versions as exceptions of one kind or another). Then, the question is, what are we to make of this pattern? Do speakers just routinely lie, and retract when they are 'caught out' by their recipients' disbelief? This is the final stage in analysing a conversational phenomenon or pattern – providing an account for the pattern. It is not easy to be prescriptive about how or where one seeks such an account; but, broadly, it involves trying to identify the contingency which the pattern systematically handles, or to which it offers a solution. Very often, this will involve another of the analytic steps outlined earlier, which is to consider where and how the object or pattern in question arose.

If we look at the sequence immediately prior to the over-strong 'incorrect' versions, it is plain that the initial versions are being 'exaggerated' in order to fit with the sequential environments in which they are produced, and the actions being done in those environments. For example, in (10), Lesley is disagreeing with Joyce, initially with Joyce's assessment that their friend is clever *mentally*: this is shown here in (14), line 1 (they have been talking previously about how clever she is with her hands, making her family's clothes and so on).

```
(14)   (expansion of (10)) [Holt:2:15:4–5]
1      Joy:    =eh Well surely she's clever ↓ mentally isn't s[he
2      Les:                                                   [Oh I don't
3              know'bout ↑ that, I mean uh I don'think it's all that
4              difficult really
```

```
5           (0.4)
6    Joy:   What.
7           (0.5)
8    Les:   If you've got- if you got the schooling an' the
9           back↑grou:nd ih-uh (.) (        )-
10          (0.4)
11   Joy:   Oh[no(h)o perhaps that's what it is I don't know
12   Les:      [(        )
13   Les:   ↓No[: : : ,
14   Joy:       [(     ) Oh well I don't ↓ know though I d- I should
15          imagine she is clever her children'r clever aren't they,
16          .hhhh yih know I[mean]
17   Les:                    [NO::]↑: no they're not. Only: one is
18          outst↓andingly clever wuh- an:' the other- .hh an:'°Rebecca
19          didn't get t'college,°
```

After Lesley's initial disagreement in lines 2–3, and subsequent elaboration (lines 8–9), Joyce pursues her assessment of their friend's likely cleverness, stating as supporting evidence that *her children are clever* (line 15). Without tracing this in detail, it is reasonably clear that neither is entirely letting go of her position regarding their friend's cleverness, and that they have, in effect, 'upped the ante'. At this point, in line 17, Lesley further pursues and escalates the disagreement by very strongly contesting Joyce's claim that the children are smart: the extent to which she has escalated the strength of her disagreement is evident in its being strongly marked – lexically, through the outright negative tokens, and direct rejection of Joyce's statement; prosodically, through raised pitch and amplitude. So it is in this environment, in pursuing her disagreement, and doing so in a strongly marked form, that Lesley produces her rebuttal of Joyce's claim that *her children are clever*. Her rebuttal is designed to equal the strength of her (escalated) disagreement. Thus, the completeness and strength of her rejection *('NO::↑: no they're not.')* is matched by her claim that one of the children did not even get into college – while the fact that both children are at college (that is, university) would hardly be commensurate with or support her claim, against Joyce, that they are not clever.

One further example: recall that in (11), line 3, Sandra claims initially *never to have been* to a disco. Looking at the sequence leading up to this claim, we see that she and Becky are talking about their friends/housemates going to a local club that night ([15], lines 1–7).

```
(15)  (Expansion of (11) [Drew:St:1] ('Silks' is a local disco club)
1     Bec:   We were all talking about going out t- Silks tonight'cause
2            everyone's got the day off tomorrow?
3     San:   Are you- cz my house is all going t- Silks tonight?=
4     Bec:   =Really
5     San:   Yea:h E[mma un Ces um Ge
```

```
6    Bec:          [Bet it's gonner be absolutely pa:cked though isn't it.
7    San:   Yeah and Ces has been ra:iding my war:drobe. So: hh[h
8    Bec:                                                        [.hhh Are
9           you going.
10   San:   No::,
11   Bec:   ↑Why::
12   San:   I don't know hhh hu hu .hhh I dunno it's not really me
13   Bec:   Mw:rh
14   San:   (          ) like it .hh I've never been to one yet,
```

In response to her inquiry in lines 8–9, Sandra tells Becky that she is not going; and when Becky pursues this with an expression of evident disbelief (line 11), Sandra explains that *it's not really me* – which she supports by adding that *I've never been to one yet* (line 14). Thus, her declining to go on the grounds that *it's not really me* is made more credible by her claiming never to have been to such a place; of course, this also detaches her reasons for not going this evening from anything which might relate to this particular occasion. In this way, her claim that she has *never been to one yet* is fitted to a sequence in which her friend has responded to her declining to go (in line 10) with disbelief: Sandra matches the strength of that disbelief with an account which seems incontrovertible.

What emerges, then, is that these strong, dramatic or perhaps exaggerated claims arise from, or are fitted to, the contingencies of the particular action sequence in which they are produced. They are constructed to 'work' in terms of the 'requirements' of the slots in which they are done. The 'weaker' versions to which they subsequently retreat would not have done the job *in the slot in which they are produced*. For instance, in the case with which we initially began, when she confirms that *not a word* has been heard from her ex-husband, Nancy is simultaneously both agreeing with Emma, and complaining about him (simultaneously, because she is joining or collaborating with Emma's implied complaint about him, on her, Nancy's, behalf). The strong version *not a word* works to agree/complain; had she began, in line 38 in extract (8), by reporting that his mother had heard from him, she would not have been agreeing/complaining – indeed, she might have been heard as disaffiliating, or disassociating, herself from Emma's (sympathetic) implied complaint. Thus, the weaker version which she comes to would not have achieved the responsive action which Emma's prior turn is built to get – that is, confirmation, agreement and collaboration in a complaint about her ex-husband. Hence, the subsequent weaker versions would not have accomplished, in a coherent fashion, the work of reporting, disagreeing, confirming/agreeing, complaining, giving an account, etc., in the particular positions in which speakers construct those actions. Therefore, these initial (over-) strong versions are fitted to the slot in which speakers are announcing, disagreeing, declining, etc.; here, we can see that the speakers are dealing, through these claims, with the exigencies which have arisen in the immediate (prior) sequential environments. Speakers produce versions which are fitted to those sequential moments. When the moment is past, so, too, is the 'requirement' for that strong version: the speaker can put the record straight and retreat to a 'weaker' version (albeit in a manner which maintains an essential consistency with the initial 'false' claims). You'll find published accounts of this pattern of exaggerated versions in Drew (2003; 2005).

Conclusion

I have tried here to give an account of the principal stages of analysis in CA research – the stages involved when developing research findings about the ways in which interaction, and particularly verbal interaction, are organized. Space has not allowed me to say much about the significance of what we are looking for, or about the theoretical standpoint which this perspective adopts towards people's activities in talk – for instance, the reasons for considering talk as action rather than communication, and our identifying patterns associated with manifest behaviour, and *not* inner cognitive states and other states such as intentions, motives, personality, etc. However, I hope that showing how Nancy's apparent inconsistency in extract (8) is simply one in a recurrent pattern in which speakers initially produce over-strong versions, in order to fit the contingencies of the particular interactional sequences in which they are engaged, helps to illustrate that CA resists psychological accounts of behaviour which turn out to be general (rather than individual), systematic (and not particularistic) and interactional (rather than arising from the psyche of one of the participants, as though she were acting independently of the other and the interaction between them). What Nancy does here is what people – of whatever psychological dispositions or types – do generally, given these interactional circumstances.

Nor have I been able to give any account of another very important aspect of CA research, which is to *distributionalize* phenomena – that is, to try to identify where in conversations certain devices or patterns tend to occur. We take the view that everything about conversation (and other forms of verbal interaction) is thoroughly organized, so that what people say, and how they say it, is not random or chance (see Chapter 8 in Heritage, 1984, for a beautifully clear account of this fundamental assumption of CA). An example of research showing that a device in conversation is systematically distributed is Drew and Holt's account of the way in which idioms and figures of speech are used to terminate topics of conversations: hence, figures of speech are distributed in an organized fashion, occurring predominantly at points where speakers move from one topic to another (that is, topic transition) (Drew and Holt, 1998).

I have, though, tried to describe how we cut in to looking at data, and start to make analytic observations about (verbal) conduct. Starting with a transcript of a recording of natural conversation, we begin by looking at the activities which participants may be managing through their talk; then, we examine in as much detail as possible how their talk is designed or constructed, in an effort to map the organized properties through which participants conduct their affairs in talk-in-interaction. And I have illustrated how we develop an analysis of such organized properties (patterns, devices and practices) by focusing on what at first sight appears to be an incidental curiosity in the extract with which I began – that is, Nancy's initially confirming that *no one heard a word* (from her ex-husband), but subsequently reporting that his mother had heard from him. This was to give you some feeling for how we can move from making observations about the details of talk, to developing an analysis of a conversational phenomenon or practice – in other words, arriving at findings about stable and systematic patterns in talk. If only it were as easy as this! I have to admit that the process or steps from beginning to notice things about the detail to be found in talk, to the end product of a publishable research finding, are not nearly as smooth as this account might have suggested. For one thing, there is the difficulty of knowing what kinds of details one might begin noticing, and what to say about them. The next hurdle is to decide whether what one is focusing on is actually a phenomenon (that is, a systematically organized pattern or practice). Afterwards, building a collection of the phenomenon can involve comparative questions, including what kinds of cases the phenomenon encompasses and what cases might be used for comparison and contrast – all of which are not dissimilar from the decisions which need to be made in experimental design. This is too brief an account of CA's methodological approach to do any justice to these complexities: the only way to find out more is to survey the research which has been published (see below), collect some naturally occurring interactional data relating to some topic in which you are interested, and have a go at doing it yourself.

Box 7.3 presents three examples of CA in action.

Box 7.3   Three good examples of CA

Here are three studies illustrating clearly the application of CA's approach to moments in interaction that have a real (social) psychological significance – teasing, claiming knowledge (as one's own), and avoiding seeming to be paranoid!

Teasing

There is generally supposed to be a psychological dimension to teasing, associated partly with the ways in which teasing, like other forms of humour, can convey a more serious message of hostility towards the tease recipient, and partly also with

(Continued)

(Continued)

the relational tensions which can generate that hostility (in the anthropological literature, the structural relationship to which teasing is frequently attributed is that between mother-in-law and son-in-law). Drew (1987) showed that there is a systematic interactional rather than structural basis for teasing. In ordinary interactions someone is teased when they have been complaining, extolling or bragging in a somewhat overdone or exaggerated fashion. Teasing is, therefore, a form of social control of minor conversational transgressions. Teasing jokingly attributes certain (mildly) deviant identities to joke recipients who, finding themselves conceivably portrayed as deviant, generally respond in a serious, 'po-faced' manner. The 'standard' sequence that emerges is

A: *Exaggerated* (*complaining bragging* etc.)
B: *Tease*
A: *Po-faced* (serious) *response.*

At first I thought ...

Witnesses and others caught up in dramatic, tragic, criminal or otherwise frightening events – such as earthquakes, assassinations, robberies and murders – regularly describe themselves as not at first frightened. Indeed, they often report that initially they thought something humorous was happening, that it was a joke, or at least something quite innocuous, unthreatening. Piecing together evidence from a whole range of sources – ordinary interactions, newspaper stories of such events and the like – and building on the work of Sacks, Jefferson (2004) shows that people report *At first I thought X, then I realized Y.* This device involves a *thought/realized* alternation, itself of psychological interest. However, it has further psychological significance; Jefferson analyses *at first I thought* ... as being a 'normalizing device' – demonstrating that the speaker or witness (first) takes the world to be ordinary, unexceptional. That a witness's initial explanation is that something humorous is happening, or something which can be explained as 'normal' (e.g. during the Los Angeles earthquake of 1988 people sitting in a football stadium reported thinking that the shaking was caused by the rock concert being held in an adjacent stadium!), displays their being 'normal', not someone who immediately sees things as threatening – and so not paranoid.

Epistemic authority

'How we know things' is referred to as epistemics; and the epistemics of what we (think we) know are very much involved in the struggles which can sometimes occur between people in interaction about 'who knows best', what I know and how I know it, whether what you (or I) know is correct or accurate, between first-hand knowledge (seeing or experiencing it) and what we have been told or heard from others, how recent my information is and the like. In their study of assessment sequences in interaction, Heritage and Raymond (2005) show that

(Continued)

when agreeing to a first speaker's assessment, recipients can index (in a variety of ways documented in their analysis) their epistemic authority – that their assessments are independent of first speakers, that they know (about) whatever is being assessed independently. Recipients thereby resist any claim to epistemic authority that the first speaker may have made. (See also Raymond and Heritage, 2006.)

Further Reading

Heritage, J. (1984) *Garfinkel and Ethnomethodology*. Cambridge: Polity Press, Chapter 8.
Drew, P. (2005) 'Conversation analysis', in K.L. Fitch and R.E. Sanders (eds) *Handbook of Language and Social Interaction*. Mawah, NJ: Lawrence Erlbaum, pp. 71–102.
Both offer concise overviews of conversation analysis.

Atkinson, J.M. and Heritage, J. (eds) (1984) *Structures of Social Action: Studies in Conversation Analysis*. Cambridge: Cambridge University Press.
The editor's introduction gives an invaluable brief guide, and many of the studies (e.g. by Pomerantz, on agreeing/disagreeing), are key works in CA's programme.

Sacks, H. (1992) *Lectures on Conversation*, G. Jefferson (ed.), Vols 1 and 2. Oxford: Blackwell.
See Schegloff's introductions for a definitive account of Sacks's work and the development of the field, and the distinctiveness of CA's approach.
Sacks's lectures themselves are an essential resource for anyone interested in CA's analytic approach.

Ten Have, P. (1999) *Doing Conversation Analysis: A Practical Guide*. London: Sage.
Hutchby, I. and Wooffitt, R. (1998) *Conversation Analysis: Principles, Practices and Applications*. Cambridge: Polity Press.
These are useful overview texts.

Drew, P. and Heritage, J. (eds) (1992) *Talk at Work*. Cambridge: Cambridge University Press.
Heritage, J. (2005) 'Conversation analysis and institutional talk', in K.L. Fitch and R.E. Sanders (eds) *Handbook of Language and Social Interaction*. Mawah, NJ: Lawrence Erlbaum, pp. 103–147.

CA is widely applied to forms of talk-in-interaction other than 'ordinary conversation' – for instance, to the study of interactions in such 'institutional' settings as courts, classrooms, medical consultations, news media, counselling and therapy. This book, and Heritage's article, give useful introductions to studies covering a wide range of settings.

EIGHT

Discourse Analysis

Carla Willig

In recent years, discourse analysis has gained popularity and acceptance as a qualitative research method in psychology. As an increasing number of researchers turn to the analysis of discourse, it is worth exploring what a discursive analysis can actually deliver and what kinds of research questions it can, and cannot, address.

In this chapter, I introduce two versions of the discourse analytic method: *discursive psychology* and *Foucauldian discourse analysis*. Even though these two approaches share a concern with the role of language in the construction of social reality, the two versions address different sorts of research questions. They also identify with different theoretical traditions. Burr (1995; 2003) and Parker (1997) provide detailed discussions of the distinction between the two versions of discourse analysis. However, some discourse analysts do not welcome such a strong conceptual separation. For example, Potter and Wetherell (1995: 81) argue that the distinction between the two versions 'should not be painted too sharply' while Wetherell (1998; 2001) also advocates a synthesis of the two versions. This chapter introduces and describes the two approaches to discourse analysis and illustrates each with a worked example. The two versions of discourse analysis are applied to the same interview extract in order to highlight similarities and differences between them. The chapter concludes with a comparison between the two discursive methods (see also Langdridge, 2004, Chapter 18 for more on the relationship between the two approaches).

Psychology's Turn to Language

Psychologists' turn to language was inspired by theories and research which had emerged within other disciplines over a period of time. From the 1950s onwards, philosophers, communication theorists, historians and sociologists became increasingly interested in language as a social performance. The assumption that language provides a set of unambiguous signs with which to label internal states and with which to describe external reality began to be challenged. Instead, language was reconceptualized as productive; that is to say, language was seen to construct versions of social reality, and it was seen to achieve social objectives. The focus of inquiry shifted from individuals and their intentions to language and its productive potential. Wittgenstein's philosophy, Austin's speech-act theory and Foucault's historical studies of discursive practices are important examples of this shift. However, psychology remained relatively untouched by these intellectual developments throughout the 1950s and 1960s. Instead, it was concerned with the study of mental representations and the rules which control cognitive mediation of various types of input from the environment. In the 1970s, social psychologists began to challenge psychology's cognitivism (e.g., Gergen, 1973; 1989), and in the 1980s the 'turn to language' gained a serious foothold in psychology.

Discursive Psychology

This version of discourse analysis was introduced into social psychology with the publication of Potter and Wetherell's *Discourse and Social Psychology: Beyond Attitudes and Behaviour* in 1987. The label 'discursive psychology' was provided later by Edwards and Potter (1992). As the method evolved, changes in emphasis also emerged. These are largely to do with an increasing emphasis on the flexibility of discursive resources and a preference for the use of naturalistic materials. Recent developments in discursive psychology continue to be strongly influenced by conversation analytic principles (see Wooffitt, 2005; Wiggins and Potter, forthcoming). Potter and Wetherell's book presented a wide-ranging critique of cognitivism, followed by a detailed analysis of interview transcripts using a discourse analytic approach. Later publications developed the critique of psychology's preoccupation with cognition and its use as an all-purpose explanatory strategy which involved 'claiming for the cognitive processes of individuals the central role in shaping perception and action' (Edwards and Potter, 1992: 13). The critique of cognitivism argues that the cognitive approach is based upon a number of unfounded assumptions about the relationship between language and representation. These include: (1) that talk is a route to cognition; (2) that cognitions are based on perception; (3) that an objective perception of reality is theoretically possible; (4) that there are consensual objects of thought; and (5) that there are cognitive structures which are relatively enduring. Each of these assumptions can be challenged from a discursive psychology perspective.

Talk is a Route to Cognition

From a cognitive point of view, people's verbal expression of their beliefs and attitudes provides information about the cognitions which reside in their minds. In other words, talk is a route to cognition. As long as the researcher ensures that participants have no reason to lie, their words are taken to constitute true representations of their mental state (such as the beliefs they subscribe to or the attitudes they hold). Discourse analysts do not share this view of language. They argue that when people state a belief or express an opinion, they are taking part in a conversation which has a purpose and in which all participants have a stake. In other words, in order to make sense of what people say, we need to take into account the social context within which they speak. For example, when male participants are interviewed by a female researcher with the aim of identifying men's attitudes towards sharing housework, their responses may be best understood as a way of disclaiming undesirable social identities (as 'sexist slob', as dependent upon their female partners or as lazy). This is not to say that they are lying to the researcher about the amount of housework that they do; rather, it suggests that, in their responses, participants *orient towards* a particular reading of the questions they are being asked (such as a challenge, a criticism or an opportunity to complain), and that the accounts they provide need to be understood in relation to such a reading. As a result, we should not be surprised to find that people's expressed attitudes are not necessarily consistent across social contexts.

Cognitions are Based on Perception

Ultimately, cognitivism has to assume that *cognitions are based on perceptions*. Cognitions are mental representations of real objects, events and processes which occur in the world. Even though cognitions are abstractions, and therefore often simplifications and distortions of such external events, they do constitute attempts to capture reality. Once established, cognitive schemata and representations facilitate perception and interpretation of novel experiences and observations. By contrast, discourse analysts argue that the world can be 'read' in an unlimited number of ways, and that, far from giving rise to mental representations, objects and events are, in fact, constructed through language itself. As a result, it is discourse and conversation which should be the focus of study, because that is where meanings are created and negotiated.

Objective Perception of Reality is Theoretically Possible

If cognitions are based on perceptions, as proposed by cognitivism, it follows that *an objective perception of reality is theoretically possible*. Errors and simplifications in representation are the result of the application of time-saving heuristics which introduce bias into cognition. Given the right circumstances, it should be possible to eliminate such biases from cognitive processes. Again, discourse analysts take issue with this assumption. If language constructs, rather than represents, social reality, it follows that there can be no objective perception of this reality. Instead, emphasis is placed upon the ways in which social categories are constructed and with what consequences they are deployed in conversation.

There are Consensual Objects of Thought

Attitudes describe how people feel about objects and events in the social world, whereas attribution theory is concerned with how people account for actions and events. In both cases, researchers assume that the social object or event towards which participants have different attitudes and which participants attribute to different causes is itself consensual. That is to say, even though people hold different attitudes and attributions in relation to something (for example, European Monetary Union, same-sex marriages or the break-up of the Soviet Union), that 'something' itself is not disputed. In other words, there are *consensual objects of thought*, in relation to which people form opinions. People agree on what it is they are talking about, but they disagree about why it happened (attributions) and whether or not it is a good thing (attitudes). Discourse analysts do not accept that there are such consensual objects of thought. They argue that the social objects themselves are constructed through language and that one person's version of, say, 'the break-up of the Soviet Union' may be quite different from another person's. From this point of view, what have traditionally been referred to as 'attitudes' and 'attributions' are, in fact, aspects of the discursive construction of the object itself.

There are Relatively Enduring Cognitive Structures

Finally, cognitivism is based upon the assumption that somewhere inside the human mind there are *cognitive structures which are relatively enduring*. People are said to hold views and have cognitive styles. Cognitive structures can change, but such change needs to be explained in terms of intervening variables such as persuasive messages or novel experiences. The assumption is that, in the normal course of events, beliefs, attitudes, attributions and so forth remain stable and predictable from day to day. Discourse analysts' conceptualization of language as productive and performative is not compatible with such a view. Instead, they argue that people's accounts, the views they express and the explanations they provide, depend upon the discursive context within which they are produced. Thus, what people say tells us something about what they are *doing* with their words (disclaiming, excusing, justifying, persuading, pleading, etc.) rather than about the cognitive structures these words represent.

Discourse analysts' challenge to cognitivism shows that discourse analysis is not simply a research method. It is a critique of mainstream psychology, it provides an alternative way of conceptualizing language, and it indicates a method of data analysis which can tell us something about the discursive construction of social reality. Discourse analysis is more than a methodology because 'it involves a theoretical way of understanding the nature of discourse and the nature of psychological phenomena' (Billig, 1997: 43). However, discursive psychology is still a *psychology* because it is concerned with psychological phenomena such as memory, attribution and identity. But, in line with its critique of cognitivism, discursive psychology conceptualizes these phenomena as *discursive actions* rather than as cognitive processes. Psychological activities such as justification, rationalization, categorization, attribution, naming and blaming are understood as ways in which participants manage their interests. They are discursive practices which are used by participants within particular contexts in order to achieve social and interpersonal objectives. As a result, psychological concepts such as prejudice, identity, memory or trust become something people do rather than something people *have*.

The focus of analysis in discursive psychology is on how participants use discursive resources and with what effects. In other words, discursive psychologists pay attention to the *action orientation* of talk. They are concerned with the ways in which speakers manage issues of stake and interest. They identify discursive strategies such as 'disclaiming' or 'footing' and explore their function in a particular discursive context. For example, an interviewee may disclaim a racist social identity by saying 'I am not racist, but I think immigration controls should be strengthened' and then legitimate the statement by referring to a higher authority: 'I agree with the Prime Minister's statement that the situation requires urgent action.' Other discursive devices used to manage interest and accountability include the use of metaphors and analogies, direct quotations, extreme case formulations, graphic descriptions, consensus formulations, stake inoculation and many more (see Edwards and Potter, 1992; Potter, 1996, for a detailed discussion of such devices). Box 8.1 summarizes discursive psychology's major concerns.

Box 8.1   Discursive psychology

Discursive psychology

- emerged from ethnomethodology and conversation analysis
- is concerned with discourse practices
- emphasizes the performative qualities of discourse
- emphasizes the fluidity and variability of discourse
- prioritizes action orientation and stake
- asks, 'What are participants doing with their talk?'

How to do Discursive Psychology

Ideally, this type of analysis should be used to analyse naturally occurring text and talk (Potter and Hepburn, 2005). This is because the research questions addressed by discursive psychologists are concerned with how people manage accountability and stake in everyday life. For example, tape recordings of naturally occurring conversations in informal (for example, friends chatting on the telephone, families having meals together) and formal (for example, medical consultations, radio interviews) 'real-world' settings constitute suitable data for discursive analysis. However, both ethical and practical difficulties in obtaining such naturally occurring data have led many discourse analysts to carry out semi-structured interviews to generate data for analysis. In any case, discourse analysis works with texts, most of which are generated by transcribing tape recordings of some form of conversation (see Potter and Wetherell, 1987; O'Connell and Kowal, 1995; Jefferson, 2004b, for guidance on transcription). It is important that the transcript contain at least some information about non-linguistic aspects of the conversation such as delay, hesitation or emphasis. This is because the way in which something is said can affect its meaning. Discourse analysis may be described as a way of reading a text. This reading is informed by a conceptualization of language as *performative*. This means that the reader focuses upon the internal organization of the discourse in order to find out what the discourse is doing. It means moving beyond an understanding of its content and to trace its *action orientation*. Discourse analysis requires us to adopt an orientation to talk and text as *social action*, and it is this orientation which directs our analytic work. Although there is no universally agreed set of methodological procedures, the following guidelines for the analysis of discourse can help the analyst get started (see also Potter and Wetherell, 1987: 160–76; Billig, 1997: 54; Edwards and Potter, 2001, for guidance).

Reading

First of all, the researcher needs to take the time to *read* the transcripts carefully. Although the researcher will continue to read and reread the transcripts throughout the process of coding and analysis, it is important that the transcripts are read, at least once, without any attempt at analysis. This is because such a reading allows us to experience *as a reader* some of the discursive effects of the text. For example, a text may come across as an apology even though the words 'I am sorry' are not actually spoken. We may feel that a text 'makes it sound like' there is a war going on even though the topic of the transcribed speech was a forthcoming election. Reading a text before analysing it allows us to become aware of what a text is doing. The purpose of analysis is to identify exactly how the text manages to accomplish this.

Coding

Reading and rereading of the transcripts is followed by the selection of material for analysis, or *coding*. Coding of the transcripts is done in the light of the research question. All relevant sections of text are highlighted, copied and filed for analysis. At this stage, it is important to make sure that all material which is potentially relevant is included. This means that even instances which are indirectly or only vaguely related to the research question should be identified. Most importantly, use of certain key words is *not* required for selection of textual material. All implicit constructions (MacNaghten, 1993) must be included at this stage.

The need for coding before analysis illustrates that we can never produce a complete discourse analysis of a text. Our research question identifies a particular aspect of the discourse which we decide to explore in detail. Coding helps us to select relevant sections of the texts which constitute our data. There are always many aspects of the discourse which we will not analyse. This means that the same material can be analysed again, generating further insights.

Analysis

Discourse analysis proceeds on the basis of the researcher's interaction with the text. Potter and Wetherell (1987: 168) recommend that throughout the process of analysis the researcher asks, 'Why am I reading this passage in this way? What features [of the text] produce this reading?' Analysis of textual data is generated by paying close attention to the constructive and functional dimensions of discourse. In order to facilitate a systematic and sustained exploration of these dimensions, *context*, *variability* and *construction* of discursive accounts need to be attended to. The researcher looks at how the text constructs its objects and subjects, how such constructions vary across discursive contexts, and with what consequences they may be deployed. In order to identify diverse constructions of subjects and objects in the text, we need to pay attention to terminology, stylistic and grammatical features, and preferred metaphors and other figures of speech which may be used in their construction. Potter and Wetherell (1987: 149) refer to such systems of terms as 'interpretative repertoires'. Different repertoires are used to construct different versions of events. For example, a newspaper article may refer to young offenders as 'young tearaways', while defending lawyers may describe their clients as 'no-hope kids'. The former construction emphasizes the uncontrollability of young offenders and implies the need for stricter parenting and policing, while the latter draws attention to the unmet psychological and educational needs of young offenders and highlights the importance of social and economic deprivation. Different repertoires can be used by the same speaker in different discursive contexts in the pursuit of different social objectives. Part of the analysis of discourse is to identify the action orientation of accounts. In order to do this, the researcher needs to pay careful attention to the discursive contexts within which such accounts are produced and to trace their consequences for the participants in a conversation. This can be done satisfactorily only on the basis of an analysis of *both* the interviewer's and the interviewee's contribution to the conversation. It is important to remember that discourse analysis requires us to examine language in *context*.

Interpretative repertoires are used to construct alternative, and often contradictory, versions of events. Discourse analysts have identified conflicting repertoires within participants' talk about the same topic. For example, Potter and Wetherell (1995) found that their participants used two different repertoires in order to talk about Maori culture and its role in the lives of Maoris in New Zealand – 'culture-as-heritage' and 'culture-as-therapy'. Billig (1997) identifies two alternative, and contrasting, accounts of the meaning of history in participants' discussions of the British royal family: 'history as national decline' and 'history as national progress'. The presence of tensions and contradictions among the interpretative repertoires used by speakers demonstrates that the discursive resources which people draw on are inherently dilemmatic (see Billig et al., 1988; Billig, 1991). This is to say, they contain contrary themes which can be pitted against each other within rhetorical contexts. In order to understand why and how speakers are using a particular theme, we need to look to the rhetorical context within which they are deploying it. Again, the analytic focus is upon variability across contexts and the action orientation of talk.

Writing

Writing up discourse analytic research is not a process which is separate from the analysis of the texts. Both Potter and Wetherell (1987) and Billig (1997) draw attention to the fact that writing a report is itself a way of clarifying analysis. The attempt to produce a clear and coherent account of one's research in writing allows the researcher to identify inconsistencies and tensions which, in turn, may lead to new insights. Alternatively, the researcher may have to return to the data in order to address difficulties and problems raised in the process of writing.

A Worked Example

The extract in Box 8.2 is taken from the transcript of a semi-structured interview with a woman who had recently experienced the break-up of an intimate relationship. The extract represents an exchange between the interviewer (I) and the participant (R) which occurred about halfway through the hour-long interview.

Box 8.2   Extract from break-up interview

1 I: And when you made the decision um when you were actually working
2   towards finishing it did you talk to friends about it?
3 R: Oh of course
4 I: Yeah
5 R: All the time yeah it would always be a case of how do I do it
6 I: Ah right
7 R: How do I say it what do I say I know I've got to do it how do I go about doing
8   it you know and and just sort of role-playing it through and and you know just
9   sort of just preparing myself to actually say to him I don't want to go out with
10   you anymore because it's so hard even though you know it's got to be done
11   It is just so hard because there's all these you know ties and emotional
12   baggage which is which you're carrying and you you you're worrying about
13   the other person and you're thinking you invested you know he's invested
14   maybe two years in me
15 I: Yes
16 R: by going out with me and suddenly I'm dumping him what if he doesn't find
17   anyone else to go out with
18 I: Oh right yes
19 R: You you start taking responsibility for them and for how they'll cope
20   afterwards you know maybe to the detriment to your own personal sort of
21   well-being
22 I: Right
23 R: And it was a case of how is he going to cope what's going to happen to him
24   what if no one goes out with him what if this and what if that and it's all a
25   case of ifs anyway and you know as far as I was concerned I was I was
26   more concerned about him and how he would be [. . .] [and a little later in the interview]
27 I: [. . .] if you sort of think about it as going on through time um was there
28   anything that changed in the way you behaved towards each other or sex
29   life or anything like that? Could you say you know something changed or
30 R: No it was the way I saw it was would I want to marry him was the sort of um
31   you know foundation I would use
32 I: Right
33 R: because I thought OK we've been going out for two nearly two years if we

```
34        were going out for another two years would I want to marry him and the
35        answer was no
36   I:   Right
37   R:   And even though [...] I had no intentions of getting married say for
          another
38        you know four five whatever amount of years it was on that basis I was
39        using the criteria of my wanting to continue going out with him
40   I:   Right
41   R:   because it was a case of where is this relationship going and as far as I was
42        concerned it had hit the the brick wall and it wasn't going any further
```

Discursive Psychology: A Reading

Reading

An initial reading of the first half of the extract (lines 1–26) leaves me feeling weary. The text appears to bear testimony to the speaker's considerable efforts in coming to a decision about how to end her relationship with her partner. It invokes a decision not taken lightly. The speaker comes across as mature and responsible in her way of dealing with the task of breaking up. A first reading of the second half of the extract (lines 27–42) evokes a sense of finality. There appears to be no ambiguity in its message, and its conclusion (the end of the relationship) seems inevitable. The purpose of the analysis is to understand how the text achieves these impressions.

Coding

The material for analysis was selected in the light of the research question, which was concerned with the ways in which the participant accounted for the break-up of an intimate relationship. Both parts of the present extract (lines 1–26 and lines 27–42) represent occasions within the conversation which provided the participant with an opportunity to elaborate upon the circumstances surrounding the end of the relationship. This meant that they constituted suitable data for analysis within this context.

Analysis

Part 1 (lines 1–26). In response to the interviewer's question (I: 'did you talk to friends about it?', lines 1–2), the participant uses an extreme case formulation ('all the time'). In this way, her claim (to have discussed the situation with friends) is taken to its extreme in order to provide an effective warrant

(Pomerantz, 1986) for her ultimate decision (to end the relationship). It is suggested that this decision is based on careful consideration informed by frequent discussions with friends. In addition, the participant's use of the word 'you' (instead of 'I') in lines 11–21 serves to generalize her experience and to suggest that her actions followed an established procedure for dealing with such matters, a practice which she shares with responsible others and which will be recognized as such by the interviewer. Through the use of list-like sentence constructions and the use of repetition ('How do I do it, how do I say it, what do I say', lines 5–7; and again 'How is he going to cope, what's going to happen to him, what if no one goes out with him, what if this and what if that', lines 23–4), a commitment to thorough and careful consideration of all eventualities is demonstrated. References to 'role-playing' (line 8) and 'preparing myself' (line 9) reinforce this impression by suggesting that such consideration includes the mental anticipation and practical rehearsal of possible scenarios. Use of terminology such as 'ties and emotional baggage … which you're carrying' (lines 11–12) and repeated references to it being 'so hard' (line 10 and line 11) invoke a sense of sustained effort and serve to counteract any impression of a decision taken lightly. Talk of 'investment' (line 13) and 'responsibility' (line 19) chimes with a construction of breaking up as serious business. To summarize, part 1 of the extract uses language in such a way as to construct a version of decision- making which involves considerable effort and hard work. It is interesting to note that the interviewer's question ('And when you made the decision, when you were actually working towards finishing it, did you talk to friends about it?') mobilizes the same discursive construction of relationship endings as 'work'. Such a construction of decision-making constitutes a warrant for the decision actually taken (that is, ending the relationship) because it removes any semblance of lightness or superficiality from the account.

Part 2 (lines 27–42). The text accomplishes its sense of finality through its use of terminology and grammatical and stylistic features such as the use of metaphor. First, the use of the first person in assertions of the speaker's perspective ('the way I saw it', line 30; 'as far as I was concerned', lines 41–2) supports a singular and unambiguous point of view to which the speaker has privileged access. The use of a question ('Would I want to marry him?' line 34) that requires a categorical answer (we cannot get 'a little bit' married or choose to marry 'some of the time') also contributes to the finality of the extract; in the event, the 'answer was no' (lines 34–5), and this leaves no room for doubt or negotiation. References to the 'foundation' (line 31) and the 'basis' (line 38) of her decision to terminate the relationship invoke a bottom line beyond which considerations cannot be made. This serves as a warrant for the finality of the decision. Finally, and most dramatically, the use of the metaphor in the last sentence (line 42) provides a visual image of the inevitability of the end of the relationship: 'it had hit the brick wall and it wasn't going any further'. By invoking the image of an object hitting a physical barrier, the speaker underlines the finality of her decision. There is no room for second thoughts or reappraisals because it is simply too late: the relationship has 'hit the brick wall' and it cannot continue.

To summarize, part 2 of the extract uses language in such a way as to construct a version of the participant's decision that is characterized by inevitability and finality. Such a construction of the decision constitutes a warrant for the decision taken (that is, to end the relationship) because it does not allow for the possibility of an alternative outcome.

From a discursive psychology perspective, both parts of the extract serve as a warrant for the participant's decision to terminate her relationship with her partner. However, two different constructions of the decision are produced in the same interview (that is, as involving effort and hard work, and as final and inevitable, respectively) which demonstrates some of the variability that characterizes discourse. A look at preceding sections of text (not reproduced here) can throw further light on the variable deployment of discursive constructions of decision-making within the interview. The portion of text which constructs the decision as the product of considerable effort on the part of the participant is produced in response to a question about the involvement of friends in the decision-making process (lines 20–2, I: 'And when you made the decision um when you were actually working towards finishing it did you talk to friends about it?'). This question, in turn, is preceded by an account of how the participant's friends had 'taken a dislike' to her ex-partner and how they had 'talked about him with disdain'. As a result, the participant pointed out, 'everyone was glad when I'd finished it with him'. The participant's construction of her decision as 'hard work' could be understood, within this context, as a way of disclaiming an undesirable social identity. In order to counteract the impression that she was someone who unthinkingly follows her friends' advice, a construction of the break-up as involving effort and hard work was produced as a way of distancing herself from such negative attributions.

The portion of text which constructs the decision as inevitable and final is produced following the participant's account of how her ex-partner 'didn't think there was a problem that couldn't be worked out'. The construction of her decision to end the relationship as unequivocal and inescapable, therefore, occurs within a particular rhetorical context. It orients to, and at the same time challenges, an alternative view of how relationship difficulties ought to be dealt with (such as working to improve the relationship).

The variability in the participant's account is in line with discursive psychology's view of language as constructive and performative.

Writing

Much of the analysis presented above emerged from the process of writing about my interaction with the interview transcript. Impressions based upon my initial encounter with the text had to be worked into an account of how the text achieved its discursive objectives. Having picked out metaphors, expressions and terms which fed into particular versions of how the participant's relationship came to an end, I wrote about the ways in which the participant's account produced these versions. As a result, the process of analysis is really a deconstruction (through the identification of interpretative repertoires and discursive constructions that make up the text) followed by a reconstruction (through writing about and thus re-creating the constructions and functions that characterize the text) of discourse, and writing itself is an essential part of this process.

Foucauldian Discourse Analysis

The Foucauldian version of discourse analysis was introduced into Anglo-American psychology in the late 1970s. A group of psychologists who had been influenced by post-structuralist ideas, most notably the work of Michel Foucault, began to explore the relationship between language and subjectivity and its implications for psychological research. The publication of Henriques et al.'s *Changing the Subject: Psychology, Social Regulation and Subjectivity* in 1984 (re-issued in 1998) provided readers with a clear illustration of how post-structuralist theory could be applied to psychology. In the book, the authors critically and reflexively examine psychological theories (such as those of child development, gender differences, or individual differences) and their role in constructing the objects and subjects which they claim to explain.

Foucauldian discourse analysis is concerned with language and its role in the constitution of social and psychological life. From a Foucauldian point of view, discourses facilitate and limit, enable and constrain what can be said, by whom, where and when (Parker, 1992). Foucauldian discourse analysts focus upon the availability of discursive resources within a culture – something like a discursive economy – and its implications for those who live within it. Here, discourses may be defined as 'sets of statements that construct objects and an array of subject positions' (Parker, 1994: 245). These constructions, in turn, make available certain ways of seeing the world and certain ways of being in the world. Discourses offer *subject positions* which, when taken up, have implications for subjectivity and experience. For example, within a biomedicaldiscourse, those who experience ill health occupy the subject position of 'the patient', which locates them as the passive recipient of expert care within a trajectory of cure. The concept of *positioning* has received increasing attention in recent years (Harré and van Langenhove, 1999).

Foucauldian discourse analysis is also concerned with the role of discourse in wider social processes of legitimation and power. Since discourses make available ways of seeing and ways of being, they are strongly implicated in the exercise of power. Dominant discourses privilege those versions of social reality which legitimate existing power relations and social structures. Some discourses are so entrenched that it is very difficult to see how we may challenge them. They have become 'common sense'. At the same time, it is in the nature of language that alternative constructions are always possible and that *counter-discourses* can, and do, emerge. Foucauldian discourse analysts also take a historical perspective and explore the ways in which discourses have changed over time, and how this may have shaped historical subjectivities (see also Rose, 1999). Finally, the Foucauldian version of discourse analysis also pays attention to the relationship between discourses and institutions. Here, discourses are not conceptualized simply as ways of speaking or writing. Rather, discourses are bound up with institutional practices – that is, with ways of organizing, regulating and administering social life. Thus, while discourses legitimate and reinforce existing social and institutional structures, these structures, in turn, also support and validate the discourses. For instance, being positioned as 'the patient' within a biomedical discourse means that one's body becomes an object of legitimate interest to doctors and nurses, that it may be exposed, touched and invaded in the process of treatment which forms part of the practice of medicine and its institutions (see also Parker, 1992: 17).

The Foucauldian version of discourse analysis is concerned with language and language use; however, its interest in language takes it beyond the immediate contexts within which language may be used by speaking subjects. Thus, unlike discursive psychology which is primarily concerned with interpersonal communication, Foucauldian discourse analysis asks questions about the relationship between discourse and how people think or feel (subjectivity), what they may do (practices) and the material conditions within which such experiences may take place. Box 8.3 provides a summary of the major concerns associated with Foucauldian discourse analysis.

Box 8.3   Foucauldian discourse analysis

Foucauldian discourse analysis

- was inspired by Foucault and post-structuralism
- is concerned with discursive resources
- explores the role of discourse in the constitution of subjectivity and selfhood
- explores the relationship between discourse and power
- links discourse with institutions and social practices
- asks 'How does discourse construct subjects and objects?'

How to do Foucauldian Discourse Analysis

Foucauldian discourse analysis can be carried out 'wherever there is meaning' (Parker, 1999: 1). This means that we do not necessarily have to analyse words. While most analysts work with transcripts of speech or written documents, Foucauldian discourse analysis can be carried out on any symbolic system. Parker recommends that we 'consider all tissues of meaning as texts'. This means that 'speech, writing, non-verbal behaviour, Braille, Morse code, semaphore, runes, advertisements, fashion systems, stained glass, architecture, tarot cards and bus tickets' all constitute suitable texts for analysis (ibid.: 7).

In Chapter 1 of *Discourse Dynamics. Critical Analysis for Social and Individual Psychology* (1992), Parker identifies 20 steps in the analysis of discourse dynamics. These 20 steps take the researcher from the selection of a text for analysis (steps 1 and 2) through the systematic identification of the subjects and objects constructed in them (steps 3–12) to an examination of the ways in which the discourse(s) which structures the text reproduces power relations (steps 13–20). Parker provides us with a detailed and wide-ranging guide which helps us to distinguish discourses, their relations with one another, their historical location, and their political and social effects. Other guides to Foucauldian discourse analysis (e.g., Kendall and Wickham, 1999: 42–6) rely on fewer steps but presuppose a more advanced conceptual understanding of Foucault's method. In this section, I set out six stages in the analysis of discourse. These stages allow the researcher to map some of the discursive resources used in a text and the subject positions they contain, and to explore their implications for subjectivity and practice. Please bear in mind, however, that they do not constitute a full analysis in the Foucauldian sense. For more guidance on how to address key Foucauldian concerns such as genealogy, governmentality and subjectification, see Arribas-Ayllon and Walkerdine (2008).

Stage 1: Discursive Constructions

The first stage of analysis is concerned with the ways in which discursive objects are constructed. Which discursive object we focus on depends on our research question. For example, if we are interested in how people talk about 'love' and with what consequences, our discursive object would be 'love'. The first stage of analysis involves the identification of the different ways in which the discursive object is constructed in the text. It is important that we do not simply look for key words. Both implicit and explicit references need to be included. Our search for constructions of the discursive object is guided by shared meaning rather than lexical comparability. The fact that a text does not contain a direct reference to the discursive object can tell us a lot about the way in which the object is constructed. For example, someone may talk about a relative's terminal illness without directly naming it. Here, references to 'it', 'this awful thing' or 'the condition' construct the discursive object (that is, terminal illness) as something unspeakable and perhaps also unknowable.

Stage 2: Discourses

Having identified all sections of text which contribute to the construction of the discursive object, we focus on the differences between constructions. What appears to be one and the same discursive object can be constructed in very different ways. The second stage of analysis aims to locate the various discursive constructions of the object within wider discourses. For example, within the context of an interview about her experience of her husband's prostate cancer, a woman may draw on a biomedical discourse when she talks about the process of diagnosis and treatment, a psychological discourse when she explains why she thinks her husband developed the illness in the first place, and a romantic discourse when she describes how she and her husband find the strength to fight the illness together. Thus, the husband's illness is constructed as a biochemical disease process, as the somatic manifestation of psychological traits, and as the enemy in a battle between good (the loving couple) and evil (separation through death) within the same text.

Stage 3: Action Orientation

The third stage of analysis involves a closer examination of the discursive contexts within which the different constructions of the object are being deployed. What is gained from constructing the object in this particular way at this particular point within the text? What is its function and how does it relate to other constructions produced in the surrounding text? These questions are concerned with what discursive psychology refers to as the *action orientation* of talk and text. To return to our example of a wife talking about her husband's cancer, it may be that her use of biomedical discourse allows her to attribute responsibility for diagnosis and treatment to medical professionals and to emphasize that her husband is being taken good care of. Her use of romantic discourse may have been produced in response to a question about her own role in her husband's recovery after surgery and may have served to emphasize that she is, in fact, contributing significantly to his recovery. Finally, psychological discourse may have been used to account for her husband's cancer in order to disclaim responsibility for sharing in a carcinogenic lifestyle (for example, 'I told him to slow down and take better care of himself but he wouldn't listen'). A focus on action orientation allows us to gain a clearer understanding of what the various constructions of the discursive object are capable of achieving within the text.

Stage 4: Positionings

Having identified the various constructions of the discursive object within the text, and having located them within wider discourses, we now take a closer look at the *subject positions* which they offer. A *subject position* within a discourse identifies 'a location for persons within the structure of rights and duties for those who use that repertoire' (Davies and Harré, 1999: 35). In other words, discourses construct *subjects* as well as objects, and, as a result, make available positions within networks of meaning which speakers can take up (as well as place others within). Subject positions are different from roles in that they offer discursive locations from which to speak and act rather than prescribing a particular part to be acted out. In addition, roles can be played without subjective identification, whereas taking up a subject position has direct implications for subjectivity (see stage 6 below).

Stage 5: Practice

This stage is concerned with the relationship between discourse and practice. It requires a systematic exploration of the ways in which discursive constructions and the subject positions contained within them open up and/or close down opportunities for action. By constructing particular versions of the world, and by positioning subjects within them in particular ways, discourses limit what can be said and done. Furthermore, non-verbal practices can, and do, form part of discourses. For example, the practice of unprotected sex can be bound up with a marital discourse which constructs marriage and its equivalent, the 'long-term relationship', as incompatible with the use of condoms (Willig, 1995). Thus, certain practices become legitimate forms of behaviour from within particular discourses. Such practices, in turn, reproduce the discourses which legitimate them in the first place. In this way, speaking and doing support one another in the construction of subjects and objects. Stage 5 of the analysis of discourse maps the possibilities for action contained within the discursive constructions identified in the text.

Stage 6: Subjectivity

The final stage in the analysis explores the relationship between discourse and subjectivity. Discourses make available certain ways of seeing the world and certain ways of being in the world. They construct social as well as psychological realities. Discursive positioning plays an important role in this process. As Davies and Harré (1999: 35) put it:

Once having taken up a particular position as one's own, a person inevitably sees the world from the vantage point of that position and in terms of the particular images, metaphors, storylines and concepts which are made relevant within the particular discursive practice in which they are positioned.

This stage in the analysis traces the consequences of taking up various subject positions for the participants' subjective experience. Having asked questions about what can be said and done from within different discourses (Stage 5), we are now concerned with what can be felt, thought and experienced from within various subject positions.

Worked Example: Six Stages of Foucauldian Analysis

Let us now take a look at how the six stages of Foucauldian analysis may be applied to our interview extract.

Stage 1: Discursive Constructions

Since the study from which the interview extract is taken was concerned with how people describe and account for the break-up of an intimate relationship (Willig and dew Valour, 1999; 2000), it makes sense to ask questions about the ways in which 'the relationship' is constructed through language. In the extract above, 'the relationship' is constructed as a clearly identifiable social arrangement with a beginning and an end, which offers security in return for investment of time and emotion (lines 2–26). In the second half of the extract, 'the relationship' is also constructed as a step on the way to marriage (lines 30–42). Thus, the relationship is constructed in two different ways. On the one hand, the relationship is constructed as a social arrangement between two people who agree to invest resources (such as time and emotion) in order to gain mutual support and security. Such an arrangement is hard to extricate oneself from ('It's hard … it's just so hard', lines 10–11) because 'ties and emotional baggage' have grown over time. On the other hand, the relationship is constructed as a testing ground for, and a step on the way to, a superior form of involvement – namely, marriage. Here, the relationship has to be 'going somewhere' for it to be worthwhile ('it had hit the brick wall and it wasn't going any further', lines 41–2), and its quality is judged in the light of its future direction ('And even though … I had no intentions of getting married for another you know four five whatever amount of years it was on that basis I was using the criteria of my wanting to continue going out with him', lines 37–9).

Stage 2: Discourses

Let us attempt to locate these two constructions of the relationship (as 'social arrangement' and as 'a step on the way') within wider discourses surrounding intimate relationship. The construction of interpersonal relationships as mutually beneficial social arrangements resonates with economic discourse. Notions of investment of resources in return for long-term security and the expectation that social actors exchange goods and services with one another are prominent in contemporary talk about the economy. For example, the term 'partner', now widely used to refer to one's significant other, also describes those we share business interests with. By contrast, the construction of the relationship as 'a step on the way' to marriage draws on a romantic discourse. Here, the relationship is not conceptualized as a mutually beneficial arrangement but rather as a way of moving towards the ultimate goal: marriage. Marriage itself is not defined or explored within the text. It is interesting that there appears to be no need to account for why the participant uses suitability for marriage as a 'foundation' (line 31), a 'basis' (line 38) and 'the criteria' (line 39) in her account. She even points out that she has no intention of actually getting married in the near future. However, marriage as a goal forms part of a romantic discourse in which 'love', 'marriage' and 'monogamy' are inextricably linked with one another. By invoking one, we invoke them all. As a result, suitability for marriage becomes a legitimate basis for making decisions about intimate relationships even where there is no suggestion that marriage is a realistic option in the near or medium future.

Stage 3: Action Orientation

A closer examination of the discursive context within which the two different constructions of the relationship are deployed allows us to find out more about them. When are they used and what might be their function within the account? How do they position the speaker within the moral order invoked by the construction? (See also Stage 4: Positionings.) The portion of text which constructs the relationship as a 'social arrangement' is produced in response to a question about the involvement of friends in the decision-making process (lines 1–2, I: 'And when you made the decision um when you were actually working towards finishing it did you talk to friends about it?'). This question, in turn, is preceded by an account of how the participant's friends had 'taken a dislike' to her ex-partner and how they had 'talked about him with disdain'. As a result, the participant pointed out, 'everyone was glad when I'd finished it with him'. The participant's use of a discursive construction of the relationship as a 'social arrangement' could be seen, within this context, as a way of emphasizing her sense of responsibility for her ex-partner's well-being. Talk about her friends' dislike of her ex-partner and their joy at seeing the relationship break up may have created the impression that he, disliked and rejected, was the victim of a callous act of abandonment on the participant's part. In order to counteract such an impression, a construction of the relationship as a 'social arrangement' draws attention to its mutually supportive nature and to the participant's awareness of the emotional significance of the break-up ('It's hard … it's just so hard', lines 10–11).

The portion of text which constructs the relationship as a 'step on the way' is produced following the participant's account of how her ex-partner 'didn't think there was a problem that couldn't be worked out'. The use of romantic discourse at this point allows the participant to ward off the charge that she did not give her ex-partner a chance to 'work out' the problems and to save the relationship. From within a romantic discourse, no amount of work can transform 'liking' into 'love', or an 'OK-relationship' into 'the real thing'. The acid test of romantic love (line 30, 'would I want to marry him?') renders redundant attempts to work out problems, because, if marriage is not a goal that can be envisaged, the relationship is not worth saving (lines 41–2, 'and as far as I was concerned it had hit the brick wall and it wasn't going any further'). From within a romantic discourse, the participant cannot be blamed for not trying hard enough to make the relationship work.

Stage 4: Positionings

What are the subject positions offered by the two discursive constructions of 'the relationship'? A construction of relationships as 'social arrangement' positions partners as highly dependent on each other. Involvement in such a relationship undermines the individual's freedom and mobility; partners are tied to each other through investments, history and emotions (line 11, 'there's all these you know ties and emotional baggage which ... you're carrying'). As a result, whoever decides to withdraw from the arrangement is going to cause the other person considerable disruption, inconvenience and probably a great deal of distress. The subject positions offered by this construction are, therefore, those of responsible social actors who depend on each other for support and who are faced with the difficult task of realizing their interests within relationships of interdependence.

The romantic construction of intimate relationships as 'a step on the way' offers provisional subject positions to lovers. While involved in unmarried relationships, lovers are not fully committed to the relationship. Their involvement contains an opt-out clause which allows them to withdraw from the relationship without penalty. Everything that occurs between lovers within such an arrangement is permanently 'under review' and there is no guarantee that the relationship has a future. Therefore, the subject positions offered by this construction are those of free agents who reserve the right to withdraw from the relationship at any time and without moral sanction.

Stage 5: Practice

What are the possibilities for action mapped by the two discursive constructions of relationships? What can be said and done by the subjects positioned within them? Constructions of relationships as 'social arrangements' and their subject positions of responsible social actors require those positioned within them to act responsibly and with consideration for the consequences of their actions. Being part of a mutually beneficial social arrangement means that whatever we do affects the other party within the arrangement, and that we need to take responsibility for these effects. The participant's account of how she rehearsed breaking up (lines 5–10) and how hard it was for her to 'actually say to him I don't want to go out with you anymore' (lines 9–10) demonstrates her positioning as a responsible social actor. Taking responsibility for one's partner's well-being (line 19) and breaking up in a way that demonstrates concern for that partner's future are practices which support a construction of relationships as 'social arrangements'. By contrast, being positioned within a relationship as 'a step on the way' does not require the same preoccupation with the other's well-being. Note that the section of text which constructs the relationship as 'a step on the way' (lines 30–42) does not contain any references to the participant's ex-partner. Instead, it talks about the nature of the relationship and the criteria by which to assess its value. The subject position of a free agent who reserves the right to withdraw from the relationship at any time and without moral sanction involves a focus upon the self and its interests. This is demonstrated in lines 30–42 (note the consistent use of the first-person singular and the references to 'foundation', 'basis' and 'criteria' for decision-making in this section).

Stage 6: Subjectivity

This stage in the analysis is, of necessity, the most speculative. This is because here we are attempting to make links between the discursive constructions used by participants and their implications for subjective experience. Since there is no necessary direct relationship between language and various mental states, we can do no more than delineate what can be felt, thought and experienced from within various subject positions; whether or not, or to what extent, individual speakers actually do feel, think or experience in these ways on particular occasions is a different question (and one we probably cannot answer on the basis of a discourse analysis alone). It could be argued that feelings of guilt and regret are available to those positioning themselves within a construction of relationships as 'social arrangements' (lines 19–21, 'You start taking responsibility for them and for how they'll cope afterwards you know maybe to the detriment to your own personal sort of well-being'), while taking up a position as free agent within a construction of relationships as 'a step on the way' may involve a sense of time urgency in relation to decision-making (lines 33–5, 'because I thought OK we've been going out for two nearly two years if we were going out for another two years would I want to marry him and the answer was no').

Key Differences between Discursive Psychology and Foucauldian Discourse Analysis

Both versions of the discourse analytic method share a concern with the role of language in the construction of social reality. However, as I hope has become clear, there are also important differences between the two approaches. To conclude this chapter, I want to make a direct comparison between the two versions of discourse analysis and the analytic insights each one of them can generate. Key differences between the two versions are presented under three headings: 'Research Questions', 'Agency' and 'Experience' (see Box 8.4 for a summary).

Box 8.4   Key differences between discursive psychology (DP) and Foucauldian discourse analysis (FDA)

Research questions

- DP asks, 'How do participants use language in order to manage stake in social interactions?'
- FDA asks, 'What characterizes the discursive worlds participants inhabit and what are their implications for possible ways of being?'

Agency

Discursive psychology

- The speaker is an active agent.
- The speaker uses discourse.
- Discourse is a tool.

Foucauldian discourse analysis

- The speaker is positioned by/in discourse.
- Discourse makes available meanings.
- Discourse constructs its subjects.

Experience

Discursive psychology

- DP questions the value of the category 'experience'.
- DP conceptualizes invocations of 'experience' as a discursive move.

Foucauldian discourse analysis

- FDA attempts to theorize experience.
- Discourse is implicated in experience.
- Discourse makes available ways of being.

Research Questions

Discursive psychology and Foucauldian discourse analysis are designed to answer different sorts of research questions. Discursive psychology projects typically ask, 'How do participants use language in order to manage stake in social interactions?', while Foucauldian discourse analysis answers the question 'What characterizes the discursive worlds people inhabit and what are their implications for possible ways of being?' Our discursive analysis of the interview extract was designed to answer questions about what the participant was doing with her talk. It allowed us to observe that the extract served as a warrant for the participant's decision to terminate her relationship with her partner. By contrast, our Foucauldian analysis was concerned with the nature of the discursive constructions used by the participant and their implications for her experience of the relationship break-up. We were able to identify both economic and romantic discourses in her account, each of which offered different subject positions and different opportunities for practice and subjectivity.

Agency

Discursive psychology and Foucauldian discourse analysis emphasize different aspects of human agency. Even though discursive psychology is concerned with language and its performative aspects, rather than with speaking subjects and their intentions, its focus on action orientation presupposes a conceptualization of the speaker as an active agent who uses discursive strategies in order to manage stake in social interactions. In line with this, our discursive analysis focused upon the participant's use of discourse in the pursuit of an interpersonal objective which was to justify her decision to leave her partner within the context of a research interview. By contrast, Foucauldian discourse analysis draws attention to the power of discourse to construct its objects, including the human subject itself. The availability of subject positions constrains what can be said, done and felt by individuals. Reflecting this concern, our Foucauldian analysis was interested in the discursive resources which were available to the participant and how their availability may have shaped her experience of the break-up.

Experience

Discursive psychology questions the value of the category 'experience' itself. Instead, it conceptualizes it (along with others such as 'subjectivity' and 'identity') as a discursive move whereby speakers may refer to their 'experiences' in order to validate their claims (as in 'I know this is hard because I've been there!'). Here, 'experience' is a discursive construction, to be deployed as and when required. Anything more than this is seen to constitute a return to cognitivism and this would, therefore, not be compatible with discursive psychology. By contrast, Foucauldian discourse analysis does attempt to theorize 'experience' (and 'subjectivity'). According to this approach, discursive constructions and practices are implicated in the ways in which we experience ourselves (such as 'sick' or 'healthy', 'normal' or 'abnormal', 'disabled' or 'able-bodied', and so on). As a result, an exploration of the availability of subject positions in discourse has implications for the possibilities of selfhood and subjective experience. This difference was reflected in our worked example. Our discursive analysis was concerned with what the respondent was *doing* with her talk, whereas our Foucauldian analysis was more interested in the implications of her use of discourse for her *experience* of the break-up.

Conclusion

Discourse analysis is a relatively recent arrival in psychology. However, despite its short history, it has already generated a large body of literature. As researchers use discourse analytic approaches within different contexts, they encounter new challenges which lead them to develop new ways of applying a discursive perspective. For example, early work in discourse analysis tended to concern itself with social psychological topics such as prejudice. More recently, health psychologists have started to use the method, leading to the formulation of a material-discursive approach (e.g., Yardley, 1997), while others have attempted to find ways in which discourse analysis could inform social and psychological interventions (e.g., Willig, 1999). Wetherell (2001) identifies as many as six different ways of doing discourse analysis. This demonstrates that discourse analysis is not a method of data analysis in any simple sense. Rather, it provides us with a way of thinking about the role of discourse in the construction of social and psychological realities, and this, in turn, can help us approach research questions in new and productive ways. The two versions of the discourse analytic method introduced in this chapter are ways of approaching texts rather than recipes for producing 'correct analyses'. The choice of approach should be determined by the research question we wish to address; in some cases, this means that a combination of the two approaches is called for. The most ambitious discourse analytic studies may wish to pay attention to both the situated and shifting deployment of discursive constructions, as well as to the wider social and institutional frameworks within which they are produced and which shape their production (e.g. Edley and Wetherell, 2001). In this case, both discursive resources *and* discourse practices need to be explored in detail so that we can understand how speakers construct and negotiate meaning (discourse practices), as well as why they may draw on certain repertoires rather than others (discursive resources) (Wetherell, 1998). In any event, our choice of analytic method(s) should always emerge from careful consideration of our research question(s).

Box 8.5 presents three examples of discourse analysis in action.

Eating practices

Wiggins, S., Potter, J. and Wildsmith, A. (2001) 'Eating your words: discursive psychology and the reconstruction of eating practices', *Journal of Health Psychology*, 6(1): 5–15

This paper examines eating practices through the analysis of tape-recorded conversations from family mealtimes. The analysis demonstrates how evaluations of food, norms around eating practices and even participants' physiological states are negotiable and flexible products of discourse. The paper focuses on three discursive processes: (1) constructions of food; (2) constructions of the individual (i.e. as consumer of food); and (3) constructions of behaviour (i.e. eating/not eating). Using extracts from the transcripts of mealtime conversations, the authors demonstrate how discursive constructions are bound up with discursive practices such as urging, offering, resisting, rejecting, accepting, and so on. They conclude that food is not simply an object to be individually appraised (e.g. in terms of its taste and texture) but rather that it can be negotiated, defined, and constructed jointly, in talk. This paper is recommended because it constitutes a clear and systematic illustration of research informed by discursive psychology principles.

GPs and male patients

Seymour-Smith, S., Wetherell, M. and Phoenix, A. (2002) ' "My wife ordered me to come!": a discursive analysis of doctors' and nurses' accounts of men's use of general practitioners', *Journal of Health Psychology*, 7(3): 253–67.

This paper is concerned with the interpretative repertoires through which doctors and nurses construct their male patients. The analysis presented in the paper is based on transcripts of interviews with general practitioners and their nursing colleagues. The authors identify three linked interpretative repertoires which offer a range of subject positions. Each of these repertoires constructs a contrast between men and women, representing masculinity and femininity as obviously dichotomous binary categories. Within these repertoires, men were positioned as childlike with women as their carers and health supervisors. Hegemonic masculinity was both criticized (for preventing men from being more health-conscious) and reinforced (by colluding with the idea that to be a man, one has to resist health care). The authors conclude that these repertoires constitute powerful cultural resources readily available to health-care professionals, which inform the ways in which male patients are positioned in relation to health-care practices. This paper

(Continued)

is recommended because it demonstrates how discursive analysis can be grounded in the micro-analysis of data *and* speak to wider socio-cultural patterns and concerns.

Lessons for sex education

Willig, C. (1998) 'Constructions of sexual activity and their implications for sexual practice: lessons for sex education', *Journal of Health Psychology*, 3(3): 383–92.

This paper explores discursive constructions of sexual activity and their implications for sexual practice. The research presented in this paper was based upon semi-structured interviews with heterosexual adults about sexual risk-taking, particularly in relation to HIV/AIDS. Discursive analysis of the interview transcripts identified a range of constructions of sexual activity invoked by participants. These included 'sex as temptation', 'sex as romance' and 'sex as male preserve'. The author examines the subject positions offered to speakers by these constructions and traces their implications for subjectivity and practice. The author concludes that the positionings on offer were predominantly disempowering with regard to the practice of safer sex. The paper identifies ways in which sex education could challenge such limiting constructions of sexual activity through opening up alternative discursive spaces. This paper is recommended because it illustrates a systematic Foucauldian approach to discursive analysis and its concern with the relationship between discursive constructions, subjective experience and behavioural practices. Unusually for a discourse analytic study, it also includes recommendations for sex education interventions.

Further Reading

Wetherell, M. (1998) 'Positioning and interpretative repertoires: conversation analysis and post-structuralism in dialogue', *Discourse and Society*, 9: 387–413.
In this paper, Wetherell argues in support of an integration of the two versions of discourse analysis.

Willig, C. (2001) *Introducing Qualitative Research in Psychology: Adventures in Theory and Method*. Buckingham: Open University Press.
Chapters 6 and 7 of this book provide a more detailed discussion of the two versions of discourse analysis.

NINE

Focus Groups

Sue Wilkinson

Focus groups are now a popular and widely used method in qualitative research across the social sciences. Although the method dates back some 75 years, it was relatively uncommon until a major resurgence of interest in the late 1970s. It has become popular in psychology only within the last decade, as qualitative research has burgeoned and become more generally accepted within the predominantly quantitative discipline.

The early use of focus groups can be traced back to the 1920s, when the psychologists Emory Bogardus and Walter Thurstone used them to develop survey instruments – although their 'invention' is more often credited to sociologist Robert Merton and his colleagues Patricia Kendall and Marjorie Fiske in the 1940s. Merton's research team developed 'focused group interviews' to elicit information from audiences about their responses to radio programmes. Since then, they have been also known (variously) as 'group interviews' or 'focus group interviews', but the term 'focus groups' is the most commonly used – and serves (if nothing else) to distinguish the approach from more psychodynamically oriented forms of group work.

Prior to the late 1970s, the main use of focus groups was as a market research tool, and most published studies were in the field of business and marketing – this is still an active area of focus group research today (Greenbaum, 1998; 2000). In the 1980s, health researchers pioneered the use of focus groups in social action research, particularly in the fields of family planning and preventive health education; the method was then widely used to study sexual attitudes and behaviours, particularly in relation to HIV/AIDS; and it continues to be used extensively today in the areas of health education and health promotion (Basch, 1987), as well as in health research more generally (Carey, 1995; Wilkinson, 1998a). In the 1990s, the growing popularity of focus group research created a substantial literature on the method across a much wider range of disciplines, including education, communication and media studies, feminist research, sociology and psychology (see Morgan, 1996; Wilkinson, 1998b, for reviews).

Focus group methodology is, at first sight, deceptively simple. It is a way of collecting qualitative data, and this – essentially – involves engaging a small number of people in an informal group discussion (or discussions), 'focused' on a particular topic or set of issues. Focus group projects in which I have been involved, for example, include young women exploring how to negotiate sexual refusals; young men talking about body modification practices, such as hair removal, piercing and tattooing; nurses evaluating different types of ward management; lesbian parents discussing their children being bullied at school; women comparing their experiences of vaginal examinations and cervical smears; and partners of women with breast cancer sharing information about 'coping' with life on a day-to-day basis. There is a common misconception that people will be inhibited in revealing intimate details in the context of a group discussion – in fact, focus groups are well suited to exploring 'sensitive' topics, and the group context may actually facilitate personal disclosures (Farquhar, 1999; Frith, 2000).

The informal group discussion is usually based around a series of questions (the focus group 'schedule'), and the researcher generally acts as a 'moderator' for the group: posing the questions, keeping the discussion flowing, and encouraging people to participate fully. Although focus groups are sometimes referred to as 'group interviews', the moderator does not ask questions of each focus group participant in turn – but, rather, facilitates group discussion, actively encouraging group members to interact *with each other*. This interaction between research participants is a key feature of focus group research – and the one which most clearly distinguishes it from one-to-one interviews (Morgan, 1997). Compared with interviews, focus groups are much more 'naturalistic' (that is, closer to everyday conversation), in that they typically include a range of communicative processes – such as storytelling, joking, arguing, boasting, teasing, persuasion, challenge and disagreement. The dynamic quality of group interaction, as participants discuss, debate and (sometimes) disagree about key issues, is generally a striking feature of focus groups.

Typically, the focus group discussion is audiotaped and the data are transcribed and then analysed by conventional techniques for qualitative data – most commonly, content or thematic analysis. Focus groups are distinctive, then, primarily for the method and type of data *collection* (that is, informal group discussion), rather than for any particular method of data *analysis*.

One possible reason for the contemporary popularity of focus group research is the flexibility of the method. Focus groups can be used as a stand-alone qualitative method, or combined with quantitative techniques as part of a multi-method project. They can be used within the psychology laboratory or out in the field, to study the social world or to attempt to change it – that is, in action research projects (see Wilkinson, 1999, for a review; also Chapter 10, this volume). At almost every stage of a focus group project, there are methodological choices to be made. A good way to get a sense of this flexibility and variety is to look through one of the recent edited collections of focus group research, such as Barbour and Kitzinger (1999) and Morgan (1993).

A focus group project can involve a single group of participants meeting on a single occasion, or it can involve many groups, with single or repeated meetings. It can involve as few as two, or as many as a dozen or so participants (the norm is between four and eight). These participants may be pre-existing groups of people (such as members of families, clubs or work teams), or they may be brought together specifically for the research, as representative of a particular population, or simply on the basis of shared characteristics or experiences (for example, middle-aged men, sales assistants, and sufferers from premenstrual tension). In addition to (or instead of) a set of questions, the moderator may present group members with particular stimulus materials (such as video clips and advertisements); and, in addition to (or instead of) discussing particular questions, they may be asked to engage in a specified activity (such as a card-sorting task or a rating exercise). Kitzinger (1990) provides examples of a range of such activities in the context of researching AIDS media messages. The moderator may be relatively directive or relatively non-directive. Proceedings may be audiotaped or videotaped (the former is more common in social science research).

Data transcription may be more or less detailed, ranging from simple orthographic transcription, which preserves just the words spoken, to the more complex form of transcription favoured by conversation analysts (see Chapter 7), which also preserves a range of linguistic and paralinguistic features, such as false starts, self-corrections, overlapping speech, pauses, volume and intonation. Data analysis may be by hand (as in cutting and pasting sections of transcript) or computer-assisted (using programs such as NUD.IST or THE ETHNOGRAPH). A wide variety of different types of data analysis may be undertaken – including content, thematic, phenomenological, narrative, biographical, ethnographic, discursive or conversation analysis (some of which are discussed in more detail in other chapters of this book).

The type of analysis used depends upon the theoretical framework of the researcher rather than upon any particular feature(s) of focus group data. One particular strength of focus group research is that it is not tied to a specific theoretical framework: the method can be used either within an 'essentialist' or within a 'social constructionist' framework. Focus group research conducted within an essentialist framework, like most psychological research, rests on the assumption that individuals have their own personal ideas, opinions and understandings, and that the task of the researcher is to access or elicit these 'cognitions'. Within this framework, the particular advantage of focus groups is the more comprehensive elicitation of individuals' ideas, opinions and understandings than is possible in one-to-one interviews (more comprehensive in the sense that co-participants are likely to trigger memories, stimulate debate, facilitate disclosure and generally encourage the production of elaborated accounts). Focus group research conducted within a social constructionist framework does *not* assume preexisting cognitions located inside people's heads, but, rather, presupposes that sense-making is produced collaboratively, in the course of social interactions between people. Within this framework, the particular advantage of focus groups is the opportunity they offer for the researcher to observe how people engage in the process of collaborative sense-making: how views are constructed, expressed, defended and (sometimes) modified within the context of discussion and debate with others. The theoretical framework of the research will influence the kind of data analysis undertaken – essentialist research is likely to utilize content or thematic analysis, while social constructionist research is more likely to use ethnographic, discursive or conversation analysis.

Given this breadth and flexibility of use, focus groups are obviously a multipurpose method. However, they are not, as is sometimes assumed, 'a method for all seasons' – like any other method, they have particular advantages and disadvantages, and are demonstrably more suited to some kinds of research questions than others. Focus groups are a good choice of method when the purpose of the research is to elicit people's own understandings, opinions or views (note that this is an essentialist research question), or when it seeks to explore how these are advanced, elaborated and negotiated in a social context (note that this is a social constructionist research question). They are less appropriate if the purpose of the research is to categorize or compare types of individuals and the views they hold, or to measure attitudes, opinions or beliefs (although they are sometimes used in this way). Focus group data are voluminous, relatively unstructured, and do not readily lend themselves to summary analysis. While such data can be subjected to some limited quantification (as in some forms of content analysis, see below), they are best reported in ways which preserve (at least some of) the participants' own words – for example, by using illustrative quotations. Ideally, too, there should also be some analysis of group interactions (although, sadly, this is all too rare in the published literature: see Wilkinson, 2006, for some examples). Focus groups are unlikely to be the method of choice when statistical data and generalizable findings are required: samples are usually small and unrepresentative, and it is difficult to make a good theoretical case for aggregating data across a number of diverse groups, or for making direct comparisons between groups (although, again, this is sometimes done).

There are also practical advantages and disadvantages to the use of focus groups. They have been seen as a way of collecting a large volume of data relatively quickly and cheaply. However, it can be difficult to recruit and bring together appropriate participants; moderating a group effectively is a skilled technique, which (ideally) requires training and practice; and data transcription and analysis (of whatever kind) are extremely painstaking and time-consuming processes, which require a range of data-handling and interpretative skills. The following section of this chapter offers a more detailed practical guide to what is involved in doing focus group research.

Practical Guide

The focus group literature includes a substantial number of 'handbooks', which offer a wealth of general information and advice about the process of doing focus group research, as well as a consideration of issues specific to particular types of focus group. The most useful of these guides for the psychologist are by Bloor et al. (2001), Fern (2001), Krueger and Casey (2000), Morgan (1997), Stewart, Shamdasani and Rook (2006) and Vaughn, Schumm and Sinagub. (1996); the most comprehensive is by Morgan and Krueger (1998). Here, I draw both on the advice offered by these handbooks and on my own experience of focus group research, to review the key stages of a focus group project and to suggest the key practical considerations at each stage.

I also illustrate each stage of a focus group project with examples from my recent research on women's experiences of breast cancer (Wilkinson, 1998a; 1998b; 2000a; 2000b; 2004; 2007). In this project, a total of 77 women took part in 13 focus groups, each lasting 1–3 hours. Participants were recruited through a symptomatic breast clinic at a general hospital in the north of England. Most were working-class, middle-aged or older, and within five years of diagnosis. The focus groups were held in a university setting, and each woman attended only one group on a single occasion. Discussion ranged across the women's feelings on diagnosis, their relationships, their experiences of treatment, and the changes that cancer had created in their lives. Data were audiotaped and transcribed orthographically in the first instance, and later retranscribed in more detail and analysed by a variety of techniques (see Wilkinson, 2000b, for a comparison of three methods of analysis of one of the focus groups).

For any focus group to provide the best possible data (and to be a rewarding experience for the participants, an outcome which will also lead to better data), two things – at least – are necessary: an effective moderator and a well-prepared session.

Ideally, the moderator should have some basic interviewing skills, some knowledge of group dynamics, and some experience of running group discussions. Although some of the skills involved in moderating a focus group are similar to those involved in one-to-one interviews (for example, establishing rapport, effective use of prompts and probes, and sensitivity to non-verbal cues), the number of research participants involved in a focus group requires more in terms of active 'people management'. The shy participant must be encouraged to speak, the talkative one discouraged at times, and instances of discomfort and/or disagreement must be handled with care. The handbooks provide substantial detail on the principles of 'people management', but are no substitute for the experience of moderating a focus group in practice. The most common mistakes of novice (and/or nervous) moderators are failure to listen (and so follow up appropriately; inability to tolerate silence; talking too much; and sequential questioning.

You should not embark on a focus group project without some kind of practice run – or, preferably, a full-scale pilot study. Proper preparation for, and efficient planning of, the focus group session itself are just as essential as moderator skills for obtaining high-quality data. A well-run focus group session might *look* effortless, but it almost certainly is not: a surprising amount of preparatory work is needed before, during and after the session itself. After you have determined that focus groups are an appropriate way to address your research question, here are some of the main practical considerations in setting up an effective focus group project.

Design Issues

First, you will need to decide on the broad parameters of your project – that is, the overall timescale; how many focus groups you will run; what kind of focus groups they will be; the number and type of participants you will have (and how you will recruit them); and how you will record, transcribe and analyse your data. These parameters need to be set before you can address the more detailed practical issues below. In almost all cases, the design of the research is likely to be a compromise between what would be ideal and what is actually feasible, given the practical constraints of time, resources and your own expertise and energy.

Ethical Issues

Focus group research, like any other psychological research, must be conducted in accordance with the ethical guidelines of the relevant professional body (that is, in the UK, the British Psychological Society). Broadly speaking, you need to obtain the necessary permissions and ethical clearances from the institution where you are based (such as a university or human subjects ethical committee), and from the institution where you will collect your data (such as a Health Authority), as well as any key 'gate-keepers' within it (such as consultant or service manager). You must also obtain your participants' informed consent to take part; you are responsible for protecting their confidentiality, and you should take all reasonable steps to ensure that they will not be subjected to any stress or anxiety beyond and above what they might reasonably experience in their everyday lives.

Confidentiality is a particular issue within focus groups, because of the number of participants, and 'ground rules' must be set to ensure that personal details and potentially sensitive material are not discussed outside the context of the group (that is, participants should be requested to respect and preserve the confidentiality of others). There are also some ethical issues specific to the interactional nature of focus group research. For example, very occasionally a participant may be visibly worried or distressed by the experiences or opinions being aired, an argument may 'turn nasty', or several focus group members may collude to silence or intimidate a particular individual. It is important to handle such a situation immediately, within the group (this may include, in the last resort, terminating the session); it may also be necessary to address it further with the individual(s) involved once the group has finished. In practice, though, focus group research is usually an interesting, and often enjoyable, experience for all concerned, and such 'difficult situations' rarely occur. Finally, as with any research, it is a good idea to have contact details available for relevant counselling services, helplines, self-help groups and other sources of information, in case they are needed or requested following the group.

Preparing Materials

You will need (at least) a focus group schedule, perhaps also written or pictorial materials. In devising a schedule, make sure that it is likely to engage the participants, that it uses appropriate vocabulary, that the questions flow logically, that it provides the opportunity for a variety of viewpoints to be expressed, and that it allows participants to raise points which may not have occurred to the researcher. Box 9.1 shows the schedule used in my breast cancer project.

Box 9.1   Focus group schedule

Women's experience of breast cancer

Introduction (recap on purpose of project, procedure, ground rules)

Questions (used in all groups)

1. How did you feel when you first became aware of a breast problem?
2. How did you feel when you were first told it was breast cancer?
3. How did people around you react to knowing you had breast cancer?
    – Partner/family/friends/others
4. What kind of support did you need?
    – When you were first aware of a problem?
    – When you knew for sure it was cancer?

---

5. What kind of support did your partner/family/others close to you need?
   – When you were first aware of a problem?
   – When you knew for sure it was cancer?
6. What do you think caused your breast cancer?
7. What kind of effect has having breast cancer had on your life
   – Including your general outlook on life?
   – On you personally?
   – On those around you?

Supplementary questions (used in some groups, when time)

8. What is the worst thing about having breast cancer?
9. Has anything good come out of having breast cancer?
   – What?
10. Have you been concerned about your appearance?
    – In what way?
    – Those around you? In what way?
11. Is there anything else you would like to say about your experience of breast cancer?
    – Or about this research project?

Conclusion (summary, thanks and debriefing)

Try out all the materials you intend to use – to ensure they are intelligible, legible, visible and the right length. If you are intending to use slides or video clips, make sure that the appropriate projectors are readily available, and that you know how to operate them. Have back-ups available in case of equipment failure. Write out your introduction to the session (include a recap on the project, the procedure to be followed and the 'ground rules' for the focus group) and your closing comments (include a summary of the session, any necessary debriefing and a reiteration of thanks); see also the procedural points covered in 'the session itself' below.

Recruiting Participants

This is much harder than the novice focus group researcher ever imagines. Make sure that potential participants know what is involved in the focus group procedure – this is part of giving informed consent. Consider whether you will pay them (or offer other incentives – for example, simple refreshments are almost always appropriate) and/or reimburse travel expenses. Always overrecruit by about 50 per cent (that is, recruit nine participants for a six-person group) – however much enthusiasm/commitment participants express, some of them always fail to turn up on the day, for one reason or another. Make sure they have clear directions for finding the venue, and (particularly if you recruit some time in advance of the session), issue several reminders, including – most crucially – a telephone call the day before the focus group meets.

Choosing the Venue

Sometimes – particularly in action research projects – there is no choice of venue: you have to conduct the focus group on the group's own 'territory' (that is, wherever the participants usually meet, or wherever they are prepared to meet you), which may not be an ideal research environment. Where there is a choice, however, the main consideration is balancing participant comfort and a good recording environment. A few universities now have purpose-built 'focus group suites' (more often in the business school than the psychology department), and most psychology departments have a laboratory with a one-way mirror – this might be worth considering, particularly if observation/video recording is part of the project. Most important is a relatively comfortable, quiet room where you will not be disturbed or under time pressure to finish. Participants should be seated in a circle – either in easy chairs or around a table (your choice may depend on what participants will be asked to do, but note the different 'feel' of these two options). Easy access to lavatories and to a telephone is essential.

Preparing for the Session

There are two aspects to this: thinking through the logistics of the day itself and preparing supplementary materials. It is ideal to have an assistant, especially for larger focus groups. Whether or not this is possible, think through how you will handle arrivals and departures (including late arrivals and early departures), refreshments, dealing with unforeseen queries or problems, and taking notes and/or operating the recording equipment while moderating the group. Remember that Murphy's Law ('if anything can go wrong, it will') holds as much for focus groups as other types of research – but seems to apply particularly to recording equipment! This should be checked and double-checked before every group. Highly specialized recording equipment is unnecessary: a small cassette tape recorder, dictaphone, or MP3 player with a recording facility is fine. However, with a tape recorder or dictaphone, it is desirable to use an omnidirectional microphone in order to produce a recording clear enough for transcription. To minimize the risk of recording failure, it is also desirable to use *two* sets of recording equipment, if possible – this is much easier to manage if you have an assistant.

In terms of supplementary materials, you will need some or all of the following:

- refreshments: water at least, preferably tea/coffee and biscuits (*not* alcohol); depending on time of day and length of session, possibly simple food (such as sandwiches and pizza) – but nothing crunchy (this obscures the recording)
- writing materials (paper and pens) – for yourself and the participants
- informed consent forms; expenses claim forms
- a box of paper tissues
- name badges or cards (and marker pens to complete them)
- recording equipment (including spare tapes and batteries for cassette tape recorders; or extra memory for digital recorders).

Set up the room well in advance, if possible, and check the recording equipment (again) just before using it.

The Session Itself

You need to allow 1–3 hours (depending on the topics/activities to be included and the availability/commitment of the participants). The beginning and end of the focus group session entail specific practical considerations.

The following activities are needed at the *beginning* of the session (not necessarily in this exact order):

- offering thanks, a welcome and introductions
- attending to participants' comfort (refreshments, toilets, any special needs)
- signing consent forms (if not done at recruitment), including permission to record and an explanation of what will be done with the data
- reiterating issues of anonymity/confidentiality
- completing name badges
- recapping purpose of study
- outlining procedure (including confirming finishing time)
- setting ground rules for running the group
- providing an opportunity to ask questions.

You then move into the discussion itself. You should aim to create an atmosphere in which participants can relax, talk freely and enjoy themselves. Although it may take a while to 'warm up', once it gets going, a good focus group discussion will appear almost to run itself. The discussion will 'flow' well – and it will seem to move seamlessly through the schedule – sometimes even without the moderator needing to ask the questions. Such apparent 'effortlessness' rests substantially upon good preparation and effective moderating skills (as well as a measure of good luck). Although your main energies should be directed towards effective moderation of the group discussion, it is also desirable to keep notes of the main discussion points, and of any events which may not be captured in an audio recording – for example, the occasion when one of my focus group participants reached inside her bra, pulled out her prosthesis (artificial breast) and passed it around the table! An assistant will be able to take more comprehensive notes, which could include a systematic list of the sequence of speakers (this helps in transcription, especially with larger groups). It is also worth noting that a good focus group often overruns: always allow participants to leave at the agreed time, even if you have not finished.

The following activities are needed at the *end* of the focus group (again not necessarily in this exact order):

- reiterating thanks
- reiterating confidentiality
- giving a further opportunity for questions
- providing further information, or possible sources of information (as appropriate)
- debriefing (as appropriate) – including on an individual basis as necessary
- checking that participants have had a good experience (possibly formal evaluation)
- completing expenses claim forms (and making payment arrangements)
- offering appropriate farewells and/or information about any follow-ups.

Data Management and Transcription

The next step is to make back-up copies of all notes, tapes and/or data files (which should be clearly labelled with the date, time, length and nature of the session). Keep them in a separate place from the originals. If you are transcribing your own data (as is usually the case), try to do this as soon as possible after the session, while it is still fresh in your mind. Specialized transcribing equipment is not necessary – although, for audio tapes, transcription is considerably facilitated by the use of a dedicated transcribing machine. For digital recordings, specialized transcription/ editing software is available (Audacity and Amadeus are popular programs).

Transcription is really the first stage of data analysis, and a careful, detailed transcription will facilitate the next steps (although the level of detail pre- served in the transcription will depend on your research question and the type of data analysis you plan to use – see earlier discussion). Note that, whenever you present extracts from your data, you should append a transcription key listing the precise transcription conventions you have used. Box 9.2 shows a typical (simple) transcription key covering the data extracts presented in this chapter (a more elaborate transcription key, of the type used in conversation analytic studies, can be found in Atkinson and Heritage, 1984; see also Chapter 7).

Box 9.2   Sample transcription key

Transcription conventions used for data extracts in this chapter

- underlining – emphasis
- hyphen at end of word – word cut off abruptly

- ellipsis (...) – speaker trails off
- round brackets – used when transcriber is uncertain what was said, but is able to make a reasonable guess – for example, (about)
- square brackets – enclose comments made by transcriber. Such comments include inability to make out what was said [indistinct], and sounds that are difficult to transcribe – such as [tch], [stutters], as well as interactional features of note – such as [laughs], [pause], [cuts in], [turns to Edith].

Whatever type of transcription you undertake, the transcription process is likely to take much longer than you might expect. A skilled transcriber typically needs 3–4 hours' transcription time per hour of discussion to produce a simple orthographic transcript; a novice transcriber is likely to take twice or three times as long. Transcription suitable for conversation analysis typically takes many hours per *minute* of discussion (for this reason, whole discussions are rarely transcribed in this way – rather, extracts relevant to the particular phenomenon under study are selected for transcription). Focus group data are harder to transcribe than one-to-one interview data, because of overlapping talk (although the degree of accuracy with which you need to transcribe this will depend on whether it is a feature of your planned analysis). Make back-up copies of all transcripts too, and store them separately, appropriately labelled and in both electronic and paper form (a large ring-binder with dividers is useful for the latter).

Data Analysis

You should have decided long before this stage how you will analyse your data, in relation to your theoretical framework and your specific research question (see earlier for a range of possibilities). Here, I will give examples of two contrasting ways of analysing focus group data – content analysis and ethnographic[1] analysis – again drawn from my breast cancer project.

The analyses presented below are both concerned with the possible 'causes' of breast cancer. The content analysis (conducted within an essentialist framework – see above) rests on the assumption that people have (relatively stable and enduring) beliefs or opinions about the causes of breast cancer, and that these can reliably be inferred from an analysis of what they say. Its aim, then, is to identify participants' beliefs or opinions about the causes of breast cancer. The ethnographic analysis (conducted within a social constructionist framework – see above) rests on the claim that people's ideas about the causes of breast cancer are produced collaboratively, in social interactions between people, and that these collaborative productions can be observed, as they actually happen, in the course of focus group interaction. Its aim, then, is to identify the ways in which people actively construct and negotiate ideas about the causes of breast cancer.

Content Analysis

Content analysis is a commonly used approach to analysing qualitative data, including focus group data. It involves coding participants' open-ended talk into closed categories, which summarize and systematize the data. These categories may be derived either from the data itself (perhaps using grounded theory – see Chapter 5; this is known as a 'bottom-up' approach) or from the prior theoretical framework of the researcher (this is known as a 'top-down' approach, and requires prior familiarity with the literature on the topic under investigation in order to derive the categories, as in the worked example below). The end point of the analysis may be simply to illustrate each category by means of representative quotations from the data, presented either in a table (see Box 9.3a); or written up as consecutive prose (e.g. Fish and Wilkinson, 2000a; 2000b). Box 9.3a provides an example of a content analysis based on the transcript of a breast cancer focus group with three participants. All talk in this focus group about the 'causes' of breast cancer has been categorized systematically. The categories (and subcategories) are derived from Mildred Blaxter's (1983) classic study on women talking about the causes of disease, with the addition of an 'Other' category. Box 9.3a illustrates each category used by the participants with representative quotations from their talk.

Box 9.3a Content analysis – presented qualitatively

Women's beliefs about the causes of breast cancer

1. *Infection*
    Not discussed
2. *Heredity or familial tendencies*
    *   'I mean there's no family <u>history</u>'
3. *Agents in the environment:*
    a) *'poisons', working condition, climate (see also Box 9.3b)*
        *   'I was once told that if you use them aluminium pans that cause cancer'
        *   'Looking years and years ago, I mean, everybody used to [laughs] sit about sunning themselves on the beach and now all of a sudden you get cancer from sunshine'
        *   'I don't know (about) all the chemicals in what you're eating and things these days as well, and how cultivated and everything'
    b) *Drugs or the contraceptive pill*
        *   'I mean I did t-, you know, obviously I took the pill at a younger age'

(Continued)

4. *Secondary to other diseases*
   Not discussed
5. *Stress, strain and worry*
   Not discussed
6. *Caused by childbearing, the menopause*
   - 'Inverted nipples, they say that that is one thing that you could be wary of'
   - 'Until I came to the point of actually trying to breastfeed I didn't realize I had flattened nipples and one of them was nearly inverted or whatever, so I had a lot of trouble breastfeeding, and it, and I was several weeks with a breast pump trying to uhm get it right, so that he could suckle on my nipple, I did have that problem'
   - 'Over the years, every, I couldn't say it happened monthly or anything like that, it would just start throbbing this [pause] leakage, nothing to put a dressing on or anything like that, but there it was, it was coming from somewhere and it were just kind of gently crust over'
   - 'I mean, I don't know whether the age at which you have children makes a difference as well because I had my [pause] 8-year-old relatively <u>late</u>, I was an old mum'
   - 'They say that if you've only had <u>one</u> that you're more likely to get it than if you have a *big* family'
7. *Secondary to trauma or to surgery*
   - 'Sometimes I've heard that <u>knocks</u> can bring one on'
   - 'I then remembered that I'd <u>banged</u> my breast with this, uhm [tch] you know these shopping bags with a wooden rod thing, those big trolley bags?'
   - 'I always think that people go into hospital, even for an exploratory, it may be all wrong, but I do think, well the <u>air</u> gets to it, it seems to me that it's not long afterwards before they [pause] simply find that there's more to it than they thought, you know, and I often wonder if the <u>air</u> getting to your inside is- [pause] brings, brings on [pause] cancer in any form'
8. *Neglect, the constraints of poverty*
   Not discussed
9. *Inherent susceptibility, individual and not hereditary*
   Not discussed
10. *Behaviour, own responsibility*
    - 'I was also told that if you eat tomatoes and plums at the same meal that-'
11. *Ageing, natural degeneration*
    Not discussed
12. *Other*
    - 'He told them nurses in his lectures that <u>everybody</u> has a cancer, <u>and</u> [pause] it's a case of whether it lays dormant'
    - 'I don't think it could be one cause, can it? It must be multi, multifactorial'

One particular advantage of content analysis (for some researchers) is that it also allows for the conversion of qualitative data into a quantitative form. This is done by means of counting the number of responses falling within each category (that is, their frequency or 'popularity') and then summarizing the number (or percentage) of responses for each category, usually in tabular form. Box 9.3b illustrates this. It is based on the same data and the same categories as Box 9.3a, but the results of the content analysis are presented quantitatively, rather than qualitatively. Box 9.3b records the frequency with which 'causes' falling into each category are mentioned.

Box 9.3b   Content analysis – presented quantitatively

Women's beliefs about the causes of breast cancer

1. *Infection*: 0 instances
2. *Heredity or familial tendencies*: 2 instances
   family history (x2)
3. *Agents in the environment*:
   a) *'poisons', working condition, climate*: 3 instances
   aluminium pans; exposure to sun; chemicals in food
   b) *drugs or the contraceptive pill*: 1 instance
   taking the contraceptive pill
4. *Secondary to other diseases*: 0 instances
5. *Stress, strain and worry*: 0 instances
6. *Caused by childbearing*, the menopause: 22 instances
   not breastfeeding; late childbearing (x3); having only one child; being single/not having children; hormonal; trouble with breastfeeding – unspecified (x4); flattened nipples (x2); inverted nipples (x7); nipple discharge (x2)
7. *Secondary to trauma or to surgery*: 9 instances
   knocks (x4); unspecified injury; air getting inside body (x4)
8. *Neglect, the constraints of poverty*: 0 instances
9. *Inherent susceptibility, individual and not hereditary*: 0 instances
10. *Behaviour, own responsibility*: 1 instance
    mixing specific foods
11. *Ageing, natural degeneration*: 0 instances
12. *Other*: 5 instances
    'several things'; 'a lot'; 'multifactorial'; everybody has a 'dormant' cancer; 'anything' could wake a dormant cancer

---

The main advantages of undertaking a content analysis of these data, then, are that it provides a useful summary of women's beliefs about the causes of breast cancer, and offers an overview of the range and diversity of their ideas.

It also offers easy comparison with other studies undertaken within a similar framework. If the potential for quantification is taken up, content analysis also gives a sense of the relative significance women attach to different causes (if – as in Blaxter's (1983) analysis – frequency of mention is equated with perceived importance). The main disadvantages are that a great deal of detail is lost; it can be hard to select quotations which are both representative of the categories and compelling to the reader ('naturalistic' talk doesn't come in sound bites!); and (particularly in the quantified version) one loses a sense of individual participants and – especially – the interaction between participants, which is so distinctive in focus group data. (It may be possible to preserve this by doing a separate 'sweep' of the data for interactional phenomena, and attempting to 'map' these onto the content analysis in some way.)

There is also a range of coding problems associated with content analysis. For example, the analysis above categorizes as equivalent causes which the women say *do* apply to them (for example, 'I took the pill at a younger age') and those which they say *do not* (for example, 'there's no family <u>history</u>'). It also categorizes as equivalent statements which the women present as their own beliefs or opinions (for example, 'I always think ...'; 'It must be ...') and those which they attribute to others (for example, 'I was once told ...'; 'He told them ...'; 'They say ...'). Finally, it is unable to deal with inconsistencies in expressed beliefs or apparent changes of opinion during the course of the focus group – because each mention of a cause is treated as an isolated occurrence, taken out of context. These apparent 'coding problems' are actually epistemological issues arising from the framework within which this type of analysis is undertaken – and, as such, they are key to what can (and cannot) be said about the data (see Wilkinson, 2000b, for a more extended discussion). The point will become clearer as we move to a second example of focus group analysis, again drawing on some of my breast cancer data.

Ethnographic Analysis

The data extract on which the second analysis is based is shown in Box 9.4 (note that this is a simple orthographic transcription of a small part of a focus group). There are three participants in this focus group, in addition to myself as researcher/moderator. Doris and Fiona are both pub landladies (although Doris has recently retired). They arrived early for the session, met each other for the first time, and discovered their shared occupation while waiting for the other participants to arrive. During this pre-focus group conversation, they developed a joint theory about the possible role of their work in causing their breast cancer. Specifically, Doris and Fiona co-constructed the explanation that 'pulling' (drawing beer from a cask, by means of a handpump, which is quite a strenuous activity) was to blame. Immediately prior to the extract presented here, I asked the focus group participants if they had any idea about what might have caused their breast cancer.

Box 9.4 Data extract for ethnographic analysis

In the following data extract, two pub landladies (Doris and Fiona) consider the possible role of their profession in 'causing' their breast cancer (another focus group participant [Edith] and the researcher/moderator [SW] also contribute to the discussion).

Doris: Well, I uhm, like you

Edith: [Cuts in] It's not in the family

Doris: [Turns to Fiona] Like you I wondered if it was with <u>pulling</u>, you know

Fiona: Yeah

SW: [Turns to Edith] These two were talking about being pub landladies and whether that contributed Edith: Well that, oh [indistinct]

Fiona: Yeah, you know, yeah

Edith: Is it at the side where ...?

Doris: Mine's at the side where [indistinct]

Fiona: where you pulled

Doris: Yes

Fiona: and mine's the same side, and I've got two friends who are both pub landladies down south

Doris: And then

Fiona: and they're sisters and both of them have got breast cancer, both on the same side as they pull beer

Doris: And then there's the atmosphere of the smoke in the [stutters] pub

Fiona: Well I, I'm not, I don't know, I'm not so sure about that one

Doris: Well, I think I lean to that more in, what do they call him? The artist, Roy Castle

Fiona: Oh Roy Castle, yeah, with passive smoking

Doris: Mm hm, he said he got his through being in smoke, smoke filled rooms

Doris and Fiona answer my question by presenting their joint theory to the group (note that they simply continue as if everyone had been present at their earlier conversation, making no concession to Edith's later arrival – it is left to me, as group moderator, to 'fill Edith in' on what has gone before). Edith is, however, very quick to catch on (asking a clarificatory question – 'Is it at the side where ...?' – which I, as researcher, would certainly not have thought to ask). Doris and Fiona respond to Edith's question by pooling their similar experiences: Fiona even completes Doris's sentence for her, in expounding their joint theory. Fiona then offers additional information: she has two friends who are also pub landladies, and *they too* have breast cancer on the same side as they pull beer. This strengthens their joint theory still further: with the evidence of *four* pub landladies all with breast cancer on the same side as they pull beer, who could doubt that 'pulling' is a contributory factor? However, Doris then offers an alternative or additional contributory factor for breast cancer in pub landladies: 'the atmosphere of the smoke in the pub'.

There are several possibilities open to Fiona at this point: she can *reject* this new information out of hand in favour of the 'pulling' theory (in which case she will need to defend 'pulling' as the stronger contender, perhaps offering more evidence to support 'pulling' or to refute the 'smoky atmosphere' theory); she can elaborate the 'pulling' theory to incorporate 'smoky atmosphere' as an *additional* possible cause; she can engage with the new information as offering a possible *alternative* theory (perhaps exploring the parameters and implications of a 'smoky atmosphere', or challenging Doris to provide examples or additional evidence of its effects); or she can simply accept 'smoky atmosphere' as a better explanation for breast cancer. In the event, her hesitant and qualified response ('Well I, I'm not, I don't know, I'm not so sure about that one') implies disagreement (or, at the very least, uncertainty). Fiona's apparent disagreement leads Doris to marshal supporting evidence for the 'smoky atmosphere' theory, in the form of a recent television documentary featuring a celebrity with cancer. Fiona has seen the documentary too, and in her response to Doris we see the possible beginning of a shift in her views (or at least a willingness to engage seriously with the 'smoky atmosphere' theory): she recognizes – and names (as 'passive smoking') – the phenomenon Doris has identified. Doris accepts this label and goes on to relate it to the case of the TV celebrity.

This ethnographic analysis illustrates the collaborative production and negotiation of ideas about the causes of breast cancer. In its focus on the processes of constructing notions of cause through ongoing social interaction, it is epistemologically very different from a content analytic approach that sees ideas about cause as internal 'cognitions'. It is also worth noting that, although ethnographic analysis has an affinity with narrative methods (see Chapter 6), from a ethnographic perspective, a narrated story – or other contribution to a discussion – is never just a stand-alone. Rather, it is a form of social action, produced for a specific purpose (such as to amuse, inform, illustrate or explain) within the particular interactional context of a particular focus group discussion.

The main advantages of undertaking a ethnographic analysis of focus group data such as these, then, are that it takes the fullest possible account of the social context within which statements about cause are made; it does not treat such statements as unitary, static or non-contingent; and it preserves both a sense of individual participants and – particularly – the details of their interaction, which here become a central analytic concern. If video (rather than audio) data are available, a broader analysis of the group dynamics within which particular conversations are located becomes a real possibility. The very different epistemological framework of ethnographic analysis also accounts for many of the 'coding problems' identified in relation to content analysis (for example, the inconsistency and variability of accounts) – see Wilkinson (2000b) for a more extended discussion. The main disadvantages of ethnographic analysis are that it does not easily permit either a summary overview of a large data set, or a detailed focus on the lives of individuals outside the focus group context (for this, see Chapters 3, 4 and 6 on phenomenological and narrative research). Only a very small sample of data can be analysed in detail in this way, and traditional concerns about representativeness, generalizability, reliability and validity (often levelled at qualitative research) may be difficult to counter (but see Chapter 11 for ways in which qualitative researchers have reconceptualized these traditional concerns).

In sum, then, what I hope to have illustrated by these two worked examples is that there is no single canonical – or even preferred – way of analysing focus group data. Rather, such data can be analysed in a number of (very different) ways, each of which has particular benefits, and also particular costs. Further, I hope to have shown that the particular method of analysis chosen depends centrally upon the particular theoretical framework of researchers and the kinds of research question that they hope to address.

Finally, I hope that the practical guide above does not look too daunting. Focus group research does demand a great deal of planning and organization (and often, also, considerable development of analytic skills), but in my experience it is also immensely rewarding, both for the researcher and for the participants.

Box 9.5 presents three examples of focus group research in action.

Box 9.5   Three good examples of focus group research

Focussing on sex

These three examples illustrate the value of focus groups in exploring 'sensitive' topics and facilitating self-disclosure.

Sexual refusal

O'Byrne, R., Rapley, M. and Hansen, S. (2006) 'You couldn't say "No", could you?': Young men's understandings of sexual refusal', *Feminism & Psychology*, 16(2): 133–54.

This study is an important contribution to the literature on so-called 'date rape'. It draws on two focus groups with young heterosexual male students to explore their understanding of sexual refusal. The authors demonstrate that these young

(Continued)

men perfectly well understand young women's refusals to have sex with them, even when such refusals do not explicitly contain the word 'no', or when they are expressed non-verbally, through 'body language' alone. This is a good illustration of an 'ethnographic' analysis of focus group data, drawing on discursive psychology.

Heterosexual age of consent

Thomson, R. (2004) '"An adult thing"? Young people's perspectives on the heterosexual age of consent', *Sexualities*, 7(2): 133–49.

In the context of proposals to lower the heterosexual age of consent in Britain (from 16 to 14), this study explores young people's own views on this issue. In single- and mixed-sex focus groups, the 56 participants questioned the authority of the law, considered how best to protect individuals, and explored tensions in the construction of sexual maturity and agency. The study provides some valuable insights into the factors that young people believe legitimate sexual activity, and highlights the gap between the public policy agenda and the concerns of young people themselves.

Harassment

Welsh, S., Carr, J., Macquarie, B. and Huntley, A. (2006) '"I'm not thinking of it as sexual harassment": Understanding harassment across race and citizenship', *Gender and Society*, 20(1): 87–107.

This Canadian study is a good example of the use of focus groups in researching the views of socially excluded, often hard-to-reach groups: here, among others, Filipina domestic workers and African-Canadian women. The focus groups provided a safe supportive context for exploring definitions of harassment. The study revealed that, for these women, isolation due to lack of citizenship and racialized harassment are central factors in their harassment experience, which may or may not be experienced as sexual.

Note

1 There are a number of different terms that could be used for this type of analysis, which draws on the approaches of discourse analysis/discursive psychology (see Chapter 8), conversation analysis (see Chapter 7), and the sociological field of ethnomethodology (e.g. Garfinkel, 2002). For clarity and consistency, I have chosen to follow Morgan (1988: 64) in using the term 'ethnographic' here.

Further Reading

Wilkinson, S. (1998b) 'Focus group methodology: a review', *International Journal of Social Research Methodology*, 1: 181–203.
Good brief introduction to the method and the range of ways in which it has been used in various disciplinary contexts.

Barbour, R. and Kitzinger, J. (eds) (1999) *Developing Focus Group Research: Politics, Theory and Practice*. London: Sage.
A very useful edited collection, with a wider range of examples than most.
One of the two best introductions to doing focus group research, very practical.

Morgan, D.L. (1997) *Focus Groups as Qualitative Research* (2nd edn). Newbury Park, CA: Sage.
Although now rather old, this is the other best introduction to doing focus group research; covers key issues as well as practical details.

Wilkinson, S. (2000b) 'Women with breast cancer talking causes: comparing content, biographical and discursive analyses', *Feminism and Psychology*, 10: 431–60.
Useful for more examples of different types of data analysis, and discussion of their implications.

Wilkinson, S. (2006) 'Analysing interaction in focus groups', in P. Drew, G. Raymond and D. Weinberg (eds), *Talk and Interaction in Social Research Methods*. London: Sage, pp. 50–62.
Collects together some of the (few) examples of focus group research to analyse interaction, and offers a more sustained example of this.

TEN

Co-operative Inquiry

An Action Research Practice

Peter Reason and *Sarah Riley*

Introduction: Epistemological and Political Groundings

The primary tradition of research in psychology has emphasized the separation of subject and object, observer from what is observed, in a search for objective truth. In this tradition it is the researcher who makes all the decisions about what to study, how to study it, and what conclusions may be drawn; and the 'subjects' contribute only their responses to the situation in which they are observed, without knowing anything about the ideas that inform the inquiry. However, another inquiry tradition, which we can broadly call action research, has placed a contrasting emphasis on collaboration between 'researcher' and 'subject' to address practical issues of shared concern. In the full flowering of the approach, this distinction between researcher and subject fades away and *all* those involved in the inquiry endeavour act as co-researchers, contributing both to the decisions which inform the research and to the action which is to be studied. Further, the purpose is to reach not for a transcendant or objective truth in the tradition of Cartesian science (Toulmin, 1990), but practical knowing in the service of human and ecological flourishing (Heron, 1996b; Reason and Bradbury, 2001a)

In this chapter we focus on one approach – co-operative inquiry – which is part of the wider rich and diverse family of action research approaches. For some, action research is primarily an individual affair through which professionals can address questions of the kind 'How can I improve my practice?' For others, action research is strongly rooted in practices of organization development and improvement of business and public sector organizations. For many in the majority world, action research is primarily a liberationist practice aiming to redress imbalances of power and restore to ordinary people the capacities of self-reliance and ability to manage their own lives – to 'sharpen their minds' as villagers in Bangladesh described it to Peter. For some, the key questions are about how to initiate and develop face-to-face inquiry groups, while for others the primary issues are about using action research to create change on a large scale and influence policy decisions. And for some action research is primarily a form of practice in the world, while for others it belongs in the scholarly traditions of knowledge generation. According to Reason and Bradbury (2006: xxii), what these approaches all share is a view of research which does the following:

- responds to practical and often pressing issues in the lives of people in organizations and communities
- engages with people in collaborative relationships, opening new 'communicative spaces' in which dialogue and development can flourish
- draws on many ways of knowing, both in the evidence that is generated and in diverse forms of presentation as we speak to wider audiences
- is strongly value-oriented, seeking to address issues of significance concerning the flourishing of human persons, their communities, and the wider ecology in which we participate
- is a living, emergent process which cannot be pre-determined but changes and develops as those engaged deepen their understanding of the issues to be addressed and develop their capacity as co-inquirers both individually and collectively.

The many dimensions of action research are explored in the *Handbook of Action Research* (Reason and Bradbury, 2001b; 2006; in preparation 2008) and the excellent *Introduction to Action Research* by Davydd Greenwood and Morten Levin (1998; 2006)

A Science of Persons

The fundamental argument behind this action research tradition is that it is not possible to have a true science of persons unless the inquiry engages with humans *as* persons. And since persons are manifestly capable of making sense of their behaviour, the distinction between a 'researcher' who does all the thinking, and 'subjects' who do the behaving is completely inappropriate. And from a participatory perspective the 'subjects' of the traditional form are really objects – curiously the word 'subject' wraps around itself to mean both the autonomous human person and the one who is 'subject to' God, the monarch, or a scientific researcher. In a science of persons, all those engaged in the inquiry process enter the process as persons, bringing with them their intelligence, their intentionality, their ability to reflect on experience and to enter relations with others – and of course also their capacity for self-deception, for consensus collusion, for rationalization, for refusal to see the obvious, which also characterizes human persons.

A Participative World-view

A science of persons also rests on a participative view of the world:

[O]ur world does not consist of separate things but of relationships which we co-author. We participate in our world, so that the 'reality' we experience is a co-creation that involves the primal givenness of the cosmos and human feeling and construing. The participative metaphor is particularly apt for action research, because as we participate in creating our world we are already embodied and breathing beings *who are necessarily acting*—and this draws us to consider how to judge the *quality* of our acting.

A participatory worldview places human persons and communities as part of their world —both human and more-than-human—embodied in their world, co-creating their world. A participatory perspective asks us to be both situated and reflexive, to be explicit about the perspective from which knowledge is created, to see inquiry as a process of coming to know, serving the democratic, practical ethos of action research. (Reason and Bradbury, 2001a: 6–7)

A science of persons in this sense is not a science of the Enlightenment. It does not seek a transcendental truth, which Descartes and his fellows would have us pursue. A science of persons embraces a 'postmodern' sentiment in attempting to move us beyond grand narratives toward localized, pragmatic and constructed practical knowings that are based in the experience and action of those engaged in the inquiry project. Toulmin (1990) argues persuasively that this can be seen as a re-assertion of Renaissance values of practical philosophy.

An 'Extended' Epistemology and the Primacy of the Practical

Thus the evidential base of participative forms of inquiry is 'extended': extended beyond the positivist concern for the rational and the empirical to include diverse ways of knowing as persons encounter and act in their world, particularly forms of knowing which are experiential and practical.

As Eikeland (2001) points out, this notion goes right back to Aristotle, and in modern times Polanyi (1962) clearly described his concept of tacit knowledge, a type of embodied know-how that is the foundation of all cognitive action. Writing more recently, Shotter argues that in addition to Gilbert Ryle's distinction between 'knowing that' and 'knowing how' there is a 'kind of knowledge one has *only from within a social situation*, a group, or an institution, and thus takes into account ... the *others* in the social situation' (Shotter, 1993: 7, emphasis in original). It is significant that Shotter usually uses the verbal form '*knowing* of the third kind', to describe this, rather than the noun *knowledge*, emphasizing that such knowing is not a thing, to be discovered or created and stored up in journals, but rather arises in the process of living and in the voices of ordinary people in conversation.

Many writers have articulated different ways of framing an extended epistemology from pragmatic, constructionist, critical, feminist, and developmental perspectives. While these descriptions differ in detail, they all go beyond orthodox empirical and rational Western views of knowing, and embrace a multiplicity of ways of knowing that start from a relationship between self and other, through participation and intuition. They assert the importance of sensitivity and attunement in the moment of relationship, and of knowing not just as an academic pursuit but as the everyday practices of acting in relationship and creating meaning in our lives (Reason and Bradbury, 2001a).

The methodology of co-operative inquiry draws on a fourfold extended epistemology: *experiential knowing* is through direct face-to-face encounter with a person, place or thing; it is knowing through empathy and resonance, that kind of in-depth knowing which is almost impossible to put into words; *presentational knowing* grows out of experiential knowing, and provides the first form of expression through story, drawing, sculpture, movement, dance, drawing on aesthetic imagery; *propositional knowing* draws on concepts and ideas; and *practical knowing* consummates the other forms of knowing in action in the world. (Heron, 1996a; Heron and Reason, in preparation 2008). In some ways the practical has primacy since:

most of our knowledge, and all our primary knowledge, arises as an aspect of activities that have practical, not theoretical objectives; and it is this knowledge, itself an aspect of action, to which all reflective theory must refer. (MacMurray, 1957: 12)

A Liberationist Spirit

However, as well as being an expression of an extended epistemology within a participative world-view, a science of persons has a political dimension. The relationship between power and knowledge is well argued by Habermas, Foucault, Lukes and others (Gaventa and Cornwall, 2001). Participative forms of inquiry start with concerns for power and powerlessness, and aim to confront the way in which the established and power-holding elements of societies world-wide are favoured because they hold a monopoly on the definition and employment of knowledge:

This political form of participation affirms peoples' right and ability to have a say in decisions which affect them and which claim to generate knowledge about them. It asserts the importance of liberating the muted voices of those held down by class structures and neo-colonialism, by poverty, sexism, racism, and homophobia. (Reason and Bradbury, 2001a: 9)

So participatory research has a double objective. One aim is to produce knowledge and action directly useful to a group of people – through research, through adult education, and through sociopolitical action. The second aim is to empower people at a second and deeper level through the process of constructing and using their own knowledge: they 'see through' the ways in which the establishment monopolizes the production and use of knowledge for the benefit of its members. This is the meaning of consciousness raising or *conscientização*, a term popularized by Paulo Freire (1970) for a 'process of self-awareness through collective self-inquiry and reflection' (Fals Borda and

Rahman, 1991: 16). As Daniel Selener emphasizes, while a major goal of participatory research is to solve practical problems in a community, 'Another goal is the creation of shifts in the balance of power in favour of poor and marginalized groups in society' (Selener, 1997: 12). Greenwood and Levin also emphasize how action research contributes actively to processes of democratic social change (Greenwood and Levin, 1998: 3). Participative research is at its best a process that explicitly aims to educate those involved to develop their capacity for inquiry both individually and collectively.

These dimensions of a science of persons – an orientation to the practical, treating persons as persons, a participative world-view, an extended epistemology and a liberationist spirit – can be seen as the basis of contemporary action research. Action research itself is currently undergoing an exciting resurgence of interest and creativity, and there are many forms of inquiry practice within this tradition. In one attempt to provide some order to this diversity we have elsewhere described three broad pathways to this practice. First-person action research/practice skills and methods address the ability of the researcher to foster an inquiring approach to his or her own life, to act awarely and choicefully, and to assess effects in the outside world while acting. Second-person action research/practice addresses our ability to inquire face-to-face with others into issues of mutual concern. Third-person research/practice aims to extend these relatively small-scale projects to create a wider community of inquiry involving a whole organization or community (Reason and Bradbury, 2006: xxv).

Co-operative inquiry is one articulation of action research. The original initiatives into experiential inquiry were taken around 1970 by John Heron (Heron, 1971). This developed into a practice of co-operative inquiry as a methodology for a science of persons (Heron, 1996a) which places an emphasis on first-person research/practice in the context of supportive and critical second-person relationships, while having the potential to reach out toward third-person practice.

The understanding of participants as co-researchers and the focus on solving problems and thus enabling social change makes co-operative inquiry an exciting method for researchers in psychology. There is a range of concerns for researchers who tend to employ qualitative methods in psychology. For some, these issues are about doing radically different psychology that is not co-opted back into the 'mainstream'; for others, the project is less political and concern is on developing the discipline to include a broader, more humanist outlook (Stainton Rogers, et al., 1995). Co-operative inquiry offers something to both 'types' of researchers. For those who are less critical of the psychology project, co-operative inquiry offers an additional method that produces new ways of knowing through a systematic yet flexible method. In drawing on multiple levels of knowing and focusing on applying knowledge at a local level, co-operative inquiry can therefore be used to broaden the remit of psychology, without challenging that remit.

Co-operative inquiry also opens up the possibilities for a more radical psychology that celebrates multiple ways of knowing. This multiplicity shifts the understanding that both researchers and participants are people from a 'methodological horror' to a 'methodological virtue' (Parker, 1994; 1999). A more radical aspect is also incorporated through the championing of the use of research for political ends. Critical and feminist psychologists, for example, may find co-operative inquiry a useful approach in engendering social change.

Regardless of whether a more humanist or more radical approach is taken, co-operative inquiry has the potential to re-energize research in psychology (Box 10.1 offers an account of the experience of one psychology teacher). Co-operative inquiry has been used in educational, health and organizational psychology, but is also particularly relevant for social psychologists looking for ways to develop their sub-discipline and discursive, critical and feminist psychologists who seek ways of using their work to address oppressive practices (see also Willig, 1999).

In the rest of this chapter we first set out the logics of the co-operative inquiry method, and then endeavour to show how this takes place within the learning community which is a co-operative inquiry group.

Box 10.1   A comment from a psychology teacher

One of our colleagues wrote to tell us of her own experience of teaching co-operative inquiry to a psychology class:

I just wanted to tell you that I have just finished teaching a fourth year class in Community Psychology and Action Research (based on Nelson and Prilleltensky's, 2005, value-driven Community Psychology and your work). Your work not only allows Psychology students to discover a human psychology (after learning the experimental method and statistics for four years) but also that they can make a difference in the world through inspiring and engaging research. The comments made to me at the end of the class indicated that for some, their thinking had been transformed and they were rethinking their careers in light of the possibilities opened by Action Research. Others found an approach that resonated with their values. I gently moved them from the experimental method using the four ways of knowing as a guide: starting with propositional knowing, introducing them to major theorists in the field of Psychology to situate action research in their own field; then experiential knowing by giving them case studies from my practice to work on, problem solve and critique; next, presentational knowing by trying out Freire's triggers in the form of 'life statues' or tableaus, in which half the students used their bodies to create a 'still life' example of a situation where there was an unequal balance of power, the other half of the class 'decoded' the example and described what they saw; and finally, practical knowing by presenting community issues and looking at particular methods to investigate them. If I had started with the methods some of them might

---

have thought action research was 'flaky' and not real science (a few did have trouble with the presentational knowledge). I also used the four ways of knowing heuristic to review and reflect on what we were learning as I felt it might appear as chaos to those who are used to following a text chapter by chapter. Their other classes in Psychology had taken this more traditional approach. It was also reassuring to me to hear that they were appreciating the significance of the participatory orientation of this approach. I didn't have to 'sell it' too vigorously.

I anticipated more resistance (e.g. this isn't science) than I experienced. From the first day they embraced the ideas and in fact appeared hungry for a 'human psychology'. I was very careful not to begin with a critique of the experimental paradigm, as I felt I would be telling them that all they had studied and worked hard to master for four years was trivial or irrelevant, but instead to present an alternative approach as just that and to win them over with my enthusiasm and case studies. Also I tried to indicate in what ways the experimental method was useful while at the same time generating excitement for the type of knowledge and change possible with action research. One thing surprised them: they were not aware that the field of action research has a long history going back to Lewin; nor of the extensive use of action research around the world. In their four years of university classes in psychology action research had not been discussed.

Jennifer Mullett (Personal communication). Jennifer Mullett is a Community Psychologist in private practice through Action Research Consulting and an Assistant Professor in the Faculty of Human and Social Development, University of Victoria, Canada. She is engaged by non-profit agencies to teach and support community members to do action research directed towards community action.

The Logics of Co-operative Inquiry

Co-operative inquiry can be seen as cycling through four phases of reflection and action. In Phase One a group of co-researchers come together to explore an agreed area of human activity. They may be professionals who wish to develop their understanding and skill in a particular area of practice or members of a minority group who wish to articulate an aspect of their experience which has been muted by the dominant culture; they may wish to explore in depth their experience of certain states of consciousness; to assess the impact on their well-being of particular healing practices; and so on. In this first phase they agree on the focus of their inquiry, and together develop tentative questions or propositions they wish to explore. They agree to undertake some action, some practice, which will contribute to this exploration, and agree to a set of procedures by which they will observe and record their own and each other's experience.

Phase One is primarily in the mode of propositional knowing, although it will also contain important elements of presentational knowing as group members use their imagination in story, fantasy and graphics to help them articulate their interests and to focus on their purpose in the inquiry. Once they have clarified sufficiently what they want to inquire about, group members conclude Phase One with planning a method for exploring this in action, and with devising ways of gathering and recording evidence from this experience.

In Phase Two, the co-researchers engage in the actions agreed. They observe and record the process and outcomes of their own and each other's experience. In particular, they are careful to hold lightly the propositional frame from which they started, to notice both how practice does and how it does not conform to their original ideas and also the subtleties of experience. This phase involves primarily practical knowledge: knowing how (and how not) to engage in appropriate action, to bracket off the starting idea, and to exercise relevant discrimination.

Phase Three is in some ways the touchstone of the inquiry method as the co-researchers become fully immersed in and engaged with their experience. They may develop a degree of openness to what is going on so free of preconceptions that they see it in a new way. They may deepen into the experience so that superficial understandings are elaborated and developed. Or they may be led away from the original ideas and proposals into new fields, unpredicted action and creative insights. It is also possible that they may get so involved in what they are doing that they lose the awareness that they are part of an inquiry group: there may be a practical crisis, they may become enthralled, they may simply forget. Phase Three involves mainly experiential knowing, although it will be richer if new experience is expressed, when recorded, in creative presentational form through graphics, colour, sound, movement, drama, story or poetry.

In Phase Four, after an agreed period engaged in Phases Two and Three, the co-researchers re-assemble to consider their original propositions and questions in the light of their experience. As a result they may modify, develop or reframe them, or reject them and pose new questions. They may choose, for the next cycle of action, to focus on the same or on different aspects of the overall inquiry. The group may also choose to amend or develop its inquiry procedures – forms of action, ways of gathering data – in the light of experience. Phase Four again emphasizes propositional knowing, although presentational forms of knowing will form an important bridge with the experiential and practical phases.

In a full inquiry the cycle will be repeated several times. Ideas and discoveries tentatively reached in early phases can be checked and developed; investigation of one aspect of the inquiry can be related to exploration of other parts; new skills can be acquired and monitored, experiential competencies realized.

The group itself may become more cohesive and self-critical, more skilled in its work and in the practices of inquiry. Ideally the inquiry is finished when the initial questions are fully answered in practice, when there is a new congruence between the four kinds of knowing. It is, of course, rare for a group to complete an inquiry so fully. It should be noted that actual inquiry practice is not as straightforward as the model suggests: there are usually mini-cycles within major cycles; some cycles will emphasize one phase more than others; some practitioners have advocated a more emergent process of inquiry which is less structured into phases. Nevertheless, the discipline of the research cycle is fundamental.

The cycling can really start at any point. It is usual for groups to get together formally at the propositional stage often as the result of an invitation from an initiating facilitator. However, such a proposal is usually birthed in experiential knowing, at the moment that curiosity is aroused or incongruity in practice noticed. And the proposal to form an inquiry group, if it is to take flight, needs to be presented in such a way as to appeal to the experience of potential co-researchers.

The Human Process of Co-operative Inquiry

In a science of persons, the quality of inquiry practice lies far less in impersonal methodology, and far more in the emergence of a self-aware, critical community of inquiry nested within a community of practice. So, while co-operative inquiry as method is based on cycles of action and reflection engaging four dimensions of an extended epistemology as described above, co-operative inquiry as human process depends on the development of healthy human interaction in a face-to-face group. The would-be initiator of a co-operative inquiry must be willing to engage with the complexities of these human processes as well as with the logic of inquiry. This requires us to recollect our understanding of group processes.

Many theories of group development trace a series of phases of development in the life of a group. Early concerns are for inclusion and membership. When and if these needs are adequately satisfied, the group focuses on concerns for power and influence. And if these are successfully negotiated, they give way to concerns for intimacy and diversity in which flexible and tolerant relationships enable individuals to realize their own identity and the group to be effective in relation to its task (see, for example, Srivastva, Obert and Neilson, 1977). This phase progression model of group behaviour – in which the group's primary concern moves from issues of inclusion to control to intimacy, or from forming to norming to storming to performing (Tuckman, 1965), or from nurturing to energizing to relaxing (Randall and Southgate, 1980) – is a valuable way of understanding group development (although every group manifests these principles in their own unique way and the complexity of an unfolding group process will always exceed what can be said about it). In what follows we will use Randall and Southgate's model of creative group process as a vehicle for describing the process of a successful co-operative inquiry group and to indicate the kinds of leadership or facilitation choices that need to be made.

Randall and Southgate differentiated between the creative group in which there is an exciting interaction between task and people – a 'living labour cycle' – and the destructive group in which primitive emotions arise, swallow up and destroy both human needs and task accomplishment – Bion's 'basic assumption group' (Bion, 1959). The life of a creative group follows the creative organismic cycle which can be seen in all life-affirming human processes such as sexual intercourse, childbirth, preparing food and feasting, and doing good work together. In contrast, the destructive group lumbers between the basic group assumptions identified by Bion – dependency, flight/flight and messianic pairing – in its search for relief of its overwhelming anxiety. In between the creative and destructive group process is the intermediate group which is neither completely satisfying nor completely destructive, but which represents the everyday experience.

The creative group can be described as a cycle of nurturing, energizing, a peak of accomplishment, followed by relaxing (see Figure 10.1).

- The nurturing phase draws people together and helps them feel emotionally safe and bonded. At the same time early, preparatory aspects of the group task and the organizational issues which allow the group to continue its life and work are attended to. The nurturing phase is about creating a safe and effective container for the work of the group, and leadership is primarily focused on those concerns.
- In the energizing phase, interaction intensifies as the group engages in its primary task. A degree of healthy conflict may arise as different views, experiences and skills are expressed. Leadership concerns are with the requirements of the task at hand, with containing and guiding the increasing levels of emotional, physical and intellectual energy which are being expressed.
- The peak in the creative group occurs at points of accomplishment, those moments when the emotional, task and organizational energy of the group comes together and the main purpose to hand is achieved. These are moments of utter mutual spontaneity.
- In the relaxing phase members attend to those issues which will complete the emotional, task and organizational work of the group. Emotionally the group needs to wind down, to celebrate achievements, to reflect and learn. The task needs to be completed – there are always final touches that differentiate excellence from the merely adequate. And the organizational issues need completion – putting away tools, paying bills. Leadership makes space for these issues to be properly attended to, and usually those naturally gifted as 'finishers' come forward to lead celebrations and complete the task.

A group which lasts over a period of time will experience cycles at different levels: mini-cycles associated with particular tasks and major cycles of action

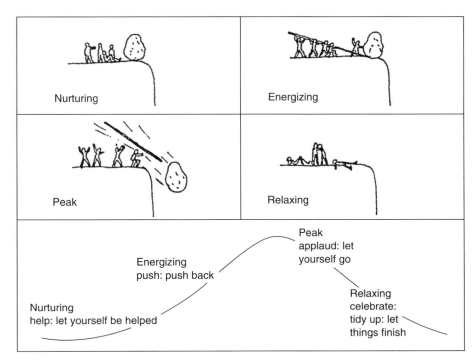

Figure 10.1 The living labour cycle and the creative group cycle. (Randall and Southgate, 1981)

and reflection. These will be set in the context of a long-term developmental cycle of birth, maturation and death, with early concern from inclusion, through conflicts and cliques of the influence stage to (possibly) the maturity of full intimacy and on to dissolution. This creative group nurturing/energizing/relaxing cycle interacts with inquiry phases of action and reflection to produce a complex rhythm of co-operative inquiry.

A creative group is also characterized by an appropriate balance of the principles of hierarchy, collaboration and autonomy: deciding for others, with others, and for oneself (Heron, 1999). Authentic hierarchy provides appropriate direction by those with greater vision, skill and experience. Collaboration roots the individual within a community of peers, offering basic support and the creative and corrective feedback of other views and possibilities. Autonomy expresses the self-directing and self-creating potential of the person. The shadow face of authority is authoritarianism: that of collaboration peer pressure and conformity; that of autonomy narcissism, wilfulness and isolation. The challenge is to design institutions which manifest valid forms of these principles, and to finds ways in which they can be maintained in self-correcting and creative tension.

Establishing Co-operative Inquiry: Focus on Nurturing

The key issues in the nurturing phase are:

- identifying potential group members and establishing a group emotional atmosphere in which potential members feel sufficiently at home to begin to contribute their creative energy
- introducing and explaining the process of co-operative inquiry
- agreeing a framework of times and places for meeting which will provide an organized framework for the major cycles of action and reflection.

A key consideration is to provide sufficient time, to create relaxed conversational spaces, and provide sufficient information for potential group members to make a considered choice about membership. Experience suggests that most inquiry groups are brought together specifically for the inquiry process – they come together around a shared interest or concern, or are members of an occupational group or an organization, so that when they assemble they will recognize their commonality and potential shared purpose. However, it is the initiating energy of one person that brings them together and creates a potential group:

Kate McArdle's doctoral research used co-operative inquiry to work with young women managers in large organizations.

At the end of October I took part in a day celebrating 'diversity' within XYZ. I was given half of a stand promoting women's interests. I covered it with bright yellow posters asking questions such as; 'What is it like to be a twenty-something woman in XYZ?' 'Does gender matter?' I littered the entire floor with bright orange flyers, which asked the same questions, gave the date of an introductory session and my contact details. I was expected to remain on the stand, but I had little interest in being interrogated or speaking to people who were not in the age bracket of my inquiry. I needed to use my voice in the right kind of conversations. I wandered around talking to people who looked as if they were in my 'target audience'. We sat on couches, drank coffee, shared stories about my research and their work and exchanged contact details. (McArdle, 2002: 180)

Carlis Douglas, exploring the question 'Is it possible for Black women to thrive in Britain?' wanted to work with the life experiences of Black women working in organizations to implement equal opportunities policies.

from my extensive network of Black women, I made a long list of managers and professionals with the type of experience I wanted to tap and outlined some criteria for achieving a successful group process. This became the basis on which I invited women to join the group. I was quickly able to identify potential women for the group, and over a period of 6/8 weeks had long face-to-face, or telephone, conversations outlining my proposal, and requesting their involvement in the research. The first five I approached accepted. (Douglas, 2002: 252)

However, some inquiry groups are actual work or living groups who choose to devote time to inquiry to address an issue of particular concern. A group of medical and complementary practitioners working together in an innovative general practice established a co-operative inquiry to explore their interdisciplinary practice (Reason, 1991); an established team of five hospital-based social workers explored the tension between prescription and discretion in front-line social work practice (Baldwin, 2001).

Whether the inquiry group arises as an independent initiative or from within an established group, the first proposal to initiate inquiry is a delicate matter: it needs to be clear enough to catch the imagination, address a felt need or interest, attract people's curiosity and interest, and at the same time be sufficiently tentative for potential members not to feel invaded or put upon by yet another demand on their busy lives. Many initiating facilitators of inquiry have spent considerable time talking through their ideas with potential members, sowing seeds in informal conversation. Some have established a reputation in their organization or community as initiators of interesting new projects and are trusted to take a lead; and others are able to attract people to their idea, and then have to work to establish an atmosphere of trust and inquiry.

One approach is to write a letter or an email which attractively summarizes the proposal and the method on one side of a sheet of paper and invites people to come to a meeting to discuss the idea in greater depth. It can be a substantial, all-day meeting, with some profile within relevant communities, or a more intimate, face-to-face affair:

Agnes Bryan and Cathy Aymer, black social work lecturers, were concerned to address issues in the development of professional identity among black social workers in the UK, issues they had identified on the basis of their experience and some prior research. They invited a large group of black social work professionals – practitioners, managers and teachers – to a day-long meeting at their university to discuss the issues and explore the establishment of inquiry groups (see Aymer, 2005; Bryan, 2000).

Elizabeth Adeline, an artist creating context-specific installations, wanted to ask questions about her practice, including the relation between the doing part of being an artist which is tactile, playing with materials, and the intellectual part which questions the associations of such materials, how they are shaped in the art-making and what it all means. She invited immediate artist friends and colleagues to a meeting at her house to explore establishing an inquiry group. (Adeline, personal communication, 2002).

Such a meeting is often the first occasion at which a potential inquiry group meets, and thus can be seen as the beginning of the creative process, and as needing to address the emotional, task, and organizational requirements of the nurturing phase.

The *emotional needs* of group members are first of all to feel safe, included and welcomed. The early stages of any group are characterized by free-floating anxiety in which every group member feels more or less isolated and is seeking to know that there are others around sufficiently like them to connect with. They will be asking questions about identity and inclusion – 'Who am I to be in this group?' and 'Who is like me?' – questions about purpose – 'Will this group meet my needs and interests?' – and questions about intimacy – 'Is this a place where I will be liked and valued?' If group members are part of an organization, there may be other questions about potential conflict between individual and organizational needs. These questions are rarely fully articulated in consciousness, they are acted out in everyday chit-chat and stereotypical interaction, but nevertheless are powerful influences on the group. It follows that careful attention to these questions is essential.

It is usually helpful if the meeting starts with opportunities for people to meet each other. There is nothing more off-putting than the silence that a new group can generate as people come into a room for the first time; and if this is followed by a meeting which launches immediately into a tasky agenda without hearing why people have come together, the new group can be off to a really bad start. In a small group it may be sufficient for the facilitator to introduce people as they come in; for a large group some structure of meeting in pairs and trios can be helpful. This can be followed by a round in which everyone is asked to say their name and what attracted them to the meeting, or some form of 'name game' that gives people an initial sense of knowing who others are. The physical arrangements for a first meeting can be important:

I arrived to find a beautiful conference room filled with large wooden tables arranged in a square, on top of which at regularly spaced intervals, were a mixture of mineral waters, glasses arranged in diamond shapes and small dishes of mints on paper doilies ... I wanted a circle of chairs. I phoned Facilities to remove the tables. Two big men in overalls arrived ... removed the tables and put the chairs back in a square. Then they all left and I was alone again. I wheeled the huge plush chairs into a circle and wondered what the women would think when they arrived. Would they be as bemused by what I had created, as I had been by what I'd seen when I'd arrived? (McArdle, 2002: 181)

The *task needs* of the group in this first meeting are to initiate people into the co-operative inquiry method, and explore together the potential focus of the proposed inquiry. Of course, these are closely related to the emotional needs explored above, because people's sense of insecurity is in part associated with uncertainty as to whether the group will meet their needs and interests. Usually both of these will have been briefly described in the invitation to the meeting, but it is likely that most people's interest will be diffuse and unformed at this stage. In particular, the methodology of co-operative inquiry can be confusing because most people associate 'research' with filling in questionnaires designed by the researcher, not with becoming co-researchers in a relationship of mutual influence.

It is here that the initiators of inquiry need to exercise authentic authority in setting out as clearly as they can the principles and practices of co-operative inquiry, and responding to questions and comments from the group. It is important that at this stage potential inquiry group members understand the logic of the inquiry method and also the personal and emotional investment that needs to be made if the inquiry is to be truly transformational. One approach is to talk through different phases of the inquiry cycle, emphasizing the different kinds of knowing that are primary at each stage, and emphasizing that the quality of the inquiry comes from the quality of engagement that group members have with the issues and their willingness to be experimental in their practices. It can be helpful to give a ten-minute talk, and then invite people to chat in pairs for a few minutes to clarify their questions before opening a general discussion. In terms of the extended epistemology we described earlier, this will give people an opportunity to draw on their tacit experiential knowing, and articulate this through a narrative (presentational knowing) which will contribute to the articulation of questions and issues that people want to address (propositional knowing). While clarity at this stage is important, one must also realize that co-operative inquiry, as an experiential process, can only be fully learned through engagement – there are important tacit learnings that take place as people enter the cycles of action and reflection, and as the group develops as a community of inquiry.

This introductory meeting needs also to attend to the inquiry topic proposed in order to generate at least an initial agreement as to the focus. Usually the initiating facilitator has done some preparatory work: they may be fired up themselves with concern for some issues, have had preliminary conversations with potential inquiry participants, and by proposing a set of questions or an arena for inquiry be playing a valuable role in initiating and focusing attention. It is important that the potential inquiry topic is put forward with clarity as an attractive and exciting venture; it is also important that a dialogue is initiated in which the initiator's vision can be explored and amended so that it becomes more generally owned and genuinely adopted by those who will join the inquiry. Geoff Mead was clear that:

> Improving the quality of leadership is a crucial issue for the police service. Learning *about* theories of leadership is not enough. What really matters is for each of us to understand and improve our own unique practice as leaders. (Mead, 2002: 191)

He therefore initiated a series of briefing meetings:

> designed to help people make a positive decision to opt in to the action inquiry or to decide, without any stigma, that it was not for them. The underlying principle was that of voluntary, informed self-selection. I spoke a little about the rationale for offering this opportunity to focus on leadership and said something about the participative and democratic ethos of action inquiry. I talked about the possibility of transformative learning and asked people to decide if they wanted to take part using their head (Do you have enough information? Does it make *sense* for you to do it?), heart (Are you intrigued, curious, drawn? Does it *feel* right for you to do it?), and will (Are you able and willing to meet the commitment? Do you really *want* to do it?). (Mead, 2002: 196)

This early process of clarifying the inquiry focus, so that the group in time meets with a clear and agreed sense of its own purpose, is a crucial stage in the establishment of an inquiry group. It is not to be rushed. Experience suggests that at least two pre-meetings, as well as informal conversations, are necessary.

The *organizational needs* of the inquiry group must also be met in these early meetings, and again these overlap with the emotional needs of nurturing the group into being, since people will feel more comfortable if they know they can meet the demands such as time and money. A first introductory meeting is often so fully engaged with discussions of method and topic that the organizational details can only be touched on, to be re-visited at a second meeting. The most significant decision usually concerns how often the group should meet and for what period of time. Ideally, the group will need enough time in meeting together at the beginning to fully clarify the topic area and details of inquiry method; enough time during the main body of the inquiry to thoroughly reflect on the information and experiences gathered; and enough time at the end to draw to some conclusion and agree about any writing or other reporting that is desired – and in addition enough time to maintain a healthy group process through social activities (eating together, going for walks, are common practices) and more formal group review sessions. Similarly, the group needs sufficient time between meetings for members to try out and observe their own and each other's behaviour, to gather experience with a thoroughness which matches the complexity of the inquiry topic.

In practice, these decisions are made pragmatically, not on the basis of what is perfect but on what is good enough under the circumstances and for the task at hand. A substantial amount of work can be accomplished in a series of 6–8 half-day meetings, but more time is desirable. As with all aspects of co-operative inquiry, the issue is not one of getting it right, because every decision has its own consequences; rather, it is a matter of being clear about the choices that are made, and their consequences for the quality of inquiry. So if a relatively small amount of time is available, it is probably better to be modest in the aims of the inquiry group, and to keep the group small, remembering always that the purpose of co-operative inquiry is to generate information and understanding that are capable of transforming action rather than generating valid but impersonal and abstract understanding on a large scale.

In practice, these decisions are usually made on a 'propose and consult' basis: the initiator, with some sense of what is required from the inquiry topic itself, may propose to the group a number of different formats for meeting, and from the group's reaction to these will come to a decision which best approximates a consensus:

The inquiry exploring the theory and practice of holistic medicine met for two extended half-day introductory meetings, agreeing then to meet for six two-day residential workshops spaced at six week intervals (see Reason, 1988).

Four young women students explored their experience in organizations entirely on the telephone as part of a university term paper (see Onyett, 1996).

Twelve facilitators and organizational consultants met to explore their practice in a combination of weekends and full half-days over two years (Reason, unpublished research diary, 1999).

Inquiries into transpersonal experience have taken place in a residential workshop over a period of a week (see Heron, 2001).

The inquiry into leadership in the police force met on eight occasions over a fifteen-month period starting and ending with a residential two-day meeting, otherwise meeting for afternoons during mid-week (see Mead, 2002).

In summary, in the introductory meetings which launch a co-operative inquiry the emotional, task and organizational needs of the group are closely intertwined. The initiating facilitator must work to establish qualities of interaction that will allow the group to grow toward a full expression of the creative cycle. This includes helping potential group members feel included in an emerging group which can meet their needs; finding a sense of purpose for the inquiry to which people can subscribe; and making organizational arrangements that enable the inquiry task to fit into people's lives. Thus the introductory meetings are both part of Phase One on the inquiry cycle, in which the inquiry questions are clarified, and an essential grounding for the whole inquiry process.

We want to emphasize the value and importance of spending time and giving careful attention to these early contracting arrangements, which is why this section on nurturing the group is substantially longer than those which follow. If you get this right (or at least 'good enough', to borrow from Winnicott), the rest will follow. We believe that more attempts at participative research fail because not enough attention is given to these early stages than for any other reason.

Cycles of Action and Reflection: Moving into Energizing

Following these initial meetings which establish the existence of the inquiry project, the group is ready to move into the inquiry proper. In terms of the major phases of the group endeavour, this means moving from a primary focus on nurturing toward greater energizing. This doesn't mean that the work of nurturing the group has been done: every meeting, almost every interaction, involves a creative cycle; and this always includes bringing the group together with a clear sense of purpose as a foundation for good work together. Throughout the life of a group the business of nurturing continues – 'Who is feeling left out?', 'Who might be feeling oppressed?', 'Are we clear about our purposes?' In particular, the first full meeting will probably be longer than subsequent ones and it may be the first occasion when the whole group is assembled: it is worth spending good time on deepening the sense of mutual knowing and discussing in more detail the dimensions of the inquiry task.

However, if the group remains in a nurturing mode, the task of inquiry doesn't get done (and the group will be at risk of smothering itself in destructive nurturing mode). The key task need is for the group to establish cycles of action and reflection since this is the major vehicle for moving the inquiry forward. This research cycling carries a fundamental rhythm of learning through which group members deepen their engagement with the inquiry, open themselves to more subtle understandings, engage with previously unsuspected aspects of the inquiry task, and so on. The research cycling, moving through the four ways of knowing described above, complements the creative group cycle.

A significant chunk of time at the first full meeting of the group is usually taken up in discussing in detail the basic ideas on which the inquiry will be founded, converting the sense of joint purpose into a practical task which can be accomplished (Phase One of the inquiry cycle). This may involve sharing experiences, concerns, hopes and fears so that group members raise their awareness and establish a sense of solidarity about what questions are important (Douglas, 2002); more formally, the group may establish a model, or a set of questions, to guide the inquiry:

The holistic medicine group, established to explore the theory and practice of holistic medicine in the NHS, spent much of its first meeting with members in small groups reflecting on their practice as doctors, and drawing from this experience themes which defined the nature of holistic practice. By the end of the weekend a tentative five-part model of holistic practice had been developed which was to guide the rest of the inquiry. (see Reason, 1988)

These ideas then need to be translated into plans for practical actions (propositional to practical knowing) which will form the basis of members' activities while away from the group. Some groups will simply agree to carefully notice aspects of their experience that fall within the scope of the inquiry:

We ended with an agreement that the time until the [next] session would be an 'exploratory' cycle, rather than taking one if the themes discussed and working solely with that. We talked about today's session as being an 'awareness-raising' one and the coming six weeks as time to mull over, digest and notice more awarely. I encouraged an already present sense of not wanting to rush the process. I believe in order for our questions to be meaningful, we have to give ourselves time to find them and give them space to grow. (McArdle, 2002: 185)

On the other hand, it may be appropriate to start more systematically:

The Hospital Group focused on a specific bureaucratic procedure to investigate differences of practice. The document chosen was a form that had to be signed by a potential service user, to give consent for the social worker to contact third parties to seek information about the user. Consent was seen by the authority as good practice in that it reflected partnership. Social workers in the Hospital Group were concerned that requesting a signature was a threatening practice for some people. When they felt that to be the case, they did not ask for a signature, even though they knew they *ought* to ...The group devised a technique of investigation and recording. Every time one of the forms *should* have been completed, participants recorded the reason why they did or did not ask service users to sign the form. In effect, they were required to justify their actions, both to themselves and to their peers in the co-operative inquiry group. (Baldwin, 2002: 290)

The holistic medicine group brainstormed ways in which each dimension of the five-part model could be applied in practice and how records of experience could be kept. Each doctor chose activities that were of greatest relevance to themselves and contracted with the rest of the group to study these (see Reason, 1988).

It may be appropriate for all members of the group to undertake the same activity, or for each to choose their own idiosyncratic path of inquiry. Whichever way, cycles of action and reflection are established. Group members leave the group with more or less specific plans: they may agree to some very specific activities, as with the social work group, or more generally to observe particular aspects of experience; they may choose to experiment with novel activities, or to deepen their understanding of their everyday practice. They may record their experience through diaries, audio or video recordings, or mutual observation; they may choose to collect quantitative data where relevant. After the agreed period, the group reassembles to reflect on the experiences, to revise and develop their propositional understandings, and to enter a second cycle:

We found that the simple act of sharing our stories, telling each other how we had been getting on with our inquiries, was enormously powerful – both to deepen the relationships between us and as a way of holding ourselves and each other to account. We quickly got into the habit of tape-recording our sessions and sending copies of relevant sections of the tapes to individuals to aid further reflection. Most sessions began with an extended 'check in' of this sort and then followed whatever themes emerged. On one occasion, following a 'spin-off' meeting arranged by several women members of the group, this lead to a fascinating exploration of gender and leadership. We learned to trust the process of action inquiry and that, in an organisational setting at least, it needs to be sustained by careful cultivation and lots of energy. (Mead, 2002: 200)

Some group members will not find it easy to enter this inquiry cycle. They may enjoy the group interaction, enter fully into the discussions about the inquiry, but be unwilling to commit in practice. Others may rush off into new activity without giving sufficient attention to the reflective side of the inquiry. The inquiry facilitator has a crucial role to play here in initiating people into the iteration of action and reflection and helping people understand the power of the research cycle.

Heron (1996a) suggests that inquiry groups need to draw on both Apollonian and Dionysian qualities in their research cycling. Apollonian inquiry is planned, ordered and rational, seeking quality through systematic search: models are developed and put in to practice; experiences are systematically recorded; different forms of presentation are regularly used. Dionysian inquiry is passionate and spontaneous, seeking quality through imagination and synchronicity: the group engages in the activity that emerges in the moment, rather than planning action; space is cleared for the unexpected to emerge; more attention is paid to dreams and imagery than to careful theory building; and so on. Apollonian inquiry carries the benefits of systematic order, while Dionysian carries the possibility of stretching the limits through play. To the extent that co-inquirers can embrace both Apollo and Dionysus in their inquiry cycling, they are able to develop diverse and rich connections with each other and with their experience.

Research cycling builds the energetic engagement of the group with its inquiry task and with each other, and thus meets the *emotional needs* of the group as it moves into energizing. As the group adventures into deeper exploration of the inquiry topic, to the extent that nurturing has built a safe container, members will become more deeply bonded and more open to conflict and difference. Deep and lasting friendships have started in inquiry groups; and relationships which are already stressed may fracture. When conflict arises between members, the group needs to find a way of working through, rather than ignoring or burying, differences, and different members will be able to offer skills of mediation, bridge-building, confrontation, and soothing hurt feelings. The deepening engagement with the inquiry task may itself raise anxieties, for as people start to question their taken-for-granted assumptions and to try out new forms of behaviour they can disturb old patterns of defence and unacknowledged distress may seriously distort inquiry. Inquiry groups will need to find some way to draw the anxieties which arise from both these sources into awareness and resolve them – one of the best ways of doing this is to allow group process time in every meeting for such issues to be raised and explored.

The *organizing needs* of the group often revolve around maintaining the schedule of meeting, and within the meetings agreeing together how much time should be devoted to different activities. Typically the structure for a meeting will be planned collaboratively, with different members taking increasing responsibility for leading different aspects. As the inquiry progresses, questions arise as to how best to complete the inquiry task, questions which often concern the validity and quality of inquiry. John Heron has explored the theoretical and practical aspects of validity in co-operative inquiry in detail (Heron, 1996a) (see Box 10.2); these may helpfully be seen within the wider context of validity in action research (Bradbury and Reason, 2001; Reason, 2006). Often the initiating facilitator will introduce these validity procedures and invite the group to consider their implications for their inquiry; this may raise questions about the appropriate balance of convergent and divergent cycling, the quality of interaction within the group, the amount of attention paid to anxiety, the degree to which the group may be colluding to avoid problematic aspects of the inquiry, and so on.

Box 10.2   Inquiry skills and validity procedures

Co-operative inquiry is based on people examining their own experience and action carefully in collaboration with people who share similar concerns and interests. But, you might say, isn't it true that people can fool themselves about their experience? Isn't this why we have professional researchers who can be detached and objective? The answer to this is that certainly people can and do fool themselves, but we find that they can also develop their attention so they can look at themselves – their way of being, their intuitions and imaginings, their beliefs and actions – critically and in this way improve the quality of their claims to four-fold knowing. We call this 'critical subjectivity'; it means that we don't have to throw away our personal, living knowledge in the search for objectivity, but are able to build on it and develop it. We can cultivate a high quality and valid individual perspective on what there is, in collaboration with others who are doing the same.

We have developed a number of inquiry skills and validity procedures that can be part of a co-operative inquiry and which can help improve the quality of knowing. The skills include:

Being present and open. This skill is about empathy, resonance and attunement, being open to the meaning we give to and find in our world.

Bracketing and reframing. The skill here is holding in abeyance the classifications and constructs we impose on our perceiving, and about trying out alternative constructs for their creative capacity; we are open to reframing the defining assumptions of any context.

Radical practice and congruence. This skill means being aware, during action, of the relationship between our purposes, the frames, norms and theories we bring, our bodily practice, and the outside world. It also means being aware of any lack of congruence between these different facets of the action and adjusting them accordingly.

Non-attachment and meta-intentionality. This is the knack of not investing one's identity and emotional security in an action, while remaining fully purposive and committed to it.

Emotional competence. This is the ability to identify and manage emotional states in various ways. It includes keeping action free from distortion driven by the unprocessed distress and conditioning of earlier years.

The co-operative inquiry group is itself a container and a discipline within which these skills can be developed. These skills can be honed and refined if the inquiry group adopts a range of validity procedures intended to free the various forms of knowing involved in the inquiry process from the distortion of uncritical subjectivity.

Research cycling. Co-operative inquiry involves going through the four phases of inquiry several times, cycling between action and reflection, looking at experience

(Continued)

(Continued)

and practice from different angles, developing different ideas, trying different ways of behaving.

Divergence and convergence. Research cycling can be convergent, in which case the co-researchers look several times at the same issue, maybe looking each time in more detail; or it can be divergent, as co-researchers decide to look at different issues on successive cycles. Many variations of convergence and divergence are possible in the course of an inquiry. It is up to each group to determine the appropriate balance for their work.

Authentic collaboration. Since intersubjective dialogue is a key component in refining the forms of knowing, it is important that the inquiry group develops an authentic form of collaboration. The inquiry will not be truly co-operative if one or two people dominate the group, or if some voices are left out altogether.

Challenging consensus collusion. This can be done with a simple procedure which authorizes any inquirer at any time to adopt formally the role of devil's advocate in order to question the group as to whether any form of collusion is afoot.

Managing distress. The group adopts some regular method for surfacing and processing repressed distress, which may get unawarely projected out, distorting thought, perception and action within the inquiry.

Reflection and action. Since inquiry process depends on alternating phases of action and reflection, it is important to find an appropriate balance, so that there is neither too much reflection on too little experience, which is armchair theorizing, nor too little reflection on too much experience, which is mere activism. Each inquiry group needs to find its own balance between action and reflection.

Chaos and order. If a group is open, adventurous and innovative, putting all at risk to reach out for the truth beyond fear and collusion, then, once the inquiry is well under way, divergence of thought and expression may descend into confusion, uncertainty, ambiguity, disorder and tension. A group needs to be prepared for chaos, tolerate it, and wait until there is a real sense of creative resolution.

(Adapted from Heron and Reason, 2001: 184)

Thus, in the major working phase of a creative co-operative inquiry, group members will continue to pay attention to nurturing each other and the group, while more attention is given to developing energetic cycles of inquiry. The task of the inquiry becomes figural, but it is nevertheless important to maintain attention for the continued health and authenticity of group interaction.

The Creative Peak

Randall and Southgate suggest that the peak is an important aspect of the creative group process, a moment when the 'living labour cycle' reaches a particular point of task accomplishment. In a co-operative inquiry group, which may be extended over weeks or months, there may be many 'mini-peaks' and if the group is successful there is likely to be an overall sense of accomplishment rather than a sharply defined moment in time. However, such moments do occur, particularly when members bring stories from the lives which show how the group is transforming their experience and practice.

Relaxing, Appreciating and Completing

Randall and Southgate call the third phase of the creative group 'relaxing', which in emotional terms means stepping back from the task, celebrating and appreciating achievements; in organizational terms, it means tying up loose ends; and in task terms, adding the final touches to group activities that move it to completion. Relaxing in this sense is an active, energetic engagement, different in quality from the feeling of 'getting out of the room and down to the pub' which so often characterizes our group experience.

We have also found that many groups express the emotional side of relaxing by choosing to give time to social activities – eating together, maybe going for walks – which provide a contrast to the intensity of inquiry and continue to build and deepen relationships:

> After this first [midwives inquiry group] meeting, having tea and coffee with cake or biscuits while we talked seemed such a normal thing to do. After all, people do this ordinarily at any social gathering where conversation is to be the primary activity. Food and fluid as a 'social lubricant' made sense for subsequent meetings as participants were in the middle of working days and their bodies needed nourishment to keep going. (Barrett and Taylor, 2002: 242)

The organizational side of relaxing often involves keeping the group's records in good order, transcribing tapes of meetings, keeping flip chart records together, providing summary statements of what has happened in meetings, and so on. This may be undertaken by each person looking after their individual records, or by one or more people taking care of this for the group:

> I found that it took a considerable amount of energy and attention to hold the whole process together. Although we shared the tasks of arranging venues and of 'rounding people up' for meetings, a good deal of the work came my way – from negotiating a budget to cover our costs for the year, to writing innumerable letters keeping members in touch with developments and making sure that those who could not get to particular meetings were kept in the picture. (Mead, 2002: 199–200)

The task requirement of the relaxing phase involves doing whatever is required to complete the inquiry, which often centres around how the learning from the project will be written or otherwise reported to a wider audience. Sometimes groups attempt to write collaboratively, but more often one person or a small group does the actual writing in consultation with other group members (e.g. Maughan and Reason, 2001). It is important to agree the basis on which group members can use the material generated by the group, attending both to issues of confidentiality and ownership. A good rule of thumb is to agree that anyone may use the experience in any form they wish, so long as they include a clear statement about how the material has arisen (e.g. 'this is my account of the XYZ inquiry group; as far as I know I have represented the group's learning but I have not checked in detail with all members').

If the inquiry project has formed part of a higher degree or other formal publication that the initiator is undertaking, ensuring an authentic representation is particularly important:

Agnes Bryan and Cathy Aymer initiated and facilitated several inquiry groups of black professionals. Agnes subsequently worked with the transcripts of the groups as part of her PhD dissertation, finding immense difficulties in arriving at an authentic representation. She offered her findings to as many group members as she could, received challenging feedback and rewrote much of her text. She recorded and explored these difficulties of sense-making at length in her dissertation (see Bryan, 2000).

The relaxing phase of a creative group also involves winding down emotionally, saying farewells, dealing with unfinished business. It is always tempting, particularly if the group has been successful, to avoid finishing properly, colluding to pretend that the group will meet again (this hints at a destructive dimension to the group's life, placing hopes in a future ideal state rather than dealing with the messy present reality). So time must be given for group members to have their final say as they separate from the group – it is often helpful to have a final 'round' at which each person can say what they have taken from the group, and leave behind any resentments or unfinished business.

By Way of Comment

We have offered two ways of seeing the inquiry process: through the logic of the inquiry process, cycling through propositional, practical, experiential and presentation knowing; and through the dynamics of the creative group cycle of nurturing, energizing, peak and relaxing. Please don't try to map these two descriptions onto each other in simple ways, but rather allow the two descriptions to interact and illuminate different aspects of the overall process. In the early life of the group, when the interpersonal emphasis will be on nurturing, the group will most likely engage with the inquiry cycle in mechanical and tentative ways. As the group matures, it will be able to engage in inquiry more energetically, robustly, adapting it to members, own needs and circumstances. There is always a complex interplay between the logic of inquiry and the process of the human group, as is described in many of the accounts of co-operative inquiry (for a collection of these, see Reason, 2001).

Outcomes

If, as we argued at the beginning of this chapter, action research places a primacy on practical knowing, on localized, pragmatic, constructed practical knowings, what is the 'outcome' in terms of a research product? Are 'research reports' (in whatever form) illegitimate, misguided, epistemologically in error? Clearly not, or the accounts of co-operative inquiry processes referred to in this chapter would never have been written. But the outcome of an inquiry is far more than can be written.

The practical knowing which is the outcome of a co-operative inquiry is part of the life experience and practice of those who participated: individual experience will be unique and reflect shared experience. The inquiry will continue to live (if it is successful), and the knowledge will be passed along, in the continuing practice of participants as informed by the inquiry experience: doctors practise differently and it affects their patients, colleagues and students; black women discover more about how to thrive and it changes how they are as professionals and as mothers; police professionals see how leadership is a practice of continued learning with others; young women are empowered to speak from their experience, and so on.

So the first thing to remember about all forms of representation is not to confuse the map with the territory. The knowing (the territory) is in the experience and in the practice, and what we write or say about it is a *re-presentation*. Sometimes action research is seen – wrongly in our view – as primarily a means to develop rich qualitative data that can be put through the processes of grounded theory or some other form of sense-making; but in action research the sense-making is in the process of the inquiry, in the cycles of action and reflection, in the dialogue of the inquiry group.

Nevertheless, we may want to write. We may want to write for ourselves, first-person inquiry, to keep records, to help make sense, to review or to deepen experience. Inquiry group members keep journals, dream diaries, write stories, draw pictures, engage in all kinds of representation as part of their inquiry. We may want to write 'for us', for the inquiry group and for the community that it represents, to pull together ideas, create frameworks of understanding, communicate what it is we think we have discovered. We may want to write for an outside audience to inform, to influence, to raise questions, to entertain. In these writing projects it is important to be clear about both authorship and audience. Rather than write in the 'voice from nowhere' (Clifford and Marcus, 1986), reports from inquiry groups are clearly authored by members and directed to a particular purpose.

An Experiment in Co-operative Inquiry

The best way to learn about co-operative inquiry is to do it. The following outline experiment is intended for a group of students to use in a classroom setting to explore together the practice of co-operative inquiry. Clearly it is not possible to describe such an activity in complete detail (if it were it would no longer be inquiry!). Rather, we invite you to try the activity out in the spirit of exploring co-operative inquiry in an experiential fashion – and, of course, you may wish to design a different experiment to explore an issue of your own choice. If your class group is large, you may wish to split into smaller groups to facilitate the process.

Improving Conversations and Dialogue in the Classroom

Undergraduate courses often have seminars running alongside formal lectures, in which students are expected to participate in discussion. But these seminars are often problematic – people don't want to or don't know how to contribute, the ground rules are unclear, and often what happens is that one or two students who are prepared to speak (and often fed up with their colleagues who won't) dominate the proceedings while the seminar leader (often a relatively inexperienced graduate student) struggles to keep things going.

Phase One (Propositional knowing): Identify an aspect of your interaction as a class you would like to improve. It might be a general issue like 'Improving the quality of our dialogue in class discussion'; or maybe better something more specific to the needs of the group. See if you can identify something you really care about. Then brainstorm practical things you might do to do this and agree on one or more to try out.

Phase Two (Practical knowing): Carry on with your normal class activities, with everyone doing what they can to implement the agreement. Keep some kind of notes of experience.

Phase Three (Experiential knowing): As you do this, allow yourself to attend to the fullness of the experience, to shyness, irritations, embarrassments, angers, delights, triumphs. Notice the subtleties of experience.

Phase Four (Presentational knowing to propositional knowing): Take some time in pairs or trios to review your experience, and then discuss together what you have noticed. What do you learn from this experience that you should take into a further cycle of inquiry? How could you develop your practices of dialogue? How does what you have learned experientially relate to formal theories you are learning?

An inquiry such as this could continue through a whole semester of seminar meetings, and could focus on skills of interpersonal practice, on questions of authority, gender, power and competition, and so on.

Box 10.3 presents three examples of co-operative inquiry in action.

Box 10.3   Three good examples of co-operative inquiry

No – you DON'T know how we feel!

Gillian Chowns, a social worker engaged in palliative care with children and families, convened a group of children, each of whom had a parent dying of cancer, as a co-operative inquiry group to research the experience of these children as they saw it. Chowns chose co-operative inquiry as an approach that offered a more ethical, respectful and democratic way of working with these children, a marginalized group in the world of palliative care. The group worked together to produce a video (Lunch and Lunch, 2006) to help make findings more readily accessible, as well as being a contemporary, attractive medium for the young co-researchers (Chowns, 2006; 2008).

Leadership for a changing world

This is a programme funded by the Ford Foundation to explore innovative, under-recognized social justice leaders, with the express intention of creating insight into the nature of effective progressive leadership. As part of this programme, researchers at New York University have established six co-operative inquiry groups consisting of academic researchers and leaders of innovative social change initiatives. Each group has focused on an issue in social change leadership of particular concern: e.g. 'How do we help our community think more strategically?'; 'How do we make space for new leadership to emerge?' Initially, many of the programme participants harboured a suspicion of the research agenda, concerned that they were not really invited as co-researchers but as subjects of research. As the programme evolved over the three-year period, these concerns lessened as participants in previous groups spoke enthusiastically of their experience (Ospina et al., 2003; Yorks et al., in press 2008; see also www.nyu.edu/wagner/leadership/change/)

Dilemmas of femininity

This is a British Academy-funded project run by Sarah Riley, Kate McArdle and Ros Gill. They wanted to examine contemporary gender relations and thus contribute

(Continued)

(Continued)

to analyses which had identified what seemed to be a number of paradoxes. For example, we are told that young women have 'never had it so good' and that they are excelling both at school and in the workplace, and indeed leaving their male peers behind. Yet, at precisely the same moment we have witnessed a dramatic and deliberate re-sexualization of women's bodies in the media, a mainstreaming and 'respectabilization' of pornography in public space and corporate culture, and a level of scrutiny of women's bodies and appearance that is historically and culturally unprecedented. Parity between men and women has been largely accepted as a value, and important steps have been made towards its achievement, yet a significant pay gap remains, there is still no easy or straightforward way of combining paid work and parenthood, and rates of mental distress, eating disorders and teenage pregnancy remain disturbingly high in the UK. Sarah, Kate and Ros invited five other female academics – all of whom had experience of doing feminist research, but who were at various points in their academic career – to explore this contradictory social landscape, through consideration of the 'dilemmas of femininity'. At the time of writing the team have met once and so are engaging in the forming of the group, nurturing relations within the group and exploring some of their experiential knowing. For example, at the end of the first session each member of the team gave themselves a task to do before the next meeting. This task originated out of the day's discussions and activities and was different for each person. Sarah's task, for example, was to notice when she felt a dilemma or contradictory pull in relation to her female identity.

ELEVEN

Demonstrating Validity in Qualitative Psychology

Lucy Yardley

The validity of research corresponds to the degree to which it is accepted as sound, legitimate and authoritative by people with an interest in research findings. This will include other researchers (in particular, those who must judge its worth for the purposes of examination or approval for funding or publication), policy-makers and practitioners who use the research, and the lay public. This chapter first discusses why there is a need to establish criteria for evaluating the validity of qualitative research, and considers why establishing the validity of research in qualitative psychology can be problematic. A variety of specific methods that can be used to increase and demonstrate the validity of qualitative research is described. Finally, a framework for evaluating the validity of qualitative psychology studies is presented, illustrated by examples of good and bad practice. The framework does not prescribe exactly what you should do in order to show that your study is valid, since each study is different and can be validated in different ways. Nevertheless, if you wish to claim that your research is valid, you may find it helpful to show that, in its own way, your study meets each of the key criteria in the framework.

Can We Judge the Validity of Qualitative Research?

Evaluating the validity of research involves making a judgement about how well the research has been carried out, and whether the findings can be regarded as trustworthy and useful. Such judgements are never easy, but can pose particular problems for qualitative research.

Differing perspectives on validity

Most qualitative researchers believe that different people have different, equally valid perspectives on 'reality', which are shaped by their context, culture and activities. But if there is no one 'true' perspective on reality, then which perspective should be used to evaluate the validity of a study? One solution to this problem might be to accept all researchers' perspectives as equally valid and useful. Some years ago I attended a qualitative research conference that appeared to have been based on this principle – it seemed as if the organizers must have accepted all the studies that were submitted for presentation. As a result, they accepted so many papers that they had to be presented in fourteen parallel sessions. To fit all these simultaneous talks into one venue there were talks given in every room, and even in the corridors between rooms! No-one was happy with this solution, since there were so many talks that only a few people attended each one, and there was no way for people to work out which of the talks would be worth going to. From this experience I concluded that it is necessary to make judgements about the value of qualitative research. Indeed, we all constantly make these judgements individually and informally: for example, when we decide whether a talk was 'worth going to' – whether it was convincing, or at least interesting or thought-provoking.

An alternative solution to the problem that we each have different perspectives on whether a study is 'really' valid is to try to agree on common criteria that can be used to judge the validity of qualitative research. However, it is not easy to identify criteria that can be applied to all qualitative studies, since there are numerous different approaches to qualitative research, each based on different assumptions and employing quite different procedures. For example, a valid grounded theory study should theoretically sample a wide enough range of people to be able to develop a detailed description and explanation of the study topic, based on an analysis of all the data obtained (see Chapter 5). In contrast, a valid discourse analysis (see Chapter 8) might be based on an in-depth analysis of just a few illuminating text excerpts. Within each broad approach, such as 'discourse analysis', there are then further differences in the methods thought to be appropriate and valid. For instance, in discursive psychology (as in conversation analysis), it is often considered important to study naturally occurring dialogue and use the way that speakers respond to each 'turn' in the conversation as one way of validating the analysis of the social and linguistic functions of what the previous speaker said. In a valid Foucauldian discourse analysis there is no imperative to use naturally occurring dialogue as data, but it is important to analyse the wider socio-cultural implications of the talk.

Using Validity Criteria from Quantitative Research

A further problem in qualitative psychology is that quantitative methods have historically been dominant within the discipline, and so there is a tendency for psychologists to assume that the criteria for validity that are relevant to quantitative studies can also be applied to qualitative studies. There are three criteria, in particular, that are often mistakenly applied to qualitative research: objectivity, reliability and (statistical) generalizability. The reasons why these criteria are relevant to most quantitative studies, but are inappropriate for most qualitative studies, are explained below (for further explanation, see Yardley, 1997b).

Most quantitative researchers seek to minimize sources of error in their data, in order to obtain as far as possible an accurate, unbiased observation of reality. Since it is known that the researcher can potentially influence the data and analysis, and this influence is seen as 'bias' or 'error', a variety of methods is used to try to reduce the influence of the researcher. These include impersonal administration of standardized questionnaires so that the researcher cannot influence how questions are asked, and statistical analysis of numerical measures to reduce the extent to which data can be shaped by the researcher's interpretation. However, most qualitative researchers believe that the researcher *inevitably* influences the production of knowledge, by formulating a research question, choosing particular measures and analyses, and interpreting findings. Moreover, attempting to eliminate the influence of the researcher would make it very difficult to retain the benefits of qualitative research, such as disclosure of subjective experiences in an in-depth interview, or insightful analysis of the hidden or oppressed meanings in talk. Consequently, rather than trying to eliminate the influence of the researcher by rigidly controlling the research process, qualitative researchers generally seek to maximize the benefits of engaging actively with the participants in the study. This means allowing the participants to influence the topic and data (for example, by using open-ended questions), while also acknowledging and analysing how the researcher may have influenced the findings of research (see section on 'coherence and transparency' below).

The aim of most quantitative research is to identify predictable causal relationships that can be observed or 'replicated' in different contexts. The reliability of measurements is therefore another important criterion for validity in quantitative research, since it is only possible to replicate a finding if the measurements used give the same results when administered by and to different people at different times. Once again, error is eliminated as far as possible through standardization of the administration and analysis of measures. But whereas quantitative researchers tend to focus on generalizable laws, qualitative researchers are often interested in the effects of context and individual differences. These are the very effects that are excluded as 'error variance' in quantitative research. For example, if you ask someone how bad their pain is, they may give a different answer depending on whether you are their employer, doctor or family member. This will cause problems if you were asking the question in order to test the effect of a treatment (in which case you need a reliable measure), but could provide very interesting insights if you want to understand the meaning and function of talk about pain in different contexts. In practice, when asked to talk about a topic, people very rarely produce 'reliable' responses; instead, they frequently offer a combination of rather different, sometimes contradictory, perspectives. This complexity in people's expressed views is suppressed and ignored when they are obliged to tick just one response to a questionnaire.

Although qualitative researchers are interested in individual differences and contextual variation, both quantitative and qualitative researchers hope that their findings will be generalizable. There would be little point in doing research if every situation was totally unique, and the findings in one study had no relevance to any other situation! Quantitative researchers usually try to ensure that their findings can be generalized from a sample to a wider population by carrying out their research on a representative random sample of the target population. However, it is seldom practical to gather and analyse in depth qualitative data from a large enough sample to be statistically representative of a wider population. In any case, qualitative researchers are typically more interested in examining subtle interactive processes occurring in particular contexts than making generalizations about population trends, and so they tend to intensively study a relatively small number of carefully selected individuals or cases. Qualitative researchers therefore aspire to what can be called 'theoretical', 'vertical' or 'logical' rather than statistical generalizations of their findings (Johnson, 1997). This means that they would not expect their findings to be exactly replicated in any other sample or context, but would hope that the insights they derived from studying one context would prove useful in other contexts that had similarities. Since contexts can share some features even if others are quite dissimilar, generalizability in qualitative research is potentially wide-ranging and flexible.

Developing Validity Criteria for Qualitative Research

Despite the difficulty of developing criteria for validity that are applicable to all types of qualitative research, there are many reasons why it is necessary to attempt to find some common criteria. Since qualitative methods have not been widely used within psychology in the past, it is essential for qualitative researchers to be able to show that their studies are sound and rigorous, and yield findings that are as valuable as those from quantitative research. Anyone, including lay people and journalists, can interview people and report what they have said, and so, if qualitative researchers are to demonstrate the value of their research, they need to show that their studies do more than this. The process of agreeing criteria for judging the value of qualitative research is useful in itself, because it involves critically reflecting on how qualitative research should be carried out, and what the essential ingredients of good qualitative research are. Publishing these criteria is an important way of disseminating best practice and improving standards. Published criteria can help novice researchers to carry out their research in a way that avoids the shortcomings and mistakes that more experienced researchers have learned to anticipate. Finally, if studies can demonstrate that they meet criteria that have been agreed and accepted by qualitative experts, this can be used as an assurance of their quality by people who are not qualitative experts. For example, policy-makers, research funders and journal editors are often not expert in qualitative methods but need to be able to make important decisions about whether qualitative studies are flawed, acceptable or outstanding.

These motives have led to the development and publication of a number of guidelines for validity criteria that qualitative studies should meet, both within qualitative psychology (e.g. Elliott, Fischer and Rennie, 1999; Henwood and Pidegon, 1992; Stiles, 1993; Yardley, 2000) and in health and social research (e.g. Malterud, 2001; Spencer et al., 2003). These guidelines are extremely useful as a set of suggestions for good practice, but the expert qualitative researchers who have produced these guidelines emphasize that they should not be used as a set of rigid rules for judging qualitative research. Simply following guidelines cannot guarantee good research; qualitative research is not simply a descriptive science but also relies on the capacity to evoke imaginative experience and reveal new meanings (Eisner, 2003) – and this core quality is not easily captured by check-list criteria. Moreover, qualitative research is constantly evolving, and it is important for qualitative researchers to be able to be flexible and creative in the way they carry out their research, provided that they can justify their departure from conventions for good practice. The framework for considering the validity of qualitative studies given later in this chapter therefore outlines the quality issues that need to be addressed, but does not restrict the ways in which they can be addressed. However, qualitative researchers have developed a range of procedures that can be used to enhance the validity of their research, and these are described in the next section.

Procedures for Enhancing Validity

The procedures described below will not be suitable for every qualitative study, but they provide a 'toolbox' from which you can select a procedure for enhancing validity that will be suitable for your study. Many of these procedures are sufficiently flexible that they can be adapted for use with a wide range of methodological approaches. However, they will only enhance the validity of your research if you use them thoughtfully to improve the depth, breadth and sensitivity of your analysis (see Barbour, 2001).

Triangulation

Triangulation is a term originally taken from navigation, where it refers to the practice of calculating location from three different reference points. As this metaphor implies, triangulation was initially viewed as a way of trying to corroborate the accounts of one person or group using the accounts of others. For example, to confirm a participant's description of their psychological problems as the consequence of external events, the researcher might interview members of their family. However, this approach to triangulation is inconsistent with the view of most qualitative researchers that people's perspectives may be different, but may each have validity. Triangulation is equally valuable from this point of view, but as a method of enriching understanding of a phenomenon by viewing it from different perspectives rather than converging on a single, consistent account of the phenomenon (Flick, 1992). For example, the participant might give a compelling and phenomenologically revealing account of their experience of external events as a cause of their problems, but family members might contribute useful insights into how the individual's personality and biography may have influenced their experiences of these events.

Enriching understanding through triangulation can be achieved by gathering data from different groups of people, or by gathering data at different times from the same people in a longitudinal study. It is also possible to triangulate different theories or methods (see Box 11.1) in a mixed methods study or 'composite analysis' (Yardley and Bishop, 2007). In addition, triangulating the perspectives of different researchers can enrich the analysis (see next section).

Box 11.1   Triangulating research on older people's attitudes to falls prevention

Research question: what do older people think of existing advice on falls prevention?
Method: Focus groups and interviews carried out with 66 people aged 61 to 94, purposively sampled to ensure a wide range of physical functioning.
Findings: Most participants (even those over 75 who have fallen) reject falls prevention as only relevant to older, frail people, and believe it means restricting activity to avoid falling (Yardley, Donovan-Hall et al., 2006).

Research question: what motivates older people to take part in falls prevention programmes based on strength and balance training?
Method: Interviewed 69 people aged 68 to 97, purposively sampled from six countries to represent a range of experience of different programmes, including people who had refused or dropped out of programmes.
Findings: Key motivations to take part were improving physical functioning to maintain independence, general health benefits and enjoyment (Yardley, Bishop et al., 2006).

Research question: Is intention to carry out strength and balance training predicted by threat appraisal (fear of falling) or coping appraisal (perceived benefits of programme)?
Method: 558 people completed questionnaires assessing threat and coping appraisal, including beliefs about strength and balance training expressed in interview study.
Findings: Structural equation modelling showed that intention to carry out strength and balance training was much more strongly related to coping

---

(Continued)

appraisal than threat appraisal, including the perceived benefits identified in the interview study (Yardley et al., 2007).

Composite analysis: The first qualitative study revealed the negative meanings that older people associated with 'falls prevention', the second qualitative study identified positive motivations that could promote uptake of falls prevention programmes, and the quantitative study confirmed that intended uptake was motivated by these perceived benefits. The PRevention Of FAlls Network Europe (www.profane.eu.org) and Help the Aged concluded from integrating these findings that to persuade older people to undertake falls prevention we need to emphasize the immediate positive benefits of strength and balance training for functioning, independence, enjoyment and health. Promoting this as 'falls prevention' may be unhelpful since people are reluctant to consider themselves as so old and frail that they need to take precautions to avoid falling.

Comparing Researchers' Coding

In qualitative research, the purpose of comparing the coding of two or more researchers is usually to triangulate their perspectives. This ensures that the analysis is not confined to one perspective, and makes sense to other people. For example, one researcher might code the data, but discuss the emerging codes in repeated meetings with other members of the research team who had read the transcripts. These discussions could help to identify potential themes in the data that may not yet have been captured by the codes, and highlight clarifications or modifications of codes that might be needed in order to increase the consistency and coherence of the analysis. This kind of inter-rater comparison is suitable for corroboration of complex and subtle coding schemes.

Sometimes a more formal procedure is used, whereby more than one researcher codes the data, and their codes are compared to determine 'inter-rater reliability' (Boyatzis, 1998). The most stringent form of inter-rater reliability requires two researchers to code the data independently. The level of agreement between their codes is then calculated by Cohen's Kappa. A Kappa of ≥.80 indicates a very good level of agreement, indicating that the data coding is reliable. This kind of inter-rater reliability calculation is appropriate if the codes are to be used for a quantitative analysis – for example, to compare the frequency of their occurrence in two groups. In this situation, coding reliability provides an assurance that the occurrence of codes has been recorded in a systematic manner that can be replicated by a second coder. However, this kind of analysis of qualitative data is unusual (except in content analysis), requires samples that are large enough to meet the requirements for statistical analysis, and is only suitable for simple codes that can be strictly defined and easily identified.

Participant Feedback

Participant feedback, sometimes known as 'respondent validation', is obtained by asking participants to comment on the analysis (Silverman, 1993). This is a valuable way of engaging participants in the research and ensuring that their views are not misrepresented, but it is not always either feasible or appropriate. Offering participants an opportunity to express their viewpoint is often an important aim of qualitative research, but most analyses go beyond this. Analyses may highlight, for example, differences and contradictions between participants' perspectives, or the suppressed meanings and functions of talk. The theories and methods these analyses draw on may be difficult for lay people to understand. Before seeking participant feedback it is therefore important to consider whether participants will be able to relate to the analysis, and whether feedback from participants can be used constructively.

Disconfirming Case Analysis

Qualitative analysis typically consists of an inductive process of identifying themes and patterns within the data. This process is inevitably influenced by the assumptions, interests and aims of the researcher. Once a set of themes and patterns have been identified, it can therefore be very useful to engage in the complementary process of seeking 'disconfirming instances', also known as 'deviant cases' or 'negative cases'. This can be considered as the qualitative equivalent of testing your emerging hypothesis, and involves systematically searching for data that does *not* fit the themes or patterns that have been identified (Creswell, 1998; Pope and Mays, 1995).

Disconfirming cases should be paid careful attention and reported whenever possible. Reporting disconfirming cases reassures the reader that you have taken into account and presented all the data, rather than just selecting the parts that fit with your viewpoint. Disconfirming cases can also provide an indication of the limits of the generalizability of the analysis. To illustrate, imagine that you have analysed the data from participants who volunteered to take part in a study of the effects of exercise. The overwhelmingly dominant themes from your interviewees consist of descriptions of how exercise makes them feel happier, healthier and more in control of their lives. However, just two people describe how exercise made them feel ill and inadequate. These two 'disconfirming cases' are an important indication that exercise may not always have positive effects. Indeed, these two cases in your sample might represent a much larger population of people who dislike exercise, and may therefore not have wanted to take part in a study of exercise. These cases could therefore suggest a valuable next step for your research – to explore the circumstances in which people do or do not have positive experiences of exercise.

A Paper Trail

While researchers are trusted to prepare reports that accurately reflect the data they gathered, it should always be possible to provide evidence linking the raw data to the final report. In qualitative research this can be done by keeping what has been called a 'paper trail' of the analysis (Flick, 1998) – although these days the 'paper trail' can be entirely electronic! If an audit of the analysis was carried out, the paper trail should allow the auditor to retrace all the stages of the analysis, based on a complete set of coded transcripts, together with a description of the development of the codes and interpretations (with records of research questions, memos, notes and diagrams detailing the reasoning behind analytic decisions, together with interim and final definitions of the codes). The paper trail cannot be published, but should be available to other researchers to examine if they want to look closely into your analysis. Availability of a paper trail serves to reassure others that you have completed and documented your study carefully and professionally.

Demonstrating the Validity of Qualitative Research

As the previous sections have explained, it can be useful to be able to refer to published criteria for demonstrating that qualitative research is valid, provided that these criteria are sufficiently flexible to be applied to a wide range of different methods and approaches. The framework outlined below (originally published in Yardley, 2000) sets out a core set of broad principles, summarized in Box 11.2, that are applicable to diverse types of qualitative research – indeed, although they were developed for qualitative research, they can even be applied to quantitative research. Some illustrations of different ways in which each of these principles might be implemented in practice are given below, and in Box 11.3. Drawing on many years of experience as a supervisor, reviewer and editor, I also provide some illustrations of common pitfalls in qualitative research to be avoided!

Box 11.2 Core principles for evaluating the validity of qualitative psychology

Sensitivity to context

- relevant theoretical and empirical literature
- socio-cultural setting
- participants' perspectives

(Continued)

(Continued)

- ethical issues
- empirical data

Commitment and rigour

- thorough data collection
- depth/breadth of analysis
- methodological competence/skill
- in-depth engagement with topic

Coherence and transparency

- clarity and power of your argument
- fit between theory and method
- transparent methods and data presentation
- reflexivity

Impact and importance

- practical/applied
- theoretical
- socio-cultural

Box 11.3   Similar hypothetical studies that demonstrate or lack features of validity

	Study lacks features of validity	Study demonstrates features of validity
Sensitivity to the context of existing theory and research in the development of a research topic	Study sets out to simply 'explore women's experiences of postnatal depression', ignoring relevant theory (e.g. feminist) and previous qualitative studies of experiences of maternity and depression in women.	Study clarifies what is already known from theory and research, formulates a specific research question that has not been addressed: 'How does the family context influence women's experiences following childbirth?'

(Continued)

Sensitivity to how the perspective and position of participants may influence whether they feel able to take part and express themselves freely	Senior male professional carries out interviews with women with postnatal depression in a clinic setting, ignoring the possibility that they may feel less able to express their feelings to a man, and may be intimidated and distressed by a clinical environment.	Participants are given the choice of taking part in focus groups (allowing solidarity with other women with similar experiences) or interviews in their own home (maximizing privacy, security and accessibility), carried out by women of about their own age.
Commitment and rigour in recruitment of participants who will represent an adequate range of views relevant to the research topic	The sample comprises twelve self-selected volunteers. Most of these women are well-educated, affluent, and married.	Twelve women are purposively sampled to include married, co-habiting and single participants from affluent and socio-economically disadvantaged backgrounds.
Transparency in the analysis of data	Little description is provided of how themes were identified and no checks on their consistency are reported.	A detailed description is provided of how data were initially coded and how codes were modified through comparison of all instances and discussions between the researchers
Coherence between the qualitative design and the analysis and presentation of data	Based on a frequency count of the occurrence of codes the researcher highlights the finding that two thirds of the single women (n = 3) but only one third of married	Based on a qualitative comparison of all instances of the codes, the researchers note that there was a

(Continued)

(Continued)

	women complain of lack of social support. Strong quantitative statements of this kind are inappropriate when the sample size is so small, and the reliability of the codes is unknown.	tendency for single women to report a lack of social support. However, disconfirming instances are discussed as revealing examples of why married and co-habiting women may feel unsupported, and how single mothers may be supported by others.
Impact of the research	The researcher simply notes that the findings are compatible with existing models and research (for example, showing that single mothers feel that they have less social support).	The researchers explain how different family structures and relationships may exert positive or negative influences on the experience of maternity, suggesting questions for further research and ways of identifying and supporting women at risk of depression.

Sensitivity to Context

Whereas the value of a quantitative scientific approach lies in hypothesis testing – the isolation and manipulation of pre-defined variables that permit causal inference – a primary motivation for using qualitative methods is to allow patterns and meanings to emerge from the study that have not been strictly specified in advance. The tremendous value of this approach is that it permits the researcher to explore new topics and discover new phenomena, to analyse subtle, interacting effects of context and time, and to engage with participants to create new understandings (Camic, Rhodes and Yardley, 2003). Demonstrating that your study has this vital characteristic is therefore central to demonstrating its validity as an example of high-quality qualitative research.

There are numerous ways in which a qualitative study can be shown to be sensitive to context. An important aspect of the context of any study is the existing relevant theoretical and empirical literature. It may be valuable to draw on basic theory relating to the meanings and concepts that are studied, referring to psychological and philosophical writers who have carried out fundamental analyses of meaning. As noted above (see comments on the generalizability of qualitative research), insights from qualitative research potentially have theoretical relevance to somewhat different contexts. Consequently, there is almost always some previous relevant qualitative research. For example, if you are carrying out research into children's feelings about taking medication for attention deficit hyperactivity disorder, then relevant qualitative research could include studies of children's attitudes to taking other kinds of medication, as well as studies of children and adults' attitudes to being diagnosed and treated for other mental health problems. Note that much good qualitative research is relevant to a range of disciplines, so you might find relevant studies carried out by sociologists, anthropologists and health and social care professionals. Familiarity with the existing literature is necessary in order to formulate a research question that addresses gaps in our current understanding, rather than re-'discovering' what is already known, and can provide comparisons and explanations that may help you interpret your findings.

Good qualitative research must show that it is sensitive to the perspective and socio-cultural context of participants. The way in which researchers engage with participants can have ethical implications as well as potentially influencing the data. At the design stage this often means considering the possible impact on participants of the characteristics of the researcher(s) and the setting in which the research is carried out. For example, if participants are interviewed by someone they see as linked with those in authority (for example, with the school that their child attends) then they may defer to the apparent expertise of the interviewer by expressing only socially acceptable views rather than their personal experiences, and may also be reluctant to disclose information that could lead to negative perceptions of their child. Another crucial way in which the design of qualitative research can demonstrate sensitivity to participants' perspectives is by the construction of open-ended questions that will encourage participants to respond freely and talk about what is important to them, rather than being constrained by the preoccupations of the researcher (Wilkinson et al., 2004).

At the analysis stage, sensitivity to the position and socio-cultural context of participants may involve consideration of the reasons why particular views may or may not be expressed, and the ways in which views are expressed. Awareness of insights from discourse analysis can be helpful in this respect, even if no discourse analysis is undertaken in the study. Most importantly, the analysis must show sensitivity to the data. This involves demonstrating that the analysis did not simply impose the researcher's categories or meanings on the data, but was open to alternative interpretations and recognized complexities and inconsistencies in the participants' talk.

Commitment and Rigour

As noted in the first section of this chapter, in order to claim that your study has validity as research you cannot simply talk to a few people and present some of what they have said – you need to show that you have carried out an analysis that has sufficient breadth and/or depth to deliver additional insight into the topic researched. The ways in which you do this will be closely linked to the purpose of your study (see next section on 'coherence'). For example, if your aim is to achieve a thorough description of a phenomenon which will have relevance to many different contexts then you will need to show that you have recruited a sufficiently broad range of people to have sampled many of the different perspectives that are likely to be encountered. However, if your aim is to study a rare but theoretically important phenomenon, then you need instead to show how and why you have carefully selected one or more individuals that have particular relevance to your research question.

The selection of your sample may be less important than the depth and insight of your analysis – which are often linked to its sensitivity to context. You may achieve unique insights because of the theoretical sophistication of your analysis, or through an empathic understanding of participants' perspectives resulting from extensive in-depth engagement with the topic (for example, based on personal experience or prolonged participant observation). Your analysis may yield insights through the painstaking and skillful application of detailed analytical methods, such as the in-depth micro-analysis of dialogue, or the systematic construction of a grounded theory.

Clearly, it is not necessary or even possible for any single study to exhibit all these qualities, and it may be useful to consider and explain which form(s) of rigour your study aims to excel in. However, a minimum quality threshold will usually be relevant even in areas where your study does not aim to demonstrate excellence. Even if the primary value of your analysis lies in the imaginative depth of your interpretation, you still need to show that you had a reasonable justification for your selection of participants or texts to study. Similarly, however comprehensive your data collection you still need to demonstrate competence in your analysis of the data. Achieving rigour therefore demands substantial personal commitment, whether to attaining methodological skills or theoretical depth, or to engaging extensively and thoughtfully with participants or data.

Coherence and Transparency

The coherence of a study means the extent to which it makes sense as a consistent whole. This is partly determined by the clarity and power of the argument you can make for the study and the way it was carried out. The clarity and power of your argument will in turn depend on the fit between the theoretical approach adopted, the research question, the methods employed, and the interpretation of the data. In order to carry out a coherent piece of qualitative research it is therefore necessary to have a solid grounding in the methods used and their theoretical background, as this will enable you to decide what is or is not compatible with the approach you have chosen. This does not mean that qualitative studies have to follow a rigid formula – it is vital that researchers are able to be flexible and innovative. However, an in-depth understanding of why different approaches employ different procedures is needed in order to coherently select, adapt and justify the methods you employ.

Sometimes using a procedure that could enhance validity in one study may actually reduce the validity of another if it is inconsistent with the approach adopted. For example, if you have adopted an interpretive approach to your data it would usually be inconsistent to carry out strict inter-rater reliability checks and report Cohen's Kappa for your codes. This is because the purpose of calculating reliability within a realist approach is to demonstrate that the codes are independent of the perspective of the coder – but within an interpretive approach it is assumed that coding can never be objective, and so even if two people code the data the same way this simply shows that the coding manual and training process have enabled them to share one particular perspective on the data.

A common mistake made by novice qualitative researchers is to present their findings in a way that is incompatible with their method. An interpretive qualitative study cannot test hypotheses or correlations. Consequently, while it may be useful to identify differences in the views of participants with different characteristics, or associations between particular sets of views, these should not be reported as if they were firm evidence of group differences or causal relationships. Similarly, since qualitative research typically offers the researchers' interpretation of people's accounts of their experiences, it is generally inappropriate to report analyses as if they are concrete 'findings' corresponding to 'reality'. Often this is simply a question of using language precisely; rather than stating that your study 'found that women were more careful drivers than men' you could report that in your study 'more women than men described themselves as careful drivers and gave examples of cautious driving behaviour'.

Incompatibility between forms of validity relevant to different methodological approaches can pose problems for 'mixed methods' studies that combine qualitative and quantitative research. It may be difficult to find a common language that can coherently integrate quantitative findings and qualitative interpretations. For example, to report the quantitative analyses it may be necessary to treat people's responses to questionnaires as accurate measures of their beliefs, whereas the qualitative analyses may highlight the complex and contradictory meanings and functions of responses to researchers' questions. One solution to this problem is to report studies using different approaches as internally coherent parts of a 'composite analysis' (Yardley and Bishop, 2007), which triangulates the findings from studies which use methods that cannot be coherently 'mixed' (see Box 11.1).

The transparency of a report of a qualitative study refers to how well the reader can see exactly what was done, and why. A clear and coherent argument contributes to transparency, but it is also necessary to provide sufficient details of the methods used, often supported by a paper trail (see section on 'Procedures for enhancing validity'). A transparent analysis presents enough data – quotations, text excerpts, and/or tables or figures summarizing themes – to show the reader what the analytic interpretations are based on.

Since qualitative research usually assumes that the researcher will influence the study, 'reflexivity' is often an important part of the transparency of the study. Reflexivity is the term used for explicit consideration of specific ways in which it is likely that the study was influenced by the researcher. This may simply mean openly describing features of the study that may have influenced the data or interpretations (such as the researchers' background and interests). Sometimes it may be appropriate to include a reflexive analysis of how these features could have influenced the conclusions reached.

Impact and Importance

There is no point in carrying out research unless the findings have the potential to make a difference. Your study may have direct practical implications, which will be immediately useful for practitioners, policy makers, or the general community. Alternatively, the importance of your research may be entirely theoretical – it may help us to understand something better, which may in turn lead to applications that achieve practical, real-world change. Some qualitative research has had a profound socio-cultural influence, changing the way we think about the position of women in society, or the way we treat people who have psychological problems. Ultimately, the key reason for taking all the steps suggested above to show that your research is valid is so that it can have an impact. Before you embark on any piece of research it may be useful to imagine how you would answer a sceptic who accepted that your findings were based on sound methods but nevertheless asked the question 'So what?'. This question leads back to the issue of being sensitive to the context of your research – your study will have impact and importance if it builds on what we already know to take us a step further, and answer questions that matter to people and to society.

Conclusion

It might at first seem daunting to contemplate criteria for high-quality research – meeting these standards may appear challenging, especially for novice researchers. It is not always possible for practical reasons to meet some of the criteria. It may be sensible or necessary to take shortcuts, to prioritize some kinds of validity and acknowledge that it may not be feasible in the circumstances to achieve others. However, the framework outlined above is not meant to intimidate or inhibit researchers but simply to provide a set of principles that can be referred to when making decisions about how to carry out and justify your research. Published criteria represent the consensus of expert qualitative researchers regarding good practice, and so can be used to support claims that what you have done is valid. These criteria continue to evolve and to provoke debate – as do the criteria for evaluating quantitative research. Nevertheless, the existence of broad principles that we can refer to for showing that our work has integrity and value marks a new confidence that qualitative methods are now sufficiently well developed to take equal place alongside quantitative methods in psychology.

Further reading

Yardley, L. (2000) 'Dilemmas in qualitative health research', *Psychology and Health*, 15: 215–28.
This paper originally set out the principles for establishing validity outlined in this chapter, and provides many referenced examples of studies that illustrate a variety of ways in which the criteria might be met.

Elliott, R., Fischer, C. T. and Rennie, D. L. (1999) 'Evolving guidelines for publication of qualitative research studies in psychology and related fields', *British Journal of Clinical Psychology*, 38: 215–29.
Another set of guidelines published specifically for qualitative psychologists. This set and mine were developed independently at much the same time, and so it is reassuring to note the close convergence between our recommendations!

Spencer, L., Ritchie, J., Lewis, J. and Dillon, L. (2003) *Quality in Qualitative Evaluation: A Framework for Assessing Research Evidence*. Government Chief Social Researcher's Office. Accessed at www.policyhub.gov.uk/docs/a_quality_framework.pdf on 26 September 2006
This report presents an integrated set of criteria based on a review of published frameworks for validity and wide consultation with qualitative experts.

References

Aanstoos, C. (1985) 'The structure of thinking in chess', in A. Giorgi (ed.), *Phenomenology and Psychological Research*. Pittsburgh, PA: Duquesne University Press, pp. 86–117.

Allahyari, R.A. (2000) *Visions of Charity: Volunteer Workers and Moral Community*. Berkeley, CA: University of California Press.

Allport, G.W. (1961) *Pattern and Growth in Personality*. New York: Holt, Rinehart and Winston.

Allport, G.W. (1962) 'The general and the unique in psychological science', *Journal of Personality*, 30: 405–22.

Allport, G.W. (1965) *Letters from Jenny*. New York: Harcourt, Brace and World.

Arendt, H. (1998) *The Human Condition* (2nd edn). Chicago: Chicago University Press.

Arribas-Ayllon, M. and Walkerdine, V. (2008) 'Foucauldian Discourse Analysis', in C. Willig and W. Stainton Rogers (eds) *The Handbook of Qualitative Research in Psychology*. London: Sage.

Ashworth, P.D. (1973) *Aspects of the psychology of professional socialisation*, unpublished PhD thesis, University of Lancaster.

Ashworth, P.D. (1979) *Social Interaction and Consciousness*. Chichester: John Wiley and Sons, Ltd.

Ashworth, P.D. (1985) '*L'enfer, c'est les autres*: Goffman's Sartrism', *Human Studies*, 8: 97–168.

Ashworth, P.D. (1996) 'Presuppose nothing! The suspension of assumptions in phenomenological psychological methodology', *Journal of Phenomenological Psychology*, 27: 1–25.

Ashworth, P.D. (2000) *Psychology and 'Human Nature'*. Hove: Psychology Press.

Ashworth, P.D. (2006) 'Seeing oneself as a carer in the activity of caring: Attending to the lifeworld of the person with Alzheimer's disease', *International Journal of Qualitative Studies in Health and Well-being*, 4.

Ashworth, P.D. and Chung, M.C. (eds) (2006) *Phenomenology and Psychological Science: Historical and Philosophical Perspectives*. New York: Springer.

Atkinson, J.M. (1984) *Our Masters' Voices: The Language and Body Language of Politics*. London: Methuen.

Atkinson, J.M. and Heritage, J. (eds) (1984) *Structures of Social Action: Studies in Conversation Analysis*. Cambridge: Cambridge University Press.

Austin, J.L. (1962) *How to Do Things with Words*. Oxford: Clarendon Press.

Aymer, C. (2005) 'Seeking knowledge for Black cultural renewal', unpublished PhD thesis, University of Bath.

Baldwin, M. (2001) 'Working together, learning together: co-operative inquiry in the development of complex practice by teams of social workers', in P. Reason and H. Bradbury (eds), *Handbook of Action Research: Participative Inquiry and Practice*. London: Sage, pp. 287–93.

Baldwin, M. (2002) 'Co-operative Inquiry as a tool for professional development', *Systemic Practice and Action Research*, 14(6).

Bannister, D. and Fransella, F. (1971) *Inquiring Man: The Psychology of Personal Constructs*. Harmondsworth: Penguin.

Barbour, R.S. (2001) 'Checklists for improving rigour in qualitative research: a case of the tail wagging the dog', *British Medical Journal,* 322: 1115–17.

Barbour, R. and Kitzinger, J. (eds) (1999) *Developing Focus Group Research: Politics, Theory and Practice*. London: Sage.

Barrett, P.A. and Taylor, B.J. (2002) 'Beyond reflection: cake and co-operative inquiry', *Systemic Practice & Action Research*, 14: 237–48.

Bartlett, F.C. (1932) *Remembering: A Study in Experimental and Social Psychology*. Cambridge: Cambridge University Press.

Basch, C.E. (1987) 'Focus-group interviews: an underutilized research technique for improving theory and practice in health education', *Health Education Quarterly*, 154: 411–48.

Becker, B. (1999) 'Narratives of pain in later life and conventions of storytelling', *Journal of Aging Studies*, 13: 73–87.

Becker, G. (1997*) Disrupted Lives: How People Create Meaning in a Chaotic World*. Berkeley, CA: University of California Press.

Benner, P. (ed.) (1994) *Interpretive Phenomenology: Embodiment, Caring and Ethics in Health and Illness*. Thousand Oaks, CA: Sage.

Berger, P. and Luckmann, T. (1967) *The Social Construction of Reality*. Harmondsworth: Penguin.

Billig, M. (1991) *Ideology and Opinions: Studies in Rhetorical Psychology*. London: Sage.

Billig, M. (1997) 'Rhetorical and discursive analysis: how families talk about the royal family', in N. Hayes (ed.), *Doing Qualitative Analysis in Psychology*. Hove: Psychology Press, pp. 39–54.

Billig, M., Condor, S., Edwards, D., Gane, M., Middleton, D. and Radley, A. (1988) *Ideological Dilemmas: A Social Psychology of Everyday Thinking*. London: Sage.

Binswanger, L. (1963) *Being-in-the-World*. New York: Basic Books.

Bion, W.R. (1959) *Experiences in Groups*. London: Tavistock.

Birren, J.E., Kenyon, G.M., Ruth, J.-E., Schroots, J.J.F. and Svensson, T. (eds) (1996) *Aging and Biography: Explorations in Adult Development*. New York: Springer.

Blaxter, M. (1983) 'The causes of disease: women talking', *Social Science and Medicine*, 17: 59–69.

Bloor, M., Frankland, J., Thomas, M. and Robson, K. (2001) *Focus Groups in Social Research*. London: Sage.

Blumer, H. (1969) *Symbolic Interactionism*. Englewood Cliffs, NJ: Prentice-Hall.

Bolton, N. (1997) *Concept Formation*: Oxford: Pergamon.

Boring, E.G. (1950) *A History of Experimental Psychology* (2nd edn). New York: Appleton-Century-Crofts.

Boss, M. (1979) *Existential Foundations of Medicine and Psychology*. New York: Jason Aronson.

Boyatzis, R.E. (1998) *Transforming Qualitative Information: Thematic Analysis and Code Development*. London: Sage.

Bradbury, H. and Reason, P. (2001) 'Conclusion: broadening the bandwidth of validity: five issues and seven choice-points for improving the quality of action research', in P. Reason and H. Bradbury (eds), *Handbook of Action Research: Participative Inquiry and Practice*. London: Sage, pp. 447–56.

Breakwell, G. (2006) 'Interviewing methods', in G. Breakwell, C. Fife-Schaw, S. Hammond and J.A. Smith (eds) *Research Methods in Psychology* (3rd edn). London: Sage.

Brenner, M., Brown, J. and Canter, D. (1985) *The Research Interview*. London: Academic Press.

Brentano, F. (1874; trans. 1973) *Psychology from an Empirical Standpoint*. London: Routledge.

Broadbent, D.E. (1958) *Perception and Communication*. London: Pergamon Press.

Brooks, P. (1985) *Reading for the Plot: Design and Intention in Narrative*. New York: Vintage.

Bruner, J. (1986) *Actual Minds, Possible Worlds*. Cambridge, MA: Harvard University Press.

Bruner, J. (1990) *Acts of Meaning*. Cambridge, MA: Harvard University Press.

Bryan, A. (2000) 'Exploring the experiences of black professionals in welfare agencies and black students in social work education', unpublished PhD dissertation, University of Bath.

Bryant, A. (2003) A constructive/ist response to Glaser. *FQS: Forum for Qualitative Social Research* 4(1): www.qualitative-research.net/fqs/www/qualitative-research.net/fqs/-texte/1–03/1–03bryant-e.htm(accessed 03/14/2003]

Bugental, J.F.T. (1964) 'The third force in psychology', *Journal of Humanistic Psychology*, 4: 19–25.

Bühler, C. (1971) 'Basic theoretical concepts of humanistic psychology', *American Psychologist*, 26: 378–86.

Burgess, R. (1984) *In the Field*. London: Unwin Hyman.

Burr, V. (1995) *An Introduction to Social Constructionism*. London: Routledge.

Burr, V. (2003) *An Introduction to Social Constructionism* (2nd edn). London: Routledge.

Byatt, A.S. (2000) *On Histories and Stories: Selected Essays*. London: Chatto and Windus.

Camic, P., Rhodes, J. and Yardley, L. (2003) 'Naming the stars: integrating qualitative methods into psychological research'. In Camic, P. Rhodes, J. and Yardley, L. *Qualitative Research in Psychology: Expanding Perspectives in Methodology and Design*. Washington, DC: APA Books. pp. 1–15.

Carey, M.A. (ed.) (1995) *Special Issue: Issues and Applications of Focus Groups. Qualitative Health Research*, 5(4).

Chapman, E. (2002) 'The social and ethical implications of changing medical technologies: the views of people living with genetic conditions', *Journal of Health Psychology*, 7: 195–206.

Charmaz, K. (1991a) *Good Days, Bad Days: The Self in Chronic Illness and Time*. New Brunswick, NJ: Rutgers University Press.

Charmaz, K. (1991b) 'Translating graduate qualitative methods into undergraduate teaching: intensive interviewing as a case example', *Teaching Sociology*, 19: 384–95.

Charmaz, K. (1995) 'Grounded theory', in J.A. Smith, R. Harré and L. Van Langenhore (eds), *Rethinking Methods in Psychology*. London: Sage, pp. 27–49.

Charmaz, K. (1999) 'Stories of suffering: subjects' tales and research narratives', *Qualitative Health Research*, 9: 369–82.

Charmaz, K. (2001) 'Grounded theory analysis', in J.F. Gubrium and J.A. Holstein (eds), *Handbook of Interviewing*. Thousand Oaks, CA: Sage, pp. 675–94.

Charmaz, K. (2006) *Constructing Grounded Theory: A Practical Guide through Qualitative Analysis*. London: Sage.

Chowns, G. (2006) '"No – You DON'T Know How We Feel": Collaborative Inquiry with children facing the life-threatening illness of a parent', unpublished doctoral thesis, University of Southampton.

Chowns, G. (in press 2008) '"No – You DON'T Know How We Feel": Collaborative Inquiry using video with children facing the life-threatening illness of a parent', in

P. Reason and H. Bradbury (eds), *Handbook of Action Research* (2nd edn). London: Sage Publications.

Clare, L. (2003) 'Managing threats to self: awareness in early stage Alzheimer's disease', *Social Science & Medicine*, 57: 1017–29.

Clarke, A.E. (2003) 'Situational analysis: grounded theory mapping after the postmodern turn'. *Symbloic Interaction* 26(4): 533–76.

Clarke, A.E. (1998) *Disciplining Reproduction: Modernity, American Life Sciences and the Problems of Sex*. Berkeley, CA: University of California Press.

Clarke, A.E. (2005) *Situational Analysis: Grounded Theory after the Postmodern Turn*. Thousand Oaks, CA: Sage.

Clayman, S. (1995) 'Defining moments, presidential debates and the dynamics of quotability', *Journal of Communication*, 45(3): 118–46.

Clayman, S. and Heritage, J. (2002) *The News Interview: Journalists and Public Figures on the Air*. Cambridge: Cambridge University Press.

Clifford, J.L. and Marcus, G.E. (1986) *Writing Culture: Poetics and Politics of Ethnography*. Berkeley, CA: University of California Press.

Cloonan, T. (1995) 'The early history of phenomenological psychological research in America', *Journal of Phenomenological Psychology*, 26: 46–126.

Conrad, P. (1987) 'The experience of illness: recent and new directions', *Research in the Sociology of Health Care*, 6: 1–31.

Corbin, J.M. and Strauss, A. (1988) *Unending Work and Care: Managing Chronic Illness at Home*. San Francisco: Jossey-Bass.

Couper-Kuhlen, E. (1996) 'The prosody of repetition: on quoting and mimicry', in E. Couper-Kuhlen and M. Selting (eds), *Prosody in Conversation*. Cambridge: Cambridge University Press, pp. 366–405.

Creswell, J.W. (1998) *Qualitative Inquiry and Research Design*. Thousand Oaks, CA: Sage.

Crossley, M.L. (1999) 'Making sense of HIV infection: discourse and adaptation to life with a long-term HIV positive diagnosis', *Health*, 3: 95–119.

Crossley, M.L. (2000) *Introducing Narrative Psychology: Self, Trauma and the Construction of Meaning*. Buckingham: Open University Press.

Davies, B. and Harré, R. (1999) 'Positioning and personhood', in R. Harré and L. Van Langenhove (eds), *Positioning Theory*. Oxford: Blackwell, pp. 32–52.

Day, M. (2004) 'The acquisition of bulimia: childhood experience', *Journal of Phenomenological Psychology*, 35.

Day, W. (1976) 'Contemporary behaviorism and the concept of intention', in J.K. Cole and W.J. Arnold (eds), *Nebraska Symposium on Motivation 1975: Conceptual Foundations of Psychology*. Lincoln, NE: University of Nebraska Press, pp. 203–62.

Denzin, N. (1995) 'Symbolic interactionism', in J.A. Smith, R. Harré and L. Van Langenhove (eds), *Rethinking Psychology*. London: Sage, pp. 43–58.

Derrida, J. (1976) *Of Grammatology*. Baltimore, MD: Johns Hopkins University Press.

Derrida, J. (1981) *Dissemination*. London: Athlone Press.

Dey, I. (1999) *Grounding Grounded Theory: Guidelines for Qualitative Inquiry*. San Diego, CA: Academic Press.

Douglas, C. (2002) 'Using co-operative inquiry with Black women managers: exploring possibilities for moving from surviving to thriving', *Systemic Practice and Action Research*, 14: 249–62.

Drew, P. (1987) 'Po-faced receipts of teases', *Linguistics*, 25: 219–53.

Drew, P. (2005) 'Conversation analysis', in K.L. Fitch and R.E. Sanders (eds), *Handbook of Language and Social Interaction*. Mawah, NJ: Lawrence Erlbaum, pp. 71–102.

Drew, P. and Heritage, J. (eds) (1992) *Talk at Work*. Cambridge: Cambridge University Press.

Drew, P. and Holt, E. (1998) 'Figures of speech: idiomatic expressions and the management of topic transition in conversation', *Language in Society*, 27(4): 495–523.

Drew, P., Collins, S. and Chatwin, J. (2001) 'Conversation analysis: a method for research in health care professional–patient interaction', *Health Expectations*, 4: 58–71.

Dunn, J.L. (2002) *Courting Disaster: Intimate Stalking, Culture, and Criminal Justice*. New York: Aldine de Gruyter.

Dunne, E.A. and Quayle, E. (2001) 'The impact of iatrogenically acquired hepatitis infection on the well-being and relationships of a group of Irish women', *Journal of Health Psychology*, 6: 679–92.

Eatough, V. and Smith, J.A. (2006a) '"I was like a wild wild person": Understanding feelings of anger using interpretative phenomenological analysis', *British Journal of Psychology*, 97: 483–98.

Eatough, V. and Smith, J.A. (2006b) '"I feel like a scrambled egg in my head": an idiographic case study of meaning making and anger using interpretative phenomenological analysis', *Psychology & Psychotherapy*, 79: 115–35.

Eatough, V. and Smith, J.A. (in press) 'Interpretative phenomenological analysis', in C. Willig and W. Stainton Rogers (eds), *Handbook of Qualitatitive Psychology*. London: Sage.

Ebbinghaus, H. (1885; trans. 1964) *Memory*. New York: Dover Publications.

Edley, N. and Wetherell, M. (2001) 'Jekyll and Hyde: men's constructions of feminism and feminists', *Feminism & Psychology*, 11(4): 439–57.

Edwards, D. (1995) 'Sacks and psychology', *Theory and Psychology*, 5(3): 579–97.

Edwards, D. (2000) 'Extreme case formulations: softeners, investment and doing non-literal', *Research on Language & Social Interaction*, 33(4): 347–73.

Edwards, D. and Potter, J. (1992) *Discursive Psychology*. London: Sage.

Edwards, D. and Potter, J. (2001) 'Discursive psychology', in A.W. McHoul and M. Rapley (eds), *How to Analyse Talk in Institutional Settings: A Casebook of Methods*. London: Continuum International.

Eikeland, O. (2001) 'Action research as the hidden curriculum of the Western tradition', in P. Reason and H. Bradbury (eds), *Handbook of Action Research: Participative Inquiry and Practice*. London: Sage, pp. 145–55.

Eisner, E.W. (2003) 'On the art and science of qualitative research in psychology', in P.M. Camic, J.E. Rhodes and L. Yardley (eds), *Qualitative Research in Psychology: Expanding Perspectives in Methodology and Design*. Washington, DC: American Psychological Association, pp. 17–30.

Elbow, P. (1981) *Writing with Power*. New York: Oxford University Press.

Elliott, R., Fischer, C. and Rennie, D. (1999) 'Evolving guidelines for publication of qualitative research studies in psychology and related fields', *British Journal of Clinical Psychology*, 38: 215–29.

Fals Borda, O. and Rahman, M.A. (eds) (1991) *Action and Knowledge: Breaking the Monopoly with Participatory Action Research*. New York: Intermediate Technology Publications/Apex Press.

Farquhar, C. (with Das, R.) (1999) 'Are focus-groups suitable for sensitive topics?', in R.S. Barbour and J. Kitzinger (eds), *Developing Focus Group Research: Politics, Theory and Practice*. London: Sage, pp. 47–63.

Fechner, G.T. (1860; trans. partially 1966) *Elements of Psychophysics*. New York: Holt, Rinehart and Winston.

Fern, E.F. (2001) *Advanced Focus Group Research*. Thousand Oaks, CA: Sage.

Fine, G.A. (1986) *With the Boys: Little League Baseball and Preadolescent Culture*. Chicago: University of Chicago Press.

Fish, J. and Wilkinson, S. (2000a) 'Cervical screening', in J.M. Ussher (ed.), *Women's Health: Contemporary International Perspectives*. Leicester: BPS Books, pp. 224–30.

Fish, J. and Wilkinson, S. (2000b) 'Lesbians and cervical screening', *Psychology of Women Section Review*, 2(2): 5–15.

Fiske, S. and Taylor, S. (1991) *Social Cognition* (2nd edn). New York: McGraw-Hill.

Flick, U. (1992) 'Triangulation revisited: strategy of validation or alternative?' *Journal for the Theory of Social Behaviour*, 22: 175–97.

Flick, U. (1998) *An Introduction to Qualitative Research*. London: Sage.

Flick, U. (2002) *An Introduction to Qualitative Research* (2nd edn). London: Sage

Flowers, P., Smith, J.A., Sheeran, P. and Beail, N. (1997) 'Health and romance: understanding unprotected sex in relationships between gay men', *British Journal of Health Psychology*, 2: 73–86.

Foucault, M. (1971) *Madness and Civilization: A History of Insanity in the Age of Reason*. London: Tavistock.

Foucault, M. (1973a) *Birth of the Clinic: An Archaeology of Medical Perception*. New York: Vintage.

Foucault, M. (1973b) *The Order of Things: An Archaeology of the Human Sciences*. New York: Vintage.

Foucault, M. (1981) *The Will to Knowledge* (*The History of Sexuality*, Vol. 1). Harmondsworth: Penguin.

Freeman, M. (1993) *Rewriting the Self: History, Memory, Narrative*. New York: Routledge.

Freire, P. (1970) *Pedagogy of the Oppressed*. New York: Herder and Herder.

Frith, H. (2000) 'Focusing on sex: using focus-groups in sex research', *Sexualities*, 3(3): 275–97.

Frye, N. (1957) *Anatomy of Criticism*. Princeton, NJ: Princeton University Press.

Fulford, R. (1999) *The Triumph of Narrative*. Toronto: Anansi.

Garfinkel, H. (1967) *Studies in Ethnomethodology*. Englewood Cliffs, NJ: Prentice-Hall.

Garfinkel, H. (2002) *Ethnomethodology's Program*. New York: Rowman and Littlefield.

Gaventa, J. and Cornwall, A. (2001) 'Power and knowledge', in P. Reason and H. Bradbury (eds), *Handbook of Action Research: Participative Inquiry and Practice*. London: Sage, pp. 70–80.

Gee, J.P. (1991) 'A linguistic approach to narrative', *Journal of Narrative & Life History*, 1: 15–39.

Geertz, C. (ed.) (1973) *The Interpretation of Culture*. New York: Basic Books.

Gergen, K.J. (1973) 'Social psychology as history', *Journal of Personality & Social Psychology*, 26 (2): 309–20.

Gergen, K.J. (1989) 'Social psychology and the wrong revolution', *European Journal of Social Psychology*, 19: 463–84.

Gergen, K.J. (1994) 'Exploring the postmodern: perils or potentials?', *American Psychologist*, 49: 412–16.

Gergen, K.J. and Gergen, M.M. (1984) 'The social construction of narrative accounts', in K.J. Gergen and M.M. Gergen (eds), *Historical Social Psychology*. Hillsdale, NJ: Lawrence Erlbaum, pp. 173–90.

Gergen, K.J. and Gergen, M.M. (1986) 'Narrative form and the construction of psychological science', in T. Sarbin (ed.), *Narrative Psychology: The Storied Nature of Human Conduct*. New York: Praeger, pp. 22–44.

Gergen, M. and Davis, S. (eds) (1997) *Toward a New Psychology of Gender: A Reader*. New York: Routledge.

Gilligan, C. (1993) *In a Different Voice: Psychological Theory and Women's Development*. Cambridge, MA: Harvard University Press.

Giorgi, A. (1970) *Psychology as a Human Science: A Phenomenologically-Based Approach*. New York: Harper and Row.

Giorgi, A. (ed.) (1985) *Phenomenology and Psychological Research*. Pittsburgh, PA: Duquesne University Press.

Giorgi, A. (1986) 'The "context of discovery/context of verification": distinction and descriptive human science', *Journal of Phenomenological Psychology*, 17: 151–66.

Giorgi, A. (1989a) 'One type of analysis of descriptive data: procedures involved in following a scientific phenomenological method', *Methods*, 1(3): 39–61.

Giorgi, A. (1989b) 'Some theoretical and practical issues regarding the psychological phenomenological method', *Saybrook Review*, 7(2): 71–85.

Giorgi, A. (1992) 'Description versus interpretation: competing alternative strategies for qualitative research', *Journal of Phenomenological Psychology*, 23: 119–35.

Giorgi, A. (1994) 'A phenomenological perspective on certain qualitative research methods', *Journal of Phenomenological Psychology*, 25: 190–220.

Giorgi, A. (1997) 'The theory, practice and evaluation of the phenomenological method as a qualitative research procedure', *Journal of Phenomenological Psychology*, 28: 235–60.

Giorgi, A. (2000) 'The similarities and differences between descriptive and interpretive methods in scientific phenomenological psychology', in B. Gupta (ed.), *The Empirical and the Transcendental: A Fusion of Horizons*. New York: Rowman and Littlefield, pp. 61–75.

Giorgi, A. and Gallegos, N. (2005) 'Living through some positive experiences of psychotherapy', *Journal of Phenomenological Psychology*, 36.

Giorgi, A. and Giorgi, B. (in press) 'The descriptive phenomenological psychological method', in P. Camic, J.E. Rhodes and L. Yardley (eds), *Qualitative Research in Psychology: Expanding Perspectives in Methodology and Design*. Washington, DC: APA Publications.

Glaser, B.G. (1978) *Theoretical Sensitivity*. Mill Valley, CA: Sociology Press.

Glaser, B.G. (1992) *Emergence vs. Forcing: Basics of Grounded Theory Analysis*. Mill Valley, CA: Sociology Press.

Glaser, B.G. (1998) *Doing Grounded Theory: Issues and Discussions*. Mill Valley, CA: Sociology Press.

Glaser, B.G. and Strauss, A.L. (1965) *Awareness of Dying*. Chicago: Aldine.

Glaser, B.G. and Strauss, A.L. (1967) *The Discovery of Grounded Theory*. Chicago: Aldine.

Goffman, E. (1959) *The Presentation of Self in Everyday Life*. Garden City, NY: Doubleday.

Goffman, E. (1983) 'The interaction order', *American Sociological Review*, 48: 1–17.

Golsworthy, R. and Coyle, A. (1999) 'Spiritual beliefs and the search for meaning among older adults following partner loss', *Mortality*, 4: 21–40.

Goodwin, C. (1993) 'Recording interaction in natural settings', *Pragmatics*, 3(2): 181–209.

Goodwin, C. (1995) 'Co-constructing meaning in conversations with an aphasic man', *Research on Language and Social Interaction*, 28(3): 233–60.

Gray, R.E., Fergus, K.D. and Fitch, M.I. (2005) 'Two Black men with prostate cancer: a narrative approach', *British Journal of Health Psychology*, 10: 71–84.

Gray, R.E., Fitch, M.I., Fergus, K.D., Mykhalovskiy, E. and Church, K. (2002) 'Hegemonic masculinity and the experience of prostate cancer: a narrative approach', *Journal of Aging & Identity*, 7: 43–62.

Greatbatch, D.L. and Dingwall, R. (1997) 'Argumentative talk in divorce mediation sessions', *American Sociological Review*, 62(1): 151–70.

Greenbaum, T.L. (1998) *The Handbook for Focus Group Research* (2nd edn). Thousand Oaks, CA: Sage.

Greenbaum, T.L. (2000) *Moderating Focus Group Research*. Thousand Oaks, CA: Sage.

Greenwood, D.J. and Levin, M. (1998) *Introduction to Action Research: Social Research for Social Change*. Thousand Oaks, CA: Sage.

Greenwood, D.J. and Levin, M. (2006) *Introduction to Action Research: Social Research for Social Change* (2nd revised edn). Thousand Oaks, CA: Sage Publications.

Gurwitsch, A. (1964) *The Field of Consciousness*. Pittsburgh, PA: Duquesne University Press.

Harré, R. and van Langenhove, L. (eds) (1999) *Positioning Theory*. Oxford: Blackwell.

Hayes, N. (1997) 'Introduction: qualitative research and research in psychology', in N. Hayes (ed.), *Doing Qualitative Analysis in Psychology*. Hove: Erlbaum.

Heath, C. (1986) *Body Movement and Speech in Medical Interaction*. Cambridge: Cambridge University Press.

Heaven, V.M. (1999) 'Narrative, believed-in imaginings and psychology's methods: an interview with Theodore R. Sarbin', *Teaching of Psychology*, 26: 300–4.

Heidegger, M. (1927; trans. 1962) *Being and Time*. Oxford: Blackwell.

Heidegger, M. (1957; trans. 1993) 'The way to language', in D.F. Krell (ed.) (1993) *Basic Writings of Martin Heidegger* (2nd edn). London: Routledge.

Heider, F. and Simmel, M. (1944) 'An experimental study of apparent behavior', *American Journal of Psychology*, 57: 243–59.

Henriques, J., Hollway, W., Urwin, C., Venn, C. and Walkerdine, V. (1984) *Changing the Subject: Psychology, Social Regulation and Subjectivity*. London: Methuen.

Henwood, K. and Pidgeon, N. (1992) 'Qualitative research and psychological theorizing', *British Journal of Psychology*, 83: 97–111.

Heritage, J. (1984) *Garfinkel and Ethnomethodology*. Cambridge: Polity Press.

Heritage, J. (2005) 'Conversation analysis and institutional talk', in K.L. Fitch and R.E. Sanders (eds), *Handbook of Language and Social Interaction*. Mahwah, NJ: Lawrence Erlbaum, pp. 103–47.

Heritage, J. and Maynard, D. (eds) (2006) *Communication in Medical Care: Interaction Between Primary Care Physicians and Patients*. Cambridge: Cambridge University Press.

Heritage, J. and Raymond, G. (2005) 'The terms of agreement: indexing epistemic authority and subordination in assessment sequences', *Social Psychology Quarterly*, 68: 15–38.

Heritage, J. and Sefi, S. (1992) 'Dilemmas of advice: aspects of the delivery and reception of advice in interactions between health visitors and first time mothers', in P. Drew and J. Heritage (eds), *Talk at Work: Interaction in Institutional Settings*. Cambridge: Cambridge University Press, pp. 359–417.

Heron, J. (1971) *Experience and Method: An Inquiry into the Concept of Experiential Research*. Human Potential Research Project, University of Surrey.

Heron, J. (1992) *Feeling and Personhood: Psychology in Another Key*. London: Sage.

Heron, J. (1996a) *Co-operative Inquiry: Research into the Human Condition*. London: Sage.

Heron, J. (1996b) 'Quality as primacy of the practical', *Qualitative Inquiry*, 2(1): 41–56.

Heron, J. (1999) *The Complete Facilitator's Handbook*. London: Kogan Page.

Heron, J. (2001) 'Transpersonal co-operative inquiry', in P. Reason and H. Bradbury (eds), *Handbook of Action Research: Participative Inquiry and Practice*. London: Sage, pp. 333–9.

Heron, J. and Reason, P. (2001) 'The practice of cooperative inquiry: research "with" rather than "on" people', in P. Reason and H. Bradbury (eds), *Handbook of Action Research: Participative Inquiry and Practice*. London: Sage.

Heron, J. and Reason, P. (in preparation 2008) 'Co-operative inquiry and ways of knowing', in P. Reason and H. Bradbury (eds), *Handbook of Action Research* (2nd edn). London: Sage.

Hollway, W. and Jefferson, T. (2000) *Doing Qualitative Research Differently: Free Association, Narrative and the Interview Method*. London: Sage.

Husserl, E. (1900; trans. 1970) *Logical Investigations, I and II*. New York: Humanities Press.

Husserl, E. (1913; trans. 1983) *Ideas Pertaining to a Pure Phenomenology and to a Phenomenological Philosophy, I*. The Hague: Martinus Nijhoff.

Husserl, E. (1925; trans. 1977) *Phenomenological Psychology*. The Hague: Martinus Nijhoff.

Husserl, E. (1931; trans. 1960) *Cartesian Meditations: An Introduction to Phenomenology*. The Hague: Martinus Nijhoff.

Husserl, E. (1936; trans. 1970) *The Crisis of European Sciences and Transcendental Phenomenology*. Euanston: Northwestern University Press.

Hutchby, I. and Wooff, H, R. (1998) *Conversation Analysis: Principles, Practices and Applications*. Cambridge: Polity Press.

James, W. (1890) *Principles of Psychology* (2 vols). London: Macmillan.

James, W. (1902) *The Varieties of Religious Experience: A Study in Human Nature. Being the Gifford Lectures on Natural Religion*. London: Longmans, Green and Company.

Jarman, M., Walsh, S. and DeLacey, G. (2005) 'Keeping safe, keeping connected: a qualitative study of HIV-positive women's experiences of partner relationships', *Psychology and Health*, 20: 533–53.

Jefferson, G. (1985) 'An exercise in the transcription and analysis of laughter', in T.A. Dijk (ed.), *Handbook of Discourse Analysis*, Vol. 3. New York: Academic Press, pp. 25–34.

Jefferson, G. (2004a) '"At first I thought": A normalizing device for extraordinary events', in G. Lerner (ed.), *Conversation Analysis: Studies from the First Generation*. Amsterdam, John Benjamins, pp. 131–67.

Jefferson, G. (2004b) 'Glossary of transcript symbols with an introduction', in G.H. Lerner (ed.), *Conversation Analysis: Studies from the First Generation*. Amsterdam: John Benjamins.

Johnson, J.M. (1997) 'Generalizability in qualitative research: excavating the discourse', in J.M. Morse (ed.), *Completing a Qualitative Project: Details and Dialogue*. London: Sage, pp. 191–208.

Jovchelovitch, S. and Bauer, M.W. (2000) 'Narrative interviewing', in M.W. Bauer and G. Gaskell (eds), *Qualitative Researching with Text, Image and Sound*. London: Sage, pp. 57–74.

Joy, M. (ed.) (1997) *Paul Ricoeur and Narrative: Context and Contestation*. Calgary: University of Calgary Press.

Kendall, G. and Wickham, G. (1999) *Using Foucault's Methods*. London: Sage.

Kitzinger, C. (2005a) 'Heteronormativity in action: reproducing the heterosexual nuclear family in after-hours medical calls', *Social Problems*, 52: 477–98.

Kitzinger, C. (2005b) '"Speaking as a heterosexual": (how) does sexuality matter for talk-in-interaction?' *Research on Language and Social Interaction*, 38: 221–65.

Kitzinger, J. (1990) 'Audience understanding of AIDS media messages: a discussion of methods', *Sociology of Health & Illness*, 12(3): 319–55.

Koffka, K. (1935) *Principles of Gestalt Psychology*. New York: Harcourt, Brace and World.

Krueger, R.A. and Casey, M.A. (2000) *Focus Groups* (3rd edn). Thousand Oaks, CA: Sage.

Kvale, S. (ed.) 1992) *Psychology and Postmodernism*. London: Sage.

Laing, R.D. (1965) *The Divided Self: An Existential Study in Sanity and Madness*. Harmondsworth: Penguin.

Langdridge, D. (2004) *Introduction to Research Methods and Data Analysis in Psychology*. Harlow: Pearson Education Limited.

Lempert, L. (1997) 'The other side of help: the negative effects of help seeking processes of abused women', *Qualitative Research*, 20: 289–309.

Lofland, J. and Lofland, L.H. (1995) *Analyzing Social Settings*. Belmont, CA: Wadsworth.

Lunch, N. and Lunch, C. (2006) *Insights in Participatory Video*. Oxford: Insightshare.

Lykes, M.B. (1997) 'Activist participatory research among the Maya of Guatemala: constructing meanings from situated knowledge', *Journal of Social Issues*, 53: 725–46.

MacMurray, J. (1957) *The Self as Agent*. London: Faber and Faber.

MacNaghten, P. (1993) 'Discourses of nature: argumentation and power', in E. Burman and I. Parker (eds), *Discourse Analytic Research*. London: Routledge, pp. 52–72.

Maines, D.R. (1993) 'Narrative's moment and sociology's phenomena: toward a narrative sociology', *Sociological Quarterly*, 34: 17–38.

Mair, M. (1989) *Between Psychology and Psychotherapy: A Poetics of Experience*. London: Routledge.

Malterud, K. (2001) 'Qualitative research: standards, challenges, and guidelines', *Lancet*, 358: 483–8.

Maslow, A.H. (1968) *Toward a Psychology of Being* (2nd edn). Princeton, NJ: Van Nostrand.

Mastain, L. (2006) 'The lived experience of spontaneous altruism: a phenomenological study', *Journal of Phenomenological Psychology*, 37.

Maughan, E. and Reason, P. (2001) 'A co-operative inquiry into deep ecology', *ReVision*, 23: 18–24.

McAdams, D. (1985) *Power, Intimacy, and the Life Story: Personological Inquiries into Identity*. New York: Guilford.

McAdams, D. (1993) *The Stories We Live By: Personal Myths and the Making of the Self*. New York: Morrow.

McArdle, K.L. (2002) 'Establishing a co-operative inquiry group; the perspective of a "first-time" inquirer', *Systemic Practice & Action Research*, 14: 177–90.

Mead, G. (2002) 'Developing ourselves as leaders: how can we inquire collaboratively in a hierarchical organization?', *Systemic Practice and Action Research*, 14: 191–206.

Mead, G.H. (1934) *Mind, Self and Society*. Chicago: University of Chicago Press.

Merleau-Ponty, M. (1962) *Phenomenology of Perception*. London: Routledge and Kegan Paul.

Merleau-Ponty, M. (1964) 'Phenomenology and the sciences of man' (trans. J. Wild), in J. Edie (ed.), *The Primacy of Perception*. Evanston, IL: Northwestern University Press, pp. 43–95.

Miller, G.A., Gallanter, E. and Pribram, K.H. (1960) *Plans and the Structure of Behavior*. New York: Holt, Rinehart and Winston.

Mischel, W. (1971) *Introduction to Personality* (5th edn). Fort Worth: Harcourt, Brace, Jouanouich.

Mishler, E.G. (1986) *Research Interviewing: Context and Narrative*. Cambridge, MA: Harvard University Press.

Misiak, H. and Sexton, V.S. (1973) *Phenomenological, Existential and Humanistic Psychologies: A Historical Survey*. New York: Grune and Stratton.

Moran, D. (2005) *Edmund Husserl Founder of Phenomenology*. Cambridge: Polity Press.

Morgan, D.L. (1988) *Focus Groups as Qualitative Research*. Newbury Park, CA: Sage.

Morgan, D.L. (ed.) (1993) *Successful Focus Groups: Advancing the State of the Art.* Newbury Park, CA: Sage.

Morgan, D.L. (1996) 'Focus groups', *Annual Review of Sociology*, 22: 129–52.

Morgan, D.L. (1997) *Focus Groups as Qualitative Research* (2nd edn). Newbury Park, CA: Sage.

Morgan, D.L. and Krueger, R.A. (1998) *The Focus Group Kit*, 6 vols. Newbury Park, CA: Sage.

Morse, J.M. (1995) 'The significance of saturation', *Qualitative Health Research*, 5: 147–9.

Murray, M. (1997a) 'A narrative approach to health psychology: background and potential', *Journal of Health Psychology*, 2: 9–20.

Murray, M. (1997b) *Narrative Health Psychology*. Visiting Scholar Series No. 7, Massey University, New Zealand.

Murray, M. (1999) 'The storied nature of health and illness', in M. Murray and K. Chamberlain (eds), *Qualitative Health Psychology: Theories and Methods*. London: Sage, pp. 47–63.

Murray, M. (2000) 'Levels of narrative analysis in health psychology', *Journal of Health Psychology*, 5: 337–48.

Murray, M. (2002) 'Narrative accounts of breast cancer'. [Interviews with women who had undergone surgery for breast cancer]. Unpublished raw data.

Natanson, M. (1973) *The Social Dynamics of George H. Mead*. The Hague: Martinus Nijhoff.

Neimeyer, R.A. (1995) 'Constructivist psychotherapies: features, foundations, and future directions', in R.A. Neimeyer and M.J. Mahoney (eds), *Constructivism in Psychotherapy*. Washington, DC: APA Books, pp. 11–38.

Neisser, U. (1967) *Cognitive Psychology*. New York: Appleton-Century-Crofts.

Nelson, G. and Prilleltensky, I. (eds) (2005) *Community Psychology: In Pursuit of Liberation and Well-being*. Basingstoke: Palgrave.

O'Connell, D.C. and Kowal, S. (1995) 'Basic principles of transcription', in J.A. Smith, R. Harré and L. Van Langenhove (eds), *Rethinking Methods in Psychology*. London: Sage, pp. 93–105.

Onyett, S. (1996) 'Young women managers: a co-operative inquiry', unpublished Coursework Project, University of Bath.

Osborn, M. and Smith, J.A. (1998) 'The personal experience of chronic benign lower back pain: an interpretative phenomenological analysis', *British Journal of Health Psychology*, 3: 65–83.

Ospina, S., Dodge, J., Godsoe, B., Minieri, J., Reza, S. and Schall, E. (2003) 'From consent to mutual inquiry: balancing democracy and authority in action research', *Action Research*, 2(1): 45–66.

Packer, M. and Addison, R. (eds) (1989) *Entering the Circle: Hermeneutic Investigations in Psychology*. Albany, NY: State University of New York.

Palmer, D. (2000) 'Identifying delusional discourse: issues of rationality, reality and power', *Sociology of Health & Illness*, 22(5): 661–78.

Palmer, R.E. (1969) *Hermeneutics: Interpretation Theory in Schleiermacher, Dilthey, Heidegger, and Gadamer*. Evanston, IL: Northwestern University Press.

Park, R.E. and Burgess, E.W. (eds) (1921) *The City*. Chicago: University of Chicago Press.

Parker, I. (1992) *Discourse Dynamics: Critical Analysis for Social and Individual Psychology*. London: Routledge.

Parker, I. (1994a) 'Reflexive research and the grounding of analysis: social psychology and the psy-complex', *Journal of Community & Applied Social Psychology*, 4(4): 239–52.

Parker, I. (1994b) 'Qualitative research', in P. Banister, E. Burman, I. Parker, M. Taylor and C. Tindall (eds), *Qualitative Methods in Psychology: A Research Guide*. Buckingham: Open University Press.

Parker, I. (1997) 'Discursive psychology', in D. Fox and I. Prilleltensky (eds), *Critical Psychology: An Introduction*. London: Sage, pp. 284–98.

Parker, I. (1999) 'Critical reflexive humanism and critical constructionist psychology', in *Social Constructionist Psychology: A Critical Analysis of Theory and Practice*. Buckingham: Open University Press.

Peräkylä, A. (1995) *AIDS Counselling: Institutional Interaction and Clinical Practice*. Cambridge: Cambridge University Press.

Plummer, K. (2000) *Documents of Life* (2nd edn). London: Sage.

Polanyi, M. (1958) *Personal Knowledge: Towards a Postcritical Philosophy*. London: Routledge and Kegan Paul.

Polanyi, M. (1962) *Personal Knowledge: Towards a Postcritical Philosophy*. 2nd edn. Chicago: University of Chicago Press.

Polkinghorne, D. (1988) *Narrative Knowing and the Human Sciences*. Albany, NY: State University of New York.

Polkinghorne, D. (1996) 'Narrative knowing and the study of human lives', in J.C. Birren, G.M. Kenyon, J.-E. Ruth, J.J.F. Schroots and T. Svensson (eds), *Aging and Biography*. New York: Springer, pp. 77–99.

Pomerantz, A. (1986) 'Extreme case formulations: a new way of legitimating claims', in G. Button, P. Drew and J. Heritage (eds), *Human Studies* (*Interaction and Language Use Special Issue*), 9: 219–30.

Pomerantz, A. and Fehr, B.J. (1996) 'Conversation analysis: an approach to the study of social action as sense-making practices', in T. Van Dijk (ed.), *Discourse as Social Interaction*, Vol. 2. London: Sage. ch. 3, pp. 64–91.

Pope, C. and Mays, N. (1995) 'Rigour and qualitative research', *British Medical Journal*, 311: 42–5.

Potter, J. (1996) *Representing Reality: Discourse, Rhetoric and Social Construction*. London: Sage.

Potter, J. and Hepburn, A. (2005) 'Qualitative interviews in psychology: problems and possibilities', *Qualitative Research in Psychology*, 2: 38–55.

Potter, J. and Wetherell, M. (1987) *Discourse and Social Psychology: Beyond Attitudes and Behaviour*. London: Sage.

Potter, J. and Wetherell, M. (1995) 'Discourse analysis', in J.A. Smith, R. Harré and L. Van Langenhove (eds), *Rethinking Methods in Psychology*. London: Sage, pp. 80–92.

Propp, V. (1928; 1968) *Morphology of the Folktale* (2nd edn). Austin, TX: University of Texas Press.

Prus, R.A. (1987) 'Generic social processes: maximizing conceptual development in ethnographic research', *Journal of Contemporary Ethnography*, 16: 250–93.

Randall, R. and Southgate, J. (1980) *Co-operative and Community Group Dynamics ... Or Your Meetings Needn't Be So Appalling*. London: Barefoot Books.

Raymond, G. and Heritage, J. (2006) 'The epistemics of social relations: owning grandchildren', *Language in Society*, 35: 677–705.

Reason, P. (1988) 'Whole person medical practice', in P. Reason (ed.), *Human Inquiry in Action*. London: Sage, pp. 102–26.

Reason, P. (1991) 'Power and conflict in multidisciplinary collaboration', *Complementary Medical Research*, 3: 144–50.

Reason, P. (2001) *Special Issue: The Practice of Co-operative Inquiry. Systemic Practice & Action Research*, 14(6).

Reason, P. (2006) 'Choice and quality in action research practice', *Journal of Management Inquiry*, 15(2): 187–203.

Reason, P. and Bradbury, H. (2001a) 'Inquiry and participation in search of a world worthy of human aspiration', in P. Reason and H. Bradbury (eds), *Handbook of Action Research: Participative Inquiry and Practice*. London: Sage, pp. 1–14.

Reason, P. and Bradbury, H. (2001b) 'Preface', in P. Reason and H. Bradbury (eds), *Handbook of Action Research: Participative Inquiry and Practice*. London: Sage, pp. xiii–xxxi.

Reason, P. and Bradbury, H. (eds) (2006) *Handbook of Action Research*. Concise paperback edn. London: Sage.

Reason, P. and Bradbury, H. (eds) (in preparation 2008). *Handbook of Action Research* (2nd edn). London: Sage.

Rhodes, J.E. and Jakes, S. (2000) 'Correspondence between delusions and personal goals: a qualitative analysis', *British Journal of Medical Psychology*, 73: 211–25.

Ricoeur, P. (1970) *Freud and Philosophy: An Essay on Interpretation*. New Haven, CT: Yale University Press.

Ricoeur, P. (1972) 'Appropriation', in M.J. Valdes (ed.), *A Ricoeur Reader: Reflection and Imagination*. Toronto: University of Toronto Press, pp. 86–98.

Ricoeur, P. (1984) *Time and Narrative*. Vol. I. trans. K. McLaughlin and D. Pellauer. Chicago: University of Chicago Press.

Ricoeur, P. (1987) 'Life: a story in search of a narrator'. In M.J. Valdes (ed.) *A Ricoeur Reader: Reflection and Imagination* (1991) Toronto: University of Toronto Press. pp. 423–37.

Ricoeur, P. (1988) *Time and Narrative*, Vol. III. Chicago: University of Chicago Press.

Ricoeur, P. (1991) 'The human experience of time and narrative', in M.J. Valdes (ed.), *A Ricoeur Reader: Reflection and Imagination*. Toronto: University of Toronto Press, pp. 99–116.

Robinson, I. (1990) 'Personal narratives, social careers and medical courses: analysing life trajectories in autobiographies of people with multiple sclerosis', *Social Science and Medicine*, 30: 1173–86.

Robrecht, L.C. (1995) 'Grounded theory – evolving methods', *Qualitative Health Research*, 5: 169–77.

Robson, F. (2002) '"Yes! – a chance to tell my side of the story": a case study of a male partner of a woman undergoing termination of pregnancy for foetal abnormality', *Journal of Health Psychology*, 7: 183–94.

Rock, P. (1979) *The Making of Symbolic Interactionism*. London: Macmillan.

Rogers, C.R. (1967) *On Becoming a Person: A Therapist's View of Psychotherapy*. London: Constable.

Rose, N. (1999) *Governing the Soul: The Shaping of the Private Self* (2nd edn). London: Free Association Books.

Sacks, H. (1992) *Lectures on Conversation*, G. Jefferson (ed.), Vols 1 and 2. Oxford: Blackwell.

Sarbin, T. (ed.) (1986*) Narrative Psychology: The Storied Nature of Human Conduct*. New York: Praeger.

Sartre, J.-P. (1958) *Being and Nothingness*. New York: Philosophical Library.

Schegloff, E.A. (1992a) 'Introduction', in G. Jefferson (ed.), *Harvey Sacks: Lectures on Conversation*, Vol. 1: *Fall 1964–Spring 1968*. Oxford: Blackwell, pp. ix–lxii.

Schegloff, E.A. (1992b) 'Repair after next turn: the last structurally provided for place for the defense of intersubjectivity in conversation', *American Journal of Sociology*, 95(5): 1295–345.

Schegloff, E.A. (1993) 'Reflections on quantification in the study of conversation', *Research on Language & Social Interaction*, 26: 99–128.

Schegloff, E.A. (1996) 'Confirming allusions: toward an empirical account of action', *American Journal of Sociology*, 104(1): 161–216.

Schutz, A. (1972) *The Phenomenology of the Social World*. London: Heinemann.

Scott, J.S. (1997) 'Dietrich Bonhoeffer, *Letters and Papers from Prison* and Paul Ricoeur's "Hermeneutics of testimony"', in M. Joy (ed.), *Paul Ricoeur and Narrative: Context and Contestation*. Calgary: University of Calgary Press, pp. 13–24.

Seidman, I.E. (2006) *Interviewing as Qualitative Research: A Guide for Researchers in Education and the Social Sciences* (2nd edn). New York: Teachers College Press.

Selener, D. (1997) *Participatory Action Research and Social Change. Cornell Participatory Action Research Network*, Ithaca, NY: Cornell University Press.

Shotter, J. (1993) *Cultural Politics of Everyday Life: Social Construction and Knowing of the Third Kind*. Buckingham: Open University Press.

Silverman, D. (1993) *Interpreting Qualitative Data*. London: Sage.

Silverman, D. (1997) *Discourses of Counselling: HIV Counselling as Social Interaction*. London: Sage.

Smith, J.A. (1990) 'Self construction: longitudinal studies in the psychology of personal identity and life transitions', D.Phil. dissertation, University of Oxford.

Smith, J.A. (1995) 'Semi-structured interviewing and qualitative analysis', in J.A. Smith, R. Harré and L. Van Langenhore (eds), *Rethinking Methods in Psychology*. London: Sage, pp. 9–26.

Smith, J.A. (1996a) 'Beyond the divide between cognition and discourse: using interpretative phenomenological analysis in health psychology', *Psychology & Health*, 11: 261–71.

Smith, J.A. (1996b) 'Evolving issues for qualitative psychology', in J. Richardson (ed.), *Handbook of Qualitative Research Methods*. Leicester: BPS, pp. 189–202.

Smith, J.A. (1999) 'Towards a relational self: social engagement during pregnancy and psychological preparation for motherhood', *British Journal of Social Psychology*, 38: 409–26.

Smith, J.A. (2004) 'Reflecting on the development of interpretative phenomenological analysis and its contribution to qualitative research in psychology', *Qualitative Research in Psychology*, 1: 39–54.

Smith, J.A. (2007) 'Hermeneutics, human sciences and health: linking theory and practice', *International Journal of Qualitative Studies on Health & Well-being*. 2: 3–11.

Smith, J.A. (2003) 'Shifting identities: the negotiation of meanings within and between texts', in B. Gough and L. Finlay (eds), *Doing Reflexivity*. Oxford: Blackwell. pp. 176–86.

Smith, J.A., Harré, R. and Van Langenhove, L. (1995) 'Idiography', in J.A. Smith, R. Harré and L. Van Langenhove (eds), *Rethinking Psychology*. London: Sage, pp. 59–69.

Smith, J.A. and Osborn, M. (2007) 'Pain as an assault on the self: an interpretative phenomenological analysis', *Psychology and Health,* 22: 517–34.

Spencer, L., Ritchie, J., Lewis, J. and Dillon, L. (2003) *Quality in Qualitative Evaluation: A Framework for Assessing Research Evidence*. Government Chief Social Researcher's Office. Available at: www.policyhub.gov.uk/docs/a_quality_framework.pdf (accessed 26 Sept. 2006).

Spiegelberg, H. (1972) *Phenomenology in Psychology and Psychiatry: A Historical Introduction*. Evanston, IL: Northwestern University Press.

Srivastva, S., Obert, S.L. and Neilson, E. (1977) 'Organizational analysis through group processes: a theoretical perspective', in C.L. Cooper (ed.), *Organizational Development in the UK and USA*. London: Macmillan, pp. 83–111.

Stainton Rogers, R., Stenner, P., Gleeson, K. and Stainton Rogers W. (1995) *Social Psychology: A Critical Agenda*. Cambridge: Polity Press.

Star, S.L. (1989) *Regions of the Mind: Brain Research and the Quest for Scientific Certainty*. Stanford, CA: Stanford University Press.

Stewart, D.W., Shamdasani, P.N. and Rook, D.W. (2006) *Focus Groups: Theory and Practice* (2nd edn). Thousand Oaks, CA: Sage.

Stiles, W. (1993) 'Quality control in qualitative research', *Clinical Psychology Review*, 13: 593–618.

Strauss, A.L. and Corbin, J.A. (1990) *Basics of Qualitative Research: Grounded Theory Procedures and Techniques*. Newbury Park, CA: Sage.

Strauss, A.L. and Glaser, B.G. (1970) *Anguish*. Mill Valley, CA: Sociology Press.

Taylor, S. and Bogdan, R. (1998) *Introduction to Qualitative Research Methods* (3rd edn). New York: Wiley.

ten Have, P. (1999) *Doing Conversation Analysis: A Practical Guide*. London: Sage.

Thomas, J. (1993) *Doing Critical Ethnography*. Newburg Park, CA: Sage.

Thomas, W.I. and Znaniecki, F. (1918) *The Polish Peasant in Europe and America*. Chicago: University of Chicago Press.

Timotigevic, L. and Breakwell, G. M. (2000) 'Migration and threat to identity', *Journal of Community & Applied Social Psychology*, 10: 355–72.

Tong, R. (1991) *Feminist Thought: A Comprehensive Introduction*. London: Routledge.

Toulmin, S. (1990) *Cosmopolis: The Hidden Agenda of Modernity*. New York: Free Press.

Tuckman, B. (1965) 'Development sequences in small groups', *Psychological Bulletin*, 63: 419–27.

Ussher, J. (ed.) (1997) *Body Talk: The Material and Discursive Regulation of Sexuality, Madness and Reproduction*. London: Routledge.

Van Manen, M. (1997) *Researching Lived Experience: Human Science for an Action Sensitive Pedagogy* (2nd edn). London, Ontario: Althouse Press.

Vaughn, S., Schumm, J.S. and Sinagub, J. (1996) *Focus Group Interviews in Education and Psychology*. Thousand Oaks, CA: Sage.

Vignoles, V., Chryssochoou, X. and Breakwell, G. (2004) 'Combining individuality and relatedness: representations of the person among the Anglican clergy', *British Journal of Social Psychology*, pp. 113–132.

Warwick, R., Joseph, S., Cordle, C. and Ashworth, P. (2004) 'Social support for women with chronic pain: what is helpful from whom?' *Psychology & Health*, 19: 117–34.

Watson, J.B. (1913) 'Psychology as a behaviorist views it', *Psychological Review*, 20: 158–77.

Welford, A.T. (1968) *Fundamentals of Skill*. London: Methuen.

Wetherell, M. (1998) 'Positioning and interpretative repertoires: conversation analysis and post-structuralism in dialogue', *Discourse & Society*, 9(3): 387–413.

Wetherell, M. (2001) 'Debates in discourse research' in M. Wetherell, S. Taylor and S.J. Yates (eds), *Discourse Theory and Practice: A Reader*. London: Sage.

Whyte, W.F. (1943/1955) *Street Corner Society*. Chicago: University of Chicago Press.

Wiggins, S., Potter, J. and Wildsmith, A. (2001) 'Eating your words: discursive psychology and the reconstruction of eating practices', *Journal of Health Psychology*, 6: 5–15.

Wilkinson, S. (1998a) 'Focus groups in health research: exploring the meanings of health and illness', *Journal of Health Psychology*, 3: 329–48.

Wilkinson, S. (1998b) 'Focus group methodology: a review', *International Journal of Social Research Methodology*, 1: 181–203.

Wilkinson, S. (1999) 'Focus groups: a feminist method', *Psychology of Women Quarterly*, 23: 221–44.

Wilkinson, S. (2000a) 'Breast cancer: a feminist perspective', in J.M. Ussher (ed.), *Women's Health: Contemporary International Perspectives*. Leicester: BPS Books, pp. 230–7.

Wilkinson, S. (2000b) 'Women with breast cancer talking causes: comparing content, biographical and discursive analyses', *Feminism and Psychology*, 10: 431–60.

Wilkinson, S. (2004) 'Focus group research', in D. Silverman (ed.) *Qualitative Research: Theory, Method and Practice*. London: Sage, pp. 177–99.

Wilkinson, S. (2006) 'Analysing interaction in focus groups,' in P. Drew, G. Raymond and D. Weinberg (eds), *Talk and Interaction in Social Research Methods*. London: Sage, pp. 50–62.

Wilkinson, S. (2007) 'Breast cancer: lived experience and feminist action', in M. Morrow, O. Hankivsky and C. Varcoe (eds), *Women's Health in Canada: Critical Theory, Policy and Practice*. Toronto, ON: University of Toronto Press, pp. 408–33.

Wilkinson, S., Joffe, H. and Yardley, L. (2004) 'Qualitative data collection', in D. Marks and L. Yardley (eds), *Research Methods for Clinical and Health Psychology*. London: Sage, pp. 39–55.

Wilkinson, S. and Kitzinger, C. (eds) (1995) *Feminism and Discourse*. London: Sage.

Williams, L., Labonte, R. and O'Brien, M. (2003) 'Empowering social action through narratives of identity and culture', *Health Promotion International*, 18: 33–40.

Willig, C. (1995) '"I wouldn't have married the guy if I'd have to do that" – heterosexual adults' accounts of condom use and their implications for sexual practice', *Journal of Community & Applied Social Psychology*, 5: 75–87.

Willig, C. (ed.) (1999) *Applied Discourse Analysis: Social and Psychological Interventions*. Buckingham: Open University Press.

Willig, C. (2001) *Introducing Qualitative Research in Psychology: Adventures in Theory and Method*. Buckingham: Open University Press.

Willig, C. and dew Valour, K. (1999) 'Love and the work ethic: constructions of intimate relationships as achievement', paper presented at the London Conference of British Psychological Society, London, 20–21 December.

Willig, C. and dew Valour, K. (2000) '"Changed circumstances", "a way out" or "to the bitter end"? A narrative analysis of 16 relationship break-ups', paper presented at the Annual Conference of Social Psychology Section of British Psychological Society, Nottingham, 6–8 September.

Wilson, M. and Sperlinger, D. (2004) 'Dropping out or dropping in? A re-examination of the concept of dropouts using qualitative methodology', *Psychoanalytic Psychotherapy*, 18: 220–37.

Wittgenstein, L. (1953) *Philosophical Investigations*. Oxford: Blackwell.

Wooffitt, R. (2005) *Conversation Analysis and Discourse Analysis: A Comparative and Critical Introduction*. London: Sage.

Wootton, A. (1997) *Interaction and the Development of Mind*. Cambridge: Cambridge University Press.

Wundt, W. (1874; trans. 1904) *Principles of Physiological Psychology*. New York: Macmillan.

Yardley, L. (ed.) (1997a) *Material Discourses of Health and Illness*. London: Routledge.

Yardley, L. (1997b) 'Introducing discursive methods', in L. Yardley (ed.), *Material Discourses of Health and Illness*. London: Routledge, pp. 25–49.

Yardley, L. (2000) 'Dilemmas in qualitative health research', *Psychology & Health*, 15: 215–28.

Yardley, L. and Bishop, F.L. (2007) 'Mixing qualitative and quantitative methods', in C. Willig and W. Stainton Rogers (eds), *Handbook of Qualitative Methods in Psychology*. London: Sage.

Yardley, L., Bishop, F.L., Beyer, N., Hauer, K. Kempen, G.I.J.M., Piot-Ziegler, C., Todd, C. Cuttelod, T., Horne, M., Lanta, K. and Rosell, A. (2006) 'Older people's views of falls prevention interventions in six European countries', *The Gerontologist*.

Yardley, L., Donovan-Hall, M., Francis, K. and Todd, C. (2006) 'Older people's views about falls prevention: a qualitative study', *Health Education Research*, 21: 508–517.

Yardley, L., Donovan-Hall, M., Francis, K. and Todd, C.J. (2007) 'Attitudes and beliefs that predict older people's intention to undertake strength and balance training', *Journal of Gerontology*, 62B: 119–125.

Yaskowich, K.M. and Stam, H.J. (2003) 'Cancer narratives and the cancer support group', *Journal of Health Psychology*, 8: 720–37.

Yin, R. (1989) *Case Study Research: Design and Methods* (2nd edn). Beverly Hills, CA: Sage.

Yorks, L., Aprill, A., James, L., Rees, A., Hoffman-Pinilla, A. and Ospina, S. (in press 2008) 'The tapestry of leadership: lessons from six cooperative inquiry groups of social justice leaders', in P. Reason and H. Bradbury (eds), *Handbook of Action Research* (2nd edn). London: Sage.

Zimmerman, D. (1992) 'The interactional organization of calls for emergency assistance', in P. Drew and J. Heritage (eds), *Talk at Work: Social Interaction in Institutional Settings*. Cambridge: Cambridge University Press, pp. 418–69.

Index

Brentano, Franz 6–7
briefings meetings 221–3
Brooks, P. 111
Bruner, Jerome 54, 112, 128
Bryan, Agnes 219, 230
Bryant, 84
Bugenthal, J.F.T. 12
Bühler, C. 12
bulimia 50–1
Burgess, E.W. 84
Burr, V. 160
Byatt, A.S. 111

Camic, 246
cancer 233
    breast 123–30, 190, 192–3, 197–204
    prostate 130
    support group 130–1
Carey, M.A. 186
Carr, J. 205
Casey, M.A. 190
categories
    focused coding 98–101
    grounded theory 98–103, 104–5, 106, 108
    memo-writing 101–3
    saturation 106
causality 237
chaos, co-operative inquiry 228
Charmaz, Kathy 24, 81–110
choice, consciousness 7
Chowns, Gillian 233
Chung, M.C. 12
Clarke, A.E. 84
Clifford, J.L. 232
clinical psychology, narrative 113
closed questions 63
clustering, themes 71–2
coding
    axial 98
    comparison 241
    conversation analysis 136
    discursive psychology 166, 169
    focused 96–101
    focus groups 201, 204
    grounded theory 92–101, 108
    line-by-line 93–6
cognitive psychology, interpretative
    phenomenological analysis 54
cognitive structures, enduring 163
cognitivism
    discourse analysis 161–4
    experience rejection 8–10
Cohen's Kappa 241
coherence 237, 244, 245, 248–50
collaboration 217, 228
collections, conversation analysis 148–53, 157
collective narratives 116, 129–30

comedy 112, 113, 121
commitment 244, 245, 248
composite analysis 240, 241
confidentiality, focus groups 191–2
congruence, co-operative inquiry 227
Conrad, P. 53
consciousness 6
    behaviourism 8–9
    co-operative inquiry 210
    existentialism 12–13
    phenomenology 22, 26, 32–3
    presentational theory 33
    stream 7–8
consensual objects of thought 163
consensus, co-operative inquiry 228
constant comparative method 93, 102–3
constructionism 14–18, 20–1, 22
    see also social constructionism
constructions
    discursive psychology 166
    Foucauldian analysis 174–5, 177, 179
constructive alternativism 15
content analysis, focus groups 197–201
context 32
    conversation analysis 135, 136, 141–2
    discourse analysis 162
    discursive psychology 166, 167
    grounded theory 88
    narrative psychology 116, 118,
        122, 123, 129
    sensitivity 243–4, 246–8
convergence, co-operative inquiry 228
conversation analysis 3, 24, 133–59, 188, 236
co-operative inquiry 25, 207–34
Corbin, J.A. 98, 104
Cornwall, A. 210
correspondence theory of truth 21
Couper-Kuhlen, E. 136
creative groups 216–17, 218–30
Cresswell, J.W. 98, 242
Crossley, M.L. 122, 124

Danforth, Christine 88–9, 91, 93–4, 97
date rape 204–5
Davies, B. 176
Day, M. 50–1
Day, W. 27
deceit, phenomenology 47, 48
Denzin, N. 54
dependency 216
Derrida, J. 21, 23
destructive groups 216
determinism 12
deviant cases 242
dew Valour, K. 177
Dey, I. 99
dialysis 59–61

Gray, R.E. 124, 130
Greenbaum, T.L. 186
Greenwood, Davydd 208, 211
grounded theory 24, 31, 81–110, 236
groups
    see also focus groups
    collective narratives 116, 129–30
    development 215–30
    narrative psychology 118, 122
guiding interests 85
Gurwitsch, A. 23

halo of relations 7
Hansen, S. 204–5
harassment 205
Harré, R. 172, 176
Hayes, N. 2
health psychology, narrative 113
health research 186
Heaven, V.M. 112
Heidegger, Martin 12, 19, 20, 24
Heider, F. 114–15
Henriques, J. 172
hepatitis C infection 79
Hepburn, A. 165
Heritage, J. 135, 136, 156, 158–9, 196
hermeneutics 18–19, 23, 53, 113
Heron, John 207, 210, 211, 217, 223, 225,
    226, 228
heterosexual age of consent 205
hierarchy 217
holistic view 46
Hollway, W. 116, 129
Holt, E. 156
horizon 7
humanistic psychology 12, 13, 14
Huntley, A. 205
Husserl, Edmund 6, 7, 10–12, 14, 19,
    24, 26, 33

identity, narrative 115–16
ideology 113
idiographic approach 9, 13–14, 25, 56, 67
imagery 113
impact 244, 246, 250
implicit meaning 91
inclusion 215, 217
inconsistency, conversation analysis 149–56
inductive strategies 82
informed consent, focus groups 193
institutions, Foucauldian analysis 173
intentionality 6, 32
interaction order 135
interpretation theory 18–19, 53
interpretative phenomenological analysis
    3, 24, 53–80

interpretative repertoires 166, 167
interpretivism 20
inter-rater reliability 241
intersubjective attitude 49
intersubjectivity 135
interviews
    cf focus groups 187
    conversation analysis 137
    deceit 48
    discursive psychology 165, 167–71
    episodic 117
    grounded theory 87, 88, 107
    guides 87
    interpretative phenomenological analysis 3,
        24, 53–80
    life-story 117–20
    narrative psychology 117–20
    phenomenology 31
    sample guides 117
    schedule 58, 59–64
    semi-structured 57–78,
        165, 167–71
    structured 57–8
introductory meetings 221–3
introspection 6
in vivo codes 99

James, William 6, 7–8, 11
Jefferson, Gail 134, 158
Jefferson, T. 116, 129
Johnson, J.M. 238
journals, narrative psychology
    118, 130
Jovchelovitch, S. 118

Kelly, George 15–16, 18, 57
Kendall, G. 174
Kendall, Patricia 186
kidney disease 59–61
Kitzinger, J. 188
Koffka, K. 27
Krueger, R.A. 190
Kvale, S. 22

Labonte, R. 131
Langdridge, D. 160
leadership 233
learning, phenomenology 28–47
Lempert, Lora Bex 109
Levin, Morten 208, 211
life-story interview 117–20
lifeworld 5, 12, 13, 15, 18, 21, 22
    phenomenology 28, 29–31
line-by-line coding 93–6
literature review, grounded theory 107
living labour cycle 218–30

localization theory 108
Lofland, J. 102
Lofland, L.H. 102
logico-deductive method 84, 85
logs, narrative psychology 118
love, narrative psychology 122
Luckmann, T. 18
Lykes, M.B. 130

McAdams, Dan 113, 122, 124, 129
McArdle, Kate 218, 220, 233–4
MacMurray, J. 210
MacNaghten, P. 166
Macquarie, B. 205
management
    conversation analysis 142–3, 147
    focus groups 190–1
Marcus, G.E. 232
market research 186
Marshall, Joyce 94
Maslow, A.H. 12
Mastain, L. 51
Maughan, E. 230
Mays, 242
Mead, Geoff 221, 225, 229, 233
Mead, George Herbert 7, 15,
        16–18, 20, 84
meaning 5, 9
    Foucauldian analysis 173–4
    grounded theory 90–2
    interpretative phenomenological analysis
        53, 54, 66
    narrative psychology 113, 114
    phenomenology 28
    recollection 18–19
    units 34–5, 44–6
membership 215
memo-writing, grounded theory
        101–3, 106, 108
Merleau-Ponty, M. 12
Merton, Robert 186
messianic pairing 216
meta-intentionality 227
metaphors, narrative psychology 111–12
migration, identity threat 78
Miller, G.A. 9
Mischel, 16
Mishler, E.G. 118, 120
Misiak, H. 12
mixed methods 240
modernism 22
morality 22–3
Moran, D. 14
Morgan, D.L. 187, 188, 190
Morse, Janice 106
Mullett, Jennifer 212–13

Murray, Michael 24, 111–32
myopathy 81

narrative identity 115–16
narrative psychology 24, 111–32
narrative therapy 113
narrative thinking 112
narrative tone 113, 122
Natanson, M. 18
negative cases 242
Neisser, U. 9
Nelson, Susan 81, 86
nomothetic approach 14, 16, 56
non-attachment 227
non-verbal data 31, 65
nurturing phase 215, 216, 217,
        218–23, 230

objectification, phenomenology 49
objectivity 8, 236–7
O'Brien, M. 131
O'Byrne, R. 204–5
ontology 24–5, 112
Onyett, S. 222
open questions 63, 87
optimistic narrative 126–7
order
    co-operative inquiry 228
    narrative psychology 115
organizational needs 222, 226
Osborn, Mike 24, 53–80
Ospina, S. 233

pain, interpretative phenomenological
        analysis 67–78
Palmer, R. E. 19
paper trail 243
paradigmatic thinking 112
Parker, I. 160, 172, 173–4, 212
Park, Robert 84
participant feedback 242
participant observation 17
participative research 209–11
participative worldview 208–9, 210
patterns, conversation analysis 148–56, 157
perception, cognition 162–3
perceptual approach 8–9, 18, 19
personal constructs 14–15, 21, 57
personal documents 14
personality 13–14
personal narrative interview 117
pessimistic narrative 124–6, 128
phase progression model 215
phenomenological reduction 33
phenomenology 3, 5, 6, 10–13, 16, 18, 19,
        21–2, 23, 24, 26–52

Phoenix, A. 184–5
pilot studies 191
Plummer, 57
pluralism 25
points of departure 85
Polanyi, M. 209
Polkinghorne, Donald 113
Pomerantz, A. 141, 151, 169
Pope, 242
positioning, Foucauldian analysis 172,
    175–6, 179–80
positivism 4, 10, 83–4
postmodernism 19–23, 209
post-structuralist theory 172
Potter, J. 160, 161, 164, 165, 166, 167, 184
power
    co-operative inquiry 210–11
    Foucauldian analysis 172
    narrative psychology 122
practical knowing 210, 214, 230, 231, 232
practice, Foucauldian analysis 176, 179–80
pragmatist philosophy 84
pre-invitations 142–3, 146, 147
presentational knowing 210, 214, 230, 232–3
presentational theory of consciousness 33
Pribram, K.H. 9
processes, grounded theory 90–2
progressive narrative 112, 121, 122, 126–7
prompts, interviews 61–2
propositional knowing 210, 214, 230, 232
propositions 4
Propp, V. 111
prostate cancer 130
Prus, R.A. 99
psychic overtone 7
psychoanalysis 23, 27
psychophysics 5–6
psychotherapy 50
purposive sampling 56

quantitative research 1–2, 236–8
Quayle, E. 79
questionnaires
    deceit 48
    interview similarity 58
questions
    see also research questions
    grounded theory 87
    interviews 61–3

radical behaviourism 27
Randall, R. 215–16, 229
Rapley, M. 204–5
Raymond, G. 158–9
Reason, Peter 25, 207–34
recruitment, focus groups 193–4
reduction 33–4, 48

reflection, co-operative inquiry 228
reflexivity 21, 250
reframing 227
regressive narrative 112, 121–2, 124–6, 127,
    128
relaxing phase 215, 216, 217, 229–30
reliability 57, 58, 236–7
representationalism 21
researcher influence 237
research questions
    discourse analysis 181–2
    discursive psychology 165
    grounded theory 85
    interpretative phenomenological
        analysis 55–7
retraction, conversation analysis 151–3
retrospective data 32, 47
Rhodes, 246
rich data 87, 88–9, 92
Ricoeur, Paul 18–19, 113, 114, 115–16, 121
rigour 244, 245, 248
Riley, Sarah 25, 207–34
Robinson, I. 121
Robrecht, L.C. 98
Rock, P. 84
Rogers, C.R. 12
role construct repertory grid 16
romance 112, 113
Rook, D.W. 190
Rose, M. 173
Ryle, Gilbert 209

Sacks, Harvey 133–4
sample size, interpretative phenomenological
    analysis 55–7, 67, 74
sampling, theoretical 103–6
Sarbin, Theodore 111–12
Sartre, J.-P. 12
satire 112, 113
schedule
    focus groups 187, 192–3
    interviews 58, 59–64
Schlegoff, Emanuel 134, 136, 137
Schutz, Alfred 18
scientific phenomenological reduction
    33–4, 48
Scott, J.S. 128
Seidman, I.E. 87
Selener, David 211
self 7–8
    idiographic psychology 14
    impairment 108–9
    symbolic interactionism 17–18
self-observation 6, 7, 8, 10
self-report 14
semi-structured interviews 57–78,
    165, 167–71

sense-making
  action research 231
  interpretative phenomenological
    analysis 54
sensitive topics 61, 187
sensitizing concepts 85
sex education 185
Sexton, V.S. 12
sexual refusal 204–5
Seymour-Smith, S. 184–5
Shamdasani, P.N. 190
Shaw, Sara 105
short cuts, grounded theory 88
Shotter, J. 209
Silverman, D. 242
Simmel, M. 114–15
single case study 56
Smith, Jonathan A. 12, 19, 24, 53–80
social cognition, interpretative
    phenomenological analysis 54
social constructionism 17–18, 21, 22, 23–4
  see also constructionism
  focus groups 188–9, 197
  narrative psychology 112
social context
  conversation analysis 135, 141–2
  discourse analysis 162
  narrative psychology 118, 122, 123
social dimensions, narrative 116
social relatedness 9
Southgate, J. 215–16, 229
Srivastva, S. 215
stable narrative 112, 121–2, 124–6, 127, 128
Stainton Rogers, R. 211
Stam, H.J. 130–1
Star, Susan Leigh 108
Stewart, D.W. 190
Strauss, Anselm L. 83, 84, 86, 93, 98, 101,
    102, 104, 107
structured interviews 57–8
subjectivity
  critical 227
  Foucauldian analysis 173, 176, 180
  phenomenology 48–9
substantive codes 99
suffering 115
superordinate themes 74–5, 76
suspicion, hermeneutics 18, 19, 23
symbolic interactionism 15, 16–18,
    20, 54, 84

tacit knowledge 209
talking aloud method 32
talk-in-interaction 134, 147, 157
tape recording 64–5
  conversation analysis 135, 136, 137
  discursive psychology 165

tape recording *cont.*
  focus groups 188, 190, 194, 196
  grounded theory 91–2
  narrative psychology 119
task needs 220
Taylor, B.J. 229
Taylor, S. 54
teasing 157–8
temporal model, narrative psychology 124
texts 21
themes
  discursive psychology 167
  interpretative phenomenological
    analysis 67–76
  narrative psychology 113,
    115, 122
theoretical sampling 103–6
thick description 1, 87, 89
Thomas, W.I. 95
Thomson, R. 205
Thurstone, Walter 186
time, grounded theory 91, 104–5
Timotijevic, L. 78
Toulmin, S. 207, 209
tragedy 112, 113, 121
transcendental phenomenological
    reduction 33
transcription 167–71
  conversation analysis 136, 137–41
  discursive psychology 165–6
  focus groups 188, 196–7
  grounded theory 87, 88, 91
  interpretative phenomenological
    analysis 64–6, 67
  key 196–7
  narrative psychology 119–20
  symbols 139
transformations
  interpretative phenomenological
    analysis 68–9
  phenomenology 35–6, 44–5, 48–9
transparency 237, 244, 245, 248–50
triangulation 239–41
Tuckman, B. 215
turn-taking 134, 136, 137, 146–7

validity 22, 25, 227–8, 235–51
Van Langenhove, L. 172
variability, discursive psychology 166
variables 4
Vaughn, S. 190
venue choice, focus groups 194
video
  conversation analysis 135, 136, 137
  focus groups 188, 203–4
  narrative psychology 118, 119
  phenomenology 31, 32